An AUSA Book

CW01501781

BATTLE FOR PANAMA

Inside Operation Just Cause

Lt. Gen. Edward M. Flanagan, Jr.,
USA (Ret.)

248149

BRASSEY's (US), Inc.
A Division of Maxwell Macmillan, Inc.
Washington • New York • London

Brassey's (US), Inc.

Editorial Offices	*Order Department*
Brassey's (US), Inc.	Brassey's Book Orders
8000 Westpark Drive	c/o Macmillan Publishing Co.
First Floor	100 Front Street, Box 500
McLean, Virginia 22102	Riverside, New Jersey 08075

Brassey's (US), Inc., books are available at special discounts for bulk purchases for sales promotions, premiums, fund-raising, or educational use through the Special Sales Director, Macmillan Publishing Company, 866 Third Avenue, New York, New York 10022.

Material from Neil C. Livingstone's "Danger in the Air" is reprinted from the June 1990 issue of the *Washingtonian*. Copyright © 1990 by the *Washingtonian*.

Library of Congress Cataloging-in-Publication Data

Flanagan, Edward M., 1921–
    Battle for Panama : inside Operation Just Cause / Edward M. Flanagan, Jr.
        p. cm.—(An AUSA book)
    Includes bibliographical references and index.
    ISBN 0-02-881039-2 :
    1. Panama—History—American Invasion, 1989. 2. United States—History, Military. I. Title. II. Series: AUSA Institute of Land Warfare book.
F1567.F57 1993
972.8705′3—dc20   92-14588
                                                                            CIP

10 9 8 7 6 5 4 3 2 1

Printed in the United States of America

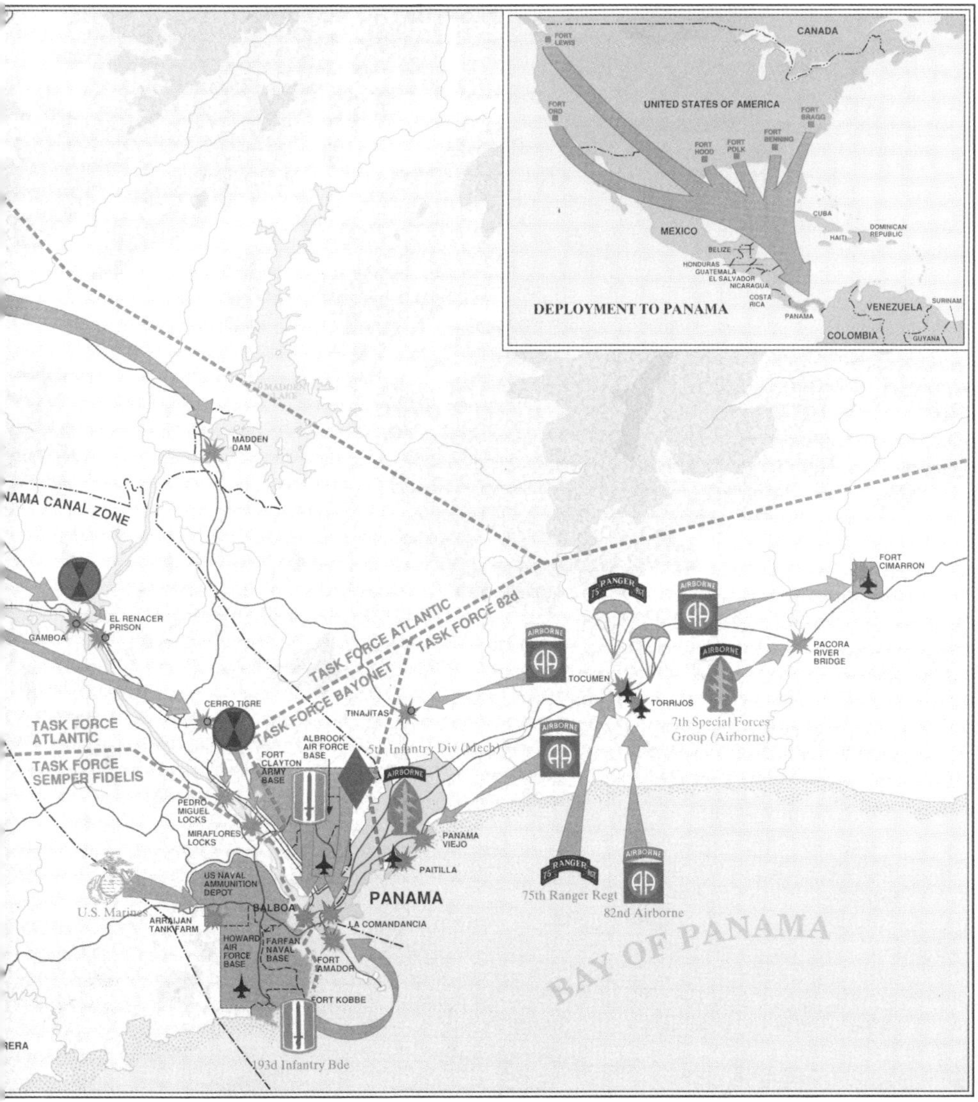

Source: U.S. Army Center for Military History

BATTLE FOR P

Also by Lt. Gen. Edward M. Flanagan, Jr.

Before the Battle (1985)

The Los Banos Raid (1986)

Corregidor: The Rock Force Assault (1988)

The Angels: A History of the 11th Airborne Division (1989)

For the Troops

An AUSA Book

The Association of the United States Army, or AUSA, was founded in 1950 as a not-for-profit organization dedicated to education concerning the role of the U.S. Army, to providing material for military professional development, and to the promotion of proper recognition and appreciation of the profession of arms. Its constituencies include those who serve in the Army today, including Army National Guard, Army Reserve, and Army civilians, and the retirees and veterans who have served in the past, and all their families. A large number of public-minded citizens and business leaders are also an important constituency. The Association seeks to educate the public, elected and appointed officials, and leaders of the defense industry on crucial issues involving the adequacy of our national defense, particularly those issues affecting land warfare.

In 1988 the AUSA established within its existing organization a new entity known as the Institute of Land Warfare. Its purpose is to extend the educational work of the AUSA by sponsoring scholarly publications, to include books, monographs, and essays on key defense issues, as well as workshops and symposia. Among the volumes chosen for designation as "An AUSA Institute of Land Warfare Book" are both new texts and reprints of titles of enduring value that are no longer in print. Topics include history, policy issues, strategy, and tactics. Publication as an AUSA Book does not indicate that the Association of the United States Army and the publisher agree with everything in the book, but does suggest that the AUSA and the publisher believe this book will stimulate the thinking of AUSA members and others concerned about important issues.

Contents

CONTENTS

Foreword

The invasion of Panama in 1989 by the United States caught the world—and a brutal dictator—by surprise. U.S. forces struck hard, struck fast, and rapidly achieved all their objectives with courage and professionalism. Operation Just Cause had been planned carefully and fully rehearsed. But the timing for execution, December 1989, had not been forecast by anyone. With essentially a "no-notice" requirement to launch, forces from all services carried out a prototypical forcible-entry parachute assault. U.S. contingency operations came of age. Many of these same units would soon be further tested during Operations Desert Shield and Desert Storm.

Lt. Gen. Edward M. Flanagan, Jr.'s *Battle for Panama* shows that Operation Just Cause was an intricate and hard-fought battle. As a career officer of impeccable credentials and a widely published military historian, General Flanagan brings a unique set of qualifications to this task. A former comrade-in-arms of many of the key participants, with access to the most recently released after-action reports, he has been able to write a uniquely perceptive account. It is an exciting read. It is about combat. It is about American soldiers, sailors, airmen, and marines compassionately and courageously accomplishing their missions. These men and women gave the citizens of Panama a chance to live and work and raise their families in a free country. It was a job well done!

Maxwell R. Thurman
General, USA (Ret.)
Washington, D.C.

Preface

"Just Cause" seemed particularly intriguing to me for one main reason. I retired from the Army in 1978, having served in combat in World War II, Korea, and Viet Nam. Some of my final years were in command positions, first of an infantry division and then of a Stateside Army. In the seventies, I must admit, the Army was not an organization of which one could be inordinately proud. We commanders suffered through some bleak times. But by the end of the eighties, the Army had regained a level of excellence with soldiers who were volunteers, soldiers who were bright, soldiers who had discipline, soldiers who were well trained, soldiers who were equipped with the most modern weapons and technology that the United States could find and buy, soldiers who were led by well-trained leaders. The Army "brass" was saying that this was "the best Army that the United States had ever fielded." And I was skeptical of such a statement. (The marines, sailors, and airmen served in equally superb units, according to their commanders.) Operation "Just Cause" had gone so well that I wanted to find out if all this were true.

Right after the completion of "Just Cause," I started to ask questions of other officers I knew at Fort Bragg. The more I learned about the operation, the more intrigued with it I became. I heard "Buck" Kernan give a briefing in Atlanta to the Airborne Association and learned of the part played by his Rangers. I talked at length to the G3's of the XVIII Airborne Corps and the 82nd Airborne Division. All of this exposure pointed to the fact that Just Cause was "well done." And when I learned of the part played by the administration, I knew it had to be a winner. The administration, from the president through the secretary of defense and the chairman of the Joint Chiefs, practiced the one principle of war that almost ensured success: Give a man a well-defined mission, give him sufficient tools with which to accomplish it, and then let him do it without "micromanaging" him.

And so after much research on the operation, many interviews, and scores of letters, I must reluctantly admit, as an "old" and undoubtly prejudiced soldier, that I can find nothing to dispute the claims of today's "brass."

This book does not try to philosophize about the basic moralilty of the operation. It does not try to determine the guilt of Manuel Noriega. It does not investigate the validity or value of the Panama Canal Treaty. It does seek simply to tell the military side of the operation—the decision, the planning, the deployments, the actions. And it does, overall, I hope, point out the competence of the "new military establishment."

Acknowledgments

Writing a book about a military operation involving over twenty-seven thousand troops assigned to many units home-based across the width and breadth of the United States, from Fort Lewis, Washington, and Fort Ord, California, to Fort Bragg, North Carolina, and Forth Benning, Georgia, and others permanently stationed in Panama requires the help, patience, and knowledge of many troops—officer and enlisted.

I am particularly grateful to the staff officers of XVIII Airborne Corps who spent time with me when I mentioned that I wanted to write a book about "Just Cause." The chief of staff at the time, MG Edison Scholes, and the G3, BG Tom Needham, provided the overview and many briefing notes and charts and reports. Lt. Col. David Huntoon, the corps planner, did yeoman service. Not only did he provide many of the details of the planning for the operation, but later he read the entire manuscript, made corrections and additions, and farmed out pertinent parts of the book to other officers in the 82nd Airborne Division and Special Operations Command who were directly involved in certain phases. Dr. Robert K. Wright, the former XVIII Airborne corps historian, answered many questions and provided maps, photos, PDF organization details, and after-action reports.

At the JCS level, Lt. Gen. Tom Kelly sent me pertinent information and called to give additional data and statistics. One of his assistants, Maj. Raymond Melnyk, sent briefing charts and notes and answered many questions.

In the 82nd Airborne Division, Col. Dan K. McNeill, the G-3 at the time, answered many questions and sent me briefing charts, chronologies, notes, and his own personal diary of the operation. Lt. Col. Gerald L. Behnke escorted me around the 82d Airborne Division and Pope Air Force Base and explained the functions of the various elements in the Personnel Holding Area near Pope. I interviewed Capt. Gary J. Ramsdell at length. Lt. Col. Harry Axson and his staff reviewed three chapters dealing with their battalion's operations and added details that only they could know about.

ACKNOWLEDGMENTS

Lt. Gen. (Maj. Gen. at the time) Wayne Downing, the commander of JSOC, spent over two hours answering my questions and telling me the details of his portion of the operation. His aide, Capt. Raymond A. Thomas, who had been the commander of A Company of the 3d Ranger Battalion, filled in many blanks in my knowledge of the Rangers' part in the operation.

Brig. Gen. (then Col.) William F. "Buck" Kernan was especially helpful. He had his Rangers write to me about their personal experiences and feelings. He also sent me charts, notes, after-action reports, and letters answering detailed questions. Maj. (then Capt.) Albert E. Dochnal read and corrected the section of the book dealing with his unit's part.

Capt. Stuart W. Bradin sat with me and explained in detail his unit's part in the Pacoro River Bridge action. Later, Maj. Kevin H. Higgins reviewed the action and added many important details.

Col. Michael G. Snell sent letters and after-action reports from all of his battalions. Lt. Col. B. R. Fitzgerald's report was especially detailed and helpful.

Lt. Col. W. J. Leszczynski took the time to write a letter explaining his battalion's part in the operation. The chief of public affairs of the 7th Division (L), Maj. L. D. Walker, sent me many newspaper clippings, handwritten journals, chronologies, and briefing notes without which I could not have reconstructed the important part played by the 7th Infantry Division (L). His successor, Maj. Steven R. Hill, answered a number of my questions. Capt. Lisa M. Kutschera, a 7th Division pilot, was especially helpful in writing to me about the details of her unit's part in Just Cause.

Lt. Col. J. W. Reed wrote a long letter describing his unit's action.

Col. C. E. Richardson, the USMC component commander, answered all my questions and went to some difficulty to discover the pertinent parts of his unit's action, particularly before he assumed command.

I know that there are others who gave me assistance, guidance, and help. To them, I am grateful. And I would be remiss if I did not thank Don McKeon, associate director of publishing at Brassey's, for his macro- and microguidance through the development of this book. His expertise made it far better than it would have been without it. I thank him and all the others who were so generous with their time, patience, and knowledge.

U.S. SOUTHERN COMMAND
JOINT TASK FORCE SOUTH
(HQ XVIII Airborne Corps)

Air Forces, Panama
Army Forces, Panama

Naval Forces, Panama
Marine Forces, Panama

TASK FORCE ATLANTIC

HQ/HQ Company, 3d Bde, 7th Inf Division	Fort Ord, Calif.
4/17 Inf	Fort Ord, Calif.
3/504 Inf (Abn)	Fort Bragg, N.C.
Battery B, 7/15 Field Artillery	Fort Ord, Calif.
Battery B, 2/62 Air Defense Artillery	Fort Ord, Calif.
Company C, 13th Engineer Bn	Fort Ord, Calif.
Company C, 7th Medical Bn	Fort Ord, Calif.
Company C, 707th Maintenance Bn	Fort Ord, Calif.
Company C, 7th Supply & Trans. Bn	Fort Ord, Calif.

TASK FORCE AVIATION (HQ Avn Bde, 7th Inf Division)

1/228 Avn	Panama
Task Force Hawk (HQ 3/123 Avn, 7th Inf Division)	
3/123 Avn (-)	Fort Ord, Calif.
Company E, 123 Avn (-)	Fort Ord, Calif.
Task Force Wolf (HQ 1/82 Avn, 82d Abn Division)	
1/82 Avn (-)	Fort Bragg, N.C.
Troop D, 1st Squadron, 17th Cavalry	Fort Bragg, N.C.
1/123 Aviation (-)	Fort Ord, Calif.

TASK FORCE SEMPER FI
(Marine Forces, Panama)

6th Marine Expeditionary Bn	Camp Lejeune, N.C.
Company K, 3/6 Marines	
Company I, 3/6 Marines	
Company D, 2d Light Armored Inf Bn (-)	
Dets. G and H, Bde Service Support Group 6	
1st Pltn, First Fleet Antiterrorist Security Team	Norfolk, Va.
Marine Corps Security Force Company	Panama
534th Military Police Company (Army)	Panama
536th Engineer Bn (Army)	Panama
Battery D, 320th Field Artillery (Army)	Panama
2/27 Inf (-) (Army)	Fort Ord, Calif.

TASK FORCE BAYONET

HQ/HQ Company, 193d Inf Brigade	Panama
5/87 Inf	Panama
1/508 Inf (Abn)	Panama
4/6 Inf (M), 5th Inf Division (M)	Fort Polk, La.
59th Engineer Company	Panama

519th MP Bn	Fort Meade, Md.
HQ/HQ Det., 519th MP Bn	Fort Meade, Md.
209th MP Company	Fort Meade, Md.
555th MP Company	Fort Lee, Va.
988th MP Company	Fort Benning, Ga.

JOINT SPECIAL OPERATIONS TASK FORCE

Task Force Red (HQ 75th Ranger Regt)	
HQ/HQ Company, 75th Rgr	Fort Benning, Ga.
1/75 Rgr	Hunter Army Afld, Ga.
2/75 Rgr	Fort Lewis, Wash.
3/75 Rgr	Fort Benning, Ga.
Task Force Green (Army Delta Force)	
Task Force Blue (Navy Special Mission Unit)	
7th SF Grp (-) (Arrived D+10)	Fort Bragg, N.C.
HQ/HQ Company, 7th SF Grp	
1/7 SF Grp (-)	
2/7 SF Grp	
Support Company, 7th SF Grp	
112th Signal Bn (-)	Fort Bragg, N.C.
528th Support Bn	Fort Bragg, N.C.
160th Aviation Grp (-)	Fort Campbell, Ky.
617th Aviation Detachment	Panama
Task Force Black (HQ 3/7 Special Forces Grp)	
3/7 SF Grp	Panama
Company A, 1/7 SF Grp	Fort Bragg, N.C.
Task Force White (HQ Nav. Spec. Warfare Grp 2)	
Teams 2, 4, Nav. Spec. War. Grp 2	Little Creek, Va.
Naval Special Warfare Unit 8	Panama
Special Boat Unit 26	Panama

ELEMENTS UNDER DIRECT CONTROL OF JTF-SOUTH

525th MI Bde (-)	Fort Bragg, N.C.
Company A, 319th MI Bn	
519th MI Bn (-)	
35th Signal Bde (-)	Fort Bragg, N.C.
1st Corps Support Command (-)	Fort Bragg, N.C.
44th Medical Bde	Fort Bragg, N.C.
5th Mobile Army Surgical Hospital	Fort Bragg, N.C.
32d Med. Supply & Optical Maint. Unit	Fort Bragg, N.C.
36th Medical Company (-)	Fort Bragg, N.C.
142d Medical Bn (-)	Panama
41st Support Group	Panama
193d Support Bn	
1097th Transportation Company	
46th Support Group (-)	Fort Bragg, N.C.
2d Support Center	Fort Bragg, N.C.
330th Transportation Center	
7th Transportation Bn	Fort Bragg, N.C.

Joint Task Force–South: Order of Battle

4th Psychological Operations Group (-)	Fort Bragg, N.C.
1st Psyop Bn	
90th Psyop Company	
94th Psyop Company	

96th Civil Affairs Bn	Fort Bragg, N.C.

1109th Signal Bde	Panama
154th Signal Bn	
1190th Signal Bn	

1st Battlefield Control Detachment (-)	Fort Bragg, N.C.

HQ/HQ Company, U.S. Army South	Panama

16th MP Bde	Fort Bragg, N.C.
503d MP Bn	Fort Bragg, N.C.
HQ/HQ Detachment, 503d MP Bn	
21st MP Company	
65th MP Company	
108th MP Company	
92d MP Bn	Panama
HQ/HQ Detachment, 92d MP Bn	
549th MP Company	

470th MI Bde	Panama
29th MI Bn	
746th MI Bn	
747th MI Bn	

NAVAL FORCES, PANAMA

Naval Security Group (Galeta Island)	Panama
Mine Division 127	Panama

AIR FORCES, PANAMA

830th Air Division	Panama
1st Special Operations Wing (AC-130)	Hurlburt Field, Fla.
24th Composite Wing	Panama
CORONET COVE (A-7D Air Nat'l Gd rotation)	
Det., 114th Tac. Fighter Grp	S.D. ANG
24th Tac. Air Support Squadron (OA-37)	Panama
61st Military Airlift Group	Panama
VOLANT OAK (C-130 rotation)	Various
310th Military Airlift Squadron	Panama
Det. 1, 480th Recon Tech. Group (FURTIVE BEAR)	Panama

ARMY FORCES, PANAMA (HQ XVIII Airborne Corps)

7th Infantry Division (LIGHT) (-)	Fort Ord, Calif.
HQ/HQ Company, 7th Inf Division	
7th MP Company (-)	

2d Squadron, 9th Cavalry (-)	

2d Bde, 7th Inf Division (-)	
HQ/HQ Company, 2d Bde	
5/21 Inf	
3/27 Inf	
6/8 Field Artillery	
Battery A, 2/62 Air Defense Artillery	
Company B, 13th Engineer Bn	
Company B, 7th Medical Bn	
Company B, 707th Maintenance Bn	
Company B, 7th Supply & Trans. Bn	

127th Signal Bn (-)	

13th Engineer Bn (-)	

107th MI Bn (-)	

TASK FORCE PACIFIC

82d Airborne Division (-)	Fort Bragg, N.C.
HQ/HQ Company, 82d Abn Division (-)	Fort Bragg, N.C.

1st Bde, 82d Abn Division (+)	Fort Bragg, N.C.
1/504 Inf (Abn)	
2/504 Inf (Abn)	
4/325 Inf (Abn) (-) (+)	
Company A, 3/505 Inf	
Battery A, 3/319 Field Artillery (-)	
Battery A, 3/4 Air Defense Artillery (-)	
Company C, 3/73 Armor	
Company A, 307th Engineer Bn	
Company A, 782d Maintenance Bn	
Company B, 307th Medical Bn	
Company A, 407th Supply & Service Bn	
Company A, 313th MI Bn	

Company B, 82d Signal Bn (-)	Fort Bragg, N.C.
82d MP Company (-)	Fort Bragg, N.C.
401st MP Company	Fort Hood, Texas
511th MP Company	Fort Drum, N.Y.

1st Bde, 7th Inf Division (Manchus)	Fort Ord, Calif.
HQ/HQ Company, 1st Bde	
1/9 Inf	
2/9 Inf	
3/9 Inf	
Company A, 13th Engineer Bn	
Company A, 707th Maintenance Bn	
Company A, 7th Medical Bn	
Company A, 7th Supply & Trans. Bn	

Joint Task Force–South: Order of Battle (continued)

Acronyms

AA	assembly area
AAR	after-action review
ALICE	all-purpose, lightweight, individual-carrier equipment
ANVIS	aviation night vision system (goggles)
AO	area of operations
AT-4	shoulder-fired antitank weapon
AWADS	all-weather air delivery system
BDU	battle-dress uniform
BSSG	brigade service support group
CCT	combat control team
CD bags	combat deployment bags
CIA	Compañia de Infanteria (Panama Defense Forces)
CDS	container delivery system
CRRC	combat rubber raiding crafts
DENI	Departmento Nacional de Investigaciónes
DIA	Defense Intelligence Agency
DNTT	Dirección Nacional de Transito Terrestre
DRB	division-ready brigade
EDRE	emergency deployment readiness exercise
EPW	enemy prisoner of war
ESIP	emergency supply issue point
FAP	Fuerza Aérea Panameña (Panamanian Air Force)
FARRP	forward area rearming and refueling point
FAST	forward area support team
FAST	fleet antiterrorist security team
FSO	fire support officer
HMMWV	high-mobility multiwheeled vehicle
HWBDU	hot-weather battle dress uniform

ACRONYMS

IAW	in accordance with
IFR	instrument flight regulations
IR tape	infrared tape
IV	intravenous
JOTC	jungle operations training center
JSOTF	joint special operations task force
LAI Bn	marine light armored infantry battalion
LAV	light assault vehicle
LAW	light antiarmor weapon
LCE	load-carrying equipment
LCM	landing craft medium
LD	line of departure
MARFORPM	Marine forces panama
MCSF	Marine Corps security force
MEB	Marine expeditionary brigade
METT-T	mission, enemy, troops, terrain, time
MOUT	military operations in urban terrain
MRE	meal ready to eat
MTT	mobile training team (Army Special Forces)
NCA	National Command Authority
NMCC	National Military Command Center (in the Pentagon)
NVG	night-vision goggles
ODA	Operational Detachment A (Special Forces A Team)
OPSEC	operational security
PCS	permanent change of station
PDF	Panama Defense Forces
PHA	personnel holding area
PPF	Panama Police Forces
PSYOPS HB team	psychological operations team
PVS-4	night scopes
PZ	pickup zone
REMAB	remote marshaling base
RGR	Ranger
RPG	rocket-propelled grenade
R&R	rest and recuperation
RSOP	reconnaissance, selection, occupation of position
RTO	radio-telephone operator
SALUTE	size, activity, location, unit, time, equipment
SATCOM	satellite communications
SAW	squad automatic weapon (machine gun)
SEAL	sea, air, land (U.S. Navy Special Forces)
SOCOM	Southern Command (General Thurman's headquarters)

SOLL	Special Operations Low-Level
SOP	standard operating procedures
TACP	tactical air control party
TA-50	Table of Allowance
TAW	tactical air wing
TEWTS	tactical exercise without troops
TOC	tactical operations center

I | BACKGROUND AND PREPARATIONS

1 | Noriega's Rise to Power

Panama. In years past, the name might have brought to one's mind a canal, weaving its circuitous way placidly through gouged-out mountains, thick jungles, and broad lakes. Perhaps one might think of a tropical country covered with a rain forest and geographically shaped like a huge "S" lying on its side, connecting Costa Rica and Colombia.

More recently, the name Panama might conjure up a different mental scenario—a picture of a slightly bewildered, unsmiling, dark-skinned, square-shouldered, five-foot-five man arrayed in a khaki uniform with the epaulets of a four-star general gracing his shoulders. Usually, in pre-December 1989 newspaper photos or on television, the man is surrounded by groups of sycophantic men, some in civilian clothes, some few in the khaki uniform of the Panama Defense Forces, the PDF. In the photos, one might also catch a glimpse of a few beautiful young ladies in the entourage. In the post-Christmas 1989 scenes, however, the man, still in uniform, but somewhat passive and befuddled, is surrounded by the agents of the U.S. Drug Enforcement Agency, and he is being led to a waiting U.S. C-130 airplane for transportation out of his country. His decline from the strutting, powerful dictator of a small, strategically important Latin American country to a subdued prisoner of the United States was swift and decisive.

Manuel Antonio Noriega Morena was born in 1934 in Terraplen, one of the poorer barrios of Panama City. His father had a Colombian background and worked as an accountant for small firms in the area. His mother was variously described as his father's "domestic" and as a cook and laundress. Noriega's dark complexion derived from his mixed blood of black, Indian, and Spanish—in simple terms, a Creole. By the time he was five, his parents had deserted him and he was reared as an orphan by a godmother.[1]

As a teenager, Noriega attended the Instituto Nacional, the premier high school in Panama. After graduation, he wanted to study medicine, but the

3

limited family finances would not permit it. Instead, after a few years' wait, he accepted a scholarship to Chorillos Military Academy in Lima, Peru. His half brother Luís Carlos, who was a minor official in the Panamanian embassy in Peru, arranged the scholarship.[2]

Noriega's career as a cadet in the military academy in Peru hardly lived up to another military academy's standards of "duty, honor, country." In the first place, he subtracted four years from his age to meet the age requirements to get into the academy. And then, during the summer of 1960, he and some fellow cadets went into town for a weekend designed to relieve them of the rigors and hardships of military academy life.

First they went to a bar, where Noriega quickly spent his small allowance on beer. Later in the evening, broke, he could not meet the price of a balky young prostitute who had already serviced two of his friends. Noriega's innate pride, his feeling of intellectual superiority, and his age—older than the other cadets—would not allow him to return to the academy without having shown his manhood in more than one way. So he took matters into his own hands—literally. Frederick Kempe, in *Divorcing the Dictator,* writes that "During the summer of 1960, an American intelligence agent, serving under diplomatic cover at the U.S. embassy in Lima, Peru, wired home a secret cable with some disturbing news. One of his more promising recent recruits, a young Panamanian cadet at Peru's Chorillos Military Academy, had been arrested for beating and raping a prostitute. She had nearly died. The recruit: Manuel Antonio Noriega." Noriega was able to ease himself out of the predicament with the police. His brutality and ability to evade the consequences thereof were beginning to become manifest.[3]

The U.S. embassy's intelligence agent had recruited Noriega, because of his high academic grades and self-confidence, to provide the U.S. Defense Intelligence Agency with data on leftist fellow students. Shortly thereafter, Noriega went on a modest monthly retainer with the agency.

On graduation and return to Panama in 1963, Noriega was commissioned a sublieutenant in the Panamanian National Guard and was posted to a military base at Colón. Here, as the fates and his luck would have it, he found the entry to his path to power. His commander at Colón was one Capt. Omar Torrijos, who, in a short time, found Noriega a kindred spirit and adopted him as one of his favorites.

Later, through the help of Torrijos and U.S. intelligence officers, Noriega received training at U.S. schools. In July of 1967 he attended a course on intelligence and counterintelligence at Fort Gulick, Canal Zone; in September of 1967 he attended a seven-week psychological operations course at the Special Warfare School at Fort Bragg, North Carolina; later that year he took a two-month course on military intelligence at the School of the Americas in Panama. By 1968 Noriega had been promoted to first lieutenant and reassigned to Chiriquí Province.

In that same year, a group of rebels of the army in Panama, called the "Combo" force, organized to resist the military realignment instituted by President Arnuflo Arias, who had been elected to the presidency on 12 May 1968 and who assumed the office on 1 October 1968. Noriega joined the rebels.

On 11 October 1968, a military coup led by Torrijos attacked the civilian government of Arias. During the coup, Lieutenant Noriega and part of the "Combo" force seized the radio and telephone centers in David, the provincial capital of Chiriquí, severing all communications with Panama City. The power struggle between the civilian structure and the military continued for a short time. In days, Torrijos emerged as the military's leading figure and the nation's strongman. The victorious junta that he headed named Col. José M. Pinilla as president and promised "economic and administrative reforms and elections by mid-1970 under a new constitution and electoral law." The reforms, of course, never happened. On the contrary, the coup introduced an era of military rule that survived until Noriega's downfall twenty-one years later.

Torrijos's grip on power, however, was not yet firmly established. In December of 1969, while he was on a trip to Mexico, three rightist colonels staged a countercoup and temporarily seized control of the government in Panama City. But Noriega, now a major and commanding a National Guard unit in Chiriquí, displayed his loyalty to the dictator with some fervor and imagination. Torrijos, aware of the coup attempt, radioed him that he would risk a night flight to Chiriquí. Unfortunately, the primitive airstrip at David had no landing lights. But that did not stop the resourceful Noriega. He assembled every available motor vehicle he could find, lined them up along the strip, and, at the sound of Torrijos's aircraft, ordered all headlights turned on. Torrijos made a safe landing, mustered Noriega's troops, and marched east to retake the capital and put down the rebellion. As a reward, Torrijos promoted Noriega to lieutenant colonel in 1970 and appointed him as chief of military intelligence. This post made him Torrijos's right-hand man and gave him great personal power over the people of Panama through control of the corrupt secret police. It also brought him into contact with the U.S. intelligence community—both the Central Intelligence Agency (CIA) and the Defense Intelligence Agency (DIA). With the promotion and assignment, Noriega's march to infamy had begun in earnest.[4]

During the 1970s, Torrijos wiped out political parties; abolished the independent newspapers, radio and television stations; and, as the commander of the armed forces, consolidated his hold on the nation.

Winston Robles was the editor of the opposition newspaper *La Prensa.* He said, "As opposed to what some people believe, we were under a dictatorship since 1968. The fact that we have had presidents does not mean anything. The thing here is we have an institutionalized dictatorship. Not the rule of one specific dictator, but the rule of whoever was in charge of the armed forces."

The ruthless dictatorship of Torrijos was only part of the problem of Panama, as viewed through the eyes of successive American administrations. Richard Nixon was deeply concerned with the war on drugs in the United States and elsewhere. In 1971 he told Congress that the war was a "national emergency" and that his drug agents had considerable evidence that Torrijos and his chief henchman, Noriega, had established a multimillion-dollar drug business in Panama through its embassies, consulates, and airports and through "custom offices in the Far East and the Americas."[5]

Nixon was also concerned about the spread of communism in Latin America and the part Torrijos was playing in it. Torrijos had known Communists in his cabinet, he had links to Fidel Castro, and he was shifting to the left in governing Panama. In 1971, Castro's henchmen had apprehended the American crews of two Miami-based freighters. Castro stubbornly refused to release them directly to U.S. authorities. Nixon, notwithstanding his abhorrence of the Panama regime, felt called upon to request Torrijos to assist in obtaining the release of the crews. On behalf of the United States and keeping his options open, Torrijos sent Noriega to Havana; Noriega dutifully secured the release of the crews.[6]

But in spite of this assistance and the intelligence furnished by Noriega's G-2 agency, the Nixon administration was becoming increasingly concerned with persistent reports that Torrijos and Noriega were deeply involved in the Colombian drug trade. In 1971 the administration went so far as to propose "decisive action . . . for destroying or immobilizing the highest level of drug traffickers." It was clear from memos of the U.S. Bureau of Narcotics and Dangerous Drugs that "decisive action" could possibly include assassination and other measures to control Noriega and Torrijos, according to a Senate Intelligence Committee report that was confirmed by John Ingersoll, the director of the Bureau of Narcotics and Dangerous Drugs. The administration rejected the assassination proposal.

As chief of the "dreaded" Panama G-2 agency, Noriega was able to keep secret and detailed files on dissidents. He and his thugs often resorted to torture, intimidation, harassment, beatings, and sexual aberrations to maintain control of Torrijos's opposition. In a major sweep of the country in 1975, Noriega's G-2 agents rounded up selected businessmen and media executives who had been critical of the government, confiscated their properties, and shipped them out to Ecuador. In 1976 Noriega and his equally demonic underlings cracked down on the Union Patriótica Feminina, a women's organization opposed to the harsh rule of the Torrijos government. One of those imprisoned was Alma Robles, daughter of a former leader of the National Assembly. For days she was held incommunicado in a filthy cell while Noriega trumped up charges against her. Even some of the officials of the Torrijos government were ashamed of the treatment.[7]

During the 1970s, when he was still in charge of the Panamanian intelligence agency, Noriega was on the payroll of both the Defense Intelligence Agency and the Central Intelligence Agency. From the CIA, he received $110,000 per year. For that money, Noriega provided data on Latin American military establishments, Castro's Cuba, and the emerging guerrilla movements in the region, particularly in Nicaragua. He was a reliable and generally the sole source for that kind of intelligence. But he was also devious and dishonest and played the role of a double and triple agent. In 1976 the Army investigated the "Singing Sergeants" scandal, in which members of the 470th Military Intelligence Group who had been taping Panamanian officials, allegedly sold copies of the reels to Noriega, who in turn passed the information to Torrijos. Washington also suspected that Noriega sold some of the information to Castro's intelligence service, which also had him on its payroll. In 1977, after a number of briefings on Noriega that detailed his methods and the barbarity of his agency's harassment of Panamanians, CIA director Adm. Stansfield Turner severed the CIA's relationship with Noriega and his intelligence agency.

But by this time, Noriega was the most feared man in Panama. On 8 March 1978, in an interview with Sally Quinn of the *Washington Post,* Noriega told her, "I know that I have an image problem. Mine is a position that doesn't attract much sympathy. But somebody must do this job. And it's a normal position in all the armies of the world. In Panama there is only one force that has control. That's my job."[8]

By the late 1970s, the crimes of Torrijos and, by now his number-two man—Noriega—were becoming clear and documented by U.S. government agencies. They included links to Colombian drugs lords, secret ties to Castro, gun-running for terrorists and insurgents in Latin America, money laundering for the drug cartels, and use of Panamanian airports as transfer points for shipment of drugs to the United States. To audit the Colombian cartel's drug accounts in Panamanian banks, Noriega placed intelligence agents on the banks' staffs.

In spite of being off the CIA payroll for the time being, Noriega managed to maintain his ties to the United States by his usual fraudulent and oblique schemes: He provided reliable intelligence, available from no other source, on Latin American insurgencies, especially in Nicaragua once the Sandinistas had taken over in 1979; he informed the United States in 1979 about a two-thousand- to three-thousand-man Soviet combat brigade in Cuba; he arrested small-level drug traffickers and shipped some of them to the United States; at the request of the U.S. government, he hosted and protected the ousted shah of Iran from December 1979 until March 1980; but he kept intact his contacts with the huge Colombian drug bosses, from whom he drew millions of dollars in recompense.

By 1981, during the first Reagan administration, Noriega was back on the payroll of the CIA, at $185,000 per year.[9] Nineteen eighty-one was also the year when Torrijos was killed in a plane crash near Penonomé, in western Panama. His death initiated a long power struggle between civilian and military leaders, with the military eventually winning. General Dario Paredes, in charge of the National Guard, emerged as the strongman; his chief of staff was Noriega. By August of 1983, Noriega had outfoxed three senior officers and became the commander of the National Guard. He also promoted himself to general. Noriega was an admirer of Israel and its military, the Israeli Defense Forces. One of his first actions, allegedly at the suggestion of his Israeli adviser, Michael Harari, was to combine the National Guard with the small navy and air force into the Panamanian Defense Forces (the PDF), which eventually numbered some fifteen-thousand men.[10]

Noriega immediately set about gaining control of the country through a number of means. He modeled his internal political network after the "Cuban- and Nicaraguan-style neighborhood spy committees." He revitalized his sub-servient military force. He secured legislation putting the military in control of airports, ports, immigration, and customs. In due time, the PDF was in control and owned hotels, liquor stores, and newspapers. In the Colón Free Zone, the military had a "protection racket" that netted some $275 million per year by charging a 1 percent tariff on exports. "Ghost employees" on the state payroll drew some $300 million annually.

Noriega may have had dealings with the top "brass" in the United States, but he was not admired—at least by one of the "brass." In the early 1980s, Oliver North had met with Noriega on a number of occasions in connection with the Iran-contra affair. In his book *Under Fire,* North makes clear his opinion of Noriega. "For me, one of the ugliest aspects of the whole Iran-contra affair was the way my meetings with Noriega were described in some quarters as though the two of us had some kind of an alliance. We didn't. Noriega was probably the single most despicable human being I ever had to deal with. After meeting with him, you just wanted to go home and take a shower."[11]

Gradually and finally, the military came to control the country totally. And, of course, Noriega controlled every aspect of the Panamanian Defense Forces. He organized and armed the "Dignity Battalions," "Digbats" (later called "dingbats" by U.S. forces involved in Just Cause)—bands of young, civilian-clad hoodlums who were intensely loyal to the dictator. The "Digbats" copied the Sandinista *turbas divinas,* who did the "regime's dirty work out of uniform." By 1985 Noriega was in total control of the nation.

In the early 1980s, Noriega fostered a number of schemes that put him in good graces with the United States. He began to assist the Reagan administration with the contra war against the Sandinistas. He permitted the Israelis to use Panama to funnel weapons to the contras. He had a fairly reliable intelligence network in Managua, whose reports he shared with the administration. And he sent arms to the contras.[12]

But under the thin layer of goodwill was a multitude of sins. He was still involved across half of the globe selling arms, intelligence, and even restricted U.S. technology to the Sandinistas, the Eastern bloc, the Cubans, the Colombians, and the opponents of the Israelis, and in running drugs for the Colombian drug cartel. An article in the 12 June 1986 issue of the *New York Times* reported that in the early 1980s Noriega had a personal stake in a drug-processing plant near the Colombian border from which he extracted millions of dollars. In addition, large drug profits, perhaps reaching half a billion dollars a year, were laundered through Panamanian banks and transferred to banks in the United States and other countries. In one deal with Eastern bloc countries, he reportedly made $3 million selling them secret U.S. technological data.[13]

At home, Noriega tightened his control. In the 1984 presidential election, Noriega's candidate was Nicolas Ardito Barletta, who holds a Ph.D. in economics from the University of Chicago, had been the minister of economic planning in the 1970s, and had served as vice president of the World Bank for Latin America and the Caribbean from 1978 to 1984. Dr. Barletta won a narrow victory over the former president, Arnuflo Arias, amid charges that Noriega's military had tampered with the ballot boxes. On 27 September 1985, Noriega forced Barletta from office, ostensibly because he did not approve of Barletta's handling of the economy. But in reality, it turned out later that Barletta was investigating the government's part in the brutal murder of Dr. Hugo Spadafora.

Spadafora had been a critic of Noriega since the two served together under

Torrijos. But in 1984, Spadafora went public with his criticism of Noriega's drug trafficking. Dr. Spadafora was last seen alive near the Costa Rican border, being dragged off a bus by Noriega's agents. He was found sometime later, decapitated and stuffed into a U.S. mailbag, inside the Costa Rican border.[14] A *New York Times* article cited DIA information that linked Noriega to the crime.

Barletta had been the first directly elected president of Panama since Torrijos's 1968 coup. The Reagan administration was deeply concerned with Noriega's flagrant actions to relieve Barletta, and in 1986 took two important steps: It cut aid to Panama by 85 percent, and it sent national security adviser John M. Poindexter to Panama City to warn Noriega to stay out of the drug business. As expected, Noriega paid no mind to Poindexter, denounced the administration for "meddling" in his internal affairs, denied all charges against him, and named Vice President Eric Arturo Delvalle to replace Barletta. Delvalle did not pursue the Spadafora investigation and was therefore no threat to Noriega.

For about a year, relations between Panama and the United States were at an apparent standoff. But in June of 1987, Col. Roberto Diaz Herrera, a former chief of staff to Noriega and who earlier had been forced into retirement, went on a public offensive. He charged that Noriega had manipulated the 1984 election, had planned and ordered the murder of Dr. Spadafora, and might even have had a part in the plane crash that killed Torrijos. Herrera admitted that he personally had bribed polling officials in the Barletta election and that he and other Panamanian military officers had become wealthy extracting exorbitant fees from Cubans desiring Panamanian visas.

Herrera's public denouncement of Noriega and his regime initiated a series of street demonstrations ("pot-bangers," they came to be called) and renewed public outcry for Noriega's ouster. A loose alliance of business, civic, and church leaders called the National Civil Crusade sprung up. Alfredo Maduro, president of the Panamanian Chamber of Commerce, said that "People wanted a change, were tired of this repressive one-man system and everything going to one little group of people. The system itself was getting more rotten. There was no law or justice."

As expected, Noriega damned the Crusaders as *rabi blancos,* literally "white butts," a term of derision for middle-class businessmen and professionals. *Rabi prietos*—"dark butts"—refers to the poor, who generally supported Noriega. But the Crusaders, nonetheless, bravely demonstrated daily. Noriega responded with speed and power: He dispatched his Dobermans—the riot police—who attacked the demonstrators with bird shot and clubs. He declared a national state of emergency, suspended the constitution, forbade public gatherings, shut down newspapers and radio stations, and arrested or shipped out of the country key opposition leaders. And to silence and punish Herrera, Noriega mounted a dawn raid with two helicopter gunships and some fifty of his Dobermans on Herrera's home. Herrera had anticipated the attack and had assembled a small company of supporters. But after a four-hour firefight, Noriega's men captured Herrera and forty-four of his supporters. Once in the hands of Noriega's thugs, and the recipient of untold "measures of persuasion," Herrera retracted his charges and confessed to "inciting antigovernment violence."[15]

But that did not quell the public uprisings. A group of business, Roman Catholic Church, and civic leaders plus numbers of students staged a successful two-day strike to protest the state of emergency and to force Noriega to return the government to civilian control. On 26 June 1987, the U.S. Senate passed a resolution calling on the Panamanian government to oust Noriega and to investigate the charges against him. In response, four days later Noriega lifted the state of emergency. But the result was not a return to calm and order in the streets. The lifting of the ban permitted some five-thousand Noriega supporters to attack the U.S. embassy, from which the Panamanian police had just minutes before withdrawn their guards. The mob stoned the embassy, painted anti-United States graffiti on the walls, and inflicted more than $100,000 in damage. The State Department closed the consular and library section to protest the action of the mob.

The attack on the embassy triggered a new U.S. approach to Panama. The Reagan administration halted all military and economic aid and indicated its strong desire to find a replacement for the Panamanian strongman. On 11 October 1987, Noriega complained to a reporter for the *Washington Post* that after years of cooperating with the CIA and other U.S. intelligence agencies, "When the Americans need something, they picture it very nicely and say you're a hero, but when they don't need you anymore, they forget you."

By the fall of 1987, Noriega's support—except for his bureaucracy and the military—was crumbling. The unrest in the nation caused depositors in Panama's banks to withdraw billions of dollars, with a resultant heavy strain on the national economy. Banking profits accounted for nearly 10 percent of Panama's gross national product. In July 1987 even Gen. Dario Paredes, a Noriega predecessor, spoke out. He supported the public charges of corruption in the government and asked Noriega to resign. Gabriel Lewis, who had been an ambassador to the United States and who had been asked by Noriega to help settle the crisis, took a different tack: He fled to Costa Rica before Noriega could arrest him and, from exile, launched a campaign to unseat the dictator.

But Noriega would not back down. He insisted that there was not "a shred of evidence" against him and adopted a slogan, "Not one step back." He even hinted that he might run for president in the 1989 elections. He railed against the United States, the Catholic Church, and the National Civil Crusade and expelled a few foreign correspondents. In the summer of 1987, he ordered the PDF routinely, and in violation of the 1977 treaties, to stop and check U.S. school buses and military and dependents' automobiles. But in December 1987, perhaps feeling the strength of his position, he permitted opposition newspapers and radio stations to reopen.

José I. Blandon was Noriega's consul general in New York. In an interview with the *New York Times* on 26 November 1988, Blandon said that he had drafted for Noriega's approval a plan that would have allowed Noriega and his leading associates to give up power without "fear of facing criminal prosecution either in Panama or the United States." Early in December, Noriega, after having first given preliminary approval to Brandon's plan, disapproved it and fired Brandon. Brandon did not go quietly. He threatened to publicize papers that would without doubt link Noriega to drug trafficking, money laundering,

10

and the murder of Dr. Spadafora if Noriega would not relinquish power. "Noriega can kill me," Blandon said in the *Times* interview, "that's the risk, but he can't kill what I know." The United States quickly put Blandon under its protection.[16]

In January 1988, Blandon testified before a Miami grand jury that was investigating drug charges against Noriega. While he was testifying in Miami, Stephen M. Kalish, a convicted American drug smuggler, was testifying in Washington, D.C., before a Senate committee investigating Noriega. Kalish admitted that in exchange for help in his own drug business in Panama, he had bribed Noriega with millions of dollars.

On 4 February 1988, two grand juries, in Miami and Tampa, returned indictments in which the U.S. Department of Justice charged Noriega with violations of U.S. racketeering and drug laws by providing protection to international drug traffickers in return for millions of dollars in payoffs, permitting the laundering of drug money through Panamanian banks, and authorizing the use of Panamanian ports and airports for the transfer of drugs.

Noriega continued to have difficulties at home, including, increasingly, the military. In March of 1988, President Delvalle, a Noriega appointee, turned against him, pledged to return the government to a democracy, and tried to oust Noriega by stripping him of command of the armed forces. For his efforts, the Army-dominated National Assembly fired Delvalle and replaced him with the former education minister, Manuel Solis Palma, a close associate of Noriega. The United States did not recognize Palma's credentials. "We had to either acquiesce in this act or call Noriega illegitimate and get into a direct confrontation with him," remembered Elliot Abrams, the assistant secretary of state for Latin America at the time. "So we sided with Delvalle, and Noriega began to teeter." In addition, the economic sanctions imposed by the United States were having a detrimental effect on Panama's economy.[17]

Shortly after Delvalle's ouster, the people of Panama began to express, with action, their resentment of Noriega's iron rule and their falling standard of living. Dissident teachers, dockworkers, electricians, and medical workers paralyzed Panama with a series of strikes. On the sixteenth of March, disgruntled officers of the PDF, led by Col. Leonidas Macias, head of the police force, staged a coup. But Noriega was still in command. His loyal forces put down the coup attempt with brutality, speed, and ease. Thereafter he banned demonstrations and "militarized a number of key public services." On the eighteenth of March, Noriega declared a "state of urgency."

"He played the multiple track system like a violinist," said Elliot Abrams in 1988. "He played us, he played the Latin Americans and the Organization of American States and the internal opposition by giving people the sense that they should play along. But it was not in his interest to leave, and he didn't leave for the most fundamental reason: He didn't want to. . . . The Panamanians who were on the fence came down on Noriega's side. And the opposition was becoming quite disturbed with us. Noriega was appearing more and more like a superman and we were tied in knots."

Noriega might have begun to "teeter" in late 1988, but he was far from falling off his self-constructed pedestal. In spite of all the pressure from the majority of the population of Panama, organizing into opposition groups increasingly, and from the United States, Noriega clung to power through his control of the bureaucracy and the PDF. The bureaucracy was a "kleptocracy." Some press accounts state that about 20 percent of the national budget was paid to *botellas,* political appointees who were paid but never worked. Luís Martins, a spokesman for Endara, thinks that estimate is too low. The 160,000-person bureaucracy was filled, he said, "with people who were on the payroll but never showed up, a lot of suspect travel expenses—that sort of thing. But on a massive scale. The one thing about the Torrijos-Noriega military rule was the institutionalization of corruption at every level, top to bottom, from richest to poorest. It was a system that didn't function without it."

In addition to control of the bureaucracy, Noriega also completely controlled the PDF, a body whose tentacles spread through the entire anatomy of the country. The PDF dominated the government; the PDF was the police force; the PDF ran businesses and banks; the PDF was corrupt; the PDF repressed dissidence with barbarity.[18]

Noriega had bought himself a respite. The United States could not topple him. Abrams said that "An amazing thing happened in the six weeks following the firing of President Delvalle by Noriega; nothing."

But 1989 would prove to be a year in which Noriega reached the extremes of absolutism: On the one hand, he rose to the heights of illegal and flagrant use of raw power in dominating Panama; on the other, by the end of the year he had sunk to the depths of impotence as a hunted, deposed, terrified, powerless, cringing former despot.

2 | 1989: The Climactic Year

After Noriega and the PDF brutally suppressed the coup attempt by Colonel Macias in March 1988, Panama entered a fourteen-month period of relative calm. Noriega abetted that atmosphere by instituting new repressive measures and even hinting that his departure from power might be "negotiable."

Several developments, however, pointed to ripples of trouble beneath the pseudoplacidity of the country. On 13 January 1989, the Panamanian government reported that the Soviet Union and Panama had signed a trade agreement that would result in the first Soviet mission in Panama. In 1988, trade between the two countries was about $2 million—mostly, curiously, Soviet automobiles. On 16 January, Noriega opened his own bank in Panama City in what was reported to be a move "to expand his control over the economy and to launder drug money." On 2 March, the opposition's first major rally drew fifty thousand anti-Noriega demonstrators. On 3 March, the Panamanian traffic police stopped 21 Department of Defense school buses and ticketed the drivers for operating vehicles with U.S. Navy license plates. On 21 March, President Delvalle, who was still recognized by the United States as the legitimate president of Panama, announced that he had taken up permanent residence in Miami. On 5 April, Kurt Muse, a U.S. citizen, was arrested and charged with violating state security. Noriega suspected him of operating a clandestine communications network that interfered with PDF and police transmissions and even became sophisticated enough to override the state radio network and broadcast opposition messages to the Panamanian people. His rescue became of prime importance to the Bush administration. Muse was, apparently, no ordinary U.S. citizen playing communications games with his fellow Rotarians. Noriega had him incarcerated in Carcelo Modelo.

On 18 April the Panamanian government announced that U.S. citizens henceforth would require visas to travel to Panama, presumably to keep U.S. observers out of Panama during the upcoming elections. On 22 April the U.S. Southern Command, the senior headquarters for all U.S. forces in Panama, announced that it planned to move its headquarters to the United States as part of the "phased withdrawal" of U.S. forces from Panama, a move dictated by the 1977 Panama treaties that required the United States to end its military presence in Panama by 1999. On 23 April U.S. officials announced that in 1988 the Senate Intelligence Committee had vetoed a covert plan that had been approved by then President Reagan to support a military coup by "dissident Panamanian military officers." The committee disapproved the plan because "it might have resulted in Noriega's assassination."

In May of 1989, the counterfeit tranquillity in Panama was shattered.

Noriega had scheduled a national election on 7 May 1989 to elect a new president, two vice presidents, 67 legislators, and 505 district representatives. Prior to the election, and in keeping with its normal means of repressive control, the Noriega-dominated hierarchy attempted to ensure the results of the election by padding the voter rosters; closing independent newspaper, radio, and TV outlets; and jimmying the electoral code.[1]

The voter turnout on 7 May was large, and the voting places calm. On one occasion during the day, a smiling, waving Noriega, dressed in dark trousers and brown jacket and wearing his military uniform cap with its gold-braided visor, led a procession of supporters down a main street of Panama City. Undoubtedly, Noriega, knowing that the election was fixed, thought of the procession as a victory parade even before the votes were counted. Clinging to his right arm was a young beauty queen with a large white sash, proclaiming her to be *reina curundu,* draped diagonally across her voluptuous body. On her right, in white formal shirt and dark trousers, was one of Noriega's candidates. On Noriega's left, arm in arm with him, was another young beauty. On her left were two more ladies. Following the entourage was an assortment of men and, a bit incongruously, one platinum-blond woman. Many large, varicolored flags backed up the whole procession and lent an air of benevolence and gaiety to the day.[2] (That Noriega was surrounded by beautiful young ladies on this occasion was no abnormality. Visitors to his office in the Comandancia were struck by the number and beauty of the young women who populated his outer office.)

Noriega's handpicked candidate for president was Carlos Duque, whose running mates were Aquilino Boyd, a former Panamanian ambassador to the United Nations, and Ramon Sieiro, Noriega's brother-in-law. Nepotism also played a part in Panamanian politics. The opposition candidate for president was Guillermo Endara, the nominee of the three-party Democratic Alliance of Civic Opposition (ADOC). His running mates were Ricardo Arias Calderon and Guillermo (Billy) Ford.

On election night, with very little to go on except the knowledge that the election had supposedly been fixed, Duque claimed victory. But Catholic Church leaders in Panama and foreign observers, including Jimmy Carter, a member of a Noriega-sanctioned international observer team representing the Council of Freely Elected Heads of Government, agreed that the opposition

14

candidate, Endara, had won by an overwhelming margin and that the Noriega regime was trying to steal the election.

The first public indication of the results of the election suggested strongly that Duque had been massively defeated. That realization triggered two reactions: On 8 May, the PDF, reasoning correctly that the vote-fixing had failed, raided vote-counting centers and delayed the start of the official count; and ten thousand people took to the streets of Panama City in support of Endara. In one attempt to break up demonstrations, the police opened fire; in the melee, a suspected government agent shot and killed a television cameraman.

Foreign journalists, opposition supporters, and other observers reported that the Noriega regime had substituted voting returns with fake records, had ordered repeated voting by the PDF, and had erased opposition names from the voting records. According to Arias, the number of people on the voting records was up 1.2 million or 29 percent from 1984, and the list contained 100,000 duplications.

On the eighth of May, Jimmy Carter charged that the government had made up fake tally sheets to give the vote to Duque. "The government has stolen the elections by fraud," he said in a statement released in Panama. "The Panamanian people have been robbed."[3]

On the ninth of May, the government began releasing the first election results that showed that Duque led his opponents; on 10 May, the government's three-member Electoral Tribunal said that Duque was ahead of Endara, 66 percent to 32 percent. Conversely, on 9 May, the ADOC released its figures, based on polling half the voting places, and gave Endara 68.6 percent and Duque 22.9 percent. The Catholic Church's sampling gave Endara 74 percent of the vote.

On that same day, after meeting with members of Jimmy Carter's group and an official U.S. observer team headed by Rep. John P. Murtha (D., Pa.), President Bush denounced the election and said that it was marked by "massive irregularities." "The opposition has won a clear-cut, overwhelming victory."

Shortly before midnight that night, Noriega reacted to the charges of fraud and vote-fixing with a simple device: He annuled the election retroactively, charging lack of tally sheets and foreign interference, "obstruction by foreigners," principally by the United States, who, he alleged, had furnished printing and advertising funds to the opposition candidates before the election.

On the tenth of May, Endara, Ford, Arias, and their supporters staged a motorcade through the streets of Panama City to protest the annulment. While TV cameras were filming the scene and newspaper photographers were flashing away, unkempt, rowdy hoodlums of the Dignity Battalions, armed with clubs and metal bars, roared into the motorcade and savagely beat the three actual winners of the election. Endara was cut in the head so severely that he required hospitalization. Reportedly he was beaten again when he returned to his vandalized office. In that second beating, the left side of his body was paralyzed and he had to return to the hospital. Ford was beaten and arrested but released the next day. The "Digbats" killed one of his bodyguards and wounded another with a bullet. Pictures of Ford with his arms raised shielding his bloody head

15

from blows by digbats brought home to Panamanians and the rest of the world the extent of the Noriega regime's brutality and corruption. Many opposition leaders, including Luís Martin, an aide to Endara, were beaten and spent time in jail after the May debacle.

The apparent lack of overt response by the United States to the obviously fraudulent election roused ire in the Panamanian people. "In 1989, when the Dignity Battalions beat up the three candidates," said Luís Martin, "and a lot of people, including myself, were in jail for a few months, there was beginning to be a strong, strong, anti-Americanism on the opposition side for not acting stronger. I'm very pro-American; I did all my schooling in the States. But it was getting very hard to be pro-American. Everybody was saying: 'My God, can't they get rid of the man? They made him, they should help us.' And I couldn't argue that."[4]

But there was response by the United States, albeit not particularly obvious to the people of Panama nor yet militantly aggressive. On the tenth of May, President Bush called several Latin American leaders to discuss with them the situation in Panama and to invite them to unite in opposing Noriega. He said that he discussed ways to remove Noriega from power and that he hoped that "regional diplomacy" would answer the crisis. On the eleventh of May, most nations in the area, with the obvious exceptions of Cuba and Nicaragua, strongly condemned Noriega and his government. President Bush recalled the U.S. ambassador, Arthur C. Davis. On the eleventh of May, President Bush ordered some two thousand additional troops to move to Panama within the following two to three weeks to protect American citizens and property.

To the U.S. military, the augmentation of troops in Panama was known as Operation Nimrod Dancer. A mechanized battalion from the 5th Infantry Division at Fort Polk, Louisiana, deployed to Panama and moved into an area across from Fort Clayton, near the western end of the zone. A brigade headquarters and one battalion from the 7th Infantry Division (Light) from Fort Ord, California, took up positions on the Atlantic side of the canal, near Colón. In April of 1988, the U.S. Marine Corps had moved some four hundred Marines to Panama and, a year later, deployed an additional Marine Corps company, equipped with light assault vehicles (LAV 25's), to Howard Air Force Base, on the western side of the canal and to the western entrance to the Bridge of the Americas.[5]

On the seventeenth of May, Noriega commented publicly for the first time on the results of the election. He flatly denied responsibility for the crimes and violence against Endara, Ford, and the other opposition candidates and denied having any voice in the annulment of the election. He attributed the violence to militants "on both sides" and strongly denounced U.S. "aggression" and "imperialism." He categorically rejected Bush's call that he resign, declaring it "an unacceptable intervention in Panama's affairs," and suggested that the United States was using the election uproar as a screen for abrogating the 1977 canal treaties.

The Bush administration was not standing idly by. For some years the Department of Defense had had contingency plans for moving additional troops into Panama to take control in various emergencies or within forty-eight

16

hours of the election violence. In May 1989, Gen. Carl Stiner, the commanding general of the XVIII Airborne Corps, the command with the major responsibility for developing the contingency plans for any U.S. operations in Panama, sent a small planning staff to Panama to review its own plan for an assault into Panama. This initial advance group consisted of Maj. David H. Huntoon, Jr. (USMA, 1973), the corps planner responsible for the Panama plan, and two other officers, Maj. Mike Findlay (USMA, 1976) from the corps G-2 section and Maj. Ed Lesnow, USMC, fire support coordinator from the corps artillery. Major Huntoon had joined the corps staff in July 1988 and had taken over planning responsibility for the XVIII Airborne Corps' six contingency plans in Central and Latin America. The trio stayed for five weeks, monitoring Noriega's activities, coordinating their plans with both U.S. Southern Command and U.S. Army South, and working with the various elements that would eventually take part in Just Cause. The original group was replaced by another "planning cell," Stiner's "eyes and ears" in the area. From then until the execution of Just Cause, Stiner kept a "planning cell" in Panama.[6]

In an operation called "Blade Jewel," Southern Command returned some dependents to the United States and ordered servicemen and -women and their families living off-base in Panama to move onto military installations. At that time a total of 51,300 Americans lived in Panama, including 10,300 military troops. None of these actions, however, was sufficient to topple Noriega nor even to cause him a loss of power. There was a temporary reduction in harassment of U.S. personnel but, on the whole, Noriega forged blithely ahead, dominating events in Panama, secure in his mastery of Panama's military and, through it, the bureaucracy and the nation's business.[7]

But during the spring and summer of 1989 there were attempts by the Organization of American States (OAS) to arbitrate a settlement between the government and the opposition. From May until July, the OAS delegation, made up of three OAS foreign ministers—one each from Ecuador, Guatemala, and Trinidad and Tobago—made three trips to Panama to meet with members of the government and the opposition. On 24 May the delegation met with Noriega and opposition members and representatives of the Catholic Church. Endara, Ford, and Arias, in defiance of a government ban, marched in protest outside the hotel where the talks were being held. On 26 May Noriega again met with the delegates and said later that he would not talk to opposition leaders and that it was up to the political parties to settle the matter. On 11 June the delegation returned to Panama and met with Noriega in an effort to transfer power from him to the winners of the May election. The session was of no avail. One member of the OAS said that the meeting was "a disaster." On 14 July the delegation returned to Panama for another attempt at settling the crisis. The meeting began on 16 July and ended in bickering and failure. The government insisted that Noriega would not step down; the opposition demanded that the results of the May election be recognized; and Noriega's representatives, going on the usual offensive, said that the meeting should attack not Noriega but the aggression of the United States against Panama.

The mediators reported to the OAS on 19 July that the situation in Panama "is a crisis which affects government institutions, the economy of the country,

17

and the Panamanian society. The Panamanian people continue to suffer from the virtual disruption of the government system, from a feeling of uncertainty and fear . . . and from violations of human rights."

On 23 August the OAS met for its fourth special session on the Panamanian crisis. At the meeting, the OAS mediators criticized the United States for its recent training exercises that had a "negative effect" on the talks with Noriega, for refusing to discuss the problems with the Panamanian government, and for its efforts to remove Noriega from power "with diplomatic and economic sanctions." At the end of the meeting on 24 August, the OAS issued a statement that reproached the United States for demanding "tough language calling on Noriega to step down" and appealed to both sides in Panama to work out a settlement by 1 September. On that same date, Panama's ruling party announced that it would install a provisional government on 1 September.

Shortly after the OAS meeting, President Bush said he would not abandon the struggle to oust Noriega and would consider further sanctions against Panama. On 31 August, at a special session of the OAS, U.S. Deputy Secretary of State Lawrence S. Eagleburger told the delegates that Noriega had a personal fortune of $200 million to $300 million and furnished details of alleged links between Noriega and the Medellín drug cartel in Colombia. He also made public a letter from Noriega to a London bank, dated 8 February 1988—three days after publication of U.S. indictments of drug charges against him—directing transfer of $14,936,426 to a Luxembourg bank.[8]

During 1988 and during the spring and summer of 1989, a number of incidents, some publicized and some little known for various reasons, escalated the tensions between Panama and the United States. When the U.S. Marines arrived in country during the buildup phase, SOUTHCOM assigned them the mission of protecting the Arraijan Tank Farm, about seven kilometers to the northwest of Howard Air Force Base and near the intersection of the Inter-American Highway and Highway 1, Carpetera Thatcher, that runs directly to the Bridge of the Americas. At the time, Col. J. J. Doyle was the commander of Marine Force, Panama. According to Col. C. E. Richardson, the commander of the Marines during Just Cause, Colonel Doyle and his Marines were involved in "one hell of a firefight with the PDF (??). I question the who because it was probably the PDF and Cubans."

The firefight was on the night of 12 April 1988. By then the Marines had been on duty guarding the tank farm about a week. That night the PDF and, according to some intelligence sources, members of the Cuban Spetznaz Special Forces—Cuban commandos—attacked the Marine outposts around the tank farm. The attack apparently started from an estate owned by a Cuban leftist, National Assembly member Rigoberto Paredes, next to the tank farm. One Marine said later that the attack was a "graduation exercise" for some PDF basic trainees. Later reports indicate that three Cubans were wounded in the attack and taken to a PDF hospital and registered under aliases. One died. The other two were allegedly put on a Cuban ship transiting the canal. ABC News, citing U.S. military intelligence sources, said that men dressed in dark uniforms were seen in a nearby town after the firefight carrying several wounded men and at least one PDF dead from a gunshot wound to the chest. The Marines

18

guarding the tank farm were from reinforced I Company, 3d Battalion, 4th Marine Regiment.

In an incident the night before, Cpl. Ricardo M. Villa Hermosa, twenty-five, a squad leader in Weapons Platoon, India Company, 3/4th Marines, was accidentally killed. One report had it that the Marines were guarding the tank farm when PDF were reported to be intruding. The Marines went out on a split patrol and one of them tripped a flare that went up, sounding like gunfire. One patrol fired on the other, and Villa Hermosa was killed, according to a Camp Lejeune public affairs release.[9]

On 18 May the U.S. Defense Department reported that there had been more than twelve hundred violations of the Panama Canal treaties in the past fifteen months, enumerating specific incidents of harassment of military personnel. On 18–19 May Panamanian security forces had detained seventeen members of the Panamanian company that provided security for the U.S. embassy. On 8 June a U.S. State Department representative disclosed that in recent months Nicaragua had sent planeloads of weapons to Panama in anticipation of possible U.S. military attack. On 8 August U.S. officials arrested twenty-nine armed Panamanians, including nine soldiers, in a restricted area during a U.S. military training exercise. Presumably in retaliation, the PDF on 9 August detained two U.S. soldiers. In reprisal, the United States sealed off Fort Amador, jointly occupied by the PDF and the U.S. military, where the two soldiers were being held. The United States lifted the seal after Panama agreed to release the two soldiers and the United States agreed to release two men seized during the 8 August arrest. In the succeeding days, similar arrests occurred. On 11 August Noriega took his gripes to the United Nations and, charging treaty violations, asked the United Nations to send observers. The United States, not to be outdone, held a "major contingency operation" in Panama City on 17 August.

In response to this increased effort by U.S. forces, the Noriega regime's controlled press tried to create a war hysteria and an anti-American response in the Panamanian populace. The newspaper *La Crítica* ran a front-page story protesting the U.S. maneuvers and claimed that they were linked to an impending invasion.

Noriega's opposition kept up its activities. On 3 August students at the University of Panama demonstrated against the government. When the police fired bird shot at the demonstrators, one student was killed. On the seventeenth of August Olimpo Saenz, publisher of the *Panamanian,* was arrested at his office and jailed for three months on charges of publishing false reports about the government. On August 29 the Panamanian police arrested five members of the opposition party near the Colombian border on charges of threating the national security.

In the face of continuing opposition from the OAS and notwithstanding the fact that many foreign countries had "recalled their ambassadors for consultation" to protest the bogus May elections, on 31 August Noriega's subservient Council of State nominated Francisco Rodriguez, fifty-one, former comptroller general of the treasury and a close crony of Noriega's, to the presidency of Panama. He was sworn in on 1 September to replace the outgoing Manuel Solis Palma. One of the opposition leaders, Ricardo Arias Calderon, said that the

Rodriguez appointment was "the equivalent of a coup d'état. . . . This becomes the seventh front man for General Noriega in seven years."

The Council of State, in naming Rodriguez, also said that it would consider a new election in six months provided U.S. economics and military pressure against Noriega ceased. It also dissolved the National Assembly and appointed a commission that would act as the legislature. Thus Noriega tightened the thumbscrews on Panama a few more turns.

On 1 September President Bush declared that the United States would not recognize the new government, would have no diplomatic relations with it, that Panama was, in effect, "without any legitimate government," and that the United States would tighten economic measures to withhold funds from the Panamanian regime. On the same day, the Bush administration announced that it would not accept any administrator of the Panama Canal (due to be selected by Panama and take the job in 1990) named by Noriega. On the fourth of September, the United States barred U.S. companies and U.S. government agencies from trading with companies owned by some 150 Panamanian officials that did business with the U.S. Southern Command military installations. On 12 September the Bush administration announced that it had reinforced a ban on sugar imports. And on 21 September the U.S. government put an additional fourteen Panamanian companies and individuals on a trade blacklist, prohibiting U.S. companies from dealing with them, establishing penalties of ten years' imprisonment and fines of $50,000 for violations.[10]

There was another authority with some power that wanted Noriega to "hang tough": the dons of the Medellín drug cartel of Colombia, who feared that a successor to Noriega might give the United States access to Panamanian bank records, their laundry slips. To emphasize their concern and, in effect, their dominance of Noriega, the lords of the cartel, gruesomely to the point, sent Noriega a miniature coffin, suggesting, rather macabrely, that the only way Noriega could leave Panama was in a life-size one.[11]

But time was beginning to run out for Noriega. Rumbles of unrest and deep discontent within the ranks of the PDF and even within the circle of the dictator's closest advisers were beginning to reach the intelligence "seismographs" of the CIA and the Department of Defense. U.S. Southern Command (USSOUTHCOM), the military headquarters in Panama, watched local developments with increased vigilance. None of the agencies keeping an eye on Panama had long to wait before the next major blip on the EKG tape monitoring the heartbeat of Panama.

3 | A Tightening Noose

In late summer of 1989, Gen. Maxwell R. Thurman, fifty-eight, who had been commissioned through ROTC at North Carolina State University in 1953, had been set to retire from the U.S. Army after finishing a two-year tour as the four-star commander of the Army's Training and Doctrine Command at Fort Monroe, Va., the command responsible for training the Army's officers and men and developing the doctrine with which it would fight its battles. This position, loaded with the heaviest of responsibility, was another in a series of top-level Army jobs that Max Thurman had held and mastered. From November of 1979 to July of 1981 he had run the Army's Recruiting Command and turned it around from a "dead end of the world for an Army officer," in the words of a retired officer who later worked for Max Thurman, to a dynamic, successful operation that asked recruits to "Be all that you can be" instead of pleading with them with the pathetic previous slogan, "Today's Army wants to join you," whatever that meant. "Be all you can be" was also Max Thurman's personal, lifetime philosophy.

After putting the Recruiting Command and, with it, the Army, on its feet in the period between the post-Viet Nam doldrums and the beginning of the Reagan massive buildup, General Thurman became the Army's deputy chief of staff for personnel in the Pentagon, a position that made him responsible for all of the Army's vast array of personnel problems. His success at that job prompted the Army's chief of staff, Gen. John Wickham, Jr., to promote Thurman to four stars and make him the Army's vice chief of staff. General Wickham, in an interview published in *Army Times,* said that he selected Max Thurman as his principal deputy because "he was a detail man" who could handle a wide number of issues. "You have to get into the detail to ensure that the policies will be carried out." Thurman was "instrumental in assuring that we were building solid programs for acquisition and modernization and particularly in the people area. It's one thing to be very brilliant and theoretical,

21

but Max's greatest capability is that he can apply his brilliance in practical ways."

General Thurman, for all his rank and positions of great responsibility, is not without a sense of humor and an ability to deprecate himself. "See me?" he asked when discussing a new slogan for Army recruiting. "The Army's not like me. The Army doesn't wear glasses. The Army hasn't got thin little necks. The Army's great big and strong." But the bespectacled, thin dynamo, with the will and determination of a Patton but the physique and the durability of a long-distance runner, worked through each of his prestigious and responsible positions with a thirst for detail and knowledge, and with skill, dedication, perseverance, and long hours for which he was famous in the Army's top-level circles and especially with those who worked for and with him. He demanded logical results based on exhaustive study and expected his officers and other soldiers to work as hard and as loyally as he did. He never told his staff to work long hours; he just seemed to have an unspoken trust and confidence in his subordinates that they would feel as committed to a project as he was: He knew, intuitively, without having to preach, that they would "do their absolute best." If he felt that a subordinate did not, that person was shortly assigned elsewhere to a less exacting clime. Max Thurman did not countenance the faults expressed in the Peter Principle. Among the officers who worked for him he was known variously, and admiringly, as Mad Max, Maxatollah, and Emperor Maximilian.

In the words of another retired general, "He does not suffer fools gladly." He simply does not accept slipshod thinking or ill-prepared studies. One officer, Col. Bill Sweeney, who worked for Thurman when he was deputy chief of staff for personnel, said, "His management style was to meticulously check you out to see if you knew what you were talking about. And once he had confidence in you, he would give you all kinds of room to succeed. He chewed my ass out once a week, whether I needed it or not. It was rarely unwarranted and usually constructive on the whole. If you had anything at all wrong with what you were working on, he usually found it. It was a painful, demoralizing, depressing experience." Some who worked for Thurman gained from the experience. Others felt somewhat abused. "Half the Army will bad-mouth him to you," Sweeney said, "and the other half will praise him to the skies." But all of them remember that for all his feistiness, his intensity, and his high expectations from his officers and soldiers, he also had compassion. He took care of his troops, looked after them when they needed it, and gave credit when and where due. He could also recognize the worthlessness of even one of his own projects and cancel it the moment a staffer could tell him the facts of its faults and inapplicability.[1]

Max Thurman seems to have little time for nonsense and relaxation. He sleeps only a few hours a night and spends the extra time in the early-morning hours in and near his quarters reading, scanning two or three newspapers, and walking his two Shetland sheep dogs. Max Thurman had never married; he seemed to epitomize that type of officer, totally devoted to the Army, who is alleged to have declared, only partially in jest, that "If the Army wanted you to have a wife, it would have issued you one with your TA-50" (Table of Allowance—basic issue of clothing and equipment). His brother, retired Lt.

Gen. John R. (Roy) Thurman III, a West Pointer, Class of 1946, never married either. They seemed to carry on the bachelor tradition of the Palmer brothers, both of whom had risen to four-star rank and for whom the Thurman brothers worked as young officers. One of the Palmers, Charles D., did eventually marry as a three-star, much to the initial chagrin of his brother, Williston B. Palmer. "Charlie Dog" eventually sired a son, and "Willie B." later recanted and treated his nephew as a grandson.[2]

Retired general William DePuy, a close friend of Thurman's and no slouch himself where energy, vitality, dedication, and productivity are concerned, said of Max Thurman: "Wherever he is, there's sort of a little dust storm of activity. You know, staff officers coming and going, day and night, unusual hours, doing jobs that no other officer would ever ask anybody to do. He gets all these jobs he never had any contact with and does them very well." Gen. Carl Vuono, the Army chief of staff, said of General Thurman: "He epitomizes selfless service, applying every ounce of his will, intellect, and ability to the challenges at hand. From the success of the volunteer force, through the victory of Just Cause, to the ongoing counternarcotics campaign, his standards of excellence set the ultimate example for our Army."[3]

Gen. Frederick F. Woerner, Jr., fifty-seven, USMA Class of 1955, had been the commander in chief of the U.S. Southern Command since April of 1987. He had had long experience in a variety of assignments in Central and South America. From 1966 to 1969 he served with the U.S. Military Group in Guatemala; he was with the Uruguay Military Institute in 1969 and 1970; he was commanding general of the 193d Infantry Brigade in Panama from 1982 to 1986. General Woerner, who spoke Spanish fluently, was intimately familiar with Panama and the Panamanians.[4]

On 17 February 1989, in a speech to a regional business group in Panama, General Woerner said that the United States was "ill prepared" to deal with the Panama situation "because, as you well know, we have a vacuum in Washington in the absence of an appointment of an assistant secretary of state for Latin American affairs." President Bush in a follow-on news conference defended his record of appointments, pointing out that he had already named sixty-seven executive branch appointees compared with fifty-five for President Reagan at the same point in his first term.

On 20 July 1989, Secretary of Defense Cheney announced that General Woerner was to retire. Apparently his criticism of the U.S. policy in Panama had antagonized the Bush administration. He is reported also to have felt that a political solution rather than a military solution to the Noriega problem was a preferred course of action.[5] At about the same time, the secretary asked General Thurman to put off his retirement and take over command of U.S. Southern Command in Panama. Given General Thurman's penchant for challenge and responsibility, he accepted willingly.

On the last weekend in September 1989, two significant command changes in the hierarchy of the U.S. military occurred: General Colin L. Powell, fifty-two, a former national security adviser to President Reagan, assumed the military's number-one position, chairman of the Joint Chiefs of Staff; in Panama, General Thurman assumed command of the U.S. Southern Command. As events were to prove, the selections of the well-rounded, universally accepted, politically "savvy" Colin Powell as the nation's top military leader and of the "aggressive," totally dedicated, widely experienced Max Thurman as the U.S. military boss in Panama were singularly propitious.

Some three days after these changes at the top of the U.S. military structure, a small group of PDF officers in Panama sought to alter their own top-level command structure more radically: They staged a coup. It began with some confidence. At about 0700 hours on 3 October, a procession of military jeeps and trucks carrying standing, armed soldiers jammed into their cargo compartments raced up Avenue A in Panama City and came to a squealing, noisy halt near the Comandancia. Out of the trucks poured about a hundred armed PDF troops who joined another two hundred already in place inside and outside the building. One of the rebel units was the PDF 4th Company. Part of the rebels stormed inside; another group stationed themselves outside. Shortly, gunfire echoed both inside and outside the Comandancia. In about an hour and a half, the firing stopped; the Comandancia was in the hands of the rebels.

One observer, a prisoner of the regime, witnessed the attack from his cellblock in a prison overlooking the Comandancia. He saw a small red helicopter land near the Comandancia. Soon he saw PDF troops set up machine guns around the headquarters. At about 0830 he heard the shooting begin. After a short firefight he saw that the PDF soldiers seemed to be surrendering to other units that had laid siege to the building. And much to his surprise, he saw that some of the so-called Dobermans, Noriega's elite riot unit dressed in riot gear and wearing helmets and carrying truncheons, were among the rebel forces.

At about 1130, the rebel leaders broadcast a communiqué on national radio announcing that General Noriega had been captured, that he and his entire high command had been forced into retirement, and that new elections would be held. The rebels added that the coup was "strictly a military movement" and that "there is no politics involved." The rebels also captured a state radio station and a Noriega-controlled TV station.

The leader of the coup was apparently Maj. Moises Giroldi Vega, the thirty-eight-year-old commander of the Urraca battalion, which was in charge of the security of the Comandancia. That Giroldi was the leader of the coup was surprising because he had been a loyalist and had been key to putting down a previous coup attempt in March of 1988. In fact, Noriega was the godfather of one of Giroldi's children. Other leaders of the coup, both of whom had signed the communiqué, were Capt. Jesús George Balma, chief of the PDF Special Forces, and Capt. Edgardo Dandoval, chief of the company responsible for public order.

The apparent success of the coup was short-lived. At about 1000 hours, a few hours after the fighting started, the elite PDF Battalion 2000, a well-equipped and well-trained unit, with many of its members Cuban-trained, left its base at Fort Cimarron, near Torrijos/Tocumen Airport, about fifteen miles northeast of the Comandancia. Battalion 2000, with some two hundred to three hundred officers and men "on a good day," according to one U.S. officer, allegedly contained 90 percent of the PDF firepower—including 120mm mortars, rocket launchers, and armored personnel carriers. Once it arrived at the Comandancia,

Battalion 2000, led by Maj. Francisco Olechea, encircled and attacked the rebels with rifle fire, grenades, and mortars. "Heavy fighting" took place in the early afternoon but, by 1400 hours, the battle was about over. Battalion 2000 was gathering up the rebels outside; the ones inside surrendered after little additional fighting. The loyalists recaptured the radio and TV station that the rebels had seized earlier in the day. Ten rebel troops, including Major Giroldi, died during the coup attempt; eighteen loyal troops and five civilians were wounded.[6]

As it so happens in even the best-laid military combat plans, the 3 October coup ran into complications, unexpected and unplanned-for developments, and failed. Murphy's Law was in effect even in Panama. In the first place, in planning the coup, Giroldi had counted on the neutrality of Olechea and Battalion 2000. But Olechea reneged and decided to come to Noriega's rescue simply because Giroldi did not get word to him that Noriega had been captured early in the fighting. Loyalist commanders then pressured Olechea to act. Giroldi's widow, who escaped to Miami after the botched coup, called Olechea a "turncoat."

In the second place, the rebels had expected over a thousand members of the PDF to join the revolt. As it turned out, fewer than three hundred troops made the scene. Nor did the coup planners seem to care much about security and secrecy. The United States, and even an exile in Miami, knew about the attempt before it was launched. Noriega reputedly had wind of the plot, but not the exact time and date.

In the third place, the rebels apparently had very limited goals. The coup leaders were midlevel officers whose goals were not the overthrow of the government—they even offered to recognize Noriega's puppet president, Francisco Rodriguez—but redress for low pay and lack of promotions. According to a spokesman for the U.S. secretary of defense, Giroldi had "no program, no civilian connection, nothing we could latch onto."

In the fourth place, the rebel leader, Giroldi, after having cornered Noriega in his office, where he was protected by two loyal bodyguards armed with submachine guns, tried to reason with him and persuade him to retire instead of killing him or turning him over to the Americans. He never placed him under arrest.

How Noriega and his loyal supporters broke the rebels' hold on the Comandancia is not clear. Certainly, the arrival of Battalion 2000 at midday had a significant effect on assisting in quelling the rebellion. In addition, apparently Noriega radioed orders to loyalists outside the building to gather up the families of the rebel leaders and hold them as hostages. Another version holds that the rebels allowed Noriega to telephone his mistress, Vicky Amado, who in turn contacted loyal army leaders, who came to his rescue. A third version may have some credibility. In this scenario, Noriega, still under control by the rebel leaders, learns that the loyal units have the building surrounded. Then he faces an armed Giroldi and yells at him: "To be a commander, you have to have balls. You don't have balls." In the face of the tirade, Giroldi wilts and surrenders. There is even some speculation that at that point Noriega "explodes in rage and orders the immediate execution of several of the coup leaders" and personally kills Giroldi. Another version—and this is probably the most exact—holds that Noriega ordered the PDF to move the leaders of the coup to Tinajitis, site of the PDF Mortar School, where they were tortured for more information on the coup leaders and then executed. Two days later, Noriega said that he had negotiated his own freedom from his captors and that "he had talked them into laying down their arms."

Noriega's reaction to the coup was swift and retributive. On the evening of 3 October he appeared on national television and called the rebellion a further attempt by the United States to prevent the implementation of the 1977 Panama Canal treaties and to "install another government of sellouts." He said that the coup "was part of the continuing aggression and penetration of the PDF by the United States." He also admitted that he had had advance knowledge of the coup. He imposed a curfew that night, and the next day Panama City was apparently "calm." On the fourth, his government announced that ten rebel soldiers, including Giroldi, had died, twenty-one had been wounded, and that thirty-seven soldiers had been taken prisoner.

Surprisingly, some of the prisoners were of high rank and held responsible positions in the PDF. Their defection indicated high-level discontent with Noriega's regime. Among the prisoners were Col. Guillermo J. Wong, the head of military intelligence; Col. Julion Ow Young, a member of the general staff of the PDF, who supervised the hated "Dobermans"; Lt. Col. Armando Palacios Gondola, head of the agency that worked with the United States on joint military operations; and two members of the Strategic Military Council set up by Noriega after the failed 1988 coup as an alternative to the general staff of the PDF. One of Noriega's close confidants said, "This was no gringo plot. This came from the general's inner core." U.S. officials said that the 4th Company, which had sided with the rebels, was "purged," and that some of the coup leaders had been tortured and then executed.

On the fifth, Noriega called for a "crackdown" on the opposition, banned unauthorized assemblies, and urged government employees to turn in traitors. He also froze the salaries of civilian government employees, some of whom had reacted too rapidly to word that the coup had succeeded and had happily torn photos of Noriega from their office walls. Noriega cautioned the Panamanians that he might impose "emergency laws" and that, under the current circumstances, this was "no time to talk democracy." Summing up his philosophy of command, certainly no surprise to the browbeaten citizens of Panama, he said that there would be "clubs for the indecisive, bullets for enemies, and money for friends" during the current crisis.

In keeping with that philosophy, on the night of the fifth, armed PDF troops attacked the offices of the opposition coalition and seized about a dozen members of the Liberal Party, including Endara, who was released by the weekend and took refuge in the Vatican diplomatic mission. The Panamanian government admitted that seventy-seven opponents had been jailed and that many others had been "beaten up" on the streets.

Noriega had regained control after a very short fall from power. But in spite of—perhaps because of—the rapidity and brutality of his "crackdown" on the rebels and the opposition, he must have sensed that his ironclad control might be cracking and that he could not know whence might come the next attempt. In a figurative sense, he had to look to his rear constantly. His daily change of sleeping quarters was an indication of his increasing paranoia.

The role of the United States in the 3 October rebellion might be described as one of studied, minor involvement almost to the point of detached passivity but nonetheless with great concern and interest, to and including the White House, in the outcome.

The U.S. administration was aware in advance that rebels were planning a coup. On Sunday, 1 October, Giroldi advised representatives of the CIA in Panama that a coup attempt was "imminent." In spite of the long connection between the PDF and U.S. intelligence agencies, this was apparently the first indication the United States had of the pending coup. Because of Giroldi's previous close ties to Noriega, however, U.S. officials were skeptical and suspected perhaps a Noriega "sting" operation, an attempt to draw the United States into committing itself prematurely, to the detriment of its relations with the rest of Latin American nations, who are always concerned about undue *yanqui* influence in the area. "Giroldi's a bastard, a sort of mini-Noriega," declared one Pentagon spokesman. "Warning signs went up. We feared a Noriega trap." The fact that both Generals Powell and Thurman had been in their posts only a couple of days added to the suspicion of a "sting." U.S. officials had learned to respect Noriega's deviousness, resiliency, and cunning.[7]

A change of command in the military establishment is a significant event—not only for the commanders involved but perhaps, more important, for the command itself. The staff and commanders are faced with a new leader whose policies, work methods, temperament, and personality are generally unknown. And the higher the level of the command, the more widespread is the impact of the new leader.

The change of command at SOUTHCOM on 30 September 1989 was such an event. General Woerner was leaving for retirement, and General Thurman was assuming command just days after he thought he was going to retire. The staff and commanders in SOUTHCOM had heard of the legendary Max Thurman and his penchant for long hours, hard work, and attention to detail and the fact that he expected the same dedication from his staff. The officers in SOUTHCOM were resigned to lost weekends and long workdays and worknights.

After the change of command ceremony on Saturday, Max Thurman went to his office. His staff gave him a series of detailed briefings on all of the nations in his command area, with emphasis on the current situation in Panama. General Thurman was in his office the next day, Sunday, just as if it were any other workday. To him, it was. At about 2230, one of his staff officers reported to him that the CIA had had a report from the wife of one of the senior PDF officers that a coup was planned for the next day. At 0200 the next morning, two men from the CIA reported to General Thurman that the leader of the coup was Maj. Moises Giroldi, who, they added, had been instrumental in putting down a coup against Noriega in March of 1988. He had handed the coup leaders over to Noriega, who had had them tortured and imprisoned. To General Thurman, the details of the coup seemed ridiculously amateurish. He thought it benevolent after the CIA representatives told him that Giroldi simply wanted Noriega to retire.

General Thurman called Lt. Gen. Thomas W. Kelly, director of operations (J-3) on General Powell's JCS staff, at his home on a secure phone at about 0230 and gave him what details he knew. He said that the rebels wanted SOUTHCOM troops to assist by blocking two access roads into Panama City, one near the jointly occupied Fort Amador and the other at the Bridge of the Americas. The rebels reasoned that by blocking these roads they would prevent the loyal 5th and 7th PDF companies from getting into Panama City and the Comandancia in time to block the coup. The rebels wanted no other U.S. assistance. Thurman recommended that the United States stay out of it. The whole setup looked too suspicious from a number of angles.[8]

General Powell had just taken over chairmanship of the Joint Chiefs of Staff at midnight on the first of October. General Kelly woke him early on Monday morning, Powell's first day on duty, with the news from Panama. General Powell relayed the news to Secretary Cheney at his home and then headed for the Pentagon in the dark of an early Monday morning.

Later that morning, after a meeting in Secretary Cheney's office, the secretary, Generals Powell and Kelly, and Rear Adm. Edward D. Sheafer, the deputy director of the Defense Intelligence Agency for support of the JCS, headed for the White House. General Powell briefed the president on the developments and recommended that, due to the nature of the coup's plan and the doubts about the leader, the United States not get involved—at least for now. The rebels would "have to do it alone."

There was no coup on Monday. Giroldi's wife said that it would happen on Tuesday, the third.[9]

On Tuesday morning, General Thurman was up before dawn and in his office in Quarry Heights. At 0740 he had a report that there was shots fired in the vicinity of the Comandancia, about a mile from Quarry Heights. As soon as Max Thurman got word that the coup was under way, he called General Powell and relayed as much information as he had—which, at that point, was probably very little. General Powell asked about Noriega's whereabouts. General Thurman at that point could not give a definitive answer. Powell ordered the roadblocks into effect, and Thurman ordered his twelve thousand in-country troops to assume "Delta" alert, wherein troops in battle gear move to previously reconnoitered positions to protect and defend U.S. installations in the area. In the blocking positions, U.S. units from Fort Amador got in the way of the PDF 5th Infantry Company, which shared a portion of Fort Amador with the Americans. Other units from the U.S. Howard Air Force Base took up a position near the Bridge of the Americas to impede the 7th Infantry Company, which was some sixty miles to the southwest of Panama City. The PDF did not confront the Americans at either roadblock.

Fort Clayton is the main U.S. Army base in Panama and the headquarters of U.S. Army South's commander, Brig. Gen. (at that time) Marc A. Cisneros. Sometime late in the morning, two rebel lieutenants reported to the gate at Fort Clayton. The MPs took them to General Cisneros's office. General Cisneros was called "The *Simpático* Soldier" by *U.S. News & World Report* in its 30 July 1990 issue. He had spent four years in Panama, spoke fluent Spanish, frequently visited small towns in Panama, and spoke to the people in their native tongue. He called Noriega a "dime-store dictator." He was a hero to the Panamanians who knew him.[10]

The rebel lieutenants told General Cisneros that the coup had been successful and that Noriega was under arrest in the Comandancia. General Cisneros passed this information to General Thurman and up the chain to the Pentagon and the White House, who decided to tell the rebels that the United States "was prepared to lift this burden from their hands." The rebels turned down the offer, apparently in keeping with the very unambitious and dangerous goals they had set for themselves. The rebels never did want to turn over Noriega to the United States, even though a botched message from Panama read that the rebels "want" to turn over Noriega instead of the correct "won't" turn over Noriega.

On 8 October Secretary of State James A. Baker and Secretary of Defense Richard Cheney confirmed a report in the *Washington Post* that early on the afternoon of 3 October, General Powell had relayed authorization to General Thurman to remove Noriega to a U.S. military base if that could be done without an overt show of American force. But by the time Max Thurman received the authority, the coup had collapsed. Thurman had also been authorized two other options: the first was to receive Noriega if the rebels handed him over, and the second was to seize Noriega by overt military force—but only on the authority of the president.

The U.S. congressional reaction to the failed coup was typical: Some members of Congress praised the Bush administration for its caution in avoiding an all-out rush to aid the rebels, while other more combative and vociferous members, both Republicans and Democrats, deplored the fact that the administration let slip through its cautious hands a unique opportunity finally to bring Noriega to justice. Congressman Dave McCurdy (D., Okla.) said, "Yesterday makes Jimmy Carter look like a man of resolve. There's a resurgence of the wimp factor." And some editorials matched the botched handling of the coup to Kennedy's Bay of Pigs fiasco and Carter's Iran hostage rescue mission.

On 4 October Secretary Cheney said that the rebels "were clearly not of a mind to turn [Noriega] over to us. They were talking about having him retire in Panama. They were not willing to have him extradited to the United States." On that same day, Marlin Fitzwater, the White House spokesman, said that the United States had "traditionally stopped short of . . . military involvement" and that President Bush did not want to interfere in the affairs of a Latin American nation. Secretary Baker testified before the Senate Finance Committee and repeated that the United States retained the option of using force but that "if you're going to risk American lives, it's the president's view that you do so on your own timetable. You do so based on your own plans, at a time of maximum opportunity and advantage."

Those assertions from the administration did not assuage the belligerency of the likes of ultraconservative senator Jesse Helms (R., N.C.), the ranking Republican on the Senate Intelligence Committee. Apparently he and other members of that committee had been briefed by the CIA that the rebels held Noriega, that they wanted to turn him over to the United States, and that they had invited U.S. troops to fight their way into the Comandancia and capture Noriega. On 5 October, after it had become clear that the administration had done little to seize Noriega or to aid the rebels, Senator Helms called the Bush team a bunch of "Keystone Kops" who showed a "total lack of planning." In rebuttal, Secretary Cheney, well aware of the reluctance of the rebels to capture Noriega or to turn him over to the United States, called Senator Helms's version of the event "hogwash" and defended the decision to avoid an open battle with the PDF.

Congressman Les Aspin (D., Wis.) was bluntly positive: "We should go in and capture Noriega." He declared that we didn't need military intervention but just a "snatch. All I want is Noriega." Senator John Kerry (D., Mass.) surprisingly described the administration's timidity as "a black mark on our diplomacy and our values."

As a final put-down to Helms, the Senate on 5 October voted 74–25 against a Helms proposal that would have allowed the president to use armed force to seize Noriega, bring him to trial in the United States, and restore democracy to Panama.[11]

One result of the coup attempt was an 11 October meeting between senior administration officials and members of the Senate Intelligence Committee. President Bush called the meeting in an attempt to smooth the relations between the administration and the committee's chairman, Senator David Boren (D., Okla.). Present at the meeting were President Bush, national security adviser Gen. Brent Scowcroft, Senator Boren, and the committee's vice chairman, William S. Cohen (R., Me.). The group discussed new guidelines for intelligence operatives in Panama in the event of another coup. The guidelines would make clear what was and what was not permissible in the intelligence-gathering activities. One guideline would provide for U.S. military, diplomatic, and intelligence officials in Panama to engage in clearer and speedier communications with the potential coup leaders. A former CIA director said that "The first, the absolute first thing you do in this case [a coup attempt] is to put somebody with a radio next to him."

The administration also decided, after reviewing Scowcroft's analysis of the 3 October debacle, to convene automatically the Deputies Committee as a crisis-management body in future emergencies. The Deputies Committee, made up of the second-highest-ranking officers of the State and Defense departments, of the Joint Chiefs of Staff, and of the CIA, would monitor the flow of information feeding into the White House Situation Room and take appropriate action.

But the 3 October coup, a blundering, low-level, limited-objective failure, was not without other benefits to the United States—both to the civilian and military sides of the administration. When the dust of the coup had settled a bit, the Bush planners in the White House could understand even more clearly the vulnerability and tenuousness of Noriega's power. They also hoped that Noriega's brutality in putting down the rebellion might "fire up" the opposition and lead to another, more successful attempt to oust him. And the White House realized that Noriega's strength, the PDF, might be waning in view of the rank and number of PDF officers who were purged by Noriega in the aftermath of the coup.

The planners in the Pentagon and in USSOUTHCOM learned a great deal from the reaction of the various elements of the PDF. According to one of the planners of Just Cause, the intelligence and operations sections of USSOUTHCOM "watched Noriega move his forces around" and learned of the loyalty and strength of the 6th and 7th companies at Rio Hato, the 5th at Fort Amador, and Battalion 2000 at Fort Cimarron. They also identified those PDF officers who were Noriega supporters and those who might assist the United States in the future. These were some of the more obvious merits emerging from the coup. But underneath these results, the planning at USSOUTHCOM went on with increased intensity and tempo.[12]

4 | The Planning Phase

       The worsening political situation in Panama sent waves of increased work loads through the planning staffs not only of the JCS and SOUTHCOM but also through the principal tactical command, the XVIII Airborne Corps at Fort Bragg, North Carolina. With each passing day it became clearer that the Bush administration might be required to take some decisive military action in its own national interest.

The XVIII Airborne Corps is the U.S. Army's primary command for quick-reaction contingency-type operations. The corps commander has under him a vast array of active Army units (with many U.S. Army Reserve and National Guard units subject to call-up to fill out the units needed for specific operations) that he can tailor to meet a wide variety of possible contingencies around the world. The divisions under the immediate command of the corps commander are the 82d Airborne Division, at Fort Bragg; the 101st Airborne Division (Air Assault), at Fort Campbell, Kentucky; the 10th Mountain Division (Light Infantry), at Fort Drum, New York; the 24th Infantry Division (Mechanized), at Fort Stewart, Georgia; and, for contingency planning, the 7th Infantry Division (Light), at Fort Ord, California. The corps also commands two separate maneuver brigades, the 197th Infantry Brigade (Mechanized) (now the 3d Brigade, 24th Mech Division), at Fort Benning, Georgia, and the 194th Armored Brigade, at Fort Knox, Kentucky. In addition, the corps commands ten separate combat support and combat service support brigades, including the 18th Aviation Brigade, the XVIII Airborne Corps Artillery, the 20th Engineer Brigade, the 525th Military Intelligence Brigade, the 16th Military Police Brigade, the 35th Signal Brigade, the 18th Personnel Group, the XVIII Corps Finance Group, the I Corps Support Command, and the Dragon Brigade, all at Fort Bragg. The entire command consists of some eighty-five thousand troops at posts scattered throughout the United States.

In August General Thurman had not yet taken over SOUTHCOM, but he made himself ready to do so in the interim. He flew into Fort Bragg to review both the Joint Special Operations Command (JSOC) and the XVIII Airborne Corps contingency plans for Panama. The staff discussed "Blue Spoon," a plan already in existence for military action by U.S. forces against the PDF. After the briefing, given by officers of the corps staff and the Joint Special Operations Command, General Thurman made some suggestions (he was not yet in the chain of command and therefore not in a position to issue directives) dealing with the size of the forces involved. He also expressed his personal view that enough force should be committed initially to overwhelm the opposition in every objective area. He pointed out that superior force and firepower save the lives of Americans as well as Panamanians. He also arranged for Maj. Gen. William A. Roosma, the XVIII Airborne Corps deputy commanding general, to visit Panama.[1]

In early September, General Roosma and a team of key commanders and staff officers from the corps flew to Panama to conduct a detailed reconnaissance of the area of operations and to meet with SOUTHCOM staff and the major commanders on the ground. Based on this reconnaissance and discussion, Lt. Gen. Carl Stiner, the XVIII Airborne Corps commander, raised to the highest level the priority of work for the corps staff on the Panama contingency plan. Col. Thomas H. Needham, the corps G-3, and Col. William H. Walters, the corps G-2, worked long hours with their staffs to revise the Blue Spoon plan, incorporating General Thurman's guidance. Colonel Needham set up a planning cell with LTC Tim McMahon, the corps director of plans, and Maj. David H. Huntoon, Jr., the corps principal planner for Panama, as the editor and author, respectively, of the new operations plan. The result was XVIII Airborne Corps Op Plan 90-2, which became the essential planning blueprint for Operation Just Cause. Although based on Blue Spoon, Op Plan 90-2 called for the rapid deployment and the simultaneous employment of overwhelming combat power—both from special operations forces and conventional forces. The planners knew that this unique combination would be effective but complex. But they also knew that they could make it work.[2]

After the failed 3 October coup, and once he was in command of SOUTHCOM, General Thurman wasted no time in accelerating the revision of the SOUTHCOM plan. His chief planner was BG William Hartzog, the J-3 for USSOUTHCOM. Thurman first gave his explicit guidance to the planners. They, in turn, set to work updating the plan and reconnoitering the entire area of operations.

On 9 October, at the request of General Thurman, General Stiner and his key staff, including Colonels Needham and Walters, flew to Panama for a contingency planning summit. Operational security was a major concern for the members of the team from Fort Bragg. They wore civilian clothes, flew in a special-mission (unmarked) aircraft, and scheduled their arrival at Howard Air Force Base in Panama during darkness. For three full days and nights, the two staffs huddled in the USSOUTHCOM Command Post at Quarry Heights, compared their plans, and ironed out operational and tactical details of potential PDF targets and U.S. responsibilities. XVIII Airborne Corps Op Plan 90-2 served as a baseline for this planning session. One salient feature emerged from the conference: In any contingency, General Stiner would be in overall command of all U.S. combat forces, regardless of service, and including Special Operations Forces. Thurman recognized the all-important principle of "unity of command"—one man in charge of all forces—neglected in such operations as Grenada and the hostage mission in Iran, and insisted on its application in this operation.[3]

While his staff was working with the SOUTHCOM staff revising the plans, General Stiner went on a personal helicopter reconnaissance of the probable areas of operation with Col. Mike Snell, the commander of the 193d Infantry Brigade, stationed permanently in Panama. Snell was intimately familiar with Panama, its terrain, road networks, cities, and force deployments. Colonel Snell's headquarters was at Fort Clayton, directly in front of the Miraflores Locks of the Panama Canal. His brigade consisted of one airborne infantry battalion, the 1st of the 508th Airborne, at Fort Kobbe (south of Howard Air Force Base), and one light infantry battalion, the 5th of the 87th Infantry, at Fort Clayton. General Stiner's air reconnaissance helped him to round out his analysis of "METT-T"—the Army's acronym for mission, enemy, troops, terrain, and time—all elements that must be carefully studied to develop a workable operational plan. He looked carefully at the various locations he thought would be significant objectives in "taking down" the PDF, Noriega's backbone of power. These sites included, as a first priority, the Comandancia, Noriega's major military and political headquarters; then Tinajitas, the location of the PDF's 1st Rifle Company and its mortar school; Panama Viejo, where several PDF elements had moved following the 3 October coup; Fort Espinar, in the "old" Canal Zone, the location of the PDF 8th Company; and the key terrain features and road networks surrounding these principal PDF locations.

General Thurman, acting on guidance from the White House and the JCS, dictated that the continency plan for Panama must include the following objectives: Protect U.S. lives and key sites and facilities; capture and deliver Noriega to competent authority; neutralize the Panamanian Defense Forces; support the establishment of a United States–recognized government in Panama; and restructure the PDF.[4]

With these objectives in mind, General Stiner and the staffs of both USSOUTHCOM and the XVIII Airborne Corps decided that Joint Task Force South (the name of General Stiner's command in the operation) would have to neutralize or protect some twenty-seven major targets simultaneously, employing surprise and minimizing collateral (i.e., not mission-essential) damage. Additional major targets outside Panama City included Río Hato, some 70 miles southwest of Panama City and the location of the elite 6th PDF Mechanized Company and the 7th PDF Ranger Company (Machos des Montes—Men of the Mountains), key players in the Noriega countercoup battle on 3 October; Torrijos-Tocumen Airport, for use as a second aerial port of embarkation (in addition to the U.S. Howard Air Force Base) on the eastern side of the Panama Canal, from which U.S. forces could block the advance of the PDF Battalion 2000 at Fort Cimarron (this battalion had been another key force in the 3 October countercoup battle); Kurt Muse; and Noriega himself, known by now for his elusiveness, use of decoys (two cars each possibly containing Noriega going in opposite directions), and the strength of his personal security forces.

Lt. Gen. Carl W. Stiner, fifty-three, is a rangy six-footer from Tennessee who has lost none of his Tennessee drawl, twang, and sense of humor. He has a vibrant personality, a down-to-earth, direct approach to problems, and a frankness that is disarming and brooks no rationalizations or compromises. Passivity is not part of his makeup. He gets the facts, makes a decision, and gets on with the mission—whatever its nature. He graduated from Tennessee Polytechnical Institute with a B.S. in agriculture and was commissioned through the ROTC program. His career has been crammed with a variety of important command and staff assignments, ranging from commanding an infantry training brigade at Fort Benning, to project manager for training the Saudi Arabian National Guard, to chief of staff of the Rapid Deployment Joint Task Force at MacDill Air Force Base, to commander of the Joint Special Operations Command at Fort Bragg, to commander of the 82d Airborne Division. He is a Ranger and a master parachutist and obviously well qualified in "special" operations.[5]

In 1985 General Stiner was the commander of JSOC (Joint Special Operations Command). It was also in 1985 that four Palestinian terrorists took over the Italian cruise ship *Achille Lauro* when it was about thirty miles from Port Said. The terrorists rounded up about a hundred passengers in the ship's dining room and, using them as hostages, demanded the release of fifty Palestinian terrorists in Israeli jails. On 8 October 1985, off the coast of Syria, the terrorists murdered Leon Klinghoffer, a retired American who had suffered a stroke and was confined to a wheelchair.

Oliver North, in his role as chief planner for antiterrorism contingencies on the NSC, recommended to the president the deployment of a JSOC special antiterrorist team to try to nab the terrorists wherever they finally arrived. In the end, the terrorists boarded an Egyptian airliner after the *Achille Lauro* docked off Alexandria. North had already gotten President Reagan's approval to have the Navy force the plane to land in Sicily—but forbade the use of any force that would harm innocent people.

General Stiner and his team in two C-141's landed just after the Egyptian 737. Stiner's men quickly surrounded the 737, which was still "buttoned up" and had one engine running. The pilot refused to open the door or turn off the engine. "Then General Stiner," according to North in his book *Under Fire*, "had a portable stairway brought over. Stiner, one of the braver men on this planet, laid down his weapon, climbed the stairway, and opened the door. He was met by an Egyptian commando officer who pointed his submachine gun straight at the general.

"'I don't want you,' Stiner said. 'I want them.'"

The commando lowered his weapon and turned over the terrorists to Stiner and his men.[6] That was not the end of the *Achille Lauro* hijacking, but it points out the part played by Stiner and the sort of dedicated special operations officer he is.

General Stiner's unique background as a commander and staff officer of both special operations and conventional forces proved to be remarkably significant for all the diverse units of Joint Task Force South. That experience meant that General Stiner was able to provide both a sound planning insight and strong, confident leadership of all his forces when the plan was executed. Just Cause was to prove one salient point: Special operations forces and conventional forces could be meshed and integrated into one cohesive, effective fighting command.

He made his "war-fighting philosophy" clear to his planners: Hit first; surprise the enemy; overwhelm him with heavy combat power; use the cover of night for surprise during the initial assault and the follow-on attack so that one's superior forces are on the objectives at dawn; and fight under favorable conditions. With that guidance, the corps planners returned to Fort Bragg on 11 October. During the next week they revised OpPlan 90-2. This revision specified new postcoup PDF targets, expanded certain specified tasks to subordinate units, and integrated the streamlined command and control of all joint war-fighting forces in Panama under the leadership of General Stiner.[7]

General Stiner also deployed forward to Fort Clayton a six-man planning staff cell as a command and control advance element. Its mission was to refine contingency planning and report to General Stiner as a "directed telescope" on PDF activity. General Stiner also placed twenty key commanders and staff at Fort Bragg on a two-hour recall alert, and sharply increased senior staff and command focus on Panama for a potential contingency crisis.

On 19 October General Stiner and his corps key staffers made another "civilian clothes" visit to Panama. This time Stiner had called for a meeting of the commanders and staffs of the major units that would be involved in the operation. These included Maj. Gen. James H. Johnson, Jr., commander of the 82d; his G-3, Lt. Col. Dan K. McNeill; and his chief of plans, Maj. Bill Caldwell; Brig. Gen. Robert L. Ord, assistant division commander of the 7th Infantry Division (Light); and the task force commanders and senior operational staff of U.S. forces in Panama—Army, Air Force, Navy, and Marine Corps—including Lt. Gen. Peter Kempf, commander of the 12th Air Force; Brig. Gen. Robin Tornow, commander of Howard Air Force Base in Panama; Rear Adm. Jerry G. Gnecknow; and Col. Charles Richardson, commander of the Marines in Panama. Stiner's purpose in calling this two-day meeting, held in the Simón Bolívar Conference Room at Fort Clayton, the home of the U.S. Army South's headquarters, was to present the plan to his war-fighting commanders and "put all of the details together."[8]

By mid-November Noriega's increased belligerency toward Americans and his arrogance toward the Bush administration were beginning to be more and more apparent. On 15 November General Stiner and his principal operational staff officers made a third planning and orientation trip to Panama. But this one took on the aspects of more than a planning conference. The team from Fort Bragg included Colonel Needham; Colonel Walters; Col. Bill Mason, the Corps signal officer; and Major Huntoon. They flew to Panama in the crew compartment of one of two C-5A Galaxy cargo planes. These giant aircraft also carried six AH-64 Apache Attack helicopters and three OH-58 Kiowa Scout helicopters, along with four M-551 Sheridan tanks. The two C-5A's arrived at Howard Air Force Base under cover of darkness on 15 and 16 November. The helicopters and tanks were quickly unloaded and moved to covered locations—a blacked-out hangar. Three days later, key commanders and staff of the 82d Airborne Division and the 7th Infantry Division joined General Stiner at Fort Clayton for another contingency conference.

During this period, General Thurman had received information about potential terrorist attacks—sponsored by the PDF—against U.S. military installations throughout Panama. In response to these threats, the CINC activated Joint Task Force South (JTFSO), with General Stiner as commander, from 18 to 27 November. SOUTHCOM's alert status was also increased. Once this crisis receded, General Stiner returned to Fort Bragg, but the week of JTSFO command post training at Fort Clayton was to prove an excellent rehearsal for Operation Just Cause.[9]

While General Stiner was not in Panama planning, reconnoitering, and talking to and briefing subordinate commanders, he was visiting various major command headquarters in the United States, briefing the details of his plan. From mid-October to mid-November he made three trips to the Pentagon to brief the chairman of the Joint Chiefs and his staff. He briefed Admiral Frank Kelso, commander of the U.S. Atlantic Command, at his headquarters in Norfolk. Admiral Kelso was responsible for providing critical air cover for the D-day MAC airlift from CONUS bases to Panama. He visited Scott Air Force Base to brief the commander in chief of the Military Airlift Command (CINCMAC), Gen. Hansford T. Johnson. He sent Colonels Needham and Walters to brief the commanding general of the U.S. Army Forces Command, Gen. Edwin H. Burba, Jr., at his headquarters in Fort McPherson, Georgia. Stiner made certain that all major commands—Army, Navy, Air Force, and Marines—were in sync on the plan. This operation, Stiner assured himself, was not going to be another Grenada.[10]

At the end of November and in the first part of December, both conventional and special operations forces conducted rehearsals of their parts of OpPlan 90-2. These rehearsals were at Fort Bragg, at Eglin Air Force Base in Florida, in Panama, and at other locations in the southeastern United States. Operational security continued to be a major concern of all the commands. Rehearsals were done as parts of routine training exercises. Only a small number of senior commanders and staff in each unit knew about the link to the actual contingency plan.

General Thurman had scheduled a fourth planning conference, for 18 December. But by that time, Noriega had lost any composure he might have had. His paranoid ranting against the United States, his provocative acts against U.S. citizens and members of the U.S. military, and his seemingly out-of-control bouts of megalomania sealed his fate.

On 15 December, the 510-member, Noriega-appointed National Assembly of Representatives voted to raise his stature to head of government and "maximum leader of the struggle for national liberation" (apparently "liberation" from the dominance of the United States). At that same session, echoing Noriega's bellicosity and chest-thumping egotism, the National Assembly approved a resolution stating that "the Republic of Panama is declared to be in a state of war" with the United States as long as U.S. "aggression," in the form of economic sanctions imposed in 1988, continued. U.S. officials, with some logic but minimum reaction to such a declaration, concluded that Noriega had in fact declared war against the United States. But the pro-Noriega clique in Panama said, with self-serving logic, that it was simply a statement of the state of affairs brought about by the actions of the Bush administration.[11]

The next day, Saturday, the sixteenth of December, words of bombast gave way to acts of brutal harassment. Some PDF guards stopped a private car, a 1981 Chevrolet with Michigan license plates and carrying four off-duty, unarmed U.S. servicemen, at a roadblock outside PDF headquarters, the Comandancia, in the old section of Panama City. The PDF and a crowd of unruly civilians milled about the car. Panamanian soldiers tried to drag the U.S. officers from the car, but the Americans, apparently in some fear, attempted to drive away through the throng. The PDF opened fire with an AK-47 and mortally wounded one of the men in the car, Marine lieutenant Robert Paz, twenty-five, and wounded another officer in the ankle. Photos of the car after the incident showed at least three bullet holes in the car—two on the driver's side and one through the trunk. Later, the other men in the car explained that they had made a wrong turn and had gotten lost; the PDF counterclaimed that they were on an unauthorized reconnaissance.

Shortly after that incident, the PDF took into custody Lt. Adam J. Curtis, a Navy lieutenant, and his wife, Bonnie, who had been stopped at the same roadblock about a half hour earlier and had witnessed the shooting of Lieutenant Paz. The PDF blindfolded both of them with masking tape, held them in custody, interrogated them repeatedly, beat the officer brutally, kicked him in the groin and the head, and threatened to kill him if he did not give them information about his unit and his activities. The PDF threatened the officer's wife with sexual harassment—fondling her neck and the backs of her legs—and then cut her head when they slammed her against a wall to emphasize their point. She collapsed on the floor. When Lieutenant Curtis protested the treatment of his wife, the PDF interrogators shoved wads of paper into his mouth. One of them put a gun to Curtis's head and kicked him repeatedly in the groin. One of the soldiers told Bonnie that her husband would never again be able "to perform in bed." After four hours of interrogation and beatings, the PDF abruptly escorted the pair to an avenue that led back to the U.S. area and released them. Lieutenant Curtis and his wife made their way back to the U.S. Naval Station at about 0215.[12]

On Monday, 18 December, a U.S. lieutenant shot and wounded a PDF military policeman, Corp. Cesar Tejada, near a U.S. installation. As an isolated incident, the circumstances might make the officer appear culpable. But given the increased tension in Panama City and Noriega's threats to Americans, the circumstances take on an entirely different look. The officer was in his car leaving a laundry in the Curundu area of western Panama City about a mile from PDF Headquarters and near Southern Command headquarters at Quarry Heights. The uniformed PDF soldier approached the officer's car and signaled him to stop. Later the officer claimed that he had felt "threatened" by the corporal, who appeared to be reaching for his gun. The officer fired two shots at

38

the PDF soldier, wounding him, according to one account, in the leg and the arm. He fell to the ground, then got up and left the scene.

On that same day, at a news conference, President Bush called the killing of Lieutenant Paz an "enormous outrage and a matter of enormous concern to this president." He refused to answer questions about a possible military response, saying, "All presidents have options. But they don't discuss what they might be." He did say, in response to a question about his possible steps: "For one, I can tell you how strongly I feel about it, which I've just done, and two, review whatever options might be available, and three, not discuss what they might be."[13]

The Bush administration had initially taken little public notice of the Panamanian National Assembly's "state of war" declaration. At the news conference, President Bush said only that "I've taken note of his statement." White House spokesman Marlin Fitzwater said that the declaration "may have been a license for harassment and threats." One top administration official described the president as "deeply disturbed" by the events in Panama. Former assistant secretary of state Abrams said, "The scuttlebutt I hear is that the sexual abuse of the Navy officer's wife sent Bush up the wall."

Noriega's days of mostly unchallenged power were winding down. His sometimes strong, sometimes tenuous ties to the United States were loosening and unraveling at a rapid pace. The CIA had played along with him because he furnished intelligence on Central America and the Caribbean. And in the war on drugs, he seemed to assist the efforts of the United States. From time to time, in the words of U.S. customs commissioner William von Raab, "they [Noriega and company] would swing some poor slob out, in effect give him away to make us feel they're cooperating [in the drug war]." And occasionally, perhaps to penalize his drug traffickers who did not pay off, Noriega would assist the United States in seizing large amounts of drugs.

He cooperated in other ways. He permitted United States–supported Nicaraguan contra rebels to train on Coiba Island, off Panama. He even suggested to Col. Oliver North, during one of North's frequent visits to Panama in 1985, that he would assassinate Nicaraguan Sandinista leaders and carry out various forms of sabotage within the country. But in exchange, he wanted the Reagan administration to improve his image in the United States. But at the same time, the devious, double- and triple-dealing Noriega was allegedly running arms to the Sandinistas and to Communist rebels in Colombia and El Salvador and supplying U.S. intelligence to Castro.[14]

Noriega had set the stage for the final act in his Panamanian drama. The cast would be drawn, for the most part, from the military forces of the United States and his own PDF and Dignity Battalions. The actuality of his declaration of a state of war against the United States was about to come to pass.

*　　*　　*

The most important item of information for any combat commander, whether he be a sergeant commanding a squad in attack or a general in command of a theater, is, "What's my mission?" Once the commander knows the answer to that vital question, he can proceed with his planning. Then he gathers intelligence on the enemy to determine the objectives he must attack to accomplish his mission; he tailors his forces to seize the objectives with the greatest surprise and speed and to minimize casualties to his own troops; he plans the logistics flow to support the operation, always keeping in mind the wisdom of Murphy; and he sets up a chain of command so that an objective or group of objectives is assigned to one subordinate commander—the time-tested and proven principle of unity of command. As the old (September 1954) Department of the Army *FM 100-5, Field Service Regulations,* so succinctly puts it, unity of command "is best achieved by vesting a single commander with requisite authority." That means "one guy's in charge."

Such was the case with the operation that became known as Just Cause. The derivation of the mission of the forces in Just Cause started at the very top of the chain of command: the national command authority (NCA), the president's own top-level planners. The national objective in Panama was long-standing, brief, and broad: Restore democracy and remove Noriega. Those two national objectives translated into four military objectives: Protect U.S. citizens; defend the canal; restore democracy; and capture Noriega. Based on these objectives, the chairman of the Joint Chiefs of Staff had developed broad planning guidance to refine the operations order that had already been approved by the NCA. Some of the guidance: Use maximum surprise; unify the command structure; minimize collateral damage; use the minimum force necessary; plan no evacuation of noncombatants; and plan for postcombat operations to restore democracy in Panama.

The command relationship at the top level for the operation was streamlined and simple: It went from the president to the secretary of defense to the chairman of the Joint Chiefs of Staff to the commander in chief of the Southern Command to the commander of Joint Task Force South. More simply stated: from Bush to Cheney to Powell to Thurman to Stiner, the commander in the field. When the president decided on 17 December to implement the plan, many pre-H-hour actions started, one of the most important of which was the prepositioning of the tactical command and control element of JTF South in Panama prior to the start of the operation.

Once the chairman of the JCS had received the broad military objectives, he converted them into this mission for General Thurman: "Conduct joint offensive operations to neutralize the PDF and other combatants, as required, so as to protect US lives, property, and interests in Panama and to assure the full treaty rights accorded by international law and the U.S. Panama Canal treaties." (One must always wonder if General Westmoreland had had any such specific guidance for the conduct of the war in Vietnam.)

The JCS staff developed the basic concept for the operation into a threefold approach. Phase 1: Combat operations at the onset designed to neutralize and fix in place the PDF, capture Noriega, install a new government, and protect and defend U.S. citizens and key facilities. Phase 2: Stability operations to ensure law and order and begin the transition to support a newly installed government. Phase 3: Nation-building that supports the Endara government to include restructuring and training the new government. This phase would eventually be turned over to the Department of State and other interagency organizations as the U.S. government would assist with the economic and political rebuilding of Panama. These phases were intended to and in fact did overlap, with no clear breaks between them.[15]

In more specific terms, General Thurman's operational tasks, inherent in his mission, were these: Protect 30,000 U.S. citizens; defend 142 key facilities along the Panama Canal; neutralize the PDF, who were spread out in some 13 key objective areas; neutralize the nonuniformed, armed Dignity Battalion hoodlums, almost unidentifiable, as they mingled with other Panamanians on the streets, in vehicles of all sorts, and in various buildings; and find and capture the elusive Noriega—who moved on a random schedule and slept in a different house every night. General Thurman's basic strategy was simply stated but complex in execution: "Simultaneously attack the Panamanian combat forces in the Panama/Colón area and force their collapse." That strategy supported the execution of the other operational tasks.

Because SOUTHCOM is based in Panama and has been there in one form or another for over thirty years, its combat situation was unique: At the start of combat operations, it was already firmly established in what was to become "enemy territory" (but with insufficient combat forces to accomplish its assigned missions). Its intelligence division, therefore, had been able to gather and refine detailed information on the strength and location of the PDF and other targets of military and political value.

The threat, as General Thurman's G-2 saw it, was this: In general, the Panamanian Defense Force was primarily infantry. It was organized into 13 military zones with two battalions; ten independent companies; a cavalry squadron; a riot control company; special forces, including UESAT (Unidad Especial de Seguridad Antiterror); and commandos. The Air Force had thirty-eight fixed-wing aircraft and seventeen helicopters; the Navy had twelve vessels and a naval infantry company (similar to Marines).[16]

The PDF over the years had extended its tentacles to assume control of numerous facets of government. Although it was composed of nearly fifteen thousand people, approximately thirty-five hundred were members of combat units. The remainder were police forces, conservation officers and forest police, customs officials, and administrative personnel. Control by the PDF had spread far and wide. For example, the entire vehicular control system, from vehicle registration to transfer of titles, licensing, and traffic control, was in the hands of the PDF. It was an institution warped to support one man: Noriega. Graft and corruption ran rampant. Those who disagreed or did not support Noriega lost their jobs.

As the crisis developed, the threat of the Dignity Battalions also grew. Over an eighteen-month period, rudimentary basic military training had been conducted and the "Digbats" increasingly indoctrinated. Rumors of PDF plans to use Digbat members to take U.S. hostages circulated. Exposed PDF Plans "Genesis" and "Exodus" called for kidnapping of Americans and transporting them to the interior. In the event of an invasion, Operation "Montana" planned for the PDF to take to the mountains and conduct guerrilla warfare. If that happened, Digbats would be well positioned to provide recruits and auxiliary support.[17]

Battalion 2000 at Fort Cimarron, fifteen miles east of Panama City, was unique and "elite" for a very good reason: With the signing of the Carter-Torrijos treaty in 1979, the United States was committed to turning over the canal to Panamanian sovereignty in 1999. During the first eight years after the signing of the treaty, relations between Panama and the United States remained friendly. Approximately three thousand Americans lived on the Panamanian economy, and the United States assisted the PDF both in training and in design. During this eight-year period, the PDF developed a modern infantry battalion designed to take over the defense of the canal in the year 2000. The well-trained and highly motivated unit was named Battalion 2000 or "Battalion Dos Mil."

The bungled 3 October coup and the reaction to it by the various PDF units and their commanders gave the SOUTHCOM intelligence division valuable information. Battalion 2000, for example, was a key unit in aiding Noriega to put down the coup. It was, however, slow to react and to move into the city. The 1st Infantry Company was a two-hundred-man force at Tinajitas. It had always been a staunch supporter of Noriega and occupied a key piece of terrain just north of Panama City. The 2d Infantry Company had two hundred men at Torrijos-Tocumen Airport. It was historically loyal to Noriega but did not participate actively in the 3 October coup. The 5th Rifle Company was a three-hundred-man unit at Fort Amador. Most troops of the unit were Military Police, and the commander of the 5th Company was also the commander of the Balboa Police Station. The 5th Company did not support Noriega on 3 October, but it was still considered loyal to him. The 6th and 7th Rifle companies, together numbering some four hundred men, were based at Río Hato and were very loyal to Noriega. Key members of the units aided Noriega on 3 October. The SOUTHCOM G-2 considered these two companies to be the best fighting units in the PDF. The 8th Rifle Company was a 175-man force at Fort Espinar and, during the 3 October coup, moved into Panama City and assisted Noriega in putting down the threat. A PDF cavalry squadron of 150 men was at Panama Viejo. It was reconstituted after the coup and consisted primarily of UESAT personnel and remnants of the PDF considered loyal to Noriega.[18]

The Comandancia was the home of the 4th Infantry Company, commanded by Major Giroldi, the leader of the 3 October coup. Following the coup, Noriega disbanded the 4th Company and executed or jailed its leaders. At the time of Just Cause, the Comandancia was guarded by about 150 men from various companies, principally the 6th, 7th, and 8th, and many UESAT personnel—all of whom were extremely loyal to Noriega.

SOUTHCOM intelligence indicated that the above units would be the major pockets of resistance during the operation. The final piece in the threat mosaic was Noriega himself. All available intelligence assets were focused on tracking his whereabouts. But some intelligence experts feel that more could have been done to locate him.

Douglas Waller, writing in the 17 June issue of *Newsweek,* said:

Special-Ops officers were frustrated that their Intelligence Support Activity, a supersecret Army spy unit, was not allowed to send agents into Panama to track Noriega before the invasion. If they had, these sources insist, Noriega might have been captured the first night of Just Cause. The command had tried to ease what it claims are cumbersome procedures imposed by the CIA and other intelligence organizations, who review all covert spying operations. Before the invasion the command wanted to sneak agents into a Panama City warehouse to check out a tip that the drug cartel was storing five car bombs to assassinate Just Cause commander General Maxwell Thurman. But the command could never get interagency approval from Washington. CIA supporters say the agency had plenty of assets in Panama to collect the information, but the Southern Command kept the CIA station at arm's length because it considered the CIA too close to Noriega.[19]

The U.S. planners had what they needed for the operation. The commander at each level of command had his mission, and intelligence on the PDF and Noriega filtered through the chain; the force was ready.

One of the senior staff officers of the XVIII Airborne Corps wrote recently that

on the 17th of December, the key members of XVIII Airborne Corps staff were called into headquarters (the former brick and concrete pre–World War II post hospital), as we had been on a high state of readiness since the shooting incident and we had been notified by the Pentagon that possibility was high that the Operation Plan would be implemented soon. We requested and received permission to deploy a small element of Corps Assault CP under the guise of attending a previously scheduled conference on the Op Plan and possible CPX (Command Post Exercise). We flew in, arriving in AM of 18 December and began initial work on establishment of Corps/JTFSouth Command Post in the Emergency Operations Center (EOC) of US Army South. Only General Thurman and a few of his staff knew of pending operation in Panama at this time. Once the execute order was received at XVIII Airborne Corps on 18 December, General Stiner issued his orders to commanders located in Panama on 19 December. Orders to relevant commanders in CONUS were issued prior to his departure from Fort Bragg. Times for orders to be issued to subordinate units in Panama were established and occurred after units were assembled and sequestered from families/ public. Because of the shooting incident and current situation, bases and units were on a high state of alert in Panama and assembly of units had become a common occurrence.[20]

Lt. Gen. Carl Stiner was General Thurman's "war fighter." As the commander in charge of all operations, he had under his command for Just Cause nearly the entire 7th Infantry Division (Light), one parachute brigade of the 82d Airborne Division, a mechanized battalion from the 5th Mech Division, a battalion-sized task force of Marines, the three battalions of the 75th Ranger Regiment, task forces of SEALs and Special Forces from Naval Special Warfare Group 2 and the Army's 7th Special Forces Group, and the in-place 193d Light Infantry Brigade. Air support came from the 830th Air Division, the 24th Composite Wing from Howard Air Force Base, and assets from the 1st Special Operations Wing from Hurlburt Air Force Base, Florida. Additional combat support and combat service support units, such as the 41st Area Support Group and 1109th Signal Brigade, provided general support to the entire operation. In all, Stiner's troops numbered over twenty-seven thousand soldiers, sailors, airmen, and marines.[21]

Stiner was faced with neutralizing the PDF, garrisoned throughout the entire country. Not every position could be attacked simultaneously. The majority of the critical command and control nodes and the majority of U.S. citizens and interests were in Panama City, however. SOUTHCOM planners thought of the old Canal Zone and Panama City as the center of the target—the bull's-eye. In October, the PDF demonstrated their capability to reinforce the Comandancia rapidly from Río Hato and Fort Cimarron. Those two locations fell into the nine ring and could only be ignored at the peril of the rest of the operation. The rest of the country fell into the four or five ring and could be handled at a later date.[22]

Stiner's plan of attack called for a number of simultaneous attacks at various locations around the country.

- Task Force Bayonet: Isolate the Comandancia in the barrio of Chorillo, about four hundred meters south of Ancon Hill and USSOUTHCOM headquarters; seize and secure the Curundu-Ancon Hill-Balboa areas; air assault into Fort Amador and neutralize the PDF's 5th Company garrisoned there.
- Task Force Semper Fi: block the western approaches to the city and secure the Bridge of the Americas.
- Task Force Atlantic: Isolate Colón; neutralize the PDF 8th Company and naval infantry company; protect Madden Dam; free a number of political prisoners at Gamboa, midway across the isthmus.
- Joint Special Operations Task Force: Parachute assault onto Río Hato; neutralize the PDF 6th and 7th companies; disable PDF patrol craft in Balboa Harbor and a TV tower at Cerro Azul; deny the use of Paitilla Airport; mount operations to capture Noriega or rescue American hostages, as required; parachute assault onto Torrijos-Tocumen Airport.
- Task Force Pacific: Parachute assault onto Torrijos-Tocumen and then air assault to Fort Cimarron, Tinajitas, and Panama Viejo.

After the accomplishment of his initial missions, Stiner had the ongoing task of restoring law and order in Panama City and the outlying parts of the country.[23]

By the 19th of December all commanders in the operation knew their individual missions. The units had rehearsed their parts. The small-unit commanders had reviewed the details with their troops and had gone over each soldier's part in the operation. Woven together, the small-unit missions made up the fabric of the plan. The entire success of the operation was totally dependent on the readiness, the training, the discipline, and the enthusiasm of the soldiers in the teams, squads, platoons, companies, and batteries. No military plan, no matter how grandiose, how thoroughly war-gamed, how detailed, how completely blessed by the chain of command, is worth more than the tabulated volume it is unless the troops at the "forward edge" are combat-ready professionals. This operation, which melded together special forces of the Army, Navy, Air Force, and Marines with conventional forces, was an exercise to test the professionalism of the troops, the planning excellence of the staffs at the higher levels, and new equipment that had never before been used in combat. On the evening of the nineteenth, all commands were on the alert; rehearsals, briefings, soul-searching, second-guessing, and rewriting plans were over.

Operation Just Cause was about to be launched.

5 | The Decision

Some 330 days into his administration, President George Bush was faced, for the first time, with a decision to commit American troops to battle—and with it the unavoidable combat deaths and wounded that would result. As he pondered the decision, he must have at least momentarily visualized and weighed the consequences of battle casualties not only to his own personal feelings but also to those of the American people. Inevitably, the TV cameras would record for the evening news scenes of body bags, flag-draped caskets, and wounded soldiers on stretchers being readied for air evacuation from the battle zone to hospitals in the States. The graphic, stifling, nightly TV coverage of the Vietnam war was not hidden in the past and lost to the American public's memory.

But Noriega's imperious conduct in Panama and his blatant, amateurish "nose-thumbing" at the United States had escalated U.S.-Panamanian relations to the "critical mass" stage. Negotiations, third-party emissaries, liaison visits from White House staffers, and empty public bantering were no longer viable courses of action for the president. By the seventeenth of December, the chairman of the Joint Chiefs of Staff, Gen. Colin L. Powell, was fully prepared to recommend a course of action that would answer the president's needs decisively.

Just Cause was the code name of the course of action that General Powell would recommend to the president. Just Cause was the contingency plan that finally evolved from a long series of plans that had been on the drawing boards of various headquarters for nearly two years. Contingency planning at the Joint Chiefs of Staff and at the headquarters of SOUTHCOM started in earnest after a U.S. federal court indicted Noriega in February 1988. At that time, the chairman of the Joint Chiefs of Staff, Admiral Crowe, issued, through his J-3, Lt. Gen. Thomas W. Kelly, a planning order, code-named "Elaborate Maze," to Gen. Frederick W. Woerner, Jr., then the commander in chief of the U.S.

46

Southern Command. Woerner's missions, according to the order, were to "protect U.S. lives and properties in Panama, assure full exercise of rights accorded by international law, and be prepared to conduct noncombat evacuation in a permissive or nonpermissive environment." After detailed examination of "Elaborate Maze" plans, both Crowe and Woerner found the plans wanting, because the plans did not consider and deal with the full panoply of possible contingencies.[1]

To accomplish the assigned missions, Woerner's staff at his headquarters in Quarry Heights, Panama, then produced a number of contingency plans, among them Post Time, Klondike Key, Blue Spoon, and Krystal Ball; collectively, these plans were known as Prayer Book. In April of 1988, Admiral Crowe approved, for "execution planning," the Prayer Book series of plans. Specifically, Blue Spoon would neutralize the PDF and other combatants as required; and Krystal Ball, changed later to Blind Logic because of operational security considerations, would stabilize the situation and restore law and order in Panama. In the original Blue Spoon plan, the equivalent of five brigades would deploy on a time-phased basis from the United States to bolster the U.S. forces already on the ground in Panama; a corps headquarters would accompany the brigades for "adequate command, control, and communications."[2]

On 8 November 1988, General Kelly called a Pentagon meeting of the members of his J-3 staff involved in contingency planning for Panama; the J-3 of SOUTHCOM, Brig. Gen. William W. Hartzog; and the director of operations of the Army's Forces Command, Maj. Gen. Jerry A. White. The group discussed "the adequacy of SOUTHCOM's plan to integrate XVIII Airborne Corps as the command and control element for Prayer Book." General Kelly decided that XVIII Airborne Corps would be the senior headquarters commanding all combat troops on the ground in Panama. From that time on, XVIII Airborne Corps headquarters was deeply involved in all phases of planning for the operation in Panama. The result of its planning was XVIII Airborne Corps Op Plan 90-2, the supporting plan for USSOUTHCOM Blue Spoon.

The election that Noriega negated in May of 1989 caused no significant changes in the Blue Spoon plans. But in the aftermath of the "stolen election," the JCS did ask General Woerner to review the "adequacy" of the Prayer Book series of plans.

What did cause a revision of SOUTHCOM's plans was the failed 3 October 1989 coup and the obvious lack of U.S. support for it. General Powell gave new guidance to General Thurman; each had just taken over his new duties. The chairman's guidance included "a need for a wider range of military options phased over time"; development of "a capability to respond on short notice to unforeseen contingencies in Panama"; integration of conventional and special operations forces; development of an operations order that "addresses increased levels of anti-U.S. activities to include active, hostile actions against U.S. lives, property, and/or interests"; and the assumption that the PDF will not be friendly. The new guidance obviously called for plans for the combat forces involved to go into Panama en masse and ready to fight for their objectives immediately. There would be no "gradual" buildup this time. General Powell's guidance thus included some time-honored and battle-tested principles of war: mass, objective, surprise, command and control, offensive, unity of command. In nonmilitary parlance that meant "Hit 'em hard, where and when they don't expect it and are not ready; give one guy all he needs to do the job and let him do it; get in, win, and get out."

The result of this guidance was a revised Blue Spoon that differed from its predecessor of April 1988 in several major ways: The 82d Airborne Division and the 75th Ranger Regiment, because of their unique capability for "forced entry" by parachute, were added to the troop list; all forces, conventional/unconventional, those already in place and those arriving after H-hour, would all be under the command of one individual—the commander of the headquarters formed specifically for this one operation, Joint Task Force South, Lieutenant General Stiner, commander of XVIII Airborne Corps; and, a significant tactical modification, the assault forces would strike their targets with maximum surprise, as "simultaneously" as possible, as opposed to the "time-phased flow of forces," a gradual buildup, called for in the old Blue Spoon. The new Blue Spoon also ordered the troops involved to "minimize collateral damage and use the minimum force necessary."

In early November, General Stiner and General Hartzog briefed the details of the new plans to the chairman. He approved the plans. On the seventh of November, the secretary authorized the augmentation of the existing forces in Panama.

Even though General Powell had been on the job as chairman of the Joint Chiefs of Staff for only a little over a month, he had kept close watch on the evolution of the plans, especially Blue Spoon. He was completely knowledgeable of the details of the plan through visits and briefings by Generals Thurman and Stiner and through his own J-3, General Kelly, who had been following the planning sequence from the time he assumed duties as the Joint Chiefs of Staff J-3 in March of 1988. Thus General Kelly was able to provide continuity between Admiral Crowe and General Powell.

The Joint Chiefs of Staff had followed in detail the buildup of the crisis in Panama precipipated by the PDF shooting of a car carrying four unarmed U.S. officers. Following are some of the entries in the J-3 chronolog, maintained in the Pentagon's Crisis Situation Room, just prior to the implementation of Just Cause:[3]

TIME   CHRONOLOG ENTRY

Saturday, 16 December 1989

TIME	CHRONOLOG ENTRY
2125	NMCC (National Military Command Center in the Pentagon) notified that four U.S. servicemen were involved in a shooting incident in Panama with PDF forces and that one serviceman was killed in the shooting.
2130	Phone call from BG Hartzog Lieutenant may die Heading out for dinner Inadvertently entered checkpoint near La Comandancia Surrounded—asked for IDs

48

	Four servicemen felt threatened; attempted to flee the area and were shot at
	Lieutenant Paz in Gorgas Hospital
2149	CJCS notified
	Directed call to General Stiner, MAC (Military Airlift Command), and JSOTF (LTG Kelly, J-3, made the call)
2151	Lieutenant Paz confirmed dead by doctors at Gorgas Hospital
	Gunfire reported in La Comandancia
	Friendly actions:
	Quick-reaction force assembling at Quarry Heights and Fort Amador
	Personnel Movement Limitation Delta set by USSOUTHCOM
	Noriega's location requested by Joint Staff
	USSOUTHCOM starting to put birds in the air
	Occasional gunshots at La Comandancia (unconfirmed)
	Gunfire reported in different places
2202	Traffic open on Bridge of the Americas
2203	Latest information given to VCJCS and CJCS
2205	MAC notified
2210	JSOTF notified with a "heads up" for warning order
2224	BG Hartzog reported:
	Apache helicopters launched
	Situation confused
	Dignity Battalion of PDF lost control
	Helos report no activity; La Comandancia blacked out, traffic flowing
2318	CDR PDF 5th In Co asks for a meeting

Sunday, 17 December 1989

0110	Joint Staff J-3 call to BG Hartzog
	Treaty Affairs meeting
	Panamanians visibly shaken
	Claim it was an isolated incident
	PDF told not to load ammo
0220	Two U.S. MPs taken custody at Tocumen Airfield by PDF and later released
0530	Official PDF statements on TV (disinformation)
	A sedan with U.S. plates broke through two security checkpoints guarding the Comandancia
	As a result of this incident a one-year-old girl, another man, and a PDF soldier were wounded
0701	Critic recap:
	The shooting had earlier been blamed on the now defunct 4th Rifle Company and Doberman Company

0800	At 0215, a USN lieutenant and his wife reported into security at Rodman.
	Reported their detention and witness to Lieutenant Paz shooting.
0900	CJCS briefed
0940	JSOTF response posture good
0945	LTG Kelly phone conversation with MG Kellum, MAC, forty-eight-hour response time

Sandwiched between meetings at the Pentagon on 17 December was an informal but significant "get-together" of the four top members of the Joint Chiefs of Staff in the study of General Powell's Quarters No. 6 at Fort Myer. His house, the traditional home of the chairman, is in a row of senior officers' quarters along the eastern edge of Fort Myer on high ground facing a magnificent view of Washington. General Vuono, the Army chief of staff, lived down the street. Senior members of the Army staff lived in houses to the left and right of the chairman's.

General Powell asked the chiefs to meet him for coffee at 1130. He elected to have the meeting at home instead of the Pentagon to avoid alerting the media that "something might be up" if all of the chiefs arrived at about the same time at the Pentagon on a Sunday morning.

The chief of naval operations, Adm. Carl Trost; the Marine Corps commandant, Alfred M. Gray, Jr.; the Army chief of staff, Carl Vuono; and the Air Force chief of staff, Larry Welch, arrived promptly and were greeted warmly by the chairman. While sitting around in easy chairs in the study and drinking coffee, General Kelly briefed them for about ten minutes on the current situation in Panama, the killing of Lieutenant Paz, the harassment of the Curtises, and a summary of the Blue Spoon plan. The chiefs, who had been briefed on the plan within the past month, were familiar at least with its broad outline.

General Powell reported that he had met with the secretary and his staff earlier that morning and that they were in general agreement that Blue Spoon should be a "go." But, he said, he wanted the chiefs to know exactly what was going on and he wanted to have their personal views.

General Vuono was in general agreement with the plans, he said, and, although he recognized its complexities, he also realized that the troops were trained, ready, and able to accomplish the mission. He also recognized that the bulk of the forces were Army, under the command of an Army general, and he felt that added responsibility.

Admiral Trost, while generally supporting the plan, the timing, and the necessity, wondered if the plan wasn't a bit of "overkill" and if it were really necessary to parachute in all of the paratroopers. Perhaps the first echelons could be jumped into Río Hato and Torrijos/Tocumen to seize the airfields, and then follow-on echelons could be airlanded on the captured strips. Well, maybe, he mused, they all wanted the bronze "combat jump" star on their jump wings. But he strongly supported the operation.

General Welch spoke very seriously and listed a number of disadvantages of the operation, including adverse reactions by other Latin American nations, the possible unrecognized strength of the PDF, the "unfairness" of the fight, and the legitimacy of the threat to our own national interests. But even given these doubts, he recognized that "there was no other solution."

Gen. Al Gray, the bantam commandant of the Marine Corps, the "supreme Marine," held the floor for some time. He was, without a doubt, the top PAO (public affairs officer) of the Marine Corps. He said that the geography of Panama was ideal for a Marine invasion, that he had a Marine Expeditionary Unit (MEU) of several thousand Marines headed back from Hawaii, and that he could easily divert them to Panama and could take care of the whole problem by himself. He said that his Marines, trained, equipped, and supplied as they were, were a far more powerful force than the Rangers and the 82d who were going to parachute into the area, armed only with the equipment they were jumping with. Realizing, however, that this was an almost total Army operation, and aware of the need for speed and surprise, paratrooper prime attributes, he said that if the paratroopers got into trouble, his more heavily equipped Marines could be on call to bail them out. He also said that he could move some amphibious ships with Marines aboard off the Atlantic side of the canal just in case there were any problems elsewhere. General Powell finally said that he would "keep in mind" the commandant's suggestions and offers of help. General Powell knew that it would take the Marines a long time to get there.

After the chiefs had had their say, General Powell told them that he and General Kelly were on the way to the White House to brief the president and that he, Powell, would recommend going with Blue Spoon. He asked the chiefs again for their comments. They agreed that the execution of Blue Spoon was the legitimate and only course to follow.[4] The Joint Chiefs of Staff chronolog continues:

TIME	CHRONOLOG ENTRY
1215	BG Hartzog advises conditions were quiet.
1225	LTG Kelly briefed results of meeting with CJCS. Incident involving USN couple considered more provocative than shooting.
1230	BG White (CJCS Executive Aide to the Chairman), EA, reviews with LTG Kelly actions required prior to 1430 White House meeting. Highlighted copy of Noriega's speech declaring war on United States. Chronology of events showing escalation of incidents.
1300	LTG Kelly spoke with General Lindsay; reviewed situation and result of 1130 meeting with service chiefs.
1330	LTG Kelly and staff review Noriega's declaration of state of war.
1630	General Kelly returned and related that no decision was made regarding the situation. Possibly more NSC discussions tomorrow.

TIME	CHRONOLOG ENTRY
1700–1800	J-3 briefed J-3 staff on presidential decision. H-hour established. CAT to be formed o/a darkness Tuesday (19) Dec. CJCS contacted General Thurman, General Lindsay, General Johnson (commanding general of the Military Airlift Command), and General Burba (commanding general of FORSCOM, the Army's Forces Command). General Kelly called General Downing (Commander of the Joint Special Operations Task Force), LTG Stiner, BG Hartzog, BG Borling, and MG Kellum.

TIME	CHRONOLOG ENTRY
1715	J-3 called LTG Stiner President has authorized Blue Spoon. H-hour established. OPSEC to the maximum.
1826	J-3 phone call w/MG Downing. Rangers from Fort Lewis travel to Lawson tomorrow.

*   *   *

The president made the decision to go with Blue Spoon—or Just Cause[5]—under rather unusual circumstances considering that he was committing U.S. forces to combat. At the White House on Sunday afternoon, 17 December 1989, President Bush was playing host to a gathering of fifty close friends and family members at a Christmas party. The group sang Christmas carols, made small talk, and ate special delicacies; staffers escorted groups of children on the "ultimate" tour, a walk through the president's living quarters, excepting only the presidential bedroom. The calmness and graciousness of the president as he hosted the party belied the fact that he was well aware of the seriousness of the events that had transpired in Panama the day before.

As the Christmas party guests were leaving at about 1430, another group, far more somber, was arriving. The identity of the members of that group and the fact that they were calling at that time on a Sunday afternoon suggested that it was more than a casual visit to wish the president and his lady an early Merry Christmas. The group included General Powell; Secretary of Defense Dick Cheney; Secretary of State Baker; national security adviser Brent Scowcroft; General Tom Kelly; Bob Gates, Scowcroft's deputy; and White House spokesman Marlin Fitzwater. As inconspicuously as possible, the group headed for the elevator to the president's living quarters.

When the president arrived, General Powell briefed him on the plans for the operation in Panama. Throughout the briefing, President Bush asked him detailed questions about the plan: What kind of troops are involved? What kind of equipment do the paratroopers carry with them when they jump? Why are you taking out this target? How are you going to do it? How many helicopters are already there? What intelligence do you have on Noriega? Do you know where he is? Are you sending in enough troops? The president continued to ply General Powell with innumerable questions and to pry into all aspects of the

52

plan. Finally he was satisfied with its thoroughness and adequacy. And then, without reference to any of his half dozen or so top advisers who were at the briefing or even to ask their opinions of the plan, he said, without hesitancy, "Okay, let's do it."

Just Cause had just received the commander in chief's imprimatur. With those four words, the burden of proof shifted to troops already on alert—on the ground in Panama and scattered at bases around the United States. Their ability to react with speed and decisiveness reflected on their superb operational readiness—a gratuity from the buildup and changes engineered by the Reagan administration, resulting in the military's improved discipline, pride, top-notch training, and self-confidence. The post-Vietnam doldrums were over. The Just Cause troops were about to prove it.[6]

6 | Alerts

Col. William F. (Buck) Kernan had a problem—an OPSEC (operational security) problem he didn't know how to solve. It was Sunday afternoon, 17 December, and Colonel Kernan had just hung up the secure phone in his stuccoed, red-tile-roofed, pre–World War II quarters at Fort Benning, Georgia.

He remembers, "I had been in and out of the office (his headquarters at Fort Benning) the fifteenth and sixteenth of December responding to various phone calls and intelligence updates and was aware the situation was deteriorating, but I was at home when I was officially notified [by Maj. Gen. Wayne A. Downing, the commander of the Joint Special Operations Task Force]. I was called on the secure line at my home, given the order to execute, and immediately alerted all my battalion commanders and assembled the battle staff. Official notification was 171600R December (1600, 17 December, local time.)"[1]

Buck's problem that Sunday afternoon was his house guests, Brig. Gen. Jerry Bates and his wife, who were staying with the Kernans en route to the 7th Infantry Division at Fort Ord, where Jerry would serve as Maj. Gen. Carmen Cavezza's assistant division commander for operations. When General Downing learned that the Bateses were at Kernan's quarters, he cautioned Buck ". . . to keep the lid on this thing. You cannot tell Jerry anything—not even that I called." Downing, Bates, and Kernan had been close friends for years—ever since their duty together at Fort Lewis in the 2d Ranger Battalion. Bates would quickly piece together what was happening if he got wind of a secure phone call between Kernan and Downing on a Sunday afternoon.

So Kernan went downstairs and casually endured a maddening thirty minutes of idle conversation before he could gracefully slip out to the "office." It worked—or at least Jerry Bates was perceptive enough not to press Buck for details when he returned home that evening.

That same afternoon, Lt. Col. Alan H. Maestas, commander of the 2d Ranger

Battalion of the 75th, was unwinding in his quarters at Fort Lewis, Washington, home of the 2d Battalion. He and the battalion had just returned to Fort Lewis that same day after a week-long training exercise near Eglin Air Force Base, Florida. The exercise involved the entire regiment and was a "warm-up" rehearsal for the regiment's role in Just Cause. Gen. James J. Lindsay, the commander in chief of the U.S. Special Operations Command at MacDill Air Force Base in Florida, had, using two auxiliary runways at Eglin, duplicated, as nearly as possible, the mission and conditions that the regiment would find on its actual operation in Panama. After the exercise, during the "hot wash" session—latest military terminology for a critique or after-action review—at Hurlbut, General Lindsay and General Downing pointed out to the commanders of the regiment and other special forces involved in the rehearsal the "rights and wrongs" and then said that the situation in Panama was in a "state of flux"; that the actual operation would be a "go—anywhere in the next six to eight months"; and that the regiment must maintain a standby, increased state of readiness. His cautions were on the mark.

On Sunday afternoon, Colonel Maestas got a call from his executive officer, a very relaxed Maj. Clyde M. Newman, who said that he would be right over to show off his newly discovered two-liter beer container. "He arrived," Colonel Maestas remembers, "and Newman and Maestas went to the kitchen to draw beer from the container (pony keg). Two glasses were drawn and, as a second glass is drawn, the phone in the kitchen rings. The call is from Maj. Ken Stauss, regimental executive officer, for Colonel Maestas. Stauss and Maestas have known each other since 1977, when both were in the 2d Ranger Battalion. . . . Stauss asks Maestas if he is on secure phone. The answer is no, so Maestas and Newman depart 2391 Sixth Street (Maestas's home address) in Newman's Ford Bronco for the battalion area. En route Maestas finishes drinking his glass of beer. Newman's beer is half full when both arrive at Bn area. Maestas calls Stauss from the office on a secure phone and is told by Colonel Kernan that the Op Plan has been ordered executed on 200600Z December 90. Maestas tells staff duty NCO to initiate immediate recall of Bn. Maestas and Newman decide to return to their respective quarters to pick up ID tags, wallets, and clean T-shirts. Clean T-shirts important because battalion had just returned that same day from . . . an exercise on the East Coast.

"As Newman and Maestas left the parking lot, Newman picked up his glass with beer and emptied the contents of the beer out the window. Maestas remarked, 'You should have finished that beer. It won't be long before you regret throwing it away.'

"In the days to follow, in the Panama heat particularly in AO Diaz, Newman often remembered about the beer he had thrown away."[2]

Sgt. Andrew Spano was a squad leader in A Company, 2d Battalion of the 75th Rangers. He remembers the details of the call-up quite clearly. "It was Sunday evening, 17 December 89, at approximately 2015 when we got the alert notification," he wrote recently. "As soon as I got the notification, I called my fiancée and told her that I got called in and I would call her as soon as I got the chance. Although most of us heard on the news that the PDF had shot and killed that Marine lieutenant and beat up that soldier and his wife, it was hard to believe that we would be called to go anywhere, because battalion was going on "block leave" (all men in the battalion take leave at the same time so that only one battalion at a time is "down") in two days. Many of us were looking forward to this leave, especially three of us in 2d Platoon, because we were supposed to get married during this leave. When I got to the company, everyone was busy drawing weapons or doing other things, but everyone seemed pretty calm and orderly. As the night went on, we still weren't quite sure of what was going on.

"The next day came and the word came down that we were going to Panama. . . . I thought to myself that this couldn't be happening, I've got a wedding to be in in two weeks. As the day went on, we got the operations orders and we knew what our mission was. As you walked through the barracks, nobody was really saying much. It's funny how we train to go to combat every day, but no one ever really believes that you'll go. It hit me like a sledgehammer in the chest. One time during that day all of us squad leaders were in the platoon CP with the platoon sergeant, who happens to be a veteran of Operation Urgent Fury. He said to us, 'The first time you go to combat, it's easy cause you do everything by instinct. The second time you go, it's hard because you know what to expect.' As I sat in one of my men's room, I thought about the men in my squad. It's hard not to think about how it's possible that maybe someone won't be coming back. I sat there and wrote a letter to my fiancée, who was back in Massachusetts. I wanted her to know what I was feeling. Any one of us would be a liar if we said we weren't scared. The rest of the day was pretty much the same, yet sitting around and waiting, the waiting was the killer."[3]

Another soldier, Private First Class Bunch, 1st Platoon of B Company of the 2d of the 75th, recounted the days leading up to the Ranger regiment's deployment. On the fourteenth of December, he wrote, "The Ranger battalion deployed on one of the biggest operations in years. . . . The mission was 2d and 3d battalions were to parachute into Florida and secure the airfield, and assault and destroy all enemy personnel in buildings and on the airfield. I don't remember the times and dates the mission actually took place but we jumped in and secured the airfield in twelve minutes then assaulted the buildings and basically kicked ass. While doing all of this, generals and SOCOM and people up higher were watching to see how well the supposed 'elite force of the United States Army' did the job. They were very impressed, so impressed one of the four stars said it was the best he'd seen in his military career.

"On the sixteenth of December, we came back from Florida to Georgia by bus. Then we got on a plane late night 0100–0200 on the seventeenth of Dec. Got to Fort Lewis early morning on the seventeenth. Unpalletized and got our shit squared away by noon, then we were cut loose for the day. All the next two weeks were half days and four-day weekends. The perfect Christmas vacation— or so we thought. I went home for eight hours. The best eight hours I've ever had in a long time. I spent time with my newlywed wife, ate what was going to be a good meal, and slept a couple of hours. The news was on and they were talking about the situation in Panama. They declared war on the U.S.A. I was talking about going down there and stomping ass. Michele didn't share my opinion. No more than five minutes later the phone rang and we were alerted. I knew why, and I'm sure Michele did also. She isn't stupid. On the way to the battalion, I tried to ease her mind by saying I had no idea why we were alerted, when I knew, 'cause we just practiced the mission in Florida which was set up like the Panamanian military post. I told her everything would be fine, but I didn't believe that myself.

"Later that night all I heard through the barracks was echoes of war. Higher tried to cover by saying we were going to Fort Bliss, Texas, but we knew it was just smoke being blown up our asses. We repallitized, packed our rucksacks (again) and our CD bags (combat deployment), then drew weapons and went to sleep.

"We woke about 0545 and made ready for the day ahead. Then we got in cattle trucks and went to McChord Air Force Base again. Got on a C-141 and almost immediately took off (unusual). I began to notice a few things like the crew chiefs on the bird were wearing sidearms, and when we asked where we were going, he said, 'The East Coast is all I can say.' It began to really dawn on me what was about to happen but my mind was still thinking 'training.' We landed four hours later at Lawson Army (Airfield) in Georgia. Everything was fine, no one was jumping out the ass screaming or yelling. We went to our tents and unpacked. The day went well. The sergeants were being unusually nice, and we were treated better than we have in all my time in service. The day went well and night fell and so did the cold. We worked out the fireguard watch and got in the rack. Then the news came—we were going to Panama. Everyone got up, oiled their weapons, fixed their LCE (device for carrying combat gear), and dumped all unnecessary shit from the rucksack. All I took was a poncho, poncho liner, two-quart canteen, a PVS-4 (night scope), and an IV. I was set, then the operations order (how to) came in. They had pictures, maps, number of troops, location of antiaircraft guns—everything.

"Here's what was to happen. Second and 3d battalions were to jump into Rio Hato, Panama. Second Battalion was to take the south and 3rd the north. First Platoon (my platoon) was to assemble at point 'Buck' about one click down the southern end of the runway and two or so clicks from Noriega's home, which was supposed to be taken out by another unit. Once enough of us assembled we were to assault Objective 'Cat' with approximately 150 enemy troops. First Platoon had the building to the left and 3rd Platoon had the buildings to the right. After that we were to go on to Objective 'Lion' and 150 troops also."[4]

In Panama, Col. Michael G. Snell, the commander of the 193d Infantry Brigade (Light), permanently stationed in Panama, had been following the details of the planning for the operation for many months at his command post at Fort Clayton. It came as no surprise to him when, on the seventeenth of December, General Thurman's headquarters alerted him to carry out his preplanned and rehearsed missions. He received the execute message at 1800 on the nineteenth.

On the seventeenth of December, General Stiner called into the corps headquarters the key members of his staff. "The headquarters had been on a high state of readiness since the shooting incident," remembered General Scholes, the corps chief of staff, "and we had been notified by the Pentagon that possibility was high that the Operation Plan would be implemented soon. We requested and received permission to deploy a small element of the corps assault CP under the guise of attending previously scheduled conference on the Op Plan and possible CPX Command Post Exercise. We flew in, arriving on AM of the eighteenth, and began initial work on establishment of Corps/JTFSouth Command Post in Emergency Operations Center of U.S. Army South. Only General Thurman and a few of his staff knew of the pending operation in Panama at this time. Once the "execute order" was received at XVIII Corps on 18 December, General Stiner and remaining, previously identified staff members deployed to Panama. General Stiner issued his orders to cdrs. located in Panama on 19 December. Orders to relevant commanders in CONUS were issued prior to his departure from Fort Bragg. Times for orders to be issued to subordinates within Panama were established and occurred after units were assembled and sequestered from families/public. Because of shooting incident and arrest situation, bases and units were on a high state of alert in Panama and assembly of units had become a common occurrence."[5]

In more detail, what happened at Fort Bragg was this: General Stiner received the execute message in a phone call from General Kelly at 1800 on Sunday evening. In anticipation of that message, General Stiner had already sent Gen. Ed Scholes, his chief of staff, who had recently assumed the position after having served as assistant division commander of the 82d under Generals Stiner and Johnson, and a small advance party from his headquarters to Panama late on Sunday night via a C-141 from Pope Air Force Base, adjacent to Fort Bragg. The task of this advanced C-2 (command and control) element was to organize a small joint command post to handle a multitude of details before H-hour.

Later, General Stiner, his G-3, Col. Tom Needham, other key members of the corps staff, and an advanced command post group from the 82d took off from Pope in two C-20s. At 1930 on Monday evening they landed at Howard Air Force Base. (The corps staff did not get into their BDUs—battle dress—until Tuesday night.) The group moved to Fort Clayton, the command post of U.S. Army South, headed by Maj. Gen. Marc Cisneros, and joined the corps joint tactical operations center (JTOC) in General Cisneros' emergency operations center. Fort Clayton—unlike Fort Amador, for example, which is jointly occupied by U.S. and Panamanian forces and dependents—is totally occupied by U.S. forces. General Cisneros became the deputy commander of Joint Task Force South and integrated his staff with General Stiner's for the duration of the operation. The advanced group from the 82d moved into Building 200 (the 193d Brigade's headquarters) at Fort Clayton to prepare for the arrival of the remainder of the 82d staff.

Sunday night, General Stiner alerted Maj. Gen. James H. Johnson, Jr., commanding general of the 82d Airborne Division, that the operation was a "go." At 0900 on Monday, the eighteenth, the XVIII Airborne Corps G-3, Col. Tom Needham, under the guise of a routine EDRE (emergency deployment readiness exercise), gave the 82d Airborne Division G-3, Lt. Col. Dan McNeill, a no-notice order to execute Corps Op Plan 2-90. This order initiated the division's eighteen-hour planning and alert procedure, a routine through which the division units had moved many times in the past.[6]

At 1100 on the eighteenth, as scheduled in the division's SOP (standard operating procedure), the N+2 briefing was held in the division headquarters operations center. Col. Jack Nix was the commander of the division's 1st Brigade, the DRB (division-ready brigade) for that period. Present at the N+2 briefing were Colonel Nix and commanders of other selected division elements who would support the 1st Brigade on the operation. "Due to OPSEC (operational security) concerns, only brigade-level commanders were briefed that this no-notice EDRE was actually a cover for the execution of Op Plan 2-90" (the division referred to the plan as 2-90), reported the division's historical summary.

At 1400 hours the division assault command post moved to the PHA (personnel holding area) and continued planning and preparation for the EDRE. At about 1500, Colonel Needham alerted Colonel McNeill in the PHA to begin preparing for combat operations in Panama in accordance with the division's Op Plan 2-90. And at 1500, Brigadier General Kinzer, the assistant division commander of the 82d, and thirteen members of the division staff airlanded at Howard Air Force Base, moved to Building 200 at Clayton, and linked up with the first element of the division staff that had arrived two days earlier.

When Colonel Nix first received the alert for an EDRE, he moved his first battalion to the PHA. In the next four hours Nix alerted and moved two more battalions to the PHA. One was from his 1st Brigade; the other was the 4th of the 325th from another brigade in the 82d. The 1st Brigade's 3rd Battalion, the 3d of the 504th, had already deployed to Panama on 10 December under the guise of jungle training.[7]

The troops in the 82d had been to the PHA many times before for alerts of varying degrees of seriousness. The procedure and the route were always the same. Cargo trucks or trucks pulling eighty-passenger, aluminum-sided trailers pulled up behind their barracks along Ardennes Road and parked. The troopers, fully combat-loaded, filed out of their barracks and loaded up for the two-mile ride to the PHA. The convoy wound down Gruber Road, then turned on Butner and made a left on Gorham. Then it ran along a dirt road past rifle ranges to the PHA, a collection of six massive, canvas-covered Quonset huts, each capable of holding about two hundred men and their gear. The huts were furnished with double-deck bunks for a possible overnight stay. In addition to the troop Quonsets, the PHA had three big, canvas-covered buildings for administration and housing of the staffs. The PHA could hold about two battalions. For Just Cause, the 4th Battalion of the 325th Infantry staged through the nearby corps marshaling area.

The PHA also held an issue point where the troops drew ammunition, mosquito nets for the bunks, and rations. In the case of Just Cause, where the 82d troopers might possibly parachute onto the concrete runways of Torrijos/Tocumen Airport, the paratroopers were also issued knee and elbow pads. The PHA held another area of some importance to infantrymen: a range where they could zero their personal weapons.[8]

Colonel Nix's DRB, a reinforced parachute infantry-heavy brigade, consisted not only of his own two battalions, the 1st and 2d of the 504, but also was augmented by the 4th Battalion of the 325th, C Company of the 3d of the 505, C Company of the 3d of the 73d Armor, the 3d Battalion of the 319th Field Artillery, A Battery of the 3d Battalion of the 4th Air Defense Artillery, A Company of the 307th Engineer Battalion, a platoon from the 82d Military Police Company, a FAST (forward-area support team), and a TACP (tactical air control party).

In the PHA, rigging of heavy-drop items (artillery pieces, vehicles, Sheridan tanks, ammunition loads, and supplies) continued throughout the day to prepare twenty-eight C-141 heavy-drop aircraft for "forward staging at Charleston Air Force Base in South Carolina." The twenty-eight C-141s moved to Charleston Air Force Base prior to the departure of the parachute assault planes from Pope Air Force Base.

On the nineteenth, Colonel Nix and the DRB continued rehearsals in the PHA while the outload support personnel finished the rigging and loading of the heavy-drop platforms. At 1100, Joint Task Force South (the XVIII Airborne Corps in Panama) notified the 82d to execute Joint Task Force South's Op Plan 90-2, with D-day/H-hour as 20 Dec 890100. The three specific objectives in the plan for the 82d (now Task Force Pacific) were the UESAT/Cav Squadron at Panama Viejo (Objective One); the 1st Infantry Company (Tigers) at Tinajitas (Objective Two); and Battalion 2000 at Fort Cimarron (Objective Three). In addition, after successfully "taking down" these objectives, "the 82d was to move into Panama City and to neutralize the Dignity Battalions, specifically the Rosa Elena Landecho (REL) Battalion, staging at Tocumen; the Venceremos Battalion, staging at Panama Viejo; and the San Miguel el Archangel Battalion, staging at 11MZ Headquarters in the San Miguelito District."[9]

When word came to load aircraft, the troops marched from the PHA to Green Ramp adjacent to the Pope Air Force Base runways. The troops were loaded down with all of their personal gear for the jump, some eighty pounds' worth. At Green Ramp were parked the aircraft for the jump, and here the troops drew their main and reserve parachutes. Then the jumpmasters lined up the troops in order of exit from the planes over the drop zones and waited for the command to load up.

The 7th Infantry Division (Light) at Fort Ord has an alert procedure like the 82d's. Twenty-four hours a day, seven days a week, the division's three brigades are designated, on a rotational basis, DRB (division-ready brigade) 1, DRB 2, or DRB 3. The DRB 1's three battalions are designated DRF 1, 2, or 3. The DRF 1 Battalion must have all deployable soldiers assembled within two hours of N-hour, combat-loaded and combat-ready. The DRF 2 battalion must be ready to move in four hours and the DRF 3 battalion in six hours.

The 7th's alert sequence started at X-hour (0900) on Monday, the eighteenth, with a "crisis action team" briefing and an increase of readiness of the 2d Brigade, its DRB 1. Five hours later, an "outload support" meeting was held to plan transportation to the airfields and schedule units onto the aircraft. At 0749 on Tuesday, the nineteenth, the division commander, Maj. Gen. Carmen J. Cavezza, received an "execute order" for Just Cause from the Joint Chiefs of

Staff. N-hour, the time that General Cavezza set for starting the alert procedure, was 0900 that same morning, just seventy-one minutes later. At 1100, General Cavezza met with his staff and with Col. Linwood Burney, commander of the 2d Brigade. At 1930 that evening, the 5th Battalion of the 21st Infantry, the DRF 1 Battalion, commanded by Lt. Col. Robert Cronin, with 32 officers, a warrant officer, and 483 enlisted men, left Fort Ord by bus for Travis Air Force Base.[10]

One observer reported that "long convoys of olive-colored military vehicles snaked along Highway 1 and State Route 156 starting at about 10:00 P.M. Tuesday and then onto U.S. 101 on the way to Travis Air Force Base, 175 miles north of Fort Ord.

"By early morning, about two dozen buses loaded with soldiers arrived at Travis. Reporters said they heard jet noise as aircraft were moved at the base, but Travis was enveloped in heavy fog, and no planes had taken off as early as this morning."[11]

Another report held that

Just past midnight, the troops and weapons began arriving at Travis, just outside Fairfield. Trucks covered with tarps but bearing "explosives" signs clearly on the sides, moved through the dense fog into the rear gate of the base. The first trucks bore Navy insignia and were likely carrying arms from the nearby Concord Naval Weapons Station.

Convoys containing as many as a dozen trucks each arrived regularly throughout the night. One group contained at least five cannons being towed behind jeeps, in addition to buses full of troops. Many of the soldiers, wearing camouflage clothing—some with their faces painted—waved and smiled at the press assembled to record their arrival.

At Travis the troops were to board transports for the seven-hour flight to Panama.

The Light Fighters, whose nicknames include "Masters of the Night," carry mostly small arms, mortars, and M-16 automatic rifles on their backs. The boast: that Night Fighters can arrive combat-ready for action anywhere within 18 hours.[12]

In Panama, JTFSOUTH, General Stiner's command, had established its assault command post in the Emergency Operations Center (EOC) of U.S. Army South at Fort Clayton. The Assault CP had communications established back to the JCS in the Pentagon, with a hot line to General Tom Kelly in the JCS operations center, General Downing's command, and the U.S. embassy. It had, of course, communications to all of the major subordinate commands in the task force. Once the operation was under way, General Thurman and his J-3, General Hartzog, moved into the crowded assault CP on a full-time basis. Thurman stayed there with General Stiner through the initial assaults and through the phases of the operation that were most crucial. The small EOC was so crowded with communications gear, operational maps, and computers that General Thurman slept—catnapped is the better term—on a cot between a computer and a desk.[13]

The chain of command was working to perfection. On Sunday evening the president made the decision to implement Just Cause. Fifty-four hours later, the operation was under way. The rehearsals, the planning, the practice alerts, and the rumors were things of the past. The commander in chief had committed his military forces to combat.

7 | Initial Deployments

         The troops stationed in Panama either on a permanent- or a temporary-duty basis were well aware that "something was up" on the nineteenth of December. They had heard of and read about the murder of Lt. Robert Paz and the harassment of the Curtises on the sixteenth—the culmination of a long series of incidents in which the PDF had harassed Americans, military and civilian. The troops knew that events were rapidly cresting to a climax—or, in their words, "The shit was about to hit the fan."

On orders from General Thurman, the commanders in-country ratcheted up the level of their readiness postures so that by the nineteenth, all U.S. troops stationed in Panama were in or within two hours of their barracks areas. The commanders had their missions, they had rehearsed their operations so often and over such a widespread area that, as planned, the PDF may have become numb to them. By the nineteenth, they were ready to operate.[1]

One of General Stiner's subordinate commanders for the operation was Maj. Gen. Wayne A. Downing, forty-nine, West Point Class of 1962. General Downing, stationed at Fort Bragg, was designated the commander of the Joint Special Operations Task Force (JSOTF), reporting directly to General Stiner. Some of General Downing's Just Cause units were already in-country; some he brought with him from the States about forty-eight hours before H-hour; and some, the entire 75th Ranger Regiment, came in by parachute at H-hour.

General Downing's military background is filled with airborne, Ranger, and special operations assignments, both in combat in Viet Nam and in the States. During his two tours in Viet Nam, totaling over two years, he served with the 173d Airborne Brigade, commanded a company in the 14th Infantry, and was a battalion and brigade S-3 in the 25th Infantry Division. In the States he commanded the 2d Battalion of the 75th Rangers and later activated and commanded the 75th Ranger Regiment. Between those Ranger assignments, he commanded an armored infantry brigade in Europe.

He is a fair-haired, youngish-looking, obviously physically fit officer who has an intensity, experience, drive, and charisma that make him uniquely well suited to his current assignment—commander of and contingency planner for all Army special operations forces. He knows the "special operations business" from a variety of command and staff levels.

On Saturday night, 16 December, at about 2200, he was in his quarters in the "generals' loop" near the Officers' Club at Fort Bragg. General Kelly, the JCS J-3, called him on his secure line and alerted him to the possibility that Just Cause might be a "go." Later, he and General Stiner talked continually through the night. He remembers the sequence of events thereafter this way: "I went in to work Sunday morning and I ended up not coming home. My wife, Cindy, had pressed my suit. I told her I needed it pressed to go to Washington the following day. She got up Monday morning and my suit was still hanging there. She was puzzled as to how I got to Washington without that suit. We left like we do—quietly, without fanfare or good-byes. Cindy didn't know what was going on until she got up Wednesday morning and turned on the TV and heard that we had invaded Panama." And that's how the spouses of many of the officers and soldiers who deployed on Just Cause found out where their mates were when they failed to report home on Tuesday evening.

General Downing stayed in his office all day Sunday. At about 1300, Lt. Gen. Tom Kelly called and told him, "It's on." Kelly called him back at about 1700 and told him, "You're going. What time do you want H-hour and what time do you want the aircraft?" General Downing gave him the information and got ready to depart.

At about 0100 on Monday morning, General Downing, some additional Special Forces and Navy SEALs, a total of about 450 men, left Pope Air Force Base and Norfolk Naval Air Station in C-141s and C-130s and landed at Howard Air Force Base in Panama some six hours later. General Downing set up his command post at Howard. His total force, the Joint Special Operations Task Force, totaled about forty-four hundred and was composed of elements of almost all existing special operations, psychological operations, and civil affairs units from the Army, Air Force, and Navy. The largest component, and the principal assault force in the JSOTF, was the entire 75th Ranger Regiment, dubbed Task Force Red for Just Cause. Supporting this task force were Air Force gunships and combat controllers from the Air Force's 1st Special Operations Wing and Army loudspeaker teams.

Another part of his command and another strike force was Task Force White, composed of five sea-air-land (SEAL) platoons from Naval Special Warfare Group 2, based at Little Creek, Virginia. On the nineteenth, General Downing brought with him four SEAL platoons to join a fifth, which was on a permanent rotation to Southern Command. Successors to the "frogmen" of World War II, the SEAL, assisted by the protection and speed of patrol boats, were assigned a broad array of maritime operations in the vicinity of the canal.

One of the units of JSOTF permanently stationed in Panama was the 3d Battalion of the 7th Special Forces Group, commanded by Lt. Col. Roy R. Trumbull. This unit, assisted by helicopters from the Army's 160th Aviation Regiment, was Task Force Black. For eighteen months the 3d of the 7th had had

64

an additional Special Forces company, on a rotational basis, from the parent group at Fort Bragg attached to it because of the crisis. Trumbull's base of operations was Fort Davis on the Atlantic side of the canal, about four miles due south of Colón, near the Gatun Locks. Its primary responsibility, "eyes on targets," devolved into reconnoitering several target areas and PDF garrisons prior to H-hour. Because of the locations of some targets in and around the built-up areas, and the possibility of compromise of the reconnaissance teams, the 7th was not able to overwatch every target.

Another Task Force Black mission was the protection of the opposition leaders who had been duly elected in the May 1989 elections but never installed by the Noriega regime. One of the primary objectives of Just Cause, of course, was the capture of Noriega and his major subordinates. It was critical, therefore, that the legitimate leaders be ready to assume political power immediately, once Noriega had been dethroned. The key leaders of the opposition, President Guillermo Endara, and Vice Presidents Guillermo Ford and Ricardo Arias Calderon, obviously needed guarding, but an overt show of U.S. military protection before H-hour would certainly alert Noriega to the pending operation. The Green Berets of Task Force Black were well qualified to provide the security, but General Thurman himself solved the problem of guarding the trio while at the same time causing no alarm bells to ring in the Comandancia.

General Thurman quietly invited the three men to dine with him at his quarters at Quarry Heights on the evening of the nineteenth. In addition to providing them with dinner, General Thurman also briefed them on the upcoming operation and arranged to have them sworn into office at his headquarters by a Panamanian judge well before H-hour. The United States immediately recognized the Endara government as the legitimate political leadership of Panama.

Another of the missions assigned to Task Force Black was blocking the Pan American Highway at the Pacora River Bridge, about 30 miles east of Panama City. The bridge was important because its seizure would prevent the movement of Battalion 2000 from its barracks at Fort Cimarron to the Torrijos/ Tocumen Airport complex at Panama City, the site of the drop zone for the paratroopers slated to arrive at H-hour, 0100, in the dark of the morning of the twentieth.

Colonel Trumbull assigned the blocking mission to Maj. Kevin Higgins, who commanded A Company of the 3d Battalion of the 7th Special Forces Group. Each company of the group had six A teams of twelve men each, generally led by two officers (or one officer and a warrant officer) and ten noncommissioned officers, all experts in one or more specialties: weapons, communications, operations, intelligence, medicine, survival, demolitions-engineering, and airborne operations.

General Downing had two additional Task Forces in his Joint Special Operations Task Force: Green and Blue. These forces, specially trained for this type of mission, had several challenging missions, which included the difficult task of capturing the elusive Noriega and his key inner circle. Diligent intelligence efforts traced Noriega from place to place and greatly narrowed the possible hideouts. Prior to the operation, the SOUTHCOM intelligence operators felt that they had Noriega's hideouts spotted about 80 percent of the time. Commencing at H-hour, Task Forces Green and Blue, supported by AH-6 helicopter gunships, UH-60 Black Hawk transport helicopters, and AC-130 gunships, applied constant pressure on Noriega's entourage and key cronies and tracked them relentlessly.[2]

Col. Michael G. Snell commanded the 193d Infantry Brigade (Light), which was permanently stationed in Panama and with its headquarters at Fort Clayton. When the 4th Battalion of the 6th Infantry, organic to the 5th Infantry Division (Mechanized) at Fort Polk, Louisiana, and the 519th Military Police Battalion from Fort Meade, Maryland, arrived in Panama during the Nimrod Dancer buildup after the grossly fraudulent May 1989 national elections, they were assigned to the 193d. For Operation Just Cause, Colonel Snell then had under his command, Task Force Bayonet, four rather diverse battalions: the 4th of the 6th, a mechanized infantry battalion from the 5th Infantry Division (Mechanized) at Fort Polk, Louisiana; the 5th of the 87th (stationed at Fort Clayton and a full-time part of the 193d); the 1st Battalion of the 508th Airborne Infantry, also a regular battalion in the 193d, a parachute infantry battalion, normally stationed at Fort Kobbe, on the west side of the canal near Howard Air Force Base; and the 519th Military Police Battalion, which had five military police companies, only one of which was organic to the 519th, under its control. Also part of his task force was the 59th Engineer Company, under the command of Capt. José A. Echevarria and normally stationed at Fort Clayton, on the east side of the canal; and D Battery of the 320th Field Artillery Battalion, under the command of Capt. Felipe S. Ibarra, stationed at Fort Kobbe.

TF Bayonet had been conducting contingency planning for defensive and offensive operations in Panama for over twenty months—or since the abortive March 1988 coup attempt. The operational plan for the 193d had steadily evolved until it was well tuned. According to Colonel Snell, "The 3 October '89 coup resulted in dramatic modifications of Op Plans, generally from passive defense to offense. . . . Being forward deployed (on the ground in Panama), the TF was able to conduct TEWTS (tactical exercises without troops) and tactical exercises (with suitable deception measures) at or near all objectives. While the troops were unaware of the real purpose of the exercises, they repeatedly rehearsed each defensive action and assault. . . . Each battalion and company produced a battle book detailing every aspect of their mission and plan. The result of this effort was a detailed, tested plan that was fully understood by the chain of command and that the troops had unwittingly rehearsed on several occasions."

Colonel Snell's principal objective was the Comandancia. But he also had seven other objectives, including the 5th CIA (which has nothing to do with the well-known U.S. Central Intelligence Agency but is an abbreviation for the 5th—or Quinta Compañia de Infanteria) stationed at Fort Amador; the Balboa and Ancón DENI (Departmento Nacional de Investigaciónes), police agencies; the Ancón DNTT (Dirección Nacional de Tránsito Terrestre), road patrols; the PDF Engineer Compound; Pier 18, Balboa Harbor; and the PDF Dog Compound. With that array of missions, Colonel Snell's few days after D-day promised to be exciting, and, if successful, rewarding.

For the operation, Colonel Snell divided his command into three task forces: TF Gator, under the control of Lt. Col. James W. Reed, the CO of the 4/6, consisting of two mech infantry companies, an airborne company, a platoon of M551 Sheridans, and a Marine Corps LAV (light assault vehicle) platoon; TF Wildcat, under the command of Lt. Col. William H. Huff III, the CO of 5/87, containing one mech infantry company and three infantry companies; TF Red Devil, under the command of Lt. Col. Billy R. Fitzgerald, commanding officer of the 1/508, comprised of two airborne companies and one mechanized company, the latter an ad hoc arrangement. The 519th MP Battalion attached several platoons to each of the task forces. And the 59th Engineer Company added platoons to Task Forces Wildcat and Red Devil.

At 1800 on Tuesday the nineteenth, Colonel Snell had a call from SOUTHCOM headquarters: "The operation is a 'go.'" He now had seven hours to complete marshaling, finish planning and "troop leading procedures" below company level (units below company had not yet been briefed that all of the rehearsing they had done was "for real"), and move his units to their lines of departure for an H-hour initiation of the operation.[3]

Marine Forces Panama became an integral part of Task Force South for Operation Just Cause and, for the operation, were appropriately christened Task Force Semper Fi. Its commander was Col. Charles E. Richardson, the commander of Marine Forces Panama at the time of the operation. The Marines were based at the U.S. Naval Station, Panama Canal—more popularly referred to as Rodman Naval Station. In addition to his command element, Colonel Richardson's Marine forces included K Company of the 3d Battalion, 6th Marines; D Company of the 2d Light Armored Infantry Battalion; MCSF Company, from the Marine Corps Security Force; a FAST platoon, from the Fleet Antiterrorist Security Team; a detachment from BSSG-6, Brigade Service Support Group 6; and, attached from the Army, the 536th Engineer Battalion and the 534th Military Police Company.

During normal times—or what were purported to be normal times in Panama before 20 December—the units in Marine Forces Panama rotated to and from the States every 90 days; the majority of the command element rotated every 179 days. The Marine units on the day of the Just Cause operation had arrived during October 1989. Colonel Richardson wrote, "I was fortunate the Marines in Panama on 20 December 1989 had been in country for almost two months. They knew the terrain and respected the people's desire for freedom."[4]

While the Marines were in Panama on rotation, they trained extensively in possible combat situations. One after-action report states, "By having maintained a high-paced training tempo, the Marines of MARFORPM [Marine Forces Panama] were extremely well prepared for the hostilities that were initiated on 20 December 1989.

"Of significant importance in preparing for combat were the Contingency Readiness Exercises, the Fire Support Coordination Exercises, the Freedom of

Movement Operations, the roadblock classes, and the numerous sand-table discussions. As stated by General Thurman, 'During the tense period before 'Just Cause' the Marines spearheaded the efforts to assert our treaty rights. . . .'"

In actuality, the Marines practiced in realistic combat situations, particularly with their LAVs (light assault vehicles). A LAV is a lightly armored, eight-wheeled vehicle capable of swimming, an important characteristic in Panama, land of the "big canal." LAVs are armed with various weapons depending on their mission. Of one practice mission, Capt. Stephen J. Linder, commander of Company A of the 2d LAI Battalion, wrote:

> On 28 May, Operation Big Show demonstrated several unique capabilities of our LAVs—maneuverability, firepower, swimming, and reliable communications. Assault and security elements swam the Panama Canal from west to east, landed on the Panama Canal shore, and maneuvered into position to help secure Fort Amador, a joint U.S./Panamanian base. It was executed flawlessly. The swim of the canal caught the PDF by surprise, and confusion was the order of the day in their response.
>
> On 9 June an armed reconnaissance on the fringes of the Empire Range area was conducted to capitalize on civilian contacts that had been established earlier.
>
> Our next mission was a night swim of the Panama Canal to conduct surreptitious reinforcement of Quarry Heights, the Southern Command's headquarters compound. The intent was to demonstrate to the PDF that keeping tabs on Marine LAVs would be a full-time job.[5]

Company D of the 2d LAI Battalion, commanded by Capt. Gerald H. Gaskins, arrived in Panama in the latter part of October 1989. The company carried on its training with the same intensity as its predecessor, B Company. On 22 November, Captain Gaskins led his company on a short exercise, theoretically to familiarize his men with their area of operations. After the operation, called Rough Rider, Captain Gaskins wrote:

> The route would take us through four major towns: Nuevo Emperador, Nuevo Guarre, Vista Allegre, and Arraijan.
>
> Two U.S. Army officers from the Treaty Affairs Section, JTF, joined the company to approach roadblock agitators and negotiate. Also, JTF sent a psyops armored HMMWV (in military jargon the Hum-V, the successor to the renowned and seemingly irreplaceable jeep) to inform the Panamanians of our "goodwill" intentions and an OH-58 to screen our movement. Company D executed Rough Rider with twelve LAVs, three HMMWVs, and its Scout Platoon.
>
> Nuevo Emperador gave us our first sight of a Panamanian town and a warm reception with smiles and enthusiastic waves. In Nuevo Guarre we made a left turn on Thatcher Highway, which leads directly back to Rodman Naval Station. As we approached Vista Allegre, the lead element reported people

gathered on Thatcher Highway waving a large Panamanian flag and several banners. The deliberate roadblock had been set, undetected by our air observer. (We later discovered that the Panamanians used the helo flyover as an indicator for our movement.)

The lead platoon set in seventy-five meters from the roadblock, while the rear element immediately set in the counterblock. The crowd of agitators was isolated to our front. When the officers of Treaty Affairs approached the agitators, a shouting match erupted and excited the crowd. I informed MarFor Panama of the situation and requested permission to give a five-minute warning. My request was granted immediately. At four minutes, I told Treaty Affairs to stop talking and board the HMMWV. All LAV drivers "buttoned up," and gunners manned their weapons to prepare for coaxial machine-gun engagements. Vehicle commanders and scouts remained exposed to monitor the crowd. The agitators realized what our intentions were, and several vehicles were hit by rocks. The company formation collapsed into a single file except for the rear element, which blocked traffic until every vehicle was through. One Panamanian rammed an LAV-L with a pickup truck, puncturing the right front tire. As the LAV-L continued forward, a Panamanian female agitator tried to block our movement with her body. She fell backward, feet in the air, flipping over another roadblock vehicle. The agitators were shocked, and began beating our vehicles with their fists, flagpoles, and anything else they could wield as the column moved forward. On the other side of the roadblock was another crowd, this one friendly, cheering at what we had done. We moved away from the roadblock to change the flat tire and get a damage assessment of the LAVs. Five minutes later we were on the move.

D Company, 2d LAI, was about ready.[6]

On 3 October, K Company, 3d Battalion, 6th Marines, under the command of Capt. Don Kline, arrived in Panama on its rotation. Lt. Kenneth M. DeTreux, a platoon leader in K Company, 3/6, wrote after Just Cause: "For three months, Kilo took part in security operations in the Arraijan Tank Farm and carried out a rigid training schedule in order to be ready for an emergency situation that might arise in that troubled country. Beginning on 19 December, the hard work and training truly paid off."[7]

"To best understand the Marine Corps' mission in Just Cause," wrote Colonel Richardson recently, "one must first have an understanding of their preinvolvement. In December 1989, Marine Forces Panama had been in the country for nearly two years. Their mission: 'to protect American lives and property.' Actually, Marine Corps' involvement in Panama dates back as far as 1905, when Marines were initially sent 'to protect American lives and property.'

"Marine Forces Panama was at a strength of approximately seven hundred and was the advance element of the 6th Marine Expeditionary Brigade. The 6th MEB has a mission in the contingency plan for the defense of the Panama Canal, known as Blue Spoon. Within thirty-six hours after notification, the 6th MEB would arrive in Panama and absorb Marine Forces Panama and be ready for combat operations. Prior to the brigade's arrival, Marine Forces Panama's mission was the protection of Howard Air Force Base, the Panama Naval

69

Station, Arraijan Tank Farm, the Pacific Ammunition Supply Point, and the Bridge of the Americas. This, however, was soon to change.

"On 3 October 1989, several PDF officers attempted, and failed, in a coup to oust Gen. Manuel Antonio Noriega. With the final shots still echoing in the air, Lt. Gen. Carl Stiner and his primary staff from XVIII Airborne Corps arrived in Panama to begin planning a new operation. The result of numerous planning sessions that spanned from Lt. Gen. Stiner's first trip to Panama until H-hour was Op Plan 90-2, which was ultimately called Operation Just Cause. Blue Spoon was shelved and along with it the plan to introduce additional Marine forces into the theater.

"Marine Forces Panama was initially represented (at General Stiner's planning sessions in Panama) by my operations officer, Lt. Col. Michael Franks, and myself. Because of the operational security requirements, only one other Marine, Maj. Bron Madrigan (the JTF South/Panama liaison officer), was involved in the planning.

"After the initial concept of the plan was delivered, it was apparent that the follow-on Marine forces were not included. This and the expansion of the Marine forces mission caused me to query Lieutenant General Stiner about the changes. In my reasoning I stated that my mission had now changed from defensive to offensive, that my area of responsibility had expanded to over six hundred square miles. Lieutenant Colonel Franks and I continually attempted to get at least one additional Marine battalion included in the initial flow of forces into Panama. Lieutenant General Stiner decided that there would be no more additional Marine forces in Panama but agreed to provide me a battalion from the 82d Airborne Division no later that H+36. In subsequent planning sessions, Lieutenant General Stiner promised a battalion from the 7th Infantry Division (L) after realizing the potential heavy involvement of the 82d Airborne Division. The 7th ID(L) battalion, 2/27, was chopped OpCon to Task Force Semper Fi at H+57. Additional forces included OpCon of the 536th Engineer Battalion and 534th Military Police Company. (These were attached by H+1.)

". . . there was little similarity between Blue Spoon and OpPlan 90-2. Blue Spoon was basically a defensive plan that had offensive execution only in response to given situations. OpPlan 90-2 had as its focus the ousting of General Noriega, neutralization of the PDF, the reestablishment of the rightful democratic government of Panama, and in doing so, the protection of U.S. citizens and U.S. property. The supporting plan for Marine Forces Panama was named Ghostbusters.

"Additional taskings for Task Force Semper Fi that were in the execution order but not in the OpPlan were: The seizing of the port of Vaca Monte, and the neutralization or destruction of all PDF in zone and the seizing of PDF facilities. This mission also included the capture of key Dignity Battalion members in the AOR (area of operations). The superb intelligence obtained by Task Force Semper Fi's S-2 resulted in the capture of a number of important Dignity Battalion members and PDF officers that had gone to ground."[8]

By the twentieth of December, Marine Forces Panama were trained in the skills they would need for the operation, were well acquainted with the vagaries of their AO and the people therein, and were eager to move out on their missions. Captain Gaskins said that "At 0800 on 19 December . . . Colonel Richardson told me he wanted a complete maintenance standdown. I called my platoon commanders and staff together and informed them that until further notice all training had been canceled, and the appointed place of duty would be the company maintenance ramp. All Marines would perform maintenance on all combat-essential equipment as if 'their lives depended on it.' By 1800 on 19 December, all equipment was 100 percent ready." So were the Marines.

Given the administration's "hands off" policy, the intense and pertinent training, the detailed rehearsals, the thorough staff planning, the mix of the forces selected for the operation, the insistence on unity of command, and the specifics of the mission—by any reckoning, the operation should be a winner.[9]

II | COMBAT

8 | The Attacks Begin

The initial attacks of Operation Just Cause were launched by in-country forces.

Maj. Kevin M. Higgins commanded A Company of the 3d Battalion of the 7th Special Forces Group, normally based at Fort Davis on the Atlantic side of the canal, near Gatun. Six A Teams, each with twelve Special Forces troopers, made up A Company. Lt. Col. Roy R. Trumble commanded the 3d of the 7th. He was on his third tour in Panama and had held every possible officer position within the 3d of the 7th. His battalion was part of Task Force Black, a unit in General Downing's Joint Special Operations Task Force, commanded by Col. Jake Jacobelly, the in-country commander of Special Operations Command South (SOCSOUTH), a joint force. Normally he worked directly for the SOUTHCOM commander, General Thurman.

"The groundwork for 7th Special Forces group success in Just Cause and Promote Liberty (a follow-on, in-country, "nation-building" mission after the completion of Just Cause) was laid in the decade prior," wrote Major Higgins recently. "There were some Vietnam veterans in the 3/7, but the men of the 3/7 SFG(A) were products of the 1980s Reagan Latin American policy. It was 3/7 that executed FID program in Central America to counter Sandinista/Cuban initiatives. It was 3/7 that spearheaded the counternarcotics efforts in the source Andean countries. It was 3/7 that participated in countless joint exercises and personnel exchanges in the region. In part, this was due to the fact that SOUTHCOM could easily get their hands on 3/7, the small SF MTTs could easily and economically hitchhike to their destinations on aircraft transiting through Howard AF Base to South and Central America. The Bn Commanders, LTC Scruggs, LTC Stankovich, LTC Froberg, and finally LTC Trumble aggressively pursued mission opportunities. What eventually evolved was a very heavy work load of back-to-back 179-day real-world deployments. The men loved it. Only the most dedicated were attracted to the unit. And it was these most dedicated soldiers that kept coming back to 3/7, Panama for additional tours or just simply stayed on. The result was an impressive collection of highly motivated/trained, culturally aware Spanish-speakers, intimately familiar with the Latin American military mind. This foundation was responsible for the unit's success in Just Cause/Promote Liberty."

On the eighteenth of December, after he had received a preliminary alert, Colonel Trumble moved his forward operating base (FOB) and all available SF personnel, about half of his battalion, some nine A teams, to a hangar at Albrook Air Force Base, just north of Balboa on the Pacific end of the canal. A company's and Higgins's final mission at the bridge (one of his original missions had been simply to reconnoiter the Pacora River Bridge with four men) was to secure the Pacora River Bridge and deny it to the enemy, particularly the elite and well-trained PDF Battalion 2000, whose barracks were at Fort Cimarron, about twenty miles to the northeast of Panama City. Battalion 2000 had three companies: one armor, one airborne, and one air assault. Blocking the bridge, about eight miles to the east of Torrijos/Tocumen Airport, would prevent Battalion 2000 and other PDF units from moving troops, ammunition, and weapons along Highway 1 (locally called the Panamerican or Pan-A Highway) to reinforce the 240 soldiers of the PDF at Torrijos/Tocumen, around which were the drop zones for the 75th Rangers and the 82d Airborne units arriving later.

In the original plan, the 3/7 had been assigned approximately twelve different four-man reconnaissance missions. "On 18 December," wrote Major Higgins, "only four were selected for execution on H-hour:

"Tinajitas Recon. A four-man team was dropped off at the back gate of Fort Clayton at 19 1900 December and moved cross country on foot to place 'eyes on target' on the Tinajitas PDF *cuartel*. They were in position by 20 0100 Dec.

"Cimarron *Cuartel*. At 19 2100 December, a four-man team was placed by UH-60 five kms. outside of Cimarron *cuartel* to report PDF movement.

"Cerro Azul TV2 Antenna. An eighteen-man team was deployed at 20 0100 December to capture and temporarily disable Noriega's primary media contact with the Panamanian people. . . .

"Pacora Bridge.

"The remaining planned missions were not executed mainly because they became irrelevant when the decision was made to do a massive invasion."[1]

Capt. Stuart W. Bradin, Citadel '84, was the commander of ODA (Operational Detachment A) 775 in A Company 3/7. He is the prototype of a Green Beret captain—handsome, with well-muscled arms and chest, slender waist, strong legs. "He is one of the best," said Major Higgins. Bradin could run ten miles carrying full combat gear. In conversation, he is straightforward, positive, and gives the impression of total commitment to and understanding of the nuances of his Special Forces job. In the three months just prior to Just Cause, he had traveled at some length.

On the thirteenth of September, Captain Bradin had completed a Spanish course at the Defense Language Institute and reported for duty to the 3d of the 7th at Fort Davis, Panama. On the third of October, after he received word of the botched coup attempt ("Pot Banger No. 5, the Green Berets called it), Higgins gave Bradin a mission packet for the old Blue Spoon plan. His mission:

On order, reconnoiter Torrijos/Tocumen Airport and the Pacora River Bridge with four men from ODA 775. But on the seventh of October, Bradin left Panama for Peru with eighteen men on a counternarcotics mission; he returned to Fort Davis on the seventh of December.

It was on the eighteenth of December, in the hangar at Albrook, that Major Higgins received his new orders from Colonel Trumble: Forget the original reconnaissance missions. Instead, take and hold the Pacora River Bridge, some twenty miles northeast of Albrook. "The Pacora was changed from a four-man recon to a 'seize and deny access' on 18 December," wrote Major Higgins. "The Rangers were supposed to drop on Tocumen and then move to seize Pacora, but the planners realized that would be too late to stop the Bn 2000."

For the assignment, Major Higgins initially had two UH-60 Black Hawk helicopters, the only two left from other H-hour missions. Because the 617th's MH60s had internal fuel bladders for increased range, each helicopter could carry only eight men. Thus Higgins could plan to insert only sixteen men for the operation, including Captain Bradin and his A Team. Higgins's troops came from four different A teams, including three captains, and, according to Higgins, "that's why LTC Trumble felt it was that the major went to control the operation."

In the isolation of the hangar, Major Higgins planned and briefed the operation in detail. Higgins assigned Captain Bradin and four of his men to hold the left flank of the far side of the bridge. He assigned other detailed missions to other teams in A Company. At 2000 hours on the night of the nineteenth, less than five hours to H-hour, Major Higgins briefed his teams a final time. Shortly thereafter, while he was inspecting his men, Higgins received word that he had an additional Black Hawk from the 228th Aviation Battalion for the mission. His executive officer, Captain Glover, quickly assigned eight more men to the teams and adjusted the loading plans. Higgins and his men were obviously flexible and well trained.

Higgins began loading his two A teams, twenty-four men, into the three Black Hawks at 0010 on the twentieth. During the loading, they were fired on from an area outside the fence around Albrook Air Force Base.

"With intermittent gunfire crackling," wrote Major Higgins, "and six UH60s cranked, the SOCSOUTH J-3 informed me that an eight-vehicle convoy had just departed Cimarron *cuartel* headed toward Tocumen, and H-hour was moved up fifteen minutes and we were to depart immediately. I told the men to load. I boarded the lead helicopter, put on the headset, and before I could brief the pilot, the pilot informed me that we couldn't land on the NE edge of the bridge as planned. With the additional third helicopter we would have to land on the SW edge of the bridge, 180 degrees out! After that news, I then brought the pilot up to date on the situation. He was unaware of the firing alongside the LZ, change in H-hour, and the PDF convoy. We immediately lifted off. In the air he briefed the other pilots and likewise the SF men on these new developments. The pilots made the immediate decision to scrap the flight plan and make a beeline for the bridge, a risk since at H-hour the airspace would be crowded."

Fifteen minutes later, at 0045, the three Black Hawks were approaching the

Pacora River Bridge. "From the helicopters we saw the lights of the eight-vehicle convoy (two jeeps and six 2½-ton trucks), headlights fifty meters apart, winding like a snake, way off in the distance, about two miles off," remembers Major Higgins. "The pilots went right up the road, straight toward the convoy, looking frantically for the bridge. We reached the bridge simultaneously with the convoy. The pilots had to do a buttonhook over the top of the convoy to get us into the LZ. All the SF men had seen the convoy prior to landing, so when we hit the ground, no explanation was needed. In retrospect, we were fortunate to land on the SW of the bridge and not the NE as planned. The NE would have put us in a hand-to-hand combat situation and we would never have been able to use the standoff of the AC-130."

The troops, each with a full load of combat gear, unloaded and deployed "on the double" into three security elements on both sides of the road on the west side of the bridge. They had to run about 100 meters through tall elephant grass and weeds and then climb up a steep, thirty-five-foot embankment, along the top of which ran the road leading to the bridge. Meanwhile, the PDF convoy had moved to within a hundred meters of the other side of the bridge. Higgins said later that he and his men "arrived moments before the enemy convoy began to cross the bridge."

Once on the embankment, Higgins organized his men into a hasty ambush, using antitank weapons and grenade launchers. To fire at the convoy, Sfc. Danny MacDonald, followed by Captain McNamara and Staff Sergeant Roman, armed with LAWs, climbed to the top of the embankment and stood in the middle of the road to fire directly across the bridge. Captain Bradin remembers seeing Sergeant First Class MacDonald fire a LAW at the lead 2½-ton truck. His missile went harmlessly through the truck's tarp, but the driver screeched to a halt, blocking the movement of the convoy. The drivers of the other trucks did not turn off their headlights and thus provided targets in the black of the night.

One of the NCOs who had been on the bridge said later: "I was carrying a SAW [squad automatic weapon]. We immediately set up our weapons on the west side of the bridge facing the oncoming convoy. As I set up my SAW, I could see several vehicles of the convoy coming down the road toward the bridge. Our mission was not only to stop the convoy but to deny movement over the bridge in either direction. As the convoy neared the bridge, we fired two AT-4 antitank rounds and three LAW rounds and several bursts of light machine gun fire at it, stopping the convoy in its tracks."

Major Higgins set up a small company command post southwest of the bridge near the embankment. With him was E-7 Eckloff, a member of an Air Force CCT (combat control team). Eckloff, covered by Master Sergeant Daly, set up his SATCOM (satellite communications) dish on the extreme flank of the position, on the edge of the firing area, to give the best possible firing data to an AC-130 when it came on station. He established communications with an AC-130 Specter, and it was overhead in half an hour, making left-hand circles around the bridge. With his night-vision devices, the Specter pilot could clearly see the stalled convoy. Eckloff radioed the pilot that "All west of the bridge are friendly." Given the marginal safety limits, the pilot asked: "Do you accept friendly casualties?" Higgins told Eckloff to reply affirmatively. Then the Specter, still circling in left-hand turns, began to fire.

The Specter has a devastating array of firepower: 20mm cannon, 7.62mm Gatling guns, and a 105mm howitzer that fires from the door. The Specter can lay down seventeen thousand rounds of ammunition a minute in a formidable, ruinous stream of shells and bullets.

The PDF soldiers scrambled out of the trucks and took up firing positions on the far side of the river. They fired their AK-47s and began moving toward the Special Forces position. The Green Berets returned fire with their M-16s, M-203 grenade launchers, and LAWs. The AC-130 continued to report to Eckloff on enemy movements and provided infrared illumination to increase the utility of the Special Forces' night-vision gear. Higgins said that the "AC-130 had to go off station for a few minutes at 0200. At that point, some PDF decided to come across the bridge. They gave me a scare, because they were carrying a mortar and wearing gas masks." Higgins's men took out the PDF trying to cross the bridge. A number of the PDF in desperation jumped off the side of the bridge.

"The AC-130 reported to us that he saw the PDF dismounting the vehicles and moving to both flanks (the riverbed)," wrote Major Higgins. "I assumed the PDF were following an infantry SOP. When you receive fire from the front, dismount and move to flank the enemy. In addition to firing lengthwise along the convoy, I had the AC-130 fire up and down the riverbed to thwart any counterattack. Likewise, we periodically directed SAW and M-203 fire into the riverbed tree line. I don't recall receiving any incoming PDF fire, although I never did query the men on that during the AAR [after-action review]."

As the firefight continued, Higgins's men spotted several vehicles in the distance moving toward the bridge from the opposite direction, threatening his men from both sides. "I thought this was a PDF relief column," remembers Higgins, "but in retrospect it was probably PDF fleeing from the scene at Tocumen to try to reach 'safety' at Cimarron." Higgins told his flank security force to fire tracers over them. The AC-130 continued to circle the area.

Col. Jake Jacobelly had been monitoring his command net since midnight. He learned from the traffic that the AC-130, which had been on station for some time and had helped disperse the PDF convoy, was running out of fuel. "I called the Air Force to request another AC-130 be expeditiously tasked to move to the area before the initial aircraft would have to leave," he remembered. "The result was continuous AC-130 coverage for the soldier on the ground. The Air Force's response proved that joint operations and interservice coordination worked well. We didn't need a credit card this time to complete the mission." (During the joint operation in Grenada, communications between the Army units on the ground and the Navy offshore required the Army sometimes to use commercial phones to call their headquarters at Fort Bragg. The messages were then relayed via satellite to the Navy commander, who passed the requests on to the air controllers aboard the aircraft carriers.)

In the meantime, SSG Roman had heard some movement under the bridge. He threw several grenades underneath it. The noise stopped. By 0300, the situation began to stabilize. Major Higgins sent out a small patrol to verify that none of the PDF had made it across the bridge. At 0500, a PDF corporal on a bicycle was captured trying to cross the bridge. "The corporal seemed to have no idea of what had taken place," Higgins said. "He was visiting his girlfriend that night out in the countryside. He thought the convoy had parked to take a rest for the night."

At dawn, about 0600, a quick-reaction force (QRF) from A Company of the 1st Battalion of the 7th Special Forces Group arrived by helicopter. The QRF and Major Higgins's team made a sweep of the destroyed convoy. They found eight of the PDF dead on the bridge. Special Forces medics treated the wounded PDF soldiers that they found. Perez's men captured several PDF hiding in a house off the road. Another Special Forces team collected weapons and munitions to be moved out of the area. Higgins established local security around the bridge and set up checkpoints to inspect vehicles for enemy soldiers and weapons.[2]

Another team processed and interrogated prisoners. The interrogation revealed that there had been some fifty-six soldiers from Battalion 2000's heavy-weapons company in the convoy. (Higgins said that he had seen reports that as many as two hundred were in the convoy and that Chepo Hospital, 15 kilometers east, treated more than thirty patients that night.) They were led by the company's executive officer and were armed with 81mm mortars, 90mm recoilless weapons, and .30-caliber and MAG-58 machine guns. According to the executive officer, the company was on the way into Panama City to put down "some sort of a civil disturbance" and he had "lost control" of the company after the fighting started. He also said that a large portion of Battalion 2000 had passed over the bridge the previous evening at 2200 and were presumably on the way to Tocumen and scattered throughout the city.

At about 1545, a scout platoon from the 82d Airborne Division, on the way to Fort Cimarron, linked up with Higgins and his men—none of whom had been wounded or killed. From Fort Cimarron, a 2½-ton truck flying a white flag came to pick up the PDF dead and wounded. A few of the PDF did escape and later ran into the Rangers and the 82d Airborne units at Tocumen. At 1730 Higgins, his twenty-four Green Berets, and twenty POWs were helicoptered by three CH-53s back to Albrook Air Force Base—mission accomplished.

Shortly after midnight, other Special Forces units had conducted special reconnaissance of Fort Cimarron to report on other movements of Battalion 2000 and of the Tinajitas compound, where PDF mortar capabilities were a concern. According to a postaction report from Gen. James Lindsay's U.S. Special Operations Command,

Task Force Black also assisted our Psychological Operations effort by temporarily disabling the primary Panamanian television station's transmissions. No longer do our forces plant explosives and knock over an antenna tower. In this mission, a Special Forces A Team, with appropriate technical assistance, "fast-roped" (rappeled rapidly down a rope from a helicopter hovering above the site) into the station compound (at Cerro Azul) and removed a critical electronic module (of TV Channel 2's transmission facility) that disabled the

TV. This prevented the opposition from using this media to support their cause and allowed our EC-130 Volant Solo aircraft to broadcast supportive themes to the Panamanian populace. This method also allows us to restore normal station operations much sooner.

The Volant Solo broadcast information to the Panamanian people to remain inside and not to resist the U.S. forces whose goal was to capture Noriega.[3]

The two technicians who accompanied the Special Forces had never fast-roped before. After a very hurried five-minute explanation of the technique, they fast-roped with the team into the compound. One observer from the U.S. Southern Command remarked, "The experience must have been somewhat to their liking, since it took nine days for their unit to pry them away from the Special Forces."

"An additional force that can only be mentioned in passing is Task Force Blue and Task Force Green," wrote one of the Special Operations Command's officers. "These forces, supported by quick-reaction helicopters and AC-130 gunships, had the difficult task of capturing the elusive Noriega. Our intelligence efforts greatly narrowed the possibilities for his location and allowed this force to apply pressure to him commencing at H-hour. This pressure never let up, with our force systematically pursuing each substantive lead. This effectively denied Noriega a place to hide and prevented his escape from Panama."[4]

A later report from U.S. Special Operations Command on the peregrinations of the desperate Noriega reported,

Pre-H-hour intelligence showed Noriega to be in Colón on 19 December 89, but his precise location on the evening of 19 December, both prior to and after H-hour, was not known. Subsequent analysis and sources reveal Noriega left Colón in the early evening of 19 December. He drove to the Cerimi Military Recreation Center Hotel at Tocumen Airfield for a rendezvous with a prostitute. While at this location, he barely escaped capture by TF Red at H-hour. He departed in such a hurry that he left his shoes and uniform at the site. They were later returned to him to wear for his surrender. Allegedly, it is the same uniform he wears at the trial. Noriega traveled to several houses of close supporters in urban Panama City on 20 December 89. He spent 21 through 24 December 89 in hiding at a house on the outskirts of Panama City, his efforts to move thwarted by search operations.

Noriega's days were numbered; the countdown was under way.

9 | Task Force White

Task Force White was the U.S. Navy's contribution to Just Cause. Naval Special Warfare Group 2 (NSWG-2), a part of U.S. Special Operations Command, is based at Little Creek, Virginia. NSWG 2 normally had one SEAL platoon on rotation to Panama. For Just Cause, SEAL Team 4, under Cmdr. Tom McGrath, deployed four more platoons to the operation aboard the C-141s that General Downing brought to Panama on the eighteenth of December. TF White, a total of some 707 sailors, also included special boat units and a countermine division.

The SEALs are the Navy's elite commandos. They are carefully selected for brains, brawn, and dedication, and they undergo an arduous training program at Coronado, California. Included in the program are long hours swimming in the cold Pacific Ocean, many nights running long and difficult obstacle courses, and lengthy instruction on weapons and marksmanship. The training is so difficult and backbreaking that two thirds of the recruits flunked the course in 1988.

Task Force White had three major missions in Operation Just Cause: Deny the PDF the use of their patrol boats in Balboa Harbor; deny Noriega the use of his personal jet at Paitilla Airport; and isolate PDF forces at Flamenco Island.[1]

Balboa Harbor, just inside the Pacific Ocean entrance to the canal, normally berths large PDF patrol boats. But Task Unit Whiskey's target just after midnight of the twentieth of December was Noriega's yacht, the *Presidente Porras,* a craft that he could use to escape from Panama.

The on-scene commander of Task Unit Whiskey, made up of two dive pairs and a fire support team, was Cmdr. Norman J. Carley. At 2300 on the night of 19 December, Carley led his two teams in two CRRCs (combat rubber raiding craft) from Rodman Naval Station on the Pacific end of the canal and across the canal from Balboa Harbor toward his target docked at Pier 18 in Balboa Harbor. Each dive pair was equipped with an MK-138 Mod 1 haversack armed with a MCS-1 clock and a MK-39 safety and arming device with a MK-96 detonator. In simple language, these were explosive devices to disable the *Presidente Porras*. The four-man fire support team, armed with .50-caliber machine guns, 60mm mortars, and MK-19 40mm machine guns, was in position at Rodman and within range of the underwater swimming teams' target. Another element of TU Whiskey was a group of six SEALs in two patrol boats, led by Lt. j.g. Martin L. Strong, standing by as a contingency surface force in the event that the underwater swimmers were "compromised."

Because of unexpected boat traffic in the harbor, Carley's two boats had to take a circuitous route to the point where he would insert the divers, and because H-hour had been moved up fifteen minutes, to 0045, Carley had to insert the teams closer to the target than he had planned. Unfortunately, one of the CRRCs had motor trouble while traveling at slow speed to avoid leaving a telltale wake. Carley went on with the first boat and concealed the team at a mangrove tree line north of the target area, Pier 18 at Balboa Harbor, until it was time to insert the divers. Then, at 2330, the first CRRC, with coxswain Hospitalman Chief George P. Riley and HT-3 Christopher J. Kinney aboard, maneuvered to a point about 150 meters from Pier 18, and Carley inserted the first team. Then, with CRRC 1, he returned to CRRC 2, whose coxswain was IS-3 Scott L. Neudecker, and towed it to the insertion point. In five minutes the second team was underwater near Pier 18. Carley towed the second boat back to Rodman for a new motor.

The four swimmers dove on a compass bearing to Pier 18 and surfaced underneath it. Then each team moved independently underneath the pier toward shore, alternating above and below the surface. The *Presidente Porras* was tied to a floating dock near shore. Near the end of the pier, the swimmers dove and began an approach that would bring them under the target. Swim pair 2, ET-1 Randy L. Beausoleil and PH-2 Christopher J. Dye, arrived at the target at 0011, made a positive identification, and attached the twenty-pound haversack to the port propeller shaft and armed the system. Swim pair 1, Lt. Edward L. Coughlin and EN-3 Timothy K. Eppley, swam under the target at 0014 and attached its haversack to the starboard propeller shaft, armed the system, and tied detonating cord leads between the charges to ensure dual priming. Both pairs finished their jobs in less than two minutes.

But it was not a completely easy task. As Coughlin and Eppley were finishing the arming sequence, the target boat's engines started. Coughlin and Eppley finished their job and swam rapidly to the concealment of Pier 17. Beausoleil and Dye joined them under the pier. Just as they got there, they felt the blast of underwater detonations nearby. They swam behind pier pilings for protection. Shortly thereafter, four more detonations bounced them in the water. The men, alternating on the surface and beneath it to conserve oxygen, moved along Pier 17 to their preplanned extraction point. They had set the timers to explode beneath the *Presidente Porras* in forty-five minutes. They were still under Pier 17 when their charges detonated at 0100, precisely on time, disabling the target ship. Following the detonation, most of the ships in the harbor began churning their propellers as an antiswimmer measure. Shortly thereafter, the divers left Pier 17 and headed on a course that brought them close to the main channel of the canal, where a large-draft ship sailed overhead and forced the divers to a depth of forty-five feet. After ten minutes at that depth, they swam up to their normal operating depth of twenty feet and headed for Pier 6, their preplanned extraction point.

At 0045, Commander Carley led the two CRRCs from Rodman and headed for Pier 6. They arrived at the seaward end of the pier fifteen minutes later and floated quietly under the pier. While waiting for the dive teams, Carley and his CRRC crews heard firefights overhead near the pier and saw tracer rounds flash overhead. Nonetheless, they stayed in place. Because the swim teams were late, Carley began to worry about them and sent CRRC 2 to the next pier downcurrent to see if the divers had missed the first extraction point. CRRC 2 returned without the divers.

At 0200, Coughlin and Eppley arrived at Pier 6; five minutes later, Beausoleil and Dye surfaced near the pier. The dive pairs were equipped with MX-300 radios in watertight bags, but they had been unable to communicate with each other or with Carley because the many obstructions and vessels in the harbor interfered with their transmissions. Carley immediately loaded the dive teams into the two CRRCs and set out for Rodman Naval Station. Once they had cleared the Balboa side of the canal, Carley lit an infrared strobe to facilitate recognition at Rodman and radioed TF White that TU Whiskey was returning to base. At 0220—three hours, twenty minutes after they had left Rodman— the teams beached their boats back at Rodman, their mission accomplished. It was one of the rare incidents in battle where a unit takes off on a combat mission from its peacetime base and returns after accomplishing its task. It was also the first time since World War II that underwater swimmers attacked a docked enemy vessel.[2]

* * *

Paitilla Airport, a private airfield in the southwestern corner of downtown Panama City, almost abuts the shore of the Pacific Ocean. The airport was frequently used by Noriega, who maintained an executive-type Learjet at Paitilla. Noriega's staff also used the field and the jet for other clandestine purposes, including drug-related operations. It fell to the SEALs to "deny the use of the jet and the airfield for a possible escape" by Noriega.

At 0045, the new H-hour, Task Unit Papa, three SEAL platoons, a total of ninety-two men led by Cmdr. Tom McGrath, landed from rubber raiding boats along the beach at Paitilla. Earlier, in camouflage fatigues and jungle boots and carrying rucksacks and weapons, they had loaded up in combat rubber raiding crafts (CRRCs) on the dark beach of Rodman Naval Station on the west side of the canal, hooked onto the back of a Navy patrol boat, and were towed across the canal in the black of the night. Then, two miles offshore, the patrol boat turned them loose. For a short time the boats remained tied together on the ocean, but when word came to move up H-hour by fifteen minutes, McGrath ordered the boats to head immediately for Paitilla.

Lt. John Patrick Connors and Lt. Mike Phillips were SEAL platoon commanders. They had served together in the Persian Gulf and for four months of jungle training in Brazil. Both were superbly fit physically and extremely well qualified in the skills of a SEAL. (One requirement for SEAL qualification was an underwater swim of seven miles at night from one point to another with navigation by compass.) Connors, twenty-five, from Boston and a Boston Marathon runner, also spoke fluent Spanish. "John had a strong sense of patriotism," said his best friend, John Sheehan. "He was the kind of character who is full of life and lives it to the fullest." Before the operation, Connors was undergoing treatment for a skin disease he had contracted from a sandfly bite in Brazil. But he so much wanted to be on the operation that he faked a release from the hospital by telling his doctor at Walter Reed that he had "an emergency in his family." Connors joined his platoon the day before it moved from Little Creek.

As soon as the rubber boats beached on the hard mud of the beach at Paitilla at 0045, the SEALs unloaded and spread out in a security perimeter. The grass was low and afforded little concealment. The SEALs could see people moving under the control tower's lights, but the area of the field near them, the south side, was apparently deserted. Five minutes later, two platoons moved north on the western side of the field and one platoon and the mortar section moved north on the eastern side. They moved as they had been taught and as they had trained: One squad moved forward at a crouch, while another squad knelt in position and covered the other's advance. In the distance they could see tracers in the sky and hear the rumble of artillery and tank guns as other Just Cause forces attacked the Comandancia and parts of Fort Amador.

Phillips's platoon raced across the open strip to the PDF hangar that housed Noriega's Learjet. But an M-60 gunner in the first squad of Phillips's platoon identified and took under fire the armed guards in the adjacent Aero Perla hangar at the same time that Phillips ordered his men to disable the Learjet in the PDF hangar. The guards in both the Aero Perla hangar and the PDF hangar opened fire simultaneously with their AK-47's at the first squad at the edge of the parking ramp only thirty meters away. The fire was devastating: The Panamanians killed one man in the squad and wounded seven others. Phillips raced forward with the rest of his platoon, firing as they approached. When he saw the extent of his first squad's casualties, he called immediately for MEDEVAC. Phillips recognized that the Specter gunship on station overhead could not fire into the hangars without endangering his men. But he knew that he would need help to suppress the PDF in the hangar with heavy fire so that he could evacuate his wounded.

So did Commander McGrath. He immediately ordered the 2d and 3d platoons to reinforce and assist Phillips's platoon. Phillips had already spread out his other two squads and took both hangars under fire. In a few minutes, Connors and his platoon arrived. Connors spread out his men and led them, firing as they moved forward toward the hangars. Phillips remembered later that Connors showed no fear as he moved across the parking area from which the PDF bullets ricocheted off the hard surface and sparked all around Connors and his advancing men.

As Connors moved forward in the lead of his platoon, PDF bullets hammered against his web equipment and his ammo pouches. But he slowed only briefly. He ran forward firing his M-16 as he charged the hangar and the PDF guards. The PDF increased their fire at this new threat. The hangar was of cinder block, and the SEALs' small arms had little effect unless they caught a PDF firing from a window.

Connors decided to use his grenade launcher, slung under his M-16. He knelt on one knee and loaded a grenade. At that moment, the PDF opened fire with a machine gun and blasted Connors in the chest. Phillips ran to Connors and dragged him out of line of the PDF fire. Other SEALs carried Connors to the MEDEVAC triage point. The medics cut away his uniform and webgear and tried to resuscitate him, but it was too late.

By now the 2d Squad of the 2d Platoon maneuvered forward to reinforce the 2d Squad of the 1st Platoon and took the hangars under fire. Then the 2d Squad of the 3d Platoon reinforced the 1st Platoon. Together the 2d and 3d platoons suppressed the enemy fire in both hangars with rockets, grenades, and machine guns. On the scene, Commander McGrath consolidated his three platoons into one perimeter.

Lieutenant Phillips went back to the triage point as soon as the perimeter was secure. There he found the medics working feverishly with the wounded. But he also found Torpedoman's Mate 2d Cl. Isaac Rodriguez, twenty-four, of Missouri City, Texas, mortally wounded and, lying in the grass, three dead SEALs: Connors; Boatswain's Mate 1st Cl. Christopher Tilghman, thirty, of Kailua, Hawaii; and Engineer Chief Donald McFaul, thirty-two, of San Diego.

By 0117, all enemy fire was suppressed; the Learjet was disabled; and, at 0330, Paitilla Airport was secure.[3]

The Navy awarded Lt. John Patrick Connors the Silver Star posthumously.

In another part of the city, just three miles from Paitilla Airport, a pre-H-hour strike was under way. It had been carefully planned and meticulously rehearsed by the Army's Delta Force, a unit trained and equipped for rescues under hostile conditions. The White House and General Powell were watching this one very intently. The man the Delta Force was going to try to rescue was a special case.

10 | The Rescue of Kurt Muse

On the nineteenth of December 1989, Kurt Muse was locked up in Modelo Prison, across the street from Noriega's headquarters, La Comandancia. But Muse was no ordinary jailbird. And his release was just moments away. Nor was that ordinary.

"The CIA was deeply concerned about Muse and wanted to avoid a repeat of the 1984 kidnapping and subsequent murder of their station chief in Beirut, William Buckley," wrote Bob Woodward in *The Commanders.* "In that episode, the agency's inability to locate and rescue one of its own had made it appear weak. So CIA director William H. Webster pressed Cheney to have the military draw up a rescue plan for Muse that would be ready for execution on short notice."

Maj. Gen. Gary Luck was the commander of the Joint Special Operations Command (JSOC) during the planning phase for Just Cause. At 1000 on the sixteenth of October, General Luck met with General Powell in his Pentagon office and gave him two thirty-minute briefings. In the first, Luck outlined his capabilities: Deploy anywhere in the world on short notice with a force of about 300 trained specialists, including helicopters, Delta troopers, a SEAL team, intelligence teams, special communicators armed with very sophisticated equipment, and medics. These men, tailored to a mission's requirements, could rescue Americans or other hostages. For operations in Panama, all he needed at any time—around the clock—was four hours to assemble his force and five hours to fly there. In the second briefing, Luck detailed Operation Acid Gambit, a plan to snatch Muse from Modelo Prison.

In this briefing, Luck had aerial photos of Modelo, a detailed, three-dimensional model of the prison with walls that flapped down to show the details of the interior, intricate maps of the neighborhood, and the location of guard posts, doors, stairs, and Muse's room. Luck outlined how the rescue would take place, minute by minute. He stated confidently that Muse would be out of his cell and on a helicopter on the roof nine minutes after the assault began.

Later, Luck's Special Forces actually rehearsed the Muse rescue plan in an isolated Florida area using a three-quarter-size mock-up of the prison. The rehearsal took place near the area where, in 1970, Col. Bull Simons had built a mock-up of the North Vietnamese Son Tay prison camp prior to the raid to rescue American POWs. In that case the raid was successful except for one major point: The North Vietnamese had moved the POWs just before the Green Beret raiders descended on the camp.[1]

Kurt Muse was born in Phoenix, Arizona, in 1950. Soon after his birth, his parents, both American citizens, moved to Panama, where the senior Muse went into the graphic-arts business. Kurt had one brother and one sister, and the three of them attended grade school in Panama. Kurt became so fluent in Spanish that his parents, to improve his English, enrolled him in Balboa High School in the United States–administered Canal Zone. All the "Army brats"— the children of the U.S. Army troops permanently stationed in Panama— attended Balboa High School. There Kurt met his future bride, the queen of the junior-senior prom, Anne Castoro. After high school, where Muse had been voted the "best all-around" and most friendly student, he went on to the University of Texas at El Paso and later served as an air defense artillery officer in the U.S. Army. Thereafter, he returned to Panama with his wife.

By the early 1980s, Kurt's father had expanded the business to include three quick-print shops, a graphic-arts distribution company, and stores that sold supplies to engineers, artists, and architects. There was enough of the family business to provide comfortable livelihoods for the entire Muse family. By this time Kurt and Anne had two children, Kimberly and Erik.

True to his classmates' appraisal of him, Kurt was an outgoing man, a personable gentleman. He was a golfer, a sailor, a "four-wheeler," and very active in the Panama City Rotary Club. He was the first baseman on the Rotary Club's softball team and, one year, the chairman of the Central American convention for Rotary International, a job requiring a great expenditure of time and polished skill at management and organization. He was also on the Salvation Army's local advisory board. The Muse family had retained its American citizenship, but because of his fluency in Spanish and his business and Rotary connections, Kurt was integrated into and accepted in Panamanian society.

In spite of Noriega's increasingly tight stranglehold on Panama, Muse stayed out of politics until 1987. "Noriega was bleeding the country dry," he said later. "He was sapping its morals—it was becoming an immoral place, with institutionalized graft. And the kids were starting to emulate their parents." And the Muse family business was beginning to feel the effects of the free-wheeling crimes of the digbats. They had burned down one of the quick-print shops because, they had thought, mistakenly, that it was printing anti-Noriega propaganda. Noriega's drug indictments in the United States in 1988 and the obvious, blatant evidence of widespread corruption in the government caused Muse a great deal of concern about the threat to the well-being of the only country he really knew: Panama.

In his spare time, Muse enjoyed monitoring PDF communications on a very simple Radio Shack police scanner that he owned and operated, even though possession of such a scanner was forbidden by Noriega's entrenched autocrats. But Muse was amused by the PDF's awkward and heavy-handed attempts to control the increasing number of demonstrations against the powers that were. "The whole country was in an uproar," he said later. "Every other street corner had burning tires on it." Another Rotarian shared Muse's interest in eavesdropping on the PDF, the police. The other Rotarian was a computer specialist. "He and I found each other doing the same thing," he remembered. "We began pooling our resources and assigned different frequencies to each other."

One day in the fall of 1987, Muse attended the opening of a Salvation Army school for the blind in Panama City. Agents of the PDF were also on hand in an obviously blatant attempt to show the people that the dictatorship of Noriega was somehow benevolent and "people-caring." At the dedication, Muse met another Rotarian and suggested to him, as they watched the PDF strut around officiously, bellowing orders into their hand-held radios, that it would be "nice if we could actually get into their communications and talk to those sons of bitches."

Muse's friend owned a small communications company and told Muse that it was a lot easier than he might imagine. He said that there were other Rotarians who were also listening in to the PDF network and that somehow they ought to form a clandestine group to monitor the PDF communications. A couple of weeks later, the five Rotary listeners were a loosely organized but dedicated group.

The Rotarians started out as a bunch of amateurs armed only with police scanners. "We simply grabbed blocks of frequency and scanned them to find communications," Muse said later. In time they managed to isolate PDF channels, interpret the PDF codes, and utilize their own two-way radios, which they had bought in Miami, to communicate with each other, actually using the PDF's own codes. They became increasingly proficient at interpreting the language of the PDF network, given the fact that the soldiers communicated in militarese and code. In flipping through the frequencies, the Rotarians happened upon the cellular-telephone channels used by the PDF and government hierarchy. They listened, for example, to officials talking intimately to their girlfriends. On these and other channels they heard drug dealers making connections, military officials actually telling a newspaper that the lead editorial for the next day was en route, and a Colombian drug dealer asking that police be removed from a shopping center so that a transfer could be made in the parking lot. Shortly they heard a command go out to the police in the area to attend an emergency meeting someplace away from the shopping center.

Muse stored much of the information in his Apple II GS computer in his den at home. But the Rotarians were still passive eavesdroppers and not involved in any overt activities. That was soon to pass.

On Saturday morning, 27 February 1988, Muse and his four fellow Rotarians were meeting to mull over the preceding weeks' events. They had their scanner turned on while they talked. At one point they heard a startling PDF transmission—an order to arrest the legal president of the country, Eric Arturo

Delvalle, and Vice President Roderick Esquivel. Esquivel was a doctor and a fellow Rotarian. Immediately, Muse and some of his compatriots raced to Esquivel's office ahead of the PDF, packed him into the back of their car, and sped off past the PDF. Esquivel was safe but then went underground.

From that date on, the group became more bold, innovative, and successful. With some more sophisticated equipment that Muse bought and smuggled into Panama City, the group found to their amazement and delight that they could override the signal from Radio Nacional. They called it "nuking." And they also realized that if they could "nuke" the Radio Nacional transmitter, they might also be able to broadcast their own messages while the government station's broadcasts were off the air. They tried it, with some apprehension, when Noriega himself was about to make a statement. When the announcer said, "And here is General Noriega . . . ," Muse and his friends punched the transmit button and all Panama heard: "We interrupt this program to bring you a message from free and democratic Panamanians, a message to their oppressors. . . ." The message lasted three minutes.

Later Muse said, "Our hearts were racing. There we are, listening to our message being broadcast all over the nation, realizing that all of the agencies in the country are going apeshit. Not knowing when a helicopter gunship was going to appear on the horizon, not knowing if troops were going to storm the house. I mean, it was a major emotional event." For the time being, the group of conspirators, flushed with their initial success, hid their equipment and departed the apartment that they had leased under a false name.

But, with success, the horizon opened, and the amateur communicators became more audacious and inventive. They bought timers and tape recorders from Radio Shack and set up a studio in a vacant apartment. The mechanism worked automatically with the timers so no Rotarian need be present and therefore could not be caught. They "nuked" talk shows and music programs with one-minute broadcasts as often as seven times an hour. One talk show emcee was so frustrated by the interruptions that he offered, on the air, to sell his tormentors radio time if they would stop. They reported on antigovernment demonstrations and broadcast public-service announcements and statements from Noriega's chief opposition group, the National Civic Crusade. And with new equipment bought in the States, they could now communicate directly with the PDF, even though, of course, the PDF did not know the origin of the interruptive communications. The Rotarians often urged the troops to revolt. They sent confusing orders to the PDF during protest demonstrations. And they ridiculed and harassed Noriega's elite riot unit, the Dobermans, calling them cowards and flunkies. Muse proved it one day when he contacted a Doberman officer on his portable radio and told him to look up at the apartment building near where he stood. Muse then told him that he could see him (he could not) and he had a thirty-power scope aimed "right down your running lights" and, "if he was brave," he would do something about it. A friend of Muse's on the scene told Muse that the Dobermans in the area scrambled in a hurry and slid under trucks and hid behind bushes.

The U.S. CIA and the U.S. Southern Command knew who was behind the anti-Noriega radio operation that was causing so much heartburn and difficulty for the Noriega regime. Early in 1989, Vice President Esquivel gave Muse and his team, now six in number, a sophisticated new transmitter. Muse suspected that the transmitter came from the CIA because of its sophistication. Later they received a second radio transmitter and a television transmitter. By now they were calling themselves "Radio Voz de la Libertad" and were broadcasting at 91.5 on the FM channel, with no program longer than fifteen minutes. For their radio broadcast times, they selected periods when traffic was heaviest so they could reach the largest number of people, and the heavy traffic would hinder the PDF from trying to find Muse's transmitter.

But the PDF, using direction finders and better-trained experts, and possibly with some help from the Cubans, began to close in on the locations of the transmitters. From nearby apartments, the Rotarian conspirators could actually watch the PDF, in unmarked cars or taxis, surreptitiously scout the area where they thought the transmitters were housed. In one raid, the PDF ransacked Apartment 10A in a building and stormed adjacent apartments. But the transmitter was in Apartment 10A in a building across the street. The government finally went so far as to announce that it would pay thousands of dollars for clues leading to the arrest of the illegal broadcasters. A few days later, the Rotarians, camouflaged as beachgoers, smuggled their equipment in several drink coolers out of the apartment within sight of PDF guards.

In the spring of 1989, the broadcasts were continuing even more boldly, some going so far as to encourage the PDF to vote for the opposition. Encouraged by their continued successes, Muse and a cohort went to Miami to investigate some new equipment. But on the way back through customs at Torrijos/Tocumen Airport, Muse found that his days of freedom were over. He handed his passport to an immigration official, who passed it routinely to a member of Panama's G-2 unit. At about the same time, Muse saw a sign taped to the booth's glass window that startled him. It read: "Kurt Muse. American citizen. Arrest him on sight."

The G-2 agent checked the passport, then a book, then the sign on the booth, and left. He returned with four civilian-garbed security men. They asked Muse to come with them for a "routine" check. The security men hustled Muse into a van with darkened windows and took him to a PDF substation managed by one Major Miranda, a short, dark man who sat behind his desk and tapped on it with his riding crop. Three PDF officers stood behind Miranda.

"We know you're a big spy," Miranda said. He examined Muse's passport, asked him a lot of questions about his travels, and wanted to know if he had been spying for the Americans in Nicaragua. Muse had reasonable answers for each of the questions. Then Miranda ordered Muse into a truck, and they took him to his home.

Muse lived in a two-story, Spanish-style home. His wife was in Miami, his son was visiting a friend, and only his fifteen-year-old daughter, Kimberly, was at home. Muse ran up the steps ahead of the guards. Kimberly met him and asked about his trip. Muse hugged her and told her in a low voice that he was being arrested. "These people are here to take me to jail. I want you to leave. Now."

Later, Kimberly said: "I could hear his heart beating. It was the first time I'd ever seen my dad scared. You'd never think he could be afraid of anything."

Kimberly ran out past the PDF but fell on the pavement and skinned her knees. Two PDF caught her and pulled her back to the house. But Miranda let her go. She quickly went to a pay phone and called her mother in Miami, her grandparents who lived in the neighborhood, and her brother.

Meanwhile, the PDF ransacked the house and jammed everything they thought was important, including all the papers from Muse's desk, into canvas bags. They also confiscated Muse's weapons, a Glock pistol and a carbine, and several boxes of ammunition.

Muse thought that he had been arrested because of the illegal broadcasts and the interference with the PDF communications. What he didn't know was that Miranda didn't know of these activities. What trapped him was that the wife of a man who made broadcast tapes for the radio transmissions had told the PDF only that Muse was "involved in seditious activity." But the guns in Muse's house made Miranda think that he had captured a terrorist. Miranda then directed searches of Muse's office downtown and his parents' home.

Fortunately, word of Muse's arrest spread rapidly to his fellow Rotarians. That night, twenty-six people, the Rotarians and their families, sought asylum in the United States–controlled Panama Canal Zone. They were granted asylum by some perplexed U.S. officers who were unaware at the time of the Rotarians' exploits.

At about 0100 the next morning, the PDF took Muse to the headquarters of the DENI (Departmento Nacional de Investigación), the Panamanian FBI. For the next two and a half days, a series of interrogators fired question after question at him. If he nodded, one of the investigators would tap him on the head with a pencil or pen. They fed him and permitted him to go to the bathroom but not to shower, shave, or change his clothes. If they left, they'd turn on a "boom box" behind his ear. Finally, exhausted, he began to mix up his answers. When they showed him yet another apartment key that he had trouble passing off, he finally confessed. "I'm Radio Libertad," he told them. "In that apartment you're going to find a transmitter."

Muse was finally allowed a couple of hours of sleep. Later he underwent more intensive interrogation and harassment by the DENI. In a few days, the government held a press conference to display publicly its "Yankee spy." Later he was taken to the office of the DENI chief, Lt. Col. Nivaldo Madrinan. Inside the office were ten people, three of whom were Americans. Because Muse's wife, Anne, was a teacher in the Canal Zone, Muse was technically a U.S. dependent and entitled to some protection as outlined in the Panama Canal Treaty of 1978. One of the Americans read Muse his rights and asked him if he understood them. "Inside I'm laughing and crying," he remembered later. "I'm screaming silently that I have no rights, that that pig over there, a PDF colonel, is going to issue me my rights. He's going to kill me if he wants. I belong to him." But he said that he understood his rights.

The three Americans would be Muse's contact with the outside world for the next nine months. One was an Air Force physician, Lt. Col. Jim Ruffer. Another was Lt. Col. Robert Perry of the Army. A third was a U.S.-Panamanian lawyer, Dr. Marcus Ostrander. They met with him every other day throughout his incarceration. Muse remembers that they were most supportive and that Perry "went the whole nine yards for me, never gave up." Ruffer "became my confidant, shrink, doctor, everything."

In a few days, the DENI moved Muse to a facility in the San Felipe district of Panama City. All day long, Muse was guarded by a man with a shotgun. He watched while the DENI thugs booked and interrogated suspects. On one occasion, the PDF brought in a Colombian for booking. Apparently he was uncooperative. Two PDF men smashed him in the face and ricocheted him off the walls. They put him in handcuffs, with one arm behind his back and the other over his shoulder. They kicked him in the groin and on his back and sides until he bled. "They beat this guy mercilessly," recalled Muse. They stood on his face with their boots, mashing it the way you would mash out a cigarette. They hit him across the back with a crowbar. It was horrible, horrible. I was certain he was going to die. I just sat there praying, 'Have mercy on this guy.'"

"Hey, shouldn't we get the gringo out of here?" one of the PDF asked the officer in charge of the beating.

"Leave the gringo here," he said. "He should know what could happen to him."

Later, Muse was moved to another police substation for additional interrogation. When the police were satisfied—they told him that the Noriega crowd was "Happy with his cooperation"—they moved him to Modelo Prison. His cell was on the second floor of the prison, an eight- by twelve-foot room with an adjoining bathroom. The U.S. embassy had meals brought to him twice a day.

The PDF confined Muse to his cell for the first four months except for visits to the hospital for physical exams by Colonel Ruffer, always in the presence of PDF officers. Ruffer and Muse managed to develop a code, based on whether he was wearing socks, to alert Ruffer that Muse needed to see someone. Muse was permitted to have one book per day, and he and Colonel Ruffer developed a signal to let Ruffer know that Muse had hidden a message in the spine of the returned book. One message actually got to President Bush. "Only military force could solve the problem of Panama," he wrote. In response, President Bush wrote to Muse's wife and children, now residing in the Washington, D.C., area, and invited them to visit the White House after his release.

During his nine months in prison, Muse watched the beatings of other prisoners, particularly after the 7 May elections, in which the opposition defeated Noriega's candidate and that Noriega annulled. One hundred fifty antigovernment protesters were jailed after the election and were, at one time, lined up along a wall, four at a time, and beaten with hoses. They "just beat the bejesus out of them," Muse recalled.

The short-lived coup attempt of 3 October had disastrous results for the rebels. Muse watched a lot of the action from his prison window across the street from La Comandancia. At 0830, some troops set up machine guns around the headquarters building, and a short firefight started. To Muse, it seemed that the troops who had moved in toward the building were winning. A small red helicopter had landed outside the headquarters earlier. Then at 1000, forces loyal to Noriega arrived in armored vehicles and attacked the building. The rebels inside the building returned the fire. But by 1330, the coup had fizzled. Muse heard some shots from inside La Comandancia and assumed that the rebels inside were being murdered. That afternoon, the PDF replaced the prison guards, and about 150 rebels were brought into the prison. Every night for weeks, Muse heard the sounds of beatings as the PDF clubbed the rebel officers with fists, hoses, and clubs. Once the interrogators arrived, "the torture would begin," Muse remembered. "The sound of a man being tortured is indescribable."

After the 3 October attempt to overthrow Noriega, Muse noticed a change in the atmosphere in the prison. New guard posts on the roof and in the halls were manned. There was a new guard at a desk at the end of hall. Through one of the rebel officers, using hand signals, Muse learned that an American officer had been killed on 16 December. On Tuesday, 19 December, he watched the PDF soldiers reinforce the sandbags around La Comandancia. He realized that something drastic was about to take place in Panama. To make matters far worse, the guard at the desk in the corridor told him, in answer to Muse's pointed question, that "Yes," he would kill him if anything happened. That evening, Muse drifted off into a troubled sleep.

He was awakened at 0045 on the twentieth by the sound of machine-gun fire. He grabbed a metal bed brace that he had kept concealed. The guard, however, woke some PDF officers and yelled at them, "Something's happening!" Muse thought that "World War III broke loose outside."

He heard the sound of the AC-130 firing its 105mm gun at the Comandancia and saw the black hole in the building where it had hit. He heard machine guns firing on the ground and from the air. The lights went out in the prison. He heard a loud explosion close by, a blast that sent debris into his cell. Then there were two more explosions followed by machine-gun fire. He could hear men shouting and running. The halls were black with smoke. Then, said Muse, "this apparition comes to my cell door. The guy looks like Darth Vader. He's wearing a funny-looking helmet, funny-looking goggles, funny-looking uniform, and had a funny-looking weapon." Muse did not know it at the time, but the soldier he saw shining a light into his cell was a Delta Force commando.

"Moose!" he yelled. "You okay?"

"Yo," Muse shouted back.

"Stay down. I'm going to blow the door!"

With that, after a blast, the Delta trooper was in the cell. "We're going to take you out. We're going to the roof. We have a chopper. You're going to get in the middle. Do you understand?"

"You got it," said Muse.

Muse could hear the sound of the battle outside and see the flashes of explosions reflected on his cell walls. The Delta trooper put a flak vest and a helmet on Muse and led him out into the corridor through the smoke. They climbed up a flight of stairs and emerged onto the roof. There was a small Hughes D-500 Bumblebee helicopter, with its rotor turning, on the roof. Other Delta troopers in the same black outfits surrounded the helicopter.

At 0111 on the twentieth, Powell and Cheney were in the Pentagon's Crisis Situation Room listening to a loudspeaker broadcasting reports from Thurman's SOUTHCOM. The word was that the Delta team was on the roof of the prison. At 0113 came the message that Muse was out of prison and on the roof.[2]

Muse described the scene. "There are helicopter gunships unloading on the Comandancia. Smoke. Fire. Tracers going down, tracers going sideways, tracers coming toward us."

The Delta troopers loaded Muse into the helicopter with a soldier on each side of him. Three more troopers climbed onto the pods on either side of the helicopter. Just as the chopper lifted off the roof, it was hit by fire from the ground. The chopper flew off the top of the building and landed on the street between the prison and the Comandancia. The chopper could not lift off, but it could lumber down the street a few feet off the ground. He drove it as "though it were a car," Muse thought. The pilot veered into a parking lot and tried to take off again. It got to about thirty feet in the air when it was hit again by fire, this time from PDF around the Comandancia. The chopper fell and landed sideways on its left pod, injuring three men who had been hanging onto the pod.

At about 0130, SOUTHCOM reported that the helicopter carrying Muse and the Delta team had crashed and that all of the troops, including Muse, might be dead. Powell was clearly disappointed. One mission given by the president—rescue Muse—apparently had ended in disaster.

At the crash site, the leader of the Delta team ordered his men to evacuate the helicopter. Muse had lost his helmet and was stunned but unhurt. One of the rescuers had taken a bullet that went through his leg and up toward his chest. One of the Delta team was knocked down by the whirling rotor blade as the helicopter fell on its side.

The rest of the team placed the wounded between a building and a Jeep Wagoneer parked next to it and took up a defensive position. In spite of their wounds, the casualties insisted on helping man the position. Muse, who knew the area well, told the Delta troopers that a likely attack would come from the direction of the Comandancia. One of the Delta men held up an infrared strobe light. A few minutes later a Black Hawk helicopter flew overhead and rocked from side to side to acknowledge their position. In a few minutes, Muse heard tracked vehicles coming toward them. "It had to be the cavalry," thought Muse. "Obviously they were Plan B, waiting to pick us up if something happened."

The Delta team loaded the wounded, Muse, and themselves aboard the first armored personnel carrier, and the driver radioed his unit commander that "We have the PC." The carrier headed back up the street between Modelo Prison and the Comandancia, back toward the Canal Zone. As they lumbered down the street, Muse could see "flames everywhere," fires set by the digbats. The whole district seemed to be on fire. Muse could barely make out Panamanians on the balconies of their apartments waving white handkerchiefs, flags, and towels and banging pots and pans.

When they got to Balboa High School, they unloaded the personnel carrier, and the U.S. medics took charge. After the wounded were readied for a flight, they boarded a helicopter and landed at Howard Air Force Base next to a MASH unit. A doctor examined Muse and found him in good health, save for some bruises. Muse got permission from a somewhat reluctant colonel with

Delta Force to see his wounded rescuers. One, the man with the chest wound, was in intensive care. For the first time, Muse could see the faces of the Delta men who saved him. "These guys were beat to hell," he said later. "Blankets over them, IVs, stitches, clotted blood, casts. They really looked bad. But they were all smiling."

"You guys are the meanest and ugliest fuckers I've met in my life. But I love you. You guys saved my life and I'm eternally, eternally grateful. . . . So long, guys."

At 0220, SOUTHCOM notified the Crisis Room that Muse was safe and out. Powell called CIA director Webster and told him, "Just wanted you to know we got your man out and he's safe." Cheney called the White House. Earlier he had talked to Gen. Brent Scowcroft. But after the first call, all calls from Cheney went directly to the president. This time Cheney had the good news: "Muse was out and safe," and Delta Force had done its job in less time than their rehearsals.

After Muse came out of the ward where the injured Delta men were in beds, he ran into the Delta colonel again. The colonel told him, "I want to thank you for talking to my troops. My guys train for a lot of missions. They train long and hard, and they never get to do many of them. But for this one they trained long and they trained hard and they got to do it."

At about noontime, Muse boarded a private jet and flew to Miami still dressed in his bloody prison garb: a T-shirt, torn Levi's, worn tennis shoes. After going through customs, aided by the pilots, he was escorted to a man and woman in civilian clothes. After a lunch and a beer in a Denny's restaurant, he was flown to Dulles International Airport near Washington, D.C., where he met his wife and children in a private terminal. Muse's nightmare was over. A few days later, he and his family's meeting with President Bush climaxed his release from Modelo.[3]

Kurt Muse had obviously not been an ordinary prisoner.

11 | The Comandancia

"The 3 October '89 coup resulted in dramatic modification of OpPlans; generally from passive defense to offense," wrote Col. Mike Snell after the operation was over. And to his Panama-based 193d Infantry Brigade fell the extremely important missions of (1) defending Ancon Hill, where several U.S. installations, including U.S. Southern Command headquarters and the U.S. Gorgas General Hospital, are located, and (2) attacking and neutralizing some of the most significant targets in Panama: La Comandancia, Noriega's headquarters, the Panamanian "Pentagon," a Priority One target and less than a thousand meters from the peak of Ancon Hill; 5th Compañía de Infanteria barracks at Fort Amador; the Balboa and Ancon DENI stations; the Ancon DNTT; the PDF Engineer Compound; Pier 18, Balboa Harbor; and the PDF Dog Compound, a mission that would later take on more than passing interest to feminists and women's rights advocates throughout the country.

As Colonel Snell put it, his mission was

> to protect U.S. lives and property, defend the Panama Canal, and neutralize the PDF. TF Bayonet's area of operations varied throughout Operation Just Cause as forces were assigned and reassigned within the Joint Task Force. The focus of TF Bayonet's operations remained fairly constant and included the east bank of the Panama Canal, from Paraiso in the north to the causeway islands in the south, the bulk of which was former Canal Zone territory. In addition, TF Bayonet focused on the Santa Anna, Chorillo and San Felipe sections of Panama City, with other sections coming temporarily under the TF's control.

On 16 November 1989, four M551A1 Sheridan tanks from the 3d Platoon of C Company of the 3d Battalion, 73d Armor and six Apache helicopters, all from the 82d Airborne Division, landed in C-5 aircraft, under cover of darkness, at

Howard Air Force Base on the west side of the canal. Later, covered with canvas tarps on tank transport trailers, the Sheridans were moved to a nearby bivouac area on the west bank, at Camp Rousseau. The tank crews then stashed the Sheridans under GP medium tents to camouflage them as sleeping tents until D-day. Just prior to H-hour, the tank crews threw off the tents and drove their tanks to overwatch positions on Ancon Hill.

To carry out his missions, mostly in urban areas in and around Panama City, Colonel Snell had a formidable task force of some three thousand soldiers and Marines formed into fifteen company-size units plus the platoon of M551 Sheridan tanks from the 82d Airborne Division and one platoon of Light Armored Vehicles (LAVs) from the Marine Corps' Panama augmentation forces.[1]

One of Snell's three task forces was Lt. Col. James W. Reed's TF Gator, made up predominantly of the 4th Battalion, 6th Infantry, a battalion from the 5th Infantry Division (Mechanized) stationed at Fort Polk, Louisiana. The 4th of the 6th had been in Panama since September, when it replaced its sister battalion, the 5th of the 6th, that had been in Panama since May, when President Bush ordered a buildup of forces, called Nimrod Dancer, to counteract the increasing acts of violence and intimidation instigated by Noriega on U.S. forces, dependents, and citizens.

Prior to the beginning of hostilities, TF 4/6 was "Routinely dispersed to several locations around Panama City," according to Colonel Reed. "Our base camp was Camp Gator, a tent city immediately adjacent to Rodman Naval Station on the west side of the canal (near the Pacific end), at which we deployed one infantry company for maintenance and services. The TF's support elements were deployed at Camp Gator also. Another infantry company was also on the west side of the canal at Empire Range, which permitted them to conduct live-fire training. Two other infantry companies were deployed on the east side of the canal: a quick-reaction force located at Corozal, about two kilometers south of Fort Clayton, and a second company to reinforce the reaction force, if required, which we kept loggered in the Corundu housing area. It was highly classified at the time, but we also kept a platoon of M-551 Sheridan tanks from the 82d Airborne Division under wraps at Camp Gator. . . .

"It was our habit to rotate the infantry companies among these four locations every seven to eight days to provide each the opportunity to conduct various types of training or maintenance. This dispersal of the task force was always problematic, since each company had a unique mission under the Op Plan, and synchronization of their movements was dependent upon their starting points as they moved toward the LD (line of departure). . . .

"As we were alerted on the night of 16 December, our initial actions were to relocate the two infantry companies at Camp Gator and Empire Range to Fort Clayton on the east side of the canal (the platoon of Sheridans remained under wraps at Camp Gator). We did this as a precaution in case either of the two routes across the canal—the Bridge of the Americas or the swing bridge in the vicinity of Fort Clayton—might be denied to us. We also effected task organization with the other elements of the 193d Brigade and awaited further instructions."

Colonel Reed had been in command of "The Regulars" only since 1 December, when he took over command of the battalion from Lt. Col. William Steiger in a change-of-command ceremony at Camp Gator. Colonel Reed had previously been a Pentagon staff officer in the Directorate of Strategy, Plans, and Policy in the office of the deputy chief of staff for Operations. His metamorphosis from staffer to commander in combat was not only swift but also total.

As Colonel Reed wrote later: "My predecessor, Lt. Col. William Steiger, clearly preferred to stay in command and see the mission through to completion, and I know that the question of whether to change command in December was discussed among the senior leadership in the theater. The fact that the transition occurred so efficiently and that the battalion performed so well in combat is, I think, a remarkable tribute both to the high standards of training and discipline which Bill Steiger had instilled in the 'Regulars' as well as to the caliber of officer and NCO leadership common throughout the battalion."[2]

Task Force Gator had two mechanized companies from the 4th of the 6th, Company B, with three platoons, and Company D, with four platoons and a platoon of Engineers from the 59th Engineer Company (Combat); Capt. Timothy J. Flynn's C Company, 1/508th Airborne Infantry Battalion, permanently stationed at Fort Kobbe in Panama; two platoons of military police; a Psyops loudspeaker team; the Sheridans, under Capt. Kevin Hammond; and the platoon of Marine LAVs under Lt. Brian Colebaugh. For the operation, Colonel Reed formed the Sheridans and LAVs into Team Armor under Captain Hammond.

Colonel Snell tasked TF Gator with the main attack—the Comandancia—not only of his command but also conceivably of the entire operation, because of its significance—it was, after all, Noriega's command and control center for the country. Colonel Reed's mission statement read: "At H-hour, D-day, TF 4-6 Infantry (TF Gator) conducts offensive operations to protect U.S. lives and property, and vital Panama Canal facilities by isolating, seizing, and securing the Comandancia/Carcel Modelo complex and neutralizing PDF forces."

The Comandancia was not a single Pentagon-type structure but a compound of fifteen separate buildings, including the barracks of two PDF companies numbering some three hundred soldiers at any one time, located in the El Chorillo district of Panama City, in a two-square-block enclosure along Avenida A. The Comandancia complex was along the shoreline of Punta Mala, less than eight hundred yards across the water from the north end of Fort Amador. It was so close to Fort Amador that before the initiation of Just Cause, soldiers from the 1st Bn of the 508th, armed with telescopes, pulled three-hour guard tours sitting in a shelter, just off one of the fairways of the Fort Amador golf course, keeping tabs on the activities of the PDF around the Comandancia.

Snell's second task force was Task Force Wildcat, based around Lt. Col. William H. Huff III's 5th of the 87th Infantry, a permanent part of the 193d stationed normally at Fort Clayton, on the east bank of the canal, about four miles northwest of Panama City. Huff had three of his own infantry companies plus Capt. Isadore Bower's A Company of the 4th of the 6th, one of Reed's

99

mechanized infantry companies. Snell assigned Huff four objectives: the PDF Engineer Compound, the Ancon DNTT, and the Ancon and Balboa DENIs.

Snell's third task force was Task Force Black Devil, built around Lt. Col. Billie R. Fitzgerald's 1/508 Airborne Infantry Battalion. Colonel Fitzgerald had three of his own airborne companies plus, on an ad hoc basis, Capt. Don Tower's C Company of the 4th of the 6th, two platoons of which were retained by Colonel Snell as the brigade reserve. Fitzgerald's mission was to "isolate and fix the 5th CIA (a military police company), seize and secure PDF facilities, and neutralize all PDF forces at Fort Amador. On order, relocate noncombatants at Fort Amador and La Boca housing areas. Conduct communications linkup with forces at Flamenco Island. Be prepared to seize and secure causeway islands and conduct follow-on missions." In short, air assault into Fort Amador, jointly occupied by the PDF and the U.S. forces, and clear the area of the PDF.

Because his command, the 193d Infantry Brigade (Light), was permanently stationed in Panama, Colonel Snell was faced with the proverbial "good news-bad news" situation. The good news was that he and his men were intimately familiar with the terrain over which they might fight; they had had ample time to develop plans for and to rehearse, without compromise, their phases of the operation; they were knowledgeable about the potential enemy, his habits, and his capabilities, and, according to Colonel Snell, "Brigade CP remained at peacetime location on Fort Clayton." The bad news, as Colonel Snell put it, was that "to my knowledge, Just Cause is the first time since Korea, possibly the first time since the opening stages of World War II, where family members of U.S. servicemen have been in the middle of a combat environment." Having U.S. families in the combat area obviously necessitated the careful and adequate use of forces to protect them and certainly caused some consternation by the U.S. soldiers who left their families behind as they themselves went off to battle—an incongruous situation, reminiscent, perhaps, of Johnny Rebs going off to fight the Yankees on terrain of the South.

"The execution of H-hour assaults entailed a complex movement of fourteen companies (one company was held in reserve) over two routes and the air assault of a battalion (-), all having to be completed within a thirty-minute period," wrote one of Colonel Snell's staff officers later. "The deployment began at 2345 hours as two MP companies administratively crossed the swing bridge to the east bank, securing the bridge as they went. The first unit actually moving toward the assault objectives was TF Gator, which was assigned the Comandancia. At 0030 hours, the MP platoon scheduled to secure Balboa Harbor was fired on by PDF elements."

Task Force Gator, with its mix of mech infantry in their armored personnel carriers, paratroopers, Sheridan tanks, and a platoon of Marines in LAVs, was a force well tailored for its mission of isolating and neutralizing the Comandancia in downtown Panama City. A spokesman for U.S. Southern Command said, "Although not normally used in urban terrain, the tracks were selected for their shock action and firepower as the headquarters for the PDF (La Comandancia) was expected to be a tough nut to crack."

The expectation was correct. Sfc. Anthony Marteen of D Company, 4/6, said that his men were under fire practically from the time they rolled out of the gates at Fort Clayton, about three miles from La Comandancia.

Col. Robert Coffey, commander of the 2d Brigade of the 5th Division, and Brig. Gen. Michael S. Davison, Jr., 5th Division assistant division commander for maneuvers, "happened" to be in Panama when the operation began, apparently "checking" on the training of the 4th of the 6th. From Ancon Hill near Southern Command headquarters, they watched the beginning of the 4/6th assault toward the Comandancia. Colonel Coffey said that the amount of small-arms and mortar fire that the "Regulars" of the 4/6th faced was "tremendous. It's been twenty years since I've been shot at in anger, but it was as much as I've ever seen in any combat situation. It was a tough mission. I think it was the toughest mission in Panama." He went on to add, "The PDF had AK-47's, rocket-propelled grenades (RPGs), and hand grenades."[3]

At an intelligence briefing at 2000 hours on the night of 19 December, the troops of Task Force Gator had been informed that the PDF was much more prepared than the JTF South had at first anticipated. The briefing officer told them that they could expect up to three hundred of Noriega's handpicked soldiers to be inside the compound. And the troops were also told that the PDF may have been warned that a U.S. attack was imminent. According to Colonel Coffey, "The PDF were somewhat more prepared than in normal times. They had established roadblocks using large civilian trucks, POVs. They had sand-bags in emplacements around the built-up area of the city surrounding the headquarters. And we could see people who were well armed walking about. The vast majority were in civilian clothes carrying weapons. . . . The enemy were in the streets, they were in the balconies, they were in the windows, they were on tops of roofs. They had two very large high-rise buildings about sixteen stories high and the soldiers were receiving intense fire out of those buildings. . . . They fired not only small-arms fire and mortar fire but also RPGs, which are extremely dangerous and will take out our APCs. Two Company D tracks were hit by RPGs."

By 0015, all units of Task Force Bayonet were crossing their lines of departure (LD). "The LD for TF 4-6 Infantry was Fourth of July Avenue, which ran adjacent to the Comandancia complex," wrote Colonel Reed after the battle. "It was essential that our movement times from our various starting points to the LD be precise, since the task force LD time was closely synchronized with various activities of General Downing's JSOTF. (For the first phase of the operations, TF Gator was under the command of General Downing and his Joint Special Operations Task Force headquarters.) As we approached the LD, B/4-6, commanded by CPT Joe Goss, and D/4-6, commanded by Capt. Mike Etheridge, were both in the lead, moving on parallel axes through the heart of Panama City, and were to cross the LD precisely at 200045 Dec 89 (and, I'm proud to say, both companies hit the LD right on the mark). B/4-6 initiated movement from Corozal; D/4-6 from Fort Clayton; and their movement times to the LD were about 21 and 24 minutes, respectively, as I recall. In order to ensure that they were fully in synch, B/4-6 paused briefly at Quarry Heights and D/4-6 paused briefly at Balboa High School—we had timed the movements to the LD down to the second.

"Movement of all elements was in column formation, although, again, B/4-6 and D/4-6 moved on separate axes. About two hours prior to LD time, Team Armor pulled their Sheridans out from under their tents and prepared to move. Team Armor moved via the Swing Bridge behind D/4-6 into their overwatch position on the east side of Quarry Heights.

"C/1-508 (Abn) infiltrated in trucks behind the lead heavy teams and moved dismounted into an attack position just across Fourth of July Avenue. . . . Fire support was provided by two AC-130 gunships in orbit over the complex.

"Our basic concept," Colonel Reed continued, "was to establish a cordon around the roughly two-square-block area and firmly control all routes of ingress and egress. B/4-6 was to secure the northern one half of the complex with three infantry platoons; D/4-6 was to secure the southern one half with four infantry platoons. Team Armor provided overwatch from the east side of Quarry Heights (Ancon Hill). C/1-508 (Abn) moved dismounted into their attack position and awaited orders to begin clearing operations within the complex. A tight cordon was established by emplacing squad and section-sized blocking positions ringing the Comandancia complex. PDF soldiers who were willing to lay down their arms and surrender were invited to do so on a prerecorded message that was broadcast at LD time by our psyops HB team located on Ancon Hill. A safe route of egress was designated in the message; about six truckloads of captive PDF soldiers were evacuated by Task Force Gator throughout the night.

"Both lead infantry companies encountered heavy resistance as they crossed the LD. Substantial PDF obstacles (cars and trucks that had been parked to block the road) obstructed their route into the Comandancia complex, and soldiers were subjected to heavy volume of direct fire as they attempted to fight through or around these obstacles. Obstacles on both routes were cleared in a manner of minutes, generally by pushing our way through with our tracks.

"As soldiers attempted to move into their blocking positions, they received heavy volumes of machine-gun fire from PDF soldiers fighting from the multistory buildings above them. Many, if not most, of the PDF soldiers were dressed in civilian clothes, and many of them fought from the civilian apartment buildings which ringed the area. I recall being impressed by the fire discipline of our soldiers as they fired upon only those personnel who were actively engaging us. Fighting in built-up areas really tests small-unit leaders. I have said before that once the battle for the Comandancia was joined, it truly was a story of junior leaders taking charge, doing what had to be done, and controlling their people."[4]

Colonel Reed's mech units continued to move forward. As the tracks rolled across the four-lane street that separated the neighborhood near the PDF headquarters and the old Canal Zone, the companies came under heavy small-arms and rocket fire. "Hot and heavy," Colonel Reed described it. Barricades, narrow streets, and rooftop snipers hampered the movement of the APCs. "Bright red artillery shells arched over the city," one observer noted.

The shells filled the air over the old area of Panama City known as Chorillo. At about the same time, a bright orange glow appeared at the foot of Ancon Hill, where Noriega's barracks are located. Where usually the bay was lit with the steady soft glow of street and dock lights, now there were the trails of the bright red shells, reflected on the water. . . . Black smoke was seen rising from near the airport, illuminated by the lights of the city. Oddly, traffic in the city appeared normal for a weekday night for at least the first hour and a half of the attack. . . . Throughout the long night, machine-gun bursts and explosions continued sporadically. Two hours after the attack began, the area where Noriega's headquarters are located was bathed in a bright orange glow. . . . Flames forty and fifty feet high were visible from two miles away and bright orange and black smoke illuminated the city. Always the sound of aircraft droned overhead. Eerily, they were never seen—their navigation lights were turned off. . . . On the street below, the occasional pedestrian continued life as if it were normal.[5]

In a desperate move to slow down the American advance, PDF and Dignity Battalion troops set fire to the surrounding barrio. Many a U.S. newspaper or TV report coming out of Panama showed the flaming destruction of the barrio and attributed it to "collateral" damage done by U.S. gunships, tanks, and other fires. Panamanians, including local priests, who opposed Noriega knew the cause of the destruction and disputed the "collateral fire" accusations.

As the tracks made their way down the narrow, apartment-lined streets, sniper bullets from rifles and machine guns bounced off the skin of the tracks. An AC-130 circled overhead and, as directed by an Air Force controller in a command track, provided overhead fire support. Helicopter gunships cleared PDF fighting positions on the roof of an adjoining high-rise. And, according to a Southern Command staff officer, "In a desperate bid to stop the Americans, PDF and Dignity Battalion members set fire to the surrounding barrio. Although the smoke obscured the sights of the overwatching tanks, the attacking ground element moved on relentlessly. In one of the lead platoons (from D Company of 4/6), twenty-six of twenty-nine infantrymen were wounded. Luckily for the men, most of their wounds were on their arms and legs. Afterward they swore by the flak vests they had been wearing. Well prior to daylight, the mission (of surrounding the Comandancia compound) was accomplished. As the Barrio Chorillo continued to burn, TF Gator kept vigil in their blocking positions."

About an hour and a half after his company crossed the LD, Captain Goss reported that his company had secured the sector around the complex but that he had had one man killed. He was Cpl. Ivan Pérez, twenty-two, a track commander in the lead platoon of Captain Goss's company. Pérez's platoon leader, Lt. Harold Powers, was in the lead APC as the platoon tracks, in a single-file column, met one of the PDF roadblocks near the Comandancia. Powers attempted, with great difficulty, to drive his track through the block—under heavy machine-gun fire. Pérez saw Powers's predicament. His track was right behind Powers's. Pérez pulled his track out of the column to a position where he could better support his platoon leader as the platoon attempted to breach the obstacle. Pérez's track, with Pérez manning the .50-caliber machine gun on his track, came under heavy PDF fire. He did not move his track back even though he was exposed to the PDF fire as he stood in the track commander's open hatch. The heaviest fire was coming from the Comandancia prison yard behind two dump trucks and from the top of a building forty-five yards to Perez's left. Pérez saw the muzzle flashes overhead and opened fire with his machine gun. The return fire ricocheted off the track's aluminum skin. One round hit Pérez in the back of the head. His body slid down through the gun mount and fell against the knees of Sgt. Dave Blair, the squad leader. Sgt. Blair drove the track out of the line of fire and raced the short distance back to the top of Quarry Heights, where the medics pulled Pérez out of the track. He died shortly thereafter. Barry took Pérez's place in the TC hatch and roared back down the hill to continue the fighting. Corporal Pérez was awarded the Silver Star posthumously.[6]

In moving up to the Comandancia area, one of D Company's APCs was disabled by an RPG. Pvt. 2 Louis O. Miller, eighteen, volunteered to try to retrieve the track and the men still inside. When he reached it, Miller came under fire from PDF 40mm grenade launchers. Despite the barrage of grenades, he kept at the task and was able to bring the APC and its crew to safety. Later, at a company breakfast on Christmas Day, Secretary Cheney awarded him the Bronze Star with "V" device for his heroism. From then on, his first sergeant, William D. John, called him "Killer Miller."

Sergeant First Class Marteen, D Company, 4/6, remembers that the roadblocks around the Comandancia were covered by rocket-propelled grenades. Atop the roof of a PDF stronghold was a sniper position that menaced the U.S. soldiers as they advanced. "We took out the position with an AT-4 (shoulder-fired missile)," Marteen said. Knocking out the snipers was the job of .50-caliber gunner Sgt. John Skipworth. He was proficient at his job and "He's probably the reason our platoon made it," said Marteen.[7]

Within an hour after crossing the line of departure, Task Force Gator had secured the area around the Comandancia. "At this point," according to Colonel Coffey, "the battle became one of individual squads dealing with snipers and other people in the streets. It was dark, one o'clock in the morning. People were running around with small-arms weapons, AK-47's, RPGs, hand grenades, throwing them out at our soldiers. Despite this, soldiers were able to maintain their discipline and courage, reduce their area of responsibility, and isolate and secure the Comandancia area."

Captain Goss and his B/4-6 had secured the northern part of the area around the Comandancia by about 0200. D Company required about three hours after the start of the operation to secure its southern part of the area because "several pockets of determined PDF resistance remained. In its area, D/4-6 had sustained some twenty casualties, many from indirect fire," Colonel Reed reported. There is also a strong possibility that many of D Company's casualties were caused by a Specter gunship firing at the Comandancia but hitting short and into the tracks and on troops who had dismounted. But there was so much indirect fire in the area, both from the PDF mortars and RPGs, that it was difficult to determine the source.

One of the heroes of D/4-6th's fight around the Comandancia complex was SPC Roderick Ringstaff, a medic with the 2d Platoon of D Company. He was seriously wounded in his right arm and left foot by indirect fire during the platoon's attack. He refused to be evacuated from the area and, in the midst of continued intense indirect fire, Ringstaff began rounding up and administering first aid to five other wounded men in his platoon. According to a citation recommending him for a Silver Star, "Even as he neared exhaustion and still under devastating fire, Specialist Ringstaff dragged a severely wounded soldier to the medical evacuation vehicle. Although he physically collapsed at this point due to his own extensive wounds, he continued to provide words of encouragement and moral support to the other wounded soldiers of D Company." Only after all the wounded of D Company were evacuated did Ringstaff permit himself to be taken out.

Later he said, "You got to keep your adrenaline going, because if you just lay there, you're history. You've got to keep moving. It was very intense. To be frank, I was really scared but we pulled through and did what we had to do." The wounded he saw had mostly shrapnel wounds. "Guys with shrapnel in their legs, shoulders—basically limb injuries because the flak vest we had on protected us pretty good."

Colonel Reed said that Spc. Roderick Ringstaff is a great example of the kind of soldier we have in today's Army and that "he is about as modest and self-effacing a young man as you could ever meet, a great soldier." Gen. Carl E. Vuono, the Army chief of staff, personally awarded Ringstaff the Silver Star.[8]

A group of AH-6 helicopters had the mission of suppressing the snipers and other weapons positions on the top of the sixteen-story apartment buildings that overlooked the streets along which Task Force Gator was approaching the Comandancia. The lead helicopter was flown by Capt. George Kunkel and Chief WO Fred Horsley. As their helicopter crested Ancon Hill and neared their release point, they were greeted with heavy ground fire. Nonetheless, they flew on and, aware of the rules of engagement to use only the minimum force necessary, they used only their miniguns and no missiles to fire on the PDF troops on the roofs of the apartments. After a run along the rooftops, Kunkel turned his AH-6 to fire on the Comandancia itself.

On their run-in approach, Horsley noticed that Kunkel was having trouble pulling the helicopter out of its gun run. He grabbed the controls to assist. Despite their combined efforts, the helicopter did not respond, and it continued in a dive toward the ground. With no response from the collective and limited response from the cyclic, they tried to aim the helicopter toward an open spot to their right. The helicopter, in level flight, slammed into the ground, skidded across an open courtyard, slid into a concrete pillar, and caught fire. Horsley could not get out his side of the plane because he was blocked by a wall and by debris that entangled his flight vest and uniform. He struggled free and scrambled out Kunkel's side and joined him outside, forward of the fire.

The two men made a hasty and non-Fort Leavenworth-type "estimate of the situation." They were uninjured, they had no helicopter, they were in definitely unfriendly territory, they knew that there was an AC-130 Specter gunship overhead ready to lay waste enemy troops in the Comandancia (with themselves directly in the line of fire), they did not know exactly where they were, and they knew that they had to get out of the area "right now." Their first step was to move to the dark shadows of a building away from the heavy firing they had seen on their way to the unscheduled touchdown. They used their PRC-90 radios unsuccessfully to contact the friendlies and darted around the courtyard to avoid the PDF who were in the area and to try to find out where they were.

Their first attempt to escape by trying to scale a wall in the corner of the compound was frustrated by enemy fire from several locations and from the AC-130. In the next few minutes, fire inside the wall decreased as fire from the 4/6th outside the wall increased in tempo.

At about 0215, a lull in the firing prompted Kunkel and Horsley to make another try to get out. With some haste but with caution, they made their way between some buildings and reached a wall topped by a single roll of concertina wire. After a hasty conference, they decided that one of them should scale the wall, unarmed, and approach the "friendlies," shouting the password "Bulldog."

Before they could carry out their "battle plan," Horsley heard a movement in some nearby bushes. He turned to shoot, but held fire as an unarmed, arms-raised PDF soldier scampered out of the bushes. In broken English he explained that everyone who had not been killed had run away and that he himself wanted to surrender and go back to the American lines with them. Horsley said, "Okay, but wait here."

Kunkel, operating in the dark by peering through the one operational tube of his night-vision goggles, threw his flak jacket on the concertina wire on top of the wall and climbed over it. Once on the street, he moved along the sidewalk, hugging the wall, looking for friendly troops. He finally found some infantrymen who recognized that he was an American and not a PDF emerging from the compound. The Americans permitted him to return for Horsley and the Panamanian soldier. As Horsley was helping the Panamanian over the wall, the AC-130 Specter opened fire on the area of the compound. Horsley vaulted over the wall and clung to the underside. After the AC-130 finished its firing run, the two aviators pulled their prisoner over the wall and raced toward the friendly position.

They spent the next three hours in the command track, an armored personnel carrier, of D Company of the 4th of the 6th. Later, when the fighting near the Comandancia had slowed, the aviators made their way back to Balboa High School, where they contacted their unit.[9]

But La Comandancia itself was still not cleared; that part of the operation would require additional forces and a few more hours.

*   *   *

From Task Force South's assault CP at Fort Clayton, General Thurman had been keeping the Pentagon's NMCC informed of developing events on an almost minute-by-minute basis:

- At 2330 on the nineteenth, he reported that Noriega might be in Colón.
- At 0029, he reported gunfire at Fort Amador, Albrook, and the Bridge of the Americas.

- At 0039, he reported that Endara had been sworn in as president of Panama.
- At 0057, he reported gunfire on the Atlantic side of the canal.
- At 0100, he reported that he had moved his alert status to DEFCON 1, the highest state of readiness.
- At 0130, he reported that the Rangers had dropped at Río Hato and that the Bridge of the Americas was secure.
- At 0240, General Thurman called General Powell and told him that the Comandancia was in flames.
- At 0249, he reported that Noriega was still on the loose. General Powell was clearly miffed that one of the main objectives of the operation had not yet been accomplished.

Secretary Cheney had in turn kept the White House informed of all of the developments as he received them. The president asked questions but stayed out of micromanagement of the operation. In Panama the fighting went on.

*   *   *

By the evening of D-day, the Comandancia had still not been "taken down." After surrounding the complex in the early-morning hours of the twentieth, Colonel Reed, commander of the 4th Battalion of the 6th Infantry, and originally a part of General Downing's Joint Special Operations Task Force, received a message from Colonel Snell, the task force commander, that he was "chopped back" to Task Force Bayonet control and relieved from General Downing JSOTF. A portion of the battalion, including Maj. Jim Donivan, the battalion S-3, and six empty APCs driven by men of the 4th of the 6th, plus a couple of Sheridans from the 82d and two LAVs from the Marines, remained under the control of JSOTF. "This element would later provide transport and security for JSOTF," said Colonel Reed, "as they pursued General Noriega and eventually helped establish the cordon around the Papal Nunciature where Noriega took refuge."[10] Major Donivan's "tailored on the spot armor command" became known as the "Panzer Gruppe" in General Downing's headquarters.

General Downing gave Major Donivan and the "Panzer Gruppe" the mission of moving up Balboa Avenue from the Comandancia toward the U.S. embassy to relieve the Special Forces around the embassy early on the morning of the twentieth. General Downing expected to have the Panzer Gruppe under his control for only a few hours or, at most, a few days, but in reality he had it for eighteen days. Donivan and his small armored task force were able to respond to calls from JSOTF and move Special Forces troops to trouble spots throughout the city. Because Donivan had the armored vehicles, he was able to move almost at will through difficult, sniper-riddled streets to various objectives.[11]

Later in the morning of the twentieth, Colonel Snell returned to Reed's control his C Company, which had been Snell's brigade reserve. Reed also assumed control of C Company of the 3d Battalion of the 75th Rangers that had jumped into Tocumen. He got C Company of the Rangers for the specific purpose of clearing the Comandancia. According to Colonel Reed, "That was a mission which C/3-75 had trained specifically for for more than a year, and it was clear that they were better prepared for that tough mission than probably any other company in the Army at the time. Throughout the day, I used C/4-6 to reinforce the cordon around the complex while Team Armor and some Apache helicopters were used to fire into the buildings where we suspected that some PDF continued to hold out."[12]

Capt. Alfred E. Dochnal was the commander of C/3-75. At about 1000 on the morning of the twenty-first, he received orders detaching him from the 1st Battalion of the 75th at Torrijos/Tocumen Airport and placing him OPCON to Task Force Bayonet and further to Task Force Gator, Colonel Reed's command. From Torrijos, Dochnal moved his company by helicopter to Albrook Air Force Base, about two thousand meters to the northwest of the Comandancia and just to the north of Ancon Hill. Capt. Kevin O. Harris, the S-4 of 3-75, met Dochnal and led him to Colonel Snell's tactical CP. Colonel Reed's TAC CP was also in the same area. At the TAC CP, Dochnal got an update on the situation. "The warning order from the brigade," wrote Captain Dochnal later, "was to seize and clear Carcel Mondelo and La Comandancia before dark." Captain Dochnal and Lieutenant Pugmire reconnoitered the area and then, about 1400, Dochnal wrote a frag order for his platoons. The company moved forward to an assembly area about a block from the Comandancia. Dochnal gave the frag order to his platoon leaders from a spot overlooking the Carcel Mondelo and the Comandancia.

"After a quick recon," he wrote, "we moved out, with 1st Platoon moving to seize and clear Carcel Mondelo. Upon seizing Carcel Mondelo, we found U.S. troops in the *carcel* looking around the building. They are lucky . . . we might have killed them. I asked why they were in there. The response—they just walked into the area and started collecting weapons. I was livid at best over this weak excuse.

"The company continued to move to the gym across the street from La Comandancia. We used a breach charge to enter the gym. We quickly took up observation positions inside the gym looking at La Comandancia. The attack was slowed as we waited forty-five minutes for the AH-64's, the M-551's and the LAV 25mm to conduct pre-H-hour fires on La Comandancia to soften the target. After the fires were lifted, 2d Platoon commenced its attack on La Comandancia. Second Platoon M-203 gunners suppressed the second floor with 40mm, and Team Gold suppressed the third floor with snipers, covering the breach team's movement to the east gate and placing of their charges. Charges were set and executed. Second Platoon entered the east half and began clearing from the first floor to the third floor. Third Platoon moved through the breach to the main entrance and cleared the west half of the building. Three EPWs ran out the back of the building and were policed by C/1-508. The attack started at approximately 1550 and was over by 1700. We searched the building and found a substantial amount of evidence and weapons . . . we conducted a relief in place with C/1-508 at 1900."[13]

La Comandancia was at last cleared.

12 | Fort Amador and Balboa

A "PCS" (permanent change of assignment) to Panama had always been a choice Army assignment, particularly in the "old, brown-shoe, spit-and-polish" Army prior to World War II. For the officers and NCOs, the quarters were of the "permanent" variety, the flora and fauna were tropical and exotic, the weather was warm, and the atmosphere relaxed and congenial. Fort Amador, and the other permanent posts along the canal, had golf courses, tennis courts, swimming pools, officer and NCO clubs, yacht and sailing clubs, and a friendly city nearby. All of the old customs and courtesies of the service applied—frequent black-tie dinners for the officers, even at home, for example, were *de rigueur*. (In the "old" Army, young officers wore out their tuxedos before they wore out civilian suits.)

For the soldiers, it was hard training in the mornings, formal inspections in ranks at least weekly, frequent calls for formations all day long, KP for the lower ranks, nightly bed checks, well-coached athletic teams in many sports, buffed squad rooms in barracks, and meticulously laid-out uniforms in footlockers and clothes racks always. Officers wore pinks and greens or starched khakis—many of them changing their khakis twice a day in the heat of Panama. The troops usually wore khakis and leggins. Polo and golf were popular sports for the officers, and payday poker games a monthly event for the troops, some of whom, the privates, were trying to live on "$21 a day once a month." The unlucky poker players were broke for most of the month, but the company messes were available for three "squares" a day, and the commissaries and PXs were bargain-priced.[1]

Even after the war, soldiers still welcomed an assignment to Panama. As one sergeant stationed with the 508th put it, "As assignments go, you could do a lot worse." The better-than-adequate permanent quarters were still there, the climate was still the same, but, admittedly, in the 1980s, the political atmosphere was charged with Noriega-inspired harassment and stress. By December

109

of 1989, the congeniality and affability between the American soldiers and the PDF were long gone. But in spite of the harassment of soldiers and their families, the disciplined American troops held their tempers. Many soldiers did, however, send their families home in view of the rising friction between the U.S. and Panamanian forces.

Fort Amador, in the days since the signing of the Panama Canal Treaty, had become a "joint" post in order to facilitate the eventual and final takeover of the protection of the canal by the PDF forces. One of the by-products of this arrangement was the movement of the PDF's 5th Compañia de Infanteria into former U.S. Army four-story permanent barracks and facilities that were located along the entire south side of the peninsula, directly across the golf course from the quarters occupied by American military families on the other side. In some places, the distance from the PDF facilities to the houses was as little as a hundred yards. Maj. Gen. Marc Cisneros, the commander of U.S. Army South, for example, lived in one of those sets of quarters directly across the fairway from the PDF barracks.

Fort Amador is on a peninsula that juts into the Pacific at the western end of the canal just a few thousand yards south of Ancon Hill and Quarry Heights. It is on the Panama City side of the canal and about four air miles from Fort Kobbe, permanent base of the 1/508th, which is on the west side of the canal in the same complex as the U.S. Howard Air Force Base.[2]

Colonel Snell had assigned Lt. Col. Billie R. Fitzgerald's 1st of the 508th Airborne Infantry Battalion, less C Company, plus A Company of the 4th of the 6th, a mechanized infantry company, the task of "securing" Fort Amador. Securing Fort Amador meant a number of missions: protecting U.S. lives, property, and vital Panama Canal facilities located there; isolating and "fixing" the 5th PDF Company (sometimes referred to as the 5th CIA or Quinta Compañía de Infanteria); seizing and securing PDF facilities and neutralizing all PDF forces at Fort Amador; relocating noncombatants from the housing areas at Fort Amador and the nearby La Boca housing area; conducting communications linkup with the forces at Flamenco Island, one of three small islands about three thousand meters southeast of the tip of Fort Amador, all connected by a causeway to Fort Amador's southeastern tip; and preparing to seize and secure the three "causeway" islands. The battalion's mission, in short, was to secure the American family housing areas and eliminate the threat of the 5th Rifle Company at H-hour.[3]

Colonel Fitzgerald had prepared his battalion extensively for his mission. He had held numerous readiness exercises in the past months on the battalion's specific mission, and every soldier had been trained in detail for his part in the operation. On the evening of 16 December, Colonel Fitzgerald mustered his battalion. He wrote that "The next seventy-two hours was used to improve the posture of our forces and begin troop leading procedures for contingency plans. I intensified the final planning/coordination and level of detail of command and staff briefings. Brigade informed us that we would have a minimum of six hours' and maximum of twenty-four hours' notification to execute the Op Order. It was clear that we could no longer expect seventy-two hours' notification, and we would not execute the Op Order from a contingency readiness exercise during

110

daylight hours. The plan was further compounded by the fact that only those with top-secret clearances had access to the plan. The approval was given to brief platoon leaders/sergeants at H-7 and all soldiers at H-4." Troop leading time was thus at a minimum. At 1800 hours, Colonel Snell ordered Colonel Fitzgerald to execute his portion of Just Cause.

Colonel Fitzgerald's plan of attack was fairly simple. Part of his battalion, the Headquarters Company, would already be at Fort Amador. A and B companies would air assault from Fort Kobbe and land on LZ Ditch, a narrow stretch of land behind the Amador American housing area, on the northeastern side of the peninsula, and establish positions around the family housing area. Then, in a two-pronged attack, Capt. William R. Reagan would lead his A Company in an assault from the north end of the PDF compound, beginning with Building 1; Capt. Robert G. Zebrowski would lead his B Company in a simultaneous assault from the opposite end of the compound and begin clearing Building 46. Headquarters Company, under Capt. John H. Hort, Jr., would support the assault with teams of snipers, scouts, and antitank crews. For fire support, a howitzer crew was attached and under the supervision of the battalion fire support officer, 1st Lt. David Standridge.

Captain Hort had been in command of Headquarters Company only nine days when the operation began. He organized his company into four platoons—three combat scout platoons, and one mechanized antitank platoon from the 4th of the 6th. He had infiltrated his company into Fort Amador on the nineteenth and, according to the report of the 508th, "kept the appearance of our usual security missions conducted since the 3 October coup." That same evening, Colonel Fitzgerald and his S-2, Capt. Pedro Nuñez, also "infiltrated" into Fort Amador. At 0035 on the twentieth, Fitzgerald ordered the front gate of Fort Amador "shut down."[4]

At Fort Kobbe, "From 2100 to 2400," wrote Captain Reagan later, "there was a lot of scrambling around as additional ammunition continued to arrive from the S-4. Soldier loads and ammunition were being crossloaded up until after midnight, when the company finally moved out to the helicopters that were staged on Red Devil Field, right behind the company barracks. Takeoff time was slated for 0047 and platoons practiced loading and unloading the choppers several times. We flew with seats out of the Black Hawks, something we had never done before. We put approximately seventeen on each of our assigned seven Black Hawks. We had an eighth chopper that would fly with us as backup."

Shortly after midnight on the twentieth, Captain Reagan received a radio call from Colonel Fitzgerald that "hostilities had begun" and that he should lift off earlier than the 0047 time. According to Captain Reagan, "We relayed this to our pilots (Company A flew with 7th ID pilots). They requested (through their channels) to go early but were told to maintain our posture. We lifted as planned at 0047 and followed a route that took us south around the causeway islands and then into the high ground on the golf course. The choppers seemed to labor, and they flew close to the water. It seemed like the longest ride of our lives. Tracer rounds could be seen in the distance, and, as we approached Amador, it was quite apparent that the fight at La Comandancia had begun. As we banked for

111

the final approach to Amador, we could observe all the rounds impacting on the far shore. It was a comforting sight because it gave us faith that we did in fact possess superior firepower over the enemy. The LZ had been declared 'Hot' and the pilots relayed that to us. All soldiers could see the tracer rounds coming at the aircraft, although no aircraft were disabled by the rounds and no casualties were suffered."[5]

Colonel Fitzgerald wrote later that "The three greatest concerns of the battalion CO and the operations officer, Maj. Mike Dearborn, during the air assault were (a) that the fight on Amador would begin prior to the arrival of Alpha and Bravo companies and that HHC would be fighting overwhelming odds; (b) that a helicopter would be shot down during the overwater approach to Amador from AA fire from either the Comandancia or PDF positions on Fort Amador; and (c) that LZ Ditch would receive mortar fire resulting in casualties and delays in the mission—especially for Alpha Company and the sling loads that carried needed ammo and the 105mm howitzer."[6]

"The choppers landed as advertised at 0100," Captain Reagan continued. "They wasted no time in getting out of the AO. As soon as they hit, they were taking back off. Many soldiers loaded in the interior positions told of having to jump from as high as eight to ten feet to get off the departing birds. One soldier and three rucksacks were left on the second aircraft. The soldier later linked up with us, but we never recovered the lost equipment."[7]

One of the pilots who flew the troopers of the 1st of the 508th into Fort Amador was Lieutenant Kutschera of A Company of the 3d Battalion of the 123d Aviation Regiment of the 7th Division. After the operation, Lieutenant Kutschera wrote: "I spent Saturday, 16 December, qualifying on the 9mm range with the rest of A Company. That night, at about 2200, we were alerted in response to the shooting of a U.S. naval officer by PDF troops in Panama City. All that night I was one of three crews sitting in our aircraft ready to launch on fifteen minutes' notice, with the rest able to launch within an hour. Sunday afternoon we were backed off to a one-hour notice, and by Monday things seemed to be relaxing back to normal except the company was still on a one-hour string.

"On Tuesday morning, 19 December, the A Company commander, Captain Muir, briefed his platoon leaders and sergeants that 'Der Tag' ('The Day' in German and the code for Task Force Hawk's mission) had arrived. The seats were removed from the aircraft, and soldiers from the 1st Battalion, 508th Infantry, practiced loading and unloading aircraft loads of twenty. Shortly after dusk, all the helicopters were moved off the Howard Air Force Base airfield to make room for aircraft coming from the States to support the operation. The lights of the baseball field next to Task Force Hawk's barracks were shut off to conceal the Black Hawks that were now parked there.

"Phase one of 'Der Tag' consisted of an air assault of troops from 1-508 to secure Fort Amador from the adjacent PDF base at 0100 on 20 December. Seven Black Hawks from 1st Battalion, 228th Aviation Regiment and seven from A Company would insert troops on the golf course at Fort Amador. Then the seven aircraft from A Company would return to the PZ at Fort Kobbe and pick up seven HMMWV sling loads and take them to Fort Amador. Moderate resistance was expected from the PDF compound, which had air defense weapons.

"In the briefings we received, Captain Muir, my company commander, and Lieutenant Colonel Borum, my battalion commander, stressed that we were to fly just as we did in training, doing everything by the checklist and SOP and maintaining disciplined formations. The only risk factor that would change on our brief sheet would be the possibility of little pieces of lead flying around.

"The rules of engagement were also stressed. We were not to return fire unless we were fired upon and could positively identify the hostile target. There would be civilians and their property in close proximity to all the LZs and routes and we were to keep casualties and collateral damage to a minimum.

"As I copied information at the briefing and prepared myself and my equipment for the mission, I couldn't help feeling that it all seemed unreal. I watch this kind of stuff in the movies. It doesn't happen to me. We were all so matter-of-fact and outwardly calm it seemed more like any other big lift at Fort Hunter-Liggett on JRTC. . . . Here was a chance to prove ourselves, to prove that all the money spent by the taxpayers and all the years we had spent in training were worth it.

"We took off as scheduled, with twenty troops and their equipment packed into each Hawk. Our route took us out over the ocean in a wide arc in order to provide secrecy as well as to minimize the chances anyone would have to shoot at us. As we turned back . . . and headed for Amador we could see the lights of Panama City on our right. We could also see one huge bright spot burning in the middle of it and tracers arced out over the water in our general direction a couple of times but didn't come very close. We were flying with infrared formation lights and were invisible in the darkness to anyone without night-vision devices.

"We landed our troops on the golf course and took off again without taking any hits. Some of the crews could see fire coming from the PDF camp to our left but no one in my aircraft saw any. We returned to Fort Kobbe for the HMMWVs and headed back to Amador. The aircraft were more spaced out now because of the time it takes to hook up a sling load. I could only see one or two aircraft some distance in front of us. Again, firing came from the vicinity of the Comandancia. I couldn't tell if it came close to any of the other aircraft but suddenly tracers went out from the aircraft in front of us and the firing stopped. We dropped off our load on the golf course, and again I didn't see any firing, and we went to Empire Range north of Fort Kobbe to refuel and lagger until the 82d was ready for us.

"We shut the aircraft down in a big circle with the door guns facing out and waited for the word to go. The mood was good as we waited and compared stories. We had just passed unscathed through our first combat assault. We had also made history, since I was the first U.S. woman to fly a combat assault and we had done the first NVG sling-load operation into a hot LZ. We were concerned, though, for the crew of an OH-58 that was reported missing and sobered by the fact that we probably wouldn't be so lucky next time." Lieutenant Kutschera's first name is Lisa. She also runs marathons and sky-dives.[8]

"The troops moved very quickly off the LZ and headed for the caddy shack at the back of the golf club house," continued Captain Reagan. "Here all the soldiers got rid of the B-7 flotation devices and cached them for recovery by support personnel later. First Platoon was first in movement and had the mission to breach the wire fence into the naval headquarters parking lot. We used wire cutters, which was time-consuming. We had decided not to use explosives to reduce damage and not to draw attention to ourselves. In retrospect, there was so much noise from the explosions at the Comandancia and from other fighting that we should have just had the engineer squad conduct a breach in the wire for us."

"By 1800 hours (on the 19th), I had all four combat platoons assembled on Fort Amador," writes Captain Hort, the commander of Headquarters Company, 1-508. "By 2130, all soldiers had been briefed and were now conducting troop leading procedures to include rehearsals. The adrenaline and motivation were pumping through each soldier at this time as they began to realize that this was not just another exercise. . . .

"At 0015 hours on the twentieth, the platoon leaders and I began hearing automatic fire coming someplace to the north off Fort Amador. Lieutenant Manauis and First Lieutenant Vinyard were still unloading TOW missiles when the battalion commander called and gave me a 'be prepared to move at any time' order. Three to four minutes later the battalion commander told me to execute the closing of the front gate. Lieutenant Manauis and Sergeant First Class Cagle moved the platoon approximately thirty seconds later toward the front gate of Amador.

"Upon Team Recon's (one of the scout platoons) arrival at the front gate, the two PDF guards controlling the front entrance were not listening to the surrender ultimatums being given to them by the two U.S. MPs at the scene. The PDF guards, seeing the additional soldiers from TM Recon, surrendered and turned over their weapons to Staff Sergeant Meadows, 1st Squad leader. Before Lieutenant Manauis could establish any type of roadblock, he received a report from his platoon sergeant, who established a security position approximately five hundred meters down the road that a bus full of PDF soldiers was moving toward his location at a high rate of speed with lights off. First Lieutenant Manauis, along with Staff Sergeant Estes, Private First Class Mountain, Private First Class May, and Specialist Kemp, opened fire with M16A2 rifles. Staff Sergeant Estes, in the standing position, shot and killed the PDF bus driver. The bus swerved, nearly missing the HMMWVs and soldiers and continued to move down the road past TM Recon. The entire incident lasted approximately three to four seconds. The bus, continuing to return fire, crashed into a large coconut tree approximately five hundred meters outside the gate of Fort Amador. From the firing by the PDF soldiers in the bus, the PDF guard that was detained was accidently shot and killed while trying to run back into the guard shack." In just a few minutes, the PDF in the bus "took off," leaving their weapons, equipment, and even their uniforms behind.

"With little time to prepare the position, First Lieutenant Manauis established a hasty roadblock utilizing his three HMMWVs and road jacks. At 0032, a PDF sedan with six soldiers attempted to breach the same roadblock. The sedan began firing at Sergeant First Class Cagle and Private First Class Brown, who immediately returned fire and reported another vehicle was headed in the direction of the front gate. Private First Class Mountain, watching the vehicle approach, shot the driver with three round bursts from his weapon. The driver, shot in the face, crashed into the back of one of the TM Recon roadblock vehicles. The soldiers in the sedan continued to fire at the U.S. soldiers (Specialist Kemp, Private First Class Mountain, First Lieutenant Manauis, Private First Class May, and Private First Class Smith), who returned a massive volume of fire into the sedan. Realizing that their escape was futile, they surrendered after losing three soldiers to M-16 fire.

"At H-hour, TM TOW (the antitank platoon) moved to the back gate of Fort Amador by the Officers' Club. First Lieutenant Vinyard along with First Sergeant Hinman, Staff Sergeant Corvino, and Staff Sergeant Ramirez detained the two PDF guards and began clearing quarters 152, 153, and 154." Quarters 152, better known as the "Witch House," was a PDF house, apparently set aside for Noriega's private use, in which the troops found a bucket of blood— unknown whether human or animal—voodoo artifacts, a brewery for making concoctions and potions, and a candle still burning. At a press conference later, General Thurman said that General Noriega's "voodoo practitioners . . . practiced rituals for Noriega's protection." The troops cleared the house with concussion grenades. Some of the soldiers in the area reported that there were smoldering cigarettes in ashtrays and women had left their purses, and they believed that they might have come close to capturing Noriega himself. All duplexes and buildings were reported secured and vacant at 0230 hours, with one maid and one infant found in Quarters 154.

"Along with TM TOW," continued Hort, "the mortar platoon began moving at H-hour house to house, warning residents that this was not an exercise and to seek cover in their houses near the U.S. side of Fort Amador. TM Mech (the scout platoon from A Company of the 4th of the 6th equipped with five M113A2s and three M901s) moved into position at H-hour and had the responsibility of securing the exit ramp on the Bridge of the Americas and providing fire support and demonstration fire at the PDF barracks and buildings. This was conducted throughout the night in hopes of convincing the PDF soldiers to surrender. First Lieutenant MacDaniel and his .50-caliber machine guns and AT4s opened fire on specific buildings throughout the night without return fire from the PDF."

Sgt. Kent Long was a squad leader in A Company of 1/508. After A Company landed on LZ Ditch, Long and his squad, well rehearsed in their phase of the operation, set about clearing their portion of the housing area and moved with the company to positions behind the naval headquarters to secure the north end of Fort Amador and prevent the PDF from reinforcing the areas already cleared. A Company had moved into positions to support the front gate, and Captain Reagan sent Sergeant Long to establish an OP to control the area in front of the naval headquarters at the north end of Fort Amador. Sergeant Long and his squad passed the night at the OP hearing sporadic gunfire in the area. At about 0630, Captain Reagan sent Sergeant Long's platoon to clear the PDF housing area outside the front gate. The platoon quickly cleared the houses and moved into position to assault the PDF barracks.

Meanwhile, the Psyop teams from the 1st Battalion of the 4th Psyop Group had been continuously broadcasting surrender terms in Spanish between firepower demonstrations by the 1/508th. Colonel Fitzgerald's concept was initially to place fire on unoccupied buildings, such as a mess hall, as a demonstration and then broadcast more surrender demands. Following each broadcast, Colonel Fitzgerald stepped up the firepower demonstration.

Attached to the battalion was a howitzer section from D Battery of the 320th Field Artillery Battalion. They had flown in on the second lift from Kobbe and were now in a position to fire on the PDF barracks. Colonel Fitzgerald decided that, before B Company began its clearing operation into three of the barracks buildings, he would have the artillery fire one round into each of Buildings 7, 8, and 9. At 0545, Sergeant Brown, the section chief, fired the three howitzer rounds. "The effect," according to one observer, "was dramatic. As B Company moved into position, several dozen PDF soldiers were moving behind the buildings, throwing their weapons into the rocks on the waterfront."

While B Company continued its operation to clear Buildings 8 and 9 from one end of the street, A Company was receiving fire from Buildings 2 and 3. Sergeant Long moved his men into position and at 1000 began systematically clearing Building 1. He did it without the usual procedure of throwing in fragmentation grenades in order to reduce the damage and cut down on needless casualties on both sides. Sergeant Long's men were somewhat tense but, as Sergeant Long said later, "Everyone was really professional. They understood we didn't want to just shoot and destroy everything in sight and worked hard at using only what was necessary."

As the day wore on, the tension and heat increased, but the paratroopers of A and B companies carried on the tedious task of clearing each PDF-occupied building room by room. The Psyop's loudspeaker teams preceded each assault, and in a few hours only a few snipers were left holding out in the last buildings.

To flush them out, Colonel Fitzgerald ordered two M113s from A Company of 4/6 to move up and assist in attacking the sniper positions. After several bursts from the M113's .50-caliber machine guns, the snipers were silent, and the Psyop teams succeeded in coaxing them out of their nests.

At Building 3, A and B companies linked up and secured the area. They proceeded to search each building room by room and put out local security. They were also able to dispatch teams to the American housing area to inform them that all was secure.

During the hours of darkness, the paratroopers had some difficulty in identifying the "friendlies" from the PDF. One "After-Action Summary" from A Company reported,

> The calm professionalism demonstrated by the troops of the Moatengators was evidenced by the actions of Spc Sean Hebel, one of the company snipers. . . . There were a number of American servicemen assigned to the

Naval Station on Fort Amador who foolishly ventured into the action. One individual was an Hispanic Marine officer who left one of the Naval Station buildings dressed in battle dress trousers, jungle boots, and a green T-shirt while carrying a chrome-plated .45. Another naval lieutenant went outside to restart a generator dressed in khakis, which was incidentally the dress uniform of the PDF. Both of these officers could have easily been mistaken for enemy troops. Luckily, Specialist Hebel followed his rules of engagement by positively identifying his targets, thus preventing two incidents of fratricide.

Some of the PDF took unusual and imaginative measures to avoid identification and capture. Among other missions, Captain Reagan and his A Company were tasked to clear the Balboa Yacht Club, on the southwest side of the peninsula, behind the PDF barracks. "Sergeant Camp recalled the abnormally large number of waiters working at the club," wrote one of A Company's officers later. "Many of the PDF troops who had fled their barracks had attempted to disguise themselves as waiters. The dead giveaway was their combat boots. Prisoners were also retrieved from the boats anchored offshore. The men of A Company took 47 prisoners while clearing the Yacht Club."

Colonel Fitzgerald and his 1/508th paratroopers continued to clear Fort Amador all day on the twentieth. The resistance ended when the final twelve PDF were cornered (but not killed) in a shower of the gymnasium. "The fact that the paratrooper leaders and soldiers displayed this type of restraint," wrote Colonel Fitzgerald, "is once again a credit to the superb understanding of the USARO's CG, Major General Marc Cisnero's commander's intent. The 1-508 leaders and soldiers were still very much aware of the dangers and potential for danger when they coaxed the cornered PDF from the gym rather than choosing the easiest and safest way to negate their resistance."

At 1555, the troopers of Headquarters Company reverted to a time-tested task—police call of the battlefield. Finally, at 1749, Colonel Fitzgerald reported to Colonel Snell, "Fort Amador is secured." During the operation, the 1st Battalion of the 508th had captured more than 141 prisoners, 2,000 weapons, 2 V300 armored vehicles, and a ZPU4 AA gun. And because the battalion had been permanently stationed in Panama, it always had been subject to "unfair treatment by the Noriega government for years." With its neutralization of the PDF facilities at Fort Amador, part of what the 1/508th "suffered through the bad days of the Noriega regime" was finally redressed.

"Only when the final twelve PDF were cornered in a shower of the gymnasium did the resistance end," wrote a Southern Command staff officer later.

The resistance at 5th Company was indicative of the resistance of the PDF on many parts of the battlefield. In isolated places, professional, brave soldiers fought and fought hard despite abandonment by their leaders. Capt. Moises Cortizo, thirty-three (and a West Point graduate, Class of 1980), was the commander of the 5th Company. He had acted as Noriega's interpreter during Noriega's conference with Adm. John Poindexter in Panama in 1985. He

117

deserted his men early in the fight. Later he was seen hiding in a hospital in downtown Panama City before he ultimately surrendered.[9]

Fort Amador was now secure and back, totally, in U.S. hands.

*   *   *

"There's no jungle in downtown Panama City," said Capt. Bill Reagan, commanding officer of A Company of the 1/508th. In the days prior to Just Cause, the troops of the 193d Infantry Brigade went through an arduous series of MOUTSs (military operations in urban terrain) to prepare themselves for possible combat in the city.

Lt. Col. William H. Huff III was the commander of the 5th Battalion, 87th Infantry, a regular part of the 193d Infantry Brigade permanently stationed at Fort Clayton on the east side of the canal and about four miles northwest of the western exit of the canal.

In the weeks prior to Just Cause, the 5th of the 87th, plus other units that made up the 193d, had been engaged in around-the-clock security operations at U.S. installations in Panama and had kept a seven-day-a-week training schedule. Even at times when the troops were officially off-duty, they had remained on a two-hour "string." "That means," according to Capt. Don Currie, commander of C Company of 5/87th, "that if we get a call, we have to be equipped, loaded up, and out the door in two hours." Even though the two-hour "string" had been the norm since Panama's elections in 1989, troops had frequently been placed on one-hour or even thirty-minute strings during the anti-American demonstrations or other "potentially explosive activities."

The seven-day-a-week training schedule was rigorous and "exciting," according to some of the troops in 5/87th, in spite of the continual alerts prior to 20 December. In the weeks just prior to Just Cause, one example of training that was most beneficial was a month-long series of live-fire exercises that Huff had led his battalion through in a simulated urban environment. Colonel Huff said, "Jungle warfare used to be our big emphasis, but that was before the political situation in Panama changed. MOUTs weren't originally part of our wartime mission, but they are now."

Colonel Huff had started his MOUT training with squad-level defensive live-fire drills and then had advanced the troops to platoon-level operations. For Capt. Don Currie's company, the grand finale was a company offensive against a hastily built "enemy" camp. S Sgt. Jimmy Banks was a member of Currie's company. He was a "seasoned" infantryman, a veteran of Eleven Bravo, who had trained at Fort Benning, Fort Ord, in Hawaii, and Germany. "But nothing," he said, "approached the intensity of infantry operations in Panama."

"As C Company prepared for its mock assault against the 'enemy' camp," reported Donna Miles in *Soldiers,*

Banks crouched down behind a cluster of sawgrass and wiped raindrops from his eyes. He surveyed his rain-soaked platoon, each member locked and loaded and ready to move. Banks nodded toward the squad leaders, then watched as the troops bounded forward, one squad at a time, through the calf-deep mud. They splashed down behind the closest cover they could find, then returned fire on the enemy camp.

Despite the heavy M-16 and M-60 fire, the sound of the advancing company was muffled from behind by the ear-splintering roar of the 5th Battalion, 6th Infantry Regiment. An element of the 5th Division (Mechanized) from Fort Polk, Louisiana, the 5-6th was pulling a four-month rotation in Panama supporting the 193d "Lights." From their M-113 armored personnel carriers' support fire positions, the task force sprayed the target with .50-caliber machine-gun fire.

Covered by the barrage and the cloud of a smoke grenade, the 5-87th soldiers approached the enemy building. The first two soldiers to reach the doorway performed the entry procedure they'd been taught: Rock forward, backward, then forward into the building. When they crossed the threshold, they bellowed, "Entering the building!"

"We train them to enter in two-man teams and to yell out everything they're doing so everybody can hear it," said Capt. Bill Flynt, whose A Company of the 5th of the 87th conducted an identical operation on nearby Gallery Range. "When you're dealing with live ammo, it's critical that everyone knows what's happening. That's how you keep people from getting hurt."

Little did Flynt or anyone else realize that the following month the troops would apply the lessons in combat.[10]

At 0100 on the twentieth, Task Force Wildcat, Colonel Huff's 5th of the 87th plus A Company of the 4th of the 6th, crossed its line of departure outside the gate of Fort Clayton. Capt. Bill Flynt's A Company, the Jaguars, was headed for the PDF Engineer Battalion inside the Engineer Compound, a complex in the Curundu Heights area and just to the east of Albrook Air Force Base, about four miles from Fort Clayton. Capt. Mark Conley's B Company, the Junglecats, was headed for Balboa, just west of Quarry Heights and Ancon Hill, about five miles from Fort Clayton. Conley had the task of "seizing and securing" the PDF at the Balboa DENI (Departmento Nacional de Investigaciónes—police station) and neutralizing other PDF in the immediate area, securing Balboa, and protecting the integrated U.S., PDF and PCC (Panama Canal Commission) housing areas in Balboa Heights and Diablo Heights. Capt. Don Currie's C Company, the Panthers, was under orders to neutralize the PDF in the Ancon DENI and the Ancon DNTT (Dirección Nacional de Transito Terrestre—road police) and "prevent them from influencing the battle elsewhere." The Ancon Hill area was just to the east of Balboa. The U.S. Quarry Heights area and the U.S. Gorgas Hospital were just north of Ancon Hill.

Team Track, Capt. Isadore Bower's mechanized A Company of the 4th of the 6th, was attached to Task Force Wildcat and had the mission of blocking the main avenue of approach in Panama City and setting up roadblocks along Fourth of July Avenue so that PDF forces could not reinforce the Comandancia. Team Track's roadblocks tied in with Task Force Gator's left flank. TF Gator was the parent unit, the 4th of the 6th, of Team Track.

During the operation, the 59th Engineer Company, assigned to the 193d

119

Infantry Brigade and commanded by Capt. José Echevarria, provided direct combat engineer support to the various elements of Task Force Bayonet, 193d Brigade, by attaching separate platoons to each of the task forces in TF Bayonet.

The 519th MP Battalion, with headquarters at Fort Meade, Maryland, had been deployed just days prior to the start of the operation for a four-month tour of duty in Panama under Operation Nimrod Dancer. The 519th controlled five military police companies from various Stateside posts. Several of the MP platoons were subattached to the various units of TF Bayonet for the operation. The bulk of the battalion was responsible for rear-area security north of Erosivity Avenue and was also responsible for two H-hour targets, the PDF Dog Compound, and Balboa Harbor.

By 0100, all elements of Task Force Wildcat, including Team Track, had departed Fort Clayton by the SCN gate, a gate near a radio station and about four hundred yards from the main gate at Fort Clayton. The SCN gate was near the 5/87th barracks area and convenient to the highway into western Panama City, where its objectives were located. The Wildcats, a light infantry outfit, were mounted in trucks; Team Track was in its M113s.

En route to their objectives, the trucks of B and C companies of the 5th of the 87th were "ambushed" in the vicinity of the Albrook Air Force Base and Diablo Heights along Galliard Highway. The Panthers' convoy commander, Captain Conley, reported that he "received fire from a Chiva-Chiva bus and a PDF patrol." The Panthers "received automatic fire from the Albrook guard shack and Explonsa Building."

At 0126, A Company had reached the Engineer Compound and infiltrated into the area of some six buildings. The troopers of the company started clearing the buildings one by one, capturing PDF as they went along. They tried to "coax" the PDF out of the buildings with loudspeaker messages in Spanish and giving the PDF "countdowns." Sgt. Robert Judd of the 1st Platoon of the 59th Combat Engineer Company was with A Company. Captain Echevarria reported later that "The fighting was intense and the sappers [his engineers] fought aggressively as both engineers and infantry. The men of the 1st Squad showed their ingenuity by hot-wiring several cars and even a tractor to build a formidable defensive perimeter for the Jaguars of A Company." By 1240, Captain Flynt reported to Colonel Huff that the Engineer Compound was "cleared."

About forty minutes after the Junglecats left Fort Clayton via the SCN gate, they were in position at the Balboa DENI station, which had been the police station in the old Canal Zone. It stood opposite the YMCA, another old Canal Zone landmark. Nearby were the Christian Science building, the Marco Polo restaurant, and St. Mary's Hill. The DENI station was thus situated in a residential area, where, if the commander did not exercise care and caution, a great deal of "collateral damage" could occur.

At 0142, Captain Conley gave the DENI station PDF a five-minute warning and followed it with a "firepower demonstration." The PDF refused to surrender. Ten minutes later, Colonel Huff directed Conley to clear and secure the station. Conley gave the occupants of the station a final warning to surrender. No PDF appeared, so at 0335, Lieutenant Timotheus and his platoon assaulted the Balboa DENI. At 0359, the first building was cleared by Lieutenant Hampton and his platoon. By 0445, Captain Conley reported to Colonel Huff that the Balboa DENI was "cold." The assault on the buildings resulted in their complete destruction, but the company was so meticulous in its application of firepower that neither the YMCA nor the Christmas Nativity scene on the station lawn was touched. In the firefights in and around the station, one PDF was killed.

At 0050, Capt. Don Currie and his C Company Panthers left Fort Clayton via the SCN gate. After arriving at the Ancon DNTT building, the battalion S-3 requested his tactical operations center to phone the DNTT and persuade them to surrender. The DNTT refused. At 0300 the Panthers initiated an assault on the Ancon DENI station with the .50-caliber machine guns of A Company of the 4th of the 6th's M113's firing suppressive fire. Half an hour later, C Company prepared to enter the Ancon DENI and called for "fire for effect" on the Ancon DNTT. For the next four hours, the company worked on clearing the two station buildings. In the assault on the DNTT, Sergeant Dimoala and Private First Class Porter were wounded in an exchange of fire with the stubborn defenders of the stations. By 0802, the main building was cleared, and at 0853, Captain Currie reported to Colonel Huff that the DNTT was "cold."[11]

With that report, Captain Huff could report to Colonel Snell, "Mission accomplished."

13 | Task Force Atlantic

The Atlantic side of the canal—the Caribbean side—also had to be neutralized. It was one more phase in the multifaceted, simultaneously executed, zonewide campaign to paralyze the PDF and its operating facilities. The complexity of Just Cause, the extensive and meticulous planning, the depth of the staff work, the responsiveness and responsibility of the chain of command, and the demonstrated professionalism of the troops involved become apparent when one realizes that so many small operations, launched by a widely diverse mix of military units from all four services, from locations as far away as Fort Ord, California, Fort Lewis, Washington, Fort Bragg, North Carolina, and Hunter Army Airfield, Georgia, occurred at scattered in-country Panama sites at the same time.

Just Cause was not a classic military campaign in the sense that units were arrayed in the same general area and ready to attack at a predetermined H-hour along an enemy's more or less continuous defensive line. It was not a Desert Storm, a textbook war that was a perfectly developed and executed maneuver and attack against what was previously thought to be a formidable, dug-in enemy. Rather, Just Cause was a series of well-coordinated, relatively small-unit operations from a wide variety of in-country and Stateside commands against a diverse and many-pocketed enemy. It was an operation based on a contingency plan the likes of which the United States may possibly see more often in the wake of the almost miraculous success of Desert Storm with the attendant renewed worldwide respect for the determination and refusal of the U.S. government to compromise. With the collapse of the USSR, the United States remains the world's sole, formidable military power.

On the Atlantic side of the canal, U.S. forces had to isolate Colón, the canal's Caribbean port city; neutralize the PDF 8th Company in Colón at Fort Espinar and the PDF 1st Marine Infantry Company at the port of Coco Solo; capture the PDF patrol boats at the port; protect the Madden Dam, which stores water used to raise and lower ships in the canal's locks; seize the electrical distribution center at Cerro Tigre; secure the vital Gatun Locks and the defense installations; free a number of Panamanian political prisoners, victims of the aborted March 1988 coup attempt, incarcerated in Renacer Prison at Gamboa, midway across the isthmus; establish roadblocks on the neck of Colón Peninsula and on Boyd-Roosevelt Highway; protect the Galeta Island facility; disable all multiengine aircraft on France Airfield; and protect the U.S. housing area at Gamboa.[1]

Colón, with a population of about sixty thousand, is a port city on Limón Bay on the Atlantic side of the canal and lies at the northern tip of a half-mile-long peninsula commonly referred to as the Colón Bottleneck. One-half mile to the east across another inlet is the town of Coco Solo. Situated on the bay's shore in Coco Solo is a former joint-use facility, two identical buildings running north to south. The northern building is Cristóbal Junior/Senior High School. The southern building housed the 1st Naval Infantry Company, a garment factory, and a Chinese restaurant known as the Noodle Shop. Two hundred yards to the west, behind the PDF building, was the docking area for the PDF's five patrol boats. Fifty yards to the east, across a stretch of green grass, was a U.S. housing area—a street with about two dozen homes, many unoccupied by the twentieth of December.

The accomplishment of the myriad tasks on the Atlantic side of the canal fell to the lot of Task Force Atlantic, whose headquarters was Col. Keith Kellogg's staff of the 3d Brigade of the 7th Infantry Division (Light). His principal units were Lt. Col. Lynn Moore's 3d Battalion of the 504th Infantry of the 82d Airborne Division and Lt. Col. Johnny Brooks's 4th Battalion, 17th Infantry of the 7th Infantry Division (Light).

The 3d of the 504th, from the 82d Airborne Division at Fort Bragg, had been in Panama since 10 December training, on a rotational cycle, at the Panama Jungle Operations Training Center (JOTC) at Fort Sherman, on the Caribbean. It was about to put its training into combat reality.[2]

The 4th of the 17th had been in Panama since 27 October 1989. On 15 October, the 3d Brigade of the 7th Infantry Division, as part of Operation Nimrod Sustain, had assumed responsibility for all U.S. forces in the vicinity of Colón from the 1st Brigade of the 7th and had become Task Force Atlantic. Before the operation, TF Atlantic was involved in intense mission analysis, planning, preparation, and rehearsals. Prior to the Just Cause campaign, the brigade rotated its battalions from Fort Ord through a three-week course at the JOTC. The 4th Battalion of the 17th Infantry had finished its three-week jungle training at the JTOC but had remained in Panama as part of the Nimrod Dancer buildup. The 4th of the 17th also conducted "Sand Flea" exercises primarily to exercise U.S. freedom of movement rights under the Panama Canal treaties and to rehearse contingency plans. The battalion ran "freedom of movement" convoys twice weekly from Fort Sherman to Fort Clayton or from Howard Air Force Base across the isthmus and back to Colón. In their rehearsals for the operation, generally speaking, the troops of the 4/17 had no idea they were rehearsing a specific wartime plan, yet they knew their jobs, their team tasks, and their individual squad objectives. Field training was never so closely related to the actual combat that would occur.

At H-hour on 20 December, the 7th Infantry Division (Light) had in Panama a battalion task force (the 4th of the 17th), the 3d Brigade's headquarters, and the two-hundred-man Task Force Hawk, made up of units from the 7th's Aviation Brigade. TF Hawk had originally been deployed to Panama by President Reagan about a year earlier. Starting on D-day, 20 December, Maj. Gen. Carmen J. Cavezza, the 7th Division's commander, would deploy another four thousand soldiers from Fort Ord to Howard Air Force Base and Torrijos/Tocumen Airport in just two days.

Before that buildup would occur, however, the 7th Division troops in Panama had tasks to perform under combat conditions. "Our missions were to eliminate the Panamanian Defense Forces and seal off the Colón area," reported Col. Johnny Brooks, commanding officer of the 4/17. "We had to neutralize the Panamanian Naval Infantry Battalion at Coco Solo, neutralize the 8th Infantry Company at Fort Espinar, block off the city of Colón from the rest of Panama, neutralize all aircraft on France Airfield, secure the Coco Solo Hospital, and establish roadblocks on the Trans-Isthmus Highway between Colón and Panama City."

As Colonel Brooks remembered, one of the 4/17th's big fights was the neutralization of the naval infantry at Coco Solo. Brooks had assigned that mission to Capt. Christopher Rizzo and his C Company. C Company had been garrisoned in an unused wing of Cristóbal High School and was therefore in the same area, just one building away from its target, the naval infantry. For the previous thirty-three days, after the completion of their stint at the JOTC, the company had been patrolling the Coco Solo area. According to one of Rizzo's men, "Each day we came face to face with our future enemy, the naval infantry soldiers, and had to ignore their sneers and degrading gestures." The U.S. soldiers may possibly have used more graphic words and hand language when talking about the naval infantry among themselves.[3]

In the days prior to Just Cause, Rizzo developed the details of his plan to knock out the naval infantry. His plan was relatively simple: Surround them, initiate the attack by firing a few rounds from rifle, Vulcans, antitank weapons, and machine guns, ask them to surrender via a broadcast from a Psyops loudspeaker, and, if they refused, up the ante.

To seal off the area, he planned to use one rifle platoon and some military police. In addition, he would assemble an infantry platoon in front of the barracks, a platoon armed with rifles, machine guns, 20mm Vulcans, and some antitank weapons. To cover the rear of the barracks, he would put another platoon, which also had the mission of capturing the PDF patrol boats. In reserve he had a fourth platoon to clear the barracks after the initial assault, if necessary.

Rizzo had about two hundred men included in his three rifle platoons, a rifle platoon from the 3d Battalion of the 504th, two Vulcans from the 2d Battalion, 62d Air Defense Artillery, a signal detachment from the 127th Signal Battalion, and a platoon from the 549th Military Police Company.

Rizzo charged Lieutenant Kirk and his 2d Platoon of C Company, "Hard Rock Charlie," to clear the barracks.

In the evening hours of the nineteenth, the men of C Company were either on guard duty or relaxing in their barracks, writing letters, videotaping messages to their families, or eating in the mess hall. Then the word came down the chain to Rizzo that H-hour would be 0100 on the twentieth. He alerted the company, assembled them, announced H-hour, went over the plans one last time, issued new call signs and frequencies, and ordered his platoon leaders to execute the plan they had rehearsed so diligently in the past weeks. The men of the company suited up for combat, put on Kevlar body armor, and applied more facial camouflage paint than they ever had before. Rizzo positioned two Vulcans from the 2d of the 62d Air Defense Artillery near the barracks as he had done every night for the past several months. Colonel Brooks came over and spoke to the company, the chaplain said a prayer, and the company was ready to take its part as one piece in the jigsaw puzzle of Just Cause. Rizzo had one more mission before he executed his plan: At about 0015, he awakened the eight American families who lived in the U.S. family housing area right across the areas from the PDF barracks and evacuated them to a neighbor's house one row of buildings away.

At about 0045, as the platoons were moving into their assault positions, they heard three shots fired from the vicinity of the center entrance to the Coco Solo barracks. The platoon en route to secure the dock answered with M-60 machine-gun fire, and Rizzo gave the order for the Vulcans to open fire on the barracks with a two-minute sustained fire of ten-round bursts. The rounds tore through the walls and dispersed the defenders but did not cause them to surrender. Kirk and his 2d Platoon were crossing the gap between the high school and the naval barracks. Then the platoon would enter the barracks through the Chinese restaurant and work its way through the building and into the PDF-occupied part of the barracks.

Sgt. Chance De-Wayne "Ranger" Brooks had been the leader of the 3d Squad in the 2d Platoon for only two weeks. But the rehearsals and the training in the past two weeks made him ready for his combat assignment. He positioned himself on the second floor of the building, where he could watch the 1st Squad, the spearhead of the operation, move across the gap and into the building. Brooks threw several grenades into the courtyard to suppress enemy fire while the 1st Squad entered the building. Sgt. David Rainer, a squad leader in the 1st Platoon, said later, "Everybody's blood was pumping and we all ran across the gap at Olympic-breaking speed."

By this time the naval infantry soldiers were alert and reacting to the movement of Rizzo's company. Gunfire was coming from all around the building, and tracer rounds flashed through the night air. Rainer remembered seeing tracer rounds fly past him and between his legs.

Cpl. Joseph Legaspi, a recent graduate of the Ranger School, had been in the unit only a matter of days. He was A Team leader in the 3d Squad. When the Vulcans opened up, Legaspi said, "The ground shook." He was eagerly awaiting the loudspeaker to ask the PDF to surrender. But, he recalled, things weren't that simple. Instead of surrendering, the PDF increased their small-arms fire from the building. But by this time the 2d Platoon had raced across the gap, were all in the building, and had begun their clearing operations.

The platoon went, first of all, through the area where the seventeen-member Chinese family lived in the garment factory, of which their restaurant was a part. Without firing a shot, the platoon managed to round up the family and get them safely out of the building.

To get into the PDF section of the barracks, Private Secor used some C-4 to blast open the locked door between the factory and the PDF living area. Rainer then raced through the blazing doorway into a blacked-out gymnasium and led his squad to a stairway on the other side. Meanwhile, the 2d Squad guarded the entrance and the Chinese family.

The PDF soldiers were still unwilling to surrender. Lieutenant Kirk "upped the ante." He asked for more fire from the Vulcans. "We hit the naval headquarters building at Coco Solo with our Vulcans set on direct-fire mode," said Lt. James Leary, a platoon leader with B Battery of the 2/62 Air Defense Artillery. "We did a number on that building and knocked out the PDF guys. We also hit and crippled a PDF patrol boat with a Vulcan. The boat was in the wrong place at the wrong time. . . . The Vulcan was a pivotal weapon during the invasion." The second blast of the Vulcans encouraged the PDF to yell their belated willingness to surrender. Before he accepted the surrender, Sergeant Rainer made certain that the platoon had cleared the entire building. Lieutenant Kirk led his platoon through the building from top to bottom, and when he was certain that the entire building was clear, he had Private First Class Davis, a Spanish linguist, take the surrender from Captain Jiminez, a young Panamanian who had been in command of the Coco Solo naval infantry for only ten hours. His experience as a company commander was somewhat brief, unrewarding, and bewildering.

It took the 2d Platoon about four hours to clear the PDF naval infantry barracks. The platoon suffered no casualties and captured twenty-seven of the PDF, only two of whom were wounded. Unfortunately, the fire started by the C-4 destroyed the living quarters of the Chinese family. But C Company quickly found other housing for them and helped the family recover their belongings from the building.[4]

"Hard Rock Charlie" was not yet finished with the Just Cause campaign. It assisted Colonel Brooks with the rest of the battalion's missions, one part of which was clearing the city of Colón. "The Buffalos," the nickname of the 4th of the 17th Infantry, cleared Colón on 22 December. Originally, Colonel Brooks thought that a sweep of Colón would be difficult because of the predicted resistance of the PDF and the Digbats. Such did not prove to be the case. "We began our sweep into Colón with mortars, LAWs, and small arms," said Company B's first sergeant, Larry Durham. "We didn't meet any resistance; instead, thousands of Panamanians came out of their homes cheering and applauding us. The crowds were so thick. It was amazing, unbelievable."

"Here, four hundred PDF soldiers surrendered to us," Colonel Brooks reported later. "We captured about sixteen hundred weapons, many of them brand-new, and some others were very old. After we captured Colón, many

Panamanians started waving white flags and cheering the Americans on. Most of the information that we received from the Panamanians was unreliable and false. We referred to these rumors as 'Vicky says messages,' named after General Noriega's girlfriend. The Panamanian people were pleased because we didn't destroy the city or kill innocent people." The battalion was able to keep the "collateral" damage at a minimum because of its careful planning and "measured application of combat power." Sergeant Rainer said, after the reception in Colón, "It felt like what he had seen in pictures of the liberation of Paris."

"The Coco Solo naval infantry, 8th Infantry Company, and blocking Colón missions were the most difficult ones for us," Colonel Brooks summed up after the battle. "We encountered pretty heavy resistance at all three places, especially at Fort Espinar. We received the most casualties at Fort Espinar, mostly from grenades and rocket-propelled grenades and some AK-47 rounds. Some of the wounded soldiers will need up to thirteen months of recovery time."[5]

After securing Colón, joint teams from the 4th of the 17th and the 7th Division's 7th MP Company patrolled the streets around the clock to prevent looting and maintain law and order. The 7th's MPs also worked with, helped to equip, and trained the newly formed Panamanian Public Forces in the Colón area. The MPs also provided the reorganized and redirected PDF with the vehicles and weapons they needed to transform themselves into a police force. The metamorphosis from a Noriega supporting force to a police department focused on law and order was under way.

14 | Madden Dam, Cerro Tigre, and Renacer Prison

On 10 December, the 3d Battalion of the 504th Infantry of the 82d Airborne Division had arrived in Panama to undergo three weeks of jungle training at the Jungle Operations Training Center at Fort Sherman on the Atlantic side of the canal. On that date, the troopers of the battalion were unaware that in ten days their training would suddenly become battle-realistic, that they would find themselves firing at live targets and getting shot at in return. Never before had the JOTC provided its students with such authentic combat conditions as a graduation exercise. The 3d of the 504th would graduate with honors. The battalion's attacks were part of 27 H-hour simultaneous assaults by the United States against PDF targets in Panama.

In the early weeks of December, as the atmosphere in Panama became charged with increasing tension between the United States and Noriega, Lt. Col. Lynn Moore, the commander of the 3d of the 504th, knew that his battalion would become part of the Just Cause operation. He had been briefed on the plan that made his battalion part of Col. Keith Kellogg's 3d Brigade of the 7th Infantry Division—Task Force Atlantic. Moore's mission, in the simplest of terms, was the responsibility for all enemy objectives along the canal between the outskirts of Colón and the outskirts of Panama City, a distance of some fifty miles. "Everything in between was our responsibility," said Colonel Moore. The rest of TF Atlantic was responsible for reducing PDF resistance in and around Colón itself.

Colonel Moore broke down his objective area into submissions and assigned them as follows: A Company, the town of Gamboa on the Panama Canal; B Company, Madden Dam and the electrical plant at Cierro Tigre; C Company, the prison at El Renacer near Gamboa; and three of his other platoons plus a platoon from his Headquarters Company and attached personnel, security missions at several locations. "Of the 632 people I brought in-country," Colonel Moore said, "every man, regardless of his military occupational specialty, was

128

fighting as infantry." Col. Jack Nix was the commander of the 1st Brigade of the 82d, of which the 3/504th was a part. "The best part," he said, "was these young paratroopers. Their training paid off; it reduced casualties."

At 0030 in the early black hours of the morning of the twentieth, a task force composed of the Panama-based 1st Battalion 228 Aviation Regiment, with UH-1Hs and CH-47Bs, and B Company of the 3/504th, reinforced, lifted off from Fort Sherman, thirteen kilometers southwest of Colón. Each Huey carried ten combat-loaded soldiers; the CH-47 carried fifty. The mission of the task force was to clear and secure the Madden Dam to prevent damage to the water control system for the canal. According to one report, "Flying the mixed aircraft formation took expert training and split-second timing. At 0045, the lead helicopter touched down at the dam with the CH-47s landing nearby in a clearing. A large volume of ground fire erupted, but darkness and speedy unloading resulted in no aircraft being hit. The entire flight was conducted under blackout conditions, with all aviators using night-vision goggles (NVGs). The surprise gave the infantry a significant tactical advantage during the ground action that followed." The troops quickly overcame the PDF guards, secured the dam site, and later cleared the logistical and electrical power site at Cierro Tigre.

About halfway across the isthmus, near the town of Gamboa, sits Renacer Prison, a makeshift collection of twenty or so cinder-block and wooden buildings with tin roofs. The prison yard, marked by a cyclone fence, measures about forty by seventy meters, inside of which were the two major buildings of the prison, the prisoner barracks and a recreation building. Most of the buildings were outside the fence. As prisons go, it was relatively small and decrepit. But because it supposedly held a few Americans and some of Noriega's political prisoners, many from the aborted October 1989 coup, it was a key target in the immediate U.S. scheme of things in the early hours of Just Cause.

The guard force, reconnoitered in the past weeks by U.S. patrols and operations around the prison under the Sand Flea scenario, numbered twenty to twenty-five. "Apparently such duty was not the high point of a PDF soldier's career," according to one report, "as the force included members of the elite Battalion 2000, who, because of various discipline infractions, were serving punishment as guards. Armament consisted of a variety of automatic rifles— mostly Communist AK-47's and a version of the U.S. M-16, the T-65. One machine gun was later found."

During the days prior to the assault, Capt. Derek Johnson, commanding officer of C Company, 3/504, led his teams through repeated rehearsals of the operation and trained them in building clearance, control of firing, and helicopter loading and rapid unloading. Johnson set up a mock-up of the prison using tapes to simulate its restricted dimensions. The forays near the prison, practicing the pending operation, caused Captain Johnson some concern. "I was more scared during Sand Flea than the actual attack," he said later. "After those operations and our rehearsals, we were comfortable with the actual mission." The rehearsals, however, were important and paid off: They lulled the PDF into a false sense of security because they saw the Americans so often; the troops could see their targets, the location, construction and size of the buildings, the guard force habits, movements, and locations; and they demonstrated the determination of the United States to be present and move freely in its specified zone as guaranteed by the Panama Canal Treaty.[1]

The difficulty of seizing the prison and extracting the prisoners safely was compounded by the fact that the guards and the prisoners were intermixed in a very small area, and firing on the guards might endanger the prisoners. In addition, the prison was bounded on two sides by water and on the third by a jungle ridge. Colonel Moore and Captain Johnson knew that they must hit the prison quickly and precisely with surprise and an overwhelming force to protect the prisoners and knock out the guards.

The plan of attack called for a simultaneous air assault and amphibious landing at 0100 on the twentieth. For support and transportation, Captain Johnson had three Hueys from the 1st Battalion of the 228th Aviation, demolition elements from the 307th Engineer Battalion, two LCMs from the 1097th Transportation Company, and three MPs. Two Hueys, each carrying eleven paratroopers and whose pilots wore night-vision goggles, would land inside the cramped prison yard after flying over high-tension wires near the compound. The Huey door gunners were prepared to fire on preselected targets. Accompanying the Hueys was an AH-1 Cobra attack helicopter from the 7th Infantry Division, prepared to fire with precision rounds into the guards' barracks. On landing in the tight LZ, the assault force, part of 2d Lt. Christopher Oswalt's 2d Platoon, would search and secure the prisoners' barracks and the recreation building, the two major structures in the fenced-in area.

Simultaneously at H-hour, the remainder of the 2d Platoon, under Sergeant Niles, would land from an LCM on the canal side and provide fire support and security for the assault force. Sergeant Niles's men were armed with five M-60 machine guns and twenty AT-4 antitank weapons that could be used against sturdy buildings and any vehicles that might arrive, bringing in a reinforcing PDF unit.

Lt. Chuck Broadus's 3d Platoon of C Company was on the other LCM. Broadus's mission was to clear and secure the buildings in the prison area outside the chain link fence. In addition to those troops, also included in Johnson's command was one OH-58 scout helicopter, which carried a company sniper, and a third Huey, which carried ten scouts and would land outside the fence as reinforcement and to block any potential PDF relief force.

During the evening of 19 December, Colonel Moore received the "go" order to execute the missions. The weather was poor for night flying, with the cloud base at five hundred feet and little ambient light for optimum operation of the pilots' night-vision goggles. But the mission was "on." All elements of C Company, the helicopters, and the LCMs launched from Fort Sherman at precisely determined times to arrive on target at 0100.

Just prior to H-hour, two OH-58 observation helicopters flew down the canal and, when they came abreast of the guard positions near the prison, opened fire. Almost to the minute at H-hour, while the guards were momentarily distracted by the OH-58's, the two Hueys with the 2d Platoon's assault force aboard dropped inside the fence of the prison yard. They were met with a "hail of bullets" from the not totally distracted guards.

One observer said of the landing inside the prison fence, "It was a incredible display of airmanship. No one fired from the left side of the aircraft to prevent hitting the prisoners' barracks. On the right side of each helicopter the door gunner, two squad automatic weapons gunners, and a grenade launcher gunner all fired."

"Prison guards responded," remembered Chief Warrant Officer Michael Loats, the lead pilot. "How we never got hit, I don't know. All we saw were tracers in front, on the side, and behind us."

At the same time, the Huey with the scouts landed at the blocking position; the LCMs touched shore, and the fire support element raced off the boat's ramp; the Cobra flew in and shattered a guardpost with its 20mm Gatling gun; and a sniper with night-vision goggles was "picking off guards in a watchtower from his hovering OH-58 Kiowa chopper."

The floodlights in the yard shorted out, possibly due to a cable blowing across the power lines as the helicopters came in to land. Sergeant Coulter led his 1st Squad of the 2d Platoon to the main prisoner barracks and blew open a metal door. Specialist Reitveld was hit in the arm by a bullet or a grenade fragment. Sergeant Godfrey led his 3d Squad through the breached metal door into the interior of the building. They found the quick-thinking prisoners lying on the floor, covered with their mattresses. Sergeant Baker's 2d Squad, meanwhile, had entered and secured the recreation building, and Sergeant Niles had set up his five machine guns in a supporting-fire position outside the fence.

By this time and on schedule, Lt. Chuck Broadus had disembarked his 3d Platoon from the LCM after a two-hour ride from Fort Sherman. His force came under heavy fire within ten to fifteen meters of the boat dock and then had to move across a railroad track. "This was really a hairy, hairy mission," Lieutenant Broadus said later. "If the helicopters landed first, they would have been without support. If the boats landed first, it would have tipped our hand, and the helicopters would have come in under more fire. We called this San Juan Hill for a while. We had to come up quickly under fire."

Broadus quickly moved his men up toward the area where Sergeant Niles had set up his supporting machine guns. On the way, one of Broadus's troopers saw two PDF soldiers running between some buildings and notified Niles. Private First Class Watson, one of Niles's M-60 machine gunners, opened fire and killed both of the PDF.

One obstacle surprised Lieutenant Broadus and his platoon: a ten-foot chain link fence under the overhang of the office and headquarters buildings—part of the area Broadus was supposed to clear. Broadus tried grenades and a claymore mine to blow a hole in the wire, to no avail. "We tried to blow a hole in the fence but it was very thick," Broadus said later. Finally, "Pfcs. Derik Webster and Charles Ross, exposed to enemy fire, ran and cut a hole in the fence with their bayonets."

Sgt. Kevin Schleben led his squad into the blacked-out headquarters building, and they were met by a cloud of CS gas. They left the building, dooned their protective masks, and went right back in to press the attack. As Sergeant Schleben moved through the building, he spotted a trail of blood on the floor and followed it back outside. Next to the building, behind an air-conditioning vent and within a few feet of other paratroopers who were unaware of them, Schleben spotted two PDF soldiers, one of whom was wounded. As the PDF soldiers swung their rifles toward Schleben, he fired first and killed them both. Later Lieutenant Broadus said, "They could have shot four or five of us. He [Sergeant Schleben] went between us and them. He could have taken our fire or their fire." "Just a job," Sergeant Schleben said when he heard Lieutenant Broadus's comments.

C Company's troopers had cleared almost all of the twenty or so buildings around the prison complex. Farther away, Sergeant Wilson led his squad up a jungle ridge to clear a couple of buildings still unsecured. One of the buildings was a duplex, apparently family quarters. The squad cleared one apartment in the duplex and then heard a woman cry, "Don't shoot!" The squad held its fire. A somewhat shaken PDF lieutenant, his wife, and his child, none of whom was injured, came out of the second apartment and surrendered to Sergeant Wilson and his men.

Later, Spc. Damian Benson, whose squad had cut down three of the PDF killed in the fight, said that he was really distressed that he almost shot the wife of a Panamanian lieutenant and her baby when they emerged from the duplex. "I came close to killing that woman and her baby," he said, shaking his head.

Sgt. Christopher Castillo said after the operation that they had worked hard on the plan to clear the prison buildings. He credited Spc. Felix Huamandiaz, fluent in Spanish and acting as a translator, for talking some of the PDF into surrendering.

By 0600 the prison was totally in U.S. hands. All prisoners—two American journalists, five political prisoners from the October coup, and fifty-seven other prisoners (actual criminals?)—were accounted for and unharmed. Of the PDF guards, five had been killed and twenty-two captured, six of whom had been wounded. The total U.S. casualties were four wounded.[2]

In a follow-on recap of the mission, one report said,

> During the assault on Renacer Prison, the soldiers of 3/504 PIR engaged targets with a multitude of weapons and encountered many unfamiliar obstacles. In addition to concertina wire, there were eight- and 10-foot-high chain link fences. There were steel doors and concrete walls along with iron bars and heavy-duty padlocks. Pressed for time and under heavy fire, soldiers used their organic weapons against these obstacles. They were sometimes dismayed by the results and often were required to try new tactics.

One of the prisoners rescued from Renacer Prison was a thirty-six-year-old Miami electrical engineer, Diego J. Jiminez, who had fled illegally from Cuba in 1973. In June of 1989, he was in Panama. "I went to the immigration office to get my wife and son out of Panama," he said later. "They pulled me out of line and said I was working for the CIA. I was just another civilian caught in the wrong placed at the wrong time."

The PDF incarcerated Jiminez in the bleak prison at Renacer. In an effort to break his will, the PDF taped his eyes shut for fifteen days. During that period, his captors beat him, drugged his coffee, put electrical shocks through his body, and pulled out his toenails with pliers. "I was isolated, without any rights," Jiminez said after his rescue on the twentieth of December.

Jiminez went to work immediately with a U.S. intelligence unit and succeeded in putting "the finger" on a number of his former captors. He said that after fifteen days of torture he would never forget their faces, once they took off the tapes over his eyes. "Now they're shaking," he said as he eyed his former guards. So far he has identified thirteen of his captors.

One of the officers in the intelligence unit said, "He's really helped us on several cases. Initially, he identified prison guards and interrogators. He also identified some criminals—thieves and drug dealers—among the released prisoners. They'll probably go back to jail."

Jiminez treasured most a telephone call to his mother. "They [his captors] told me she was dead," he added.[3]

The in-country troops, fighting isolated battles in and around the Canal Zone, may have thought they were fighting alone. But at other places in Panama, U.S. soldiers had parachuted onto various drop zones in the black, predawn hours and were attacking and securing other objectives.

15 | The Jump on Río Hato

Col. "Buck" Kernan, commanding officer of the 75th Ranger Regiment, was, as he remembers it, "In and out of the office [at Fort Benning] the 15th and 16th of December responding to various phone calls and intelligence updates and was aware the situation was deteriorating but I was at home when I was officially notified. I was called on the secure line at my home, given the order to execute, given the critical times, and immediately alerted all my battalion commanders (one at Benning, one at Fort Lewis, Washington, and one at Hunter Army Air Field, Georgia) and assembled the battle staff. Official notification was 172000R December."[1]

On Monday, the eighteenth, the 2d of the 75th flew from Fort Lewis to a REMAB (remote marshaling base) at Fort Benning to join the 3d Battalion, stationed at Benning. C Company of the 3/75 then moved by bus to join the 1/75 in its REMAB at Hunter. The 2/75 plus 3/75 minus C Company would attack Río Hato; the 1/75 plus C/3/75 would attack Torrijos/Tocumen Airport.

In the marshaling areas at Lawson Field at Benning and at Hunter Army Airfield on the nineteenth, the commanders down the line made final preparations for what would be, for the majority of the Rangers, a first combat jump. (For one young man, Capt. Raymond A. Thomas, West Point Class of 1980, this was a second combat jump. He had jumped into Grenada in October 1983.) Regardless of the circumstances and the intelligence estimates of the size and potential of the enemy, a trooper's first combat jump is an event seared in memory. And a jump at night, a seven-hour flight away, adds to the trepidation and concern in the minds of the paratroopers—no matter how well trained and disciplined they are. One's first jump at jump school is exciting; but one's first combat jump is "red-letter"—memorable. The prospect grabs one's attention —no matter how macho he considers himself.

On the apron near the aircraft to which he was assigned, each man checked his weapon, his rucksack, his squad or platoon gear. All of them realized that

134

this was not another training alert. "The night of 19 December," remembers Pfc. R. T. Anderson of B Company of 2/75, "people were nervous as to how the next night was going to be. They kept reconstructing their jobs in their heads to make sure nothing was to be left out. People prayed."

Lt. Kerry D. McCown, a platoon leader in C Company of the 2/75, wrote later, "On the evening of 19 December, just prior to loading the aircraft, we had a final manifest call over by the tents. We were freezing [he was at Lawson Field, Fort Benning, Georgia] and standing in slosh and mud. We [the officers] in the battalion had just received our final intel update and had received the very disturbing news that the Stealth bombers would not be dropping their two-thousand-pound bombs (at Río Hato), a report that brought confusion and anger to my ears with a taste suspicious of rotten politics [as it happened, the bombers did drop their bombs, but only to 'scare' the PDF]. Immediately following final manifest call, I knew I had to tell my platoon. It was then that I called them together, as did the other platoon leaders with their platoons. Attempting to control the emotion I was feeling, I informed my platoon of the news about the bombs. They looked at me rather shocked and there were questions of 'Why?' etc. I replied I didn't know and that we would just have to do the best we could. There was a silence when the air was broken by Staff Sergeant Shalala, one of my squad leaders. We were just about to leave and head for the birds when he yelled, 'It doesn't matter, men, it just doesn't matter. This is all you need!' With this gesture he held his weapon over his head, indicating the rifle was all we Rangers needed to accomplish the mission. The men yelled and we ran to catch up with the formation.

"That comment broke the ice and the fear. I will never forget it as long as I live. It was the only attitude we could have going into the unknown and he had said it perfectly."[2]

Some of the Rangers arrived at Benning not certain of their destination. Pfc. Richard Fox, B Company of 2/75 at Fort Lewis, remembered, "It was the seventeenth of December. We had just gotten off from a deployment to Florida. Everyone was out doing their postdeployment partying. Then came the call. It was around 1600 hours or so and I was one of the few people in the barracks. When everyone finally arrived at the barracks, they [the commanding officer] gave us a 'bunco' story that we were going to Fort Bliss, Texas.

"It was the morning of the eighteenth when we deployed to Grey Army Airfield [at Fort Lewis, Washington]. We were all standing around in this hangar full of jeeps when we noticed they were loaded to the hilt with live rounds. That's when everyone knew that we were going somewhere, but no one knew where, until that night. It was about midnight when they told us. Around 0230 I received the Op Order. Being in antitank, we were supposed to follow the platoon leader and blow apart a wall and any vehicle. But as you know, a plan is just an idea or format of what you are going to attempt to do.

"That morning we drew ammo, and I felt like a kid in a candy store. Then we got in chalk order and rigged for the jump."[3]

Specialist Steve Stadelman of 2/75 was also not entirely certain of the mission when he got to Fort Benning. "On the eighteenth of December," he wrote, "we were staying in a tent city at Lawson Field on Fort Benning. We had just been deployed there on short notice (alerted), and of course no one in the ranks of the privates knew what was going on, but it started looking very suspicious when I walked past a jeep fully loaded with ammunition, including antitank mines and LAWs.

"We received an Op Order that night and we were all shocked and surprised. After practicing and practicing for what seemed like forever, we were finally going to do it for real.

"On the nineteenth, we drew ammo early in the morning. As RTO (radio operator), I only drew three hundred rounds for my CAR-15, one LAW, and some smoke grenades. All I had in my rucksack was my radio, poncho and liner, spare socks, and my shaving kit. I think I was probably one of the lightest-loaded people to jump into Panama."

"Different soldiers have different missions, different weapons, and different loads to carry," according to the 75th Ranger Regiment's SOP (standard operating procedure). "Additionally, for some missions the company may need LAWs, demolitions, incendiary grenades, mines, etc.; however, not everyone needs to carry the same munitions, nor are the same numbers required for each mission. The fighting load is designed to distribute the munitions required by the entire company while at the same time compensating for the heavier loads carried by RTOs, medics, grenadiers, etc."[4] The SOP also prescribes

Uniform and equipment common to all: Rucksack; sling rope with 1/ snaplink, poncho, work gloves, 2 pr socks, shaving gear, 2 full 2 × quart canteens, 4 × MRE's (Meals, Ready to Eat), weapons cleaning kit, lightweight gortex top, headnet, insect repellant, E-tool, flashlight, air items, 2 × cravats, 2 × combat dressings, 1 abdominal dressing, PC. Uniform: K-pot, K-vest (for bike and jeep teams), HWBDUs, brown T-shirt, LCE per RSOP, protective masks, ID card, dog tags, jungle boots and socks, red chem light, and 1″ strip of IR tape on left upper arm and from right eye to left ear on Kevlar helmet. Elbow and knee pads are optional. Helmets will be covered IAW Regimental guidance for "rag head."[5]

"Based on an individual's duty position," wrote Colonel Kernan, "his rucksack and LCE (load-carrying equipment—used to distribute the weight of equipment on the pistol belt and wraps over the shoulders) would weigh between approximately 60 pounds and 100 pounds. Radio operators and mortarmen carried the heaviest loads, followed closely by medics and machine gunners and 90mm recoilless rifle crews. . . . The uniform and equipment breakout does not include special-purpose items (i.e., night-vision goggles, night scopes, and special operations equipment). Breaching teams also carried demolitions and cutting devices to breach obstacles/wire." In spite of reports to the contrary, the Rangers did wear their reserve parachutes. Colonel Kernan reasoned that even though a man with an emergency—a streamer or an inverted parachute—might not have time to pull his reserve at such a low altitude—five hundred feet drop height—he gained some confidence from the reserve and, in some circumstances, might possibly be able to use it.[6]

By the afternoon of the nineteenth, preparations for the 75th to drop on Río

Hato and Torrijos/Tocumen were complete. Before mounting the planes, the troopers had "loose-rigged" their equipment and their parachutes so that on the seven-hour flight to Panama the harnesses of their equipment would not be uncomfortable or so tight that they would numb their arms and legs. Nonetheless, for the sixty-four or so paratroopers jammed into the web seats along the bulkheads of the C-130's, and in two rows of canvas seats back to back down the center of the cargo compartment, "like sardines in a can," one trooper called it, the flight was not even close to "tourist" class on a commercial liner. The toilet facilities were somewhat primitive: A five-gallon water can passed up and down the aisles served the purpose.

One of the Rangers was somewhat skeptical of the use of the water cans as a makeshift portable latrine. "While on the C-130 ride to Panama," he wrote later, "we were told we'd have to use a five-gallon water can to urinate in. There I was an hour or two from the jump of my life and I wondered, 'Will these jugs ever be used again?' So I pulled out my trusty Swiss knife and etched the letters 'RGR' on the left side near the carrying handle. To this day whenever I see a five-gallon water can, I check for the coveted 'RGR.' "[7]

From Lawson, the 837 troopers of 2/75 and 3/75 minus C Company took off in thirteen C-130's with two C-130's carrying their heavy drop equipment— destination, Río Hato. From Hunter, 731 troopers from 1/75 and C/3/75 took off in four C-130's and seven C-141's, with five C-141's for their heavy drop—destination, Torrijos/Tocumen. The C-130's were from Col. Daniel E. Sowada's 317th TAW (Tactical Airlift Wing), based at Pope Air Force Base, and the 314th TAW from Little Rock Air Force Base, Arkansas.

These aircraft were not the first to depart the States for the operation. At 1650 on the nineteenth—eight hours, ten minutes prior to H-hour—five AC-130H's launched from Hurlburt Field, Florida. These aircraft, from Hurlburt's 1st Special Operations Wing, marked the first launch of the assault force of over 148 Special Operations Force missions that originated from the continental United States and transited through the "gap" between Cuba and the Yucatán peninsula en route to their targets and stations in Panama. Col. George A. Gray, the Air Force Special Operational Force commander in Panama, said that the flight to Panama was complicated because the unpressurized AC-130's are restricted to ten thousand feet and they do not have station-keeping equipment for IFR formation flying.

Other Army and Air Force planes were already on the ground before the operation took place. At Howard Air Force Base were two AC-130H aircraft and two SC-130A's. On 18 December, five Air Force MH-53J Pave Low helicopters from the 1st Special Operations Wing and three CH-47D helicopters from the Army's Task Force 160, based at Fort Campbell, Kentucky, and commanded by Col. Billy Miller, flew from Eglin Air Force Base, Florida, to Howard Air Force Base with HC-130 air refueling tankers. The rest of the 160th's aircraft—nine MH-6 helicopters, eleven AH-6 helicopter gunships, nineteen UH-60 Black Hawks, and two MH-47's—flew from Fort Campbell to Howard on the eighteenth and nineteenth in six Military Airlift Command C-5's.[8]

On the long flight to Panama, the Rangers had ample time to think about their personal situations. Lt. Tim Nye was a support platoon leader in the 2d of the

75th. He wrote later, "On the flight from Benning to Río Hato each Ranger was given almost seven hours to reflect on the course of his life. I, like every other Ranger in the battalion, was preoccupied with thoughts of the upcoming battle, what would happen, would I be afraid, would I perform, would I follow my instincts and training, and, of course, would I survive. My mind wandered to my old platoon, the 'Black Sheep,' in my opinion the finest fighting force in the battalion. I wanted to be with them, I wanted to lead them, I worried for them. I didn't worry about the men in the S-4 shop. I knew they'd be okay, partly because I knew our mission wasn't as dangerous and partly because I knew I could control my men to some degree.

"I thought of friends and family and special events in my life. My mind raced between my wife and my children and I felt guilty for thinking of them when I should have been focusing on the mission. Finally my mind rested on the date, December 19, 1989. The date was familiar. My grandmother's eightieth birthday. I had missed it. I knew she would be expecting a call. I knew my parents would be disappointed for my not calling her. I became very angry because now I had a new burden. I pictured my mother calling my wife, my wife not knowing for sure where I was, and my mother becoming emotional.

"As I stood up and hooked up, I kept thinking how I had wrecked my grandmother's birthday. As I exited I thought to myself,—'Oh, well, maybe I'll get a chance to make it up to her.'"[9]

Pfc. Leon Erickson was in the weapons squad of the 3d Platoon of B Company of the 2/75. "The lights [in the plane] were dim and we were all restless. We had just finished getting rigged and the aircraft's constant, unconsoling drone kept me awake contemplating my fate in the hours to come. We were aboard a C-130 flying into hostile country prepared to give our lives so that others might enjoy the many freedoms most Americans take for granted. Yet, we were going to war.

"We stood up six minutes to jump time. The doors were opened and the humid, tropic air of Panama quickly replaced the cool air conditioning. The time warnings came down and out the door we went. The bird was pitch black, not even a red light. I went out, did a poor exit, scared me a bit. Thought I was going to be towed. Chute opened. Saw and heard firefights on the ground. Some brave defenders were shooting us as we descended. Didn't have time to lower my ruck. Damn ruck twisted in the air. I was stuck on the ground, couldn't get out of my equipment for over a minute. Tracers were flying close by over my head in opposite directions for almost a minute. Never felt as relieved in my life as I did when I met up with a fellow Ranger and moved out to the AA [assembly area.]"[10]

"During the seven-hour C-130 flight into Río Hato, I found myself very mentally and physically exhausted," remembers Capt. John A. Davis. "The previous thirty-six hours had been a particularly stressful period of time because, as the 2d Ranger Battalion S-4, I was responsible for getting the unit (and all its mission equipment and ammunition) from home station to the REMAB at Fort Benning, coordinating for all supporting assets to feed, provide shelter and heat, transport, break down and issue ammunition, and provide aerial delivery equipment to the unit, all the while trying to get myself and my section prepared for the mission as well.

"The REMAB at Fort Benning was a 'tent city' located on Lawson Army Airfield, in the middle of a freezing rain. Since my battalion was alerted while at home station, it seemed like we were about twenty-four hours 'behind the power curve' compared to the rest of the Ranger regiment, which basically deployed on the mission from home station. Taking into account the weather, the crude living conditions at our REMAB, the intense and compressed time schedule, and the fact that our thirty-three pallets of ammunition arrived at Fort Benning on the last aircraft (a mere three hours remained for us to accomplish the time-consuming task of breaking it down and issuing it to our Rangers), the scene at Fort Benning during those precious hours prior to loading the mission aircraft were quite much like a nightmare running at fast-forward.

"Like so many other of the sixty-four fellow Rangers packed like sardines aboard that C-130, I tried to rest during the flight with very little success. We were rigged in our parachute harnesses the entire time, and comfort became a function of frequent minor body adjustments. Of course, the closer we approached H-hour, the tighter the knot grew in many a stomach. Word came over the radio that the Panamanians knew we were coming and positioned obstacles on the runway and V150 armored vehicles around the airfield. The knot grew tighter. Finally, the jumpmasters began their time warnings. It seemed that there was no turning back at this point, and for some strange reason, I think the stress level was reduced ever so slightly because at least we now knew that we were going to do it! . . . I'm sure that like so many others, those last few moments before jumping into the dark, tropical air were spent mentally rehearsing exactly how to get my weapon out of its container rapidly, extent my light antiarmor weapon, and get out of the parachute harness to fight off of the drop zone. It all happened very quickly from this point . . . green light, out the door, chute looks okay, the sound of antiaircraft fire and tracers on the ground, weapons ready to fire, parachutes and planes and tracers thick in the night sky, explosions nearby, find a buddy, then another, move quickly to the assembly area."[11]

"Everything was perfect," said Lieutenant Dichairo, weapons platoon leader in Charlie Company of 2/75. "There were sixty-nine men jam-packed into a C-130, one of many on its way to dethrone Noriega, burdened with their loads of ammunition and curiosity of combat. It was a thing of beauty to see the initiation of a combat mission. Everyone knew exactly what to do, where to go, and when to do it. There were no final plans or last-minute changes. The only thing left to do was wait and execute the mission. As we began the time warnings and jump commands (usually an adrenaline rush all by itself), I didn't see any fear on any Ranger's face. Just a bunch of American Airborne Rangers . . . on a one-way trip. . . . At twenty minutes out my RTO turned to me and told me that if he didn't 'make it,' I was to tell his wife that he loved her. I told him to do the same. What else could I say? We continued to close on our objective, Río Hato, when the troop doors finally opened and I felt the rush of hot, humid air. My eyes were locked onto the jump light and I could hear the humming of the device

I was standing next to that was designed to protect the aircraft from heat-seeking missiles. Everything was still perfect as the green light switched on, Rangers began exiting the C-130, and the sounds of machine-gun fire echoed from the drop zone below. . . ."[12]

Maj. Clyde M. Newman, executive officer of 2/75, found himself alone for a time after the drop. "After exiting the aircraft, I knew my stick was way north of the intended drop zone. I was having extreme difficulty in determining my exact location on the way down. Suddenly I saw a tree, a fence, a road, and highline wires—'Oh, shit, don't land on the road,' I told myself. I managed to miss the highline wire by two feet and the barbed-wire fence by one foot. I thought the worst was over, but suddenly remembered I had not seen anyone else in the air on the way down. Tracers and bullets were going off all around me. I now realized I was alone. What had gone wrong? I kept hearing the bullets whiz by as I was getting out of my harness. I looked to my right, 'Oh, s——, the dirt road,' What if a V-300 comes by now—I'm dead. I quickened my pace to get rid of the harness and ready myself for combat. Suddenly I heard a noise and could barely make out a silhouette of a person. Could it be the enemy? I froze, but the shadow kept coming toward me. What to do? Should I shoot or play dead? Neither. I challenged the intruder, 'Bulldog.' He replied, 'Bulldog.' I recognized the voice—it was my longtime friend and fellow Ranger Battalion XO from the 3d Ranger Battalion, Maj. Danny McKnight. I was a happy camper. God bless Ranger McKnight."[13]

Lt. Jeffrey A. Bouais's time in combat was short-lived. "It was twelve hours after TOT and here I was lying on a stretcher on a C-141 MEDEVAC flight heading for Fort Sam Houston, Texas," he wrote later. "It wasn't how I expected my first combat experience to end.

"The jump had gone well despite the tracers flying up at the aircraft. I didn't feel my fractured ankle until eight hours later. It is amazing what a little adrenaline will do to carry one through a situation. I made it to the mortar position. I was the weapons platoon leader, and started consolidating my people. We put the mortars into operation as the crew members arrived. We weren't used much that morning because it is hard to compete with the firepower of a Specter gunship. All I could do was sit back and hope my company was sweeping its objectives without taking casualties. The men around me were nervous yet displayed an unexpected composure, full of confidence. The sounds of the battle seemed to put each one in a unique type of trance. These Rangers wanted to fire their 60mm mortar rounds so badly. It hurt them to just sit there and pull rear security. When dawn came I tried to move around, but I couldn't put any weight on it. My mortar section leader, Staff Sergeant Nichols, carried me to the Bn. aid station. Halfway there he stumbled and without my ability to help the situation, we both went sprawling. This act hurt my ankle incredibly, but at the time I think my pride was the thing that was most affected. Here I was, in enemy territory, supposedly practicing stealth to avoid any further enemy contact, and I'm sprawled out on the airfield, with my section leader, totally helpless. We both laughed, of course, mostly to hide our embarrassment, but deep down we were both thinking, 'This is not what I expected combat to be like.'

140

"I was MEDEVACed and Staff Sergeant Nichols drove on and did an excellent job as acting platoon sergeant."[14]

Capt. William C. Doukas wondered about his abilities as the battalion surgeon of 2/75. "After exiting a C-130 into a tracer-filled sky," he remembered, "my biggest fear was not being killed, but taking care of wounded Rangers in an unfamiliar country with unfavorable conditions and supplies. I managed to make it to my assembly area near TOC 1 without getting shot, now burdened with the anxiety of receiving casualties. A part of me wanted to see no injuries, and a part of me wanted to see if all the training would pay off. So I lay prone in the TOC area planning the setup of the battalion aid station concerned about the nature and severity of injuries when the first one arrived limping on one leg, saying, 'Where is the goddamn TOC?' It was the battalion commander [Lt. Col. Alan H. Maestas]."[15]

*   *   *

During the planning stage before the operation, Colonel Kernan had, of course, laid out in detail the missions of each of his battalions at Río Hato and at Torrijos/Tocumen. Originally "Río Hato had not figured prominently in the original Blue Spoon operation order," according to an after-action report from U.S. Southern Command,

> but the quick response of the 6th and 7th Infantry companies to move to Noriega's aid during the October coup attempt indicated the base had to be attacked. With the targeting of the mech battalion [Task Force 4-6, the augmented 4th Battalion, 6th Infantry from the 5th Mechanized Division, Fort Polk, Louisiana] toward the Comandancia, a force of Rangers became available to target against Río Hato. The extreme loyalty displayed by the men of the two PDF infantry companies portended a tough fight. It was a good objective for the Rangers.[16]

The Río Hato airfield complex, a commercial and military facility, lies about sixty miles southwest of Panama City and is contiguous to the Gulf of Panama. The runway runs north-northwest from a point about a thousand yards inland from the gulf coast. Slightly to the west, between the shoreline and the southern tip of the runway, lie the barracks of the 6th and 7th PDF companies, the PDF headquarters, and the administrative areas. The NCO academy and the motor pool lie just to the west of the runway between the barracks of the 6th and 7th companies and the Pan-American Highway. The Pan-Americana Highway runs east and west at a right angle across the 4,380-foot-long Río Hato runway, cutting it almost in half. North of the highway on the west side was a suspected ammunition supply point; on the east side were *bohios,* recreational areas maintained by lightly armed PDF "caretakers."

Colonel Kernan elected to use five Ranger companies for the task of "taking down" Río Hato. He assigned Lt. Col. Alan Maestas and his 2/75 the mission of neutralizing the 6th and 7th PDF companies. He gave Lt. Col. Joseph F. Hunt and his 3/75(-) the mission of isolating the airfield, clearing the NCO academy, the camp headquarters, the communications center, motor pool, and the airfield operations complex and of severing the Pan-American Highway.

The PDF 6th Company, "Expeditionary," a mechanized infantry company, had about 220 men assigned; the PDF 7th Company, "Machos des Monte" ("Men of the Mountains"), an elite light infantry company, had some 200 men, all of whom were reportedly "fiercely loyal to Noriega." Both the 6th and 7th companies were so loyal and well trained that they were sometimes mistakenly thought to be part of Noriega's elite Battalion 2000. The 75th Rangers' intelligence officer, Maj. Richard Inokuchi, expected that as many as 250 students would be in the Military Institute (the NCO academy) barracks. He also estimated that the two companies, the 6th and the 7th, would be armed with at least forty-two machine guns, nine bazookas, four recoilless rifles, twenty-three mortars, nineteen vehicles, and three ZPUs. With these figures and the knowledge that the 6th and 7th companies were part of Noriega's "top-notch" forces, the 837 Rangers jumping on Río Hato knew that it would be more than a training exercise or a routine "pay" jump.[17]

During the preliminary planning, which involved among other tasks detailed study of aerial photos of the Río Hato airfield, Colonel Kernan recognized that his Rangers faced a "severe" threat at Río Hato: The barracks were very close to the drop zone, which was along the southwestern side of the airfield. And General Stiner had emphasized the "critical importance" of neutralizing Río Hato with minimum casualties. The solution: Bomb the barracks area prior to the drop, to keep the PDF away from the drop zone. How? Use the Air Force's new and previously untested-in-combat airplane, the F-117A. But where? Both General Downing and Col. "Buck" Kernan wanted to bomb the barracks to provide the Rangers jumping on Río Hato all the advantages possible. But General Stiner made the command decision to "offset" bomb an open area near the barracks but not the barracks themselves.

General Downing spoke positively about the need for bombing the barracks area. "Buck and I violently disagreed with General Stiner about the 'offset' bombing. We wanted to bomb the barracks. We argued with General Stiner about the psychological impact. From the Ranger point of view, these guys were going in there, jumping on top of that thing. I was more worried about that operation than any of them because . . . I was really afraid that they were going to set up the fifties. They had something like fifteen armored cars there with .50-calibers on them. They could have set them up on that airfield and that would really have gone bad for us. But they didn't. We achieved surprise. There's a psychological impact of jumping right on top of the enemy. You get a psych on a guy."[18]

General Stiner's decision was based on the need "to minimize collateral damage." According to Pentagon officials, who agreed with General Stiner, the purpose of the F-117A bombing operation was to "disorient, stun, and confuse" the PDF troops in Río Hato without hitting them. An Air Force official, speaking in general terms, said, "It was absolutely essential to hit that target. We needed that target to be PDF-free, and we needed to take it."

Precisely at 0100, two F-117A fighters flying from Nellis Air Force Base at Tonopah, Nevada, each dropped a two-thousand-pound bomb with time-delay fuses in a large open field near the airstrip and the barracks area at Río Hato. "Subsequent press reports," wrote Clayton H. Snedeker, the historian of the

142

Twenty-first Air Force, "indicated that one of the bombs missed its target by several hundred yards, much to the embarrassment of TAC and the USAF. That *faux pas* was compounded when Secretary Dick Cheney, operating from erroneous data, briefed the press that the F-117s had carried out their mission flawlessly."[19]

"Pentagon officials called the operation [the bombing by the F-117A's] a success," wrote John D. Morrocco in the 1 January 1990 edition of *Aviation Week & Space Technology.*

> An Air Force official said the noise of the explosions created considerable confusion among the Panamanian infantry who were seen "running around the area in their underwear" as the Rangers landed. . . . There were conflicting reports as to the rationale for employing the sophisticated aircraft, which cost nearly $50 million apiece, to conduct what appeared to be a simple operation. The F-117A was designed to penetrate radar and air defenses and perform single-aircraft attacks on high-priority targets behind enemy lines. An A-7 attack aircraft and AC-130 gunships provided air support for U.S. paratroopers and ground units attacking other military installations throughout the country during the invasion.
>
> An Air Force official said the Stealth fighters were used rather than other attack aircraft because of the uncertainties about Panamanian air defenses at Río Hato and what air support or warning might be made available to the Panamanians by Cuba. . . . According to a Panamanian pilot who routinely flies into Río Hato, as early as four months ago the only air defenses were a pair of aging small-caliber antiaircraft guns. But prior to the U.S. invasion, a Panama Defense Forces Boeing 727 transport had been making regular runs between Havana, Cuba, and Río Hato as well as Tocumen and David airfields in Panama. . . . Pentagon officials said, however, the F-117A's were used mainly because of their bombing accuracy, not their radar evasion capabilities. Defense Secretary Richard B. Cheney, who visited Río Hato on Dec. 25 and observed the craters left by the 2,000-lb. bombs, said, "The reason we used that particular weapon is because of its great accuracy."
>
> Defense Department officials said the United States needed such pinpoint accuracy to bomb a large field to create the maximum impact without destroying the barracks.[20]

One detects a tone of skepticism in the reports on the use of the F-117A on such an apparently "trivial" mission, reportedly missing its target by as much as 160 yards. The AC-130, for example, already in the area, is highly accurate with its 105mm door guns. Admittedly, a 105mm shell does not have the wallop nor the psychological impact of a two-thousand-pound bomb. The debate on the decision to use the F-117A in combat for the first time in Panama, dropping two-thousand-pound bombs inaccurately on an open field, will no doubt continue in aviation and military command circles. (The debate was over in 1991, given the F-117A's accuracy in Desert Shield and Desert Storm.) And, according to an Associated Press report, "The chief of the Tactical Air Command [Gen. Robert D. Russ] intensified training for Stealth fighter-bomber crews after learning that they had missed their targets in Panama, but did not pass the information on to the Pentagon, a spokesman said. . . . 'General Russ eventually knew that the aircraft had missed its targets, but not early on.' He said it was at least ten to fifteen days after the operation when the general found out. Russ 'made training decisions based on that information,' he said." The accuracy of and the rationale for using the F-117A on the Río Hato mission is subject to some debate; its deterrent effect on PDF soldiers in and around the nearby barracks is not.

Before the mission, the Air Force and Army commanders were deeply concerned about the location of the PDF's ZPUs, antiaircraft weapons. Through intelligence sources, the ZPUs "were positively located as the jump aircraft were being loaded," according to a 75th Regimental after-action report. "These locations were passed on to the USAF AC-130's for targeting as soon as the information was confirmed. The AC-130's reportedly received fire from these two confirmed operational positions; however, they were quickly snuffed. An additional six ZPUs were located in a small ammunition/weapons storage area on the north end of the runway."

Capt. Philip D. Colahan, gunship coordinator for the 75th, can attest to the accuracy of the AC-130. "While orbiting over Río Hato Airfield providing fire support for the airborne insertion," he wrote, "the AC-130 gunship came under direct fire from a ZSU-4 antiaircraft gun. After a minute or two of 'juking' about the sky, not unlike a bull trying to throw a cowboy, the pilot, Capt. Phil Lebrun, was overheard on the intercom to say, 'Boys, that's what's known as a PPPD—Piss-Poor Panamanian Decision.' Shortly thereafter, the ZSU was taken out of action by the gunship, which then prompted another member of the crew to remark, 'Well, that ought to get us membership in the VFW.' "[21]

Special Operations AC-130's and one Army Apache and two AH-6 helicopter gunships from the Army's 160th Task Force were orbiting at the Río Hato airfield before the drop and before the F-117A's arrived. The AC-130H can hit targets precisely with its 105mm howitzer or 40mm cannon while orbiting a target in a 30-degree bank turn at six thousand to ten thousand feet altitude. The plane uses a low-light-level television to aim and fire. Col. Billy Miller, commander of the 160th, explained that the AH-6 can move in on targets at night at low level using terrain masking. The helicopter has a low-level-noise signature. The pilot uses an Aviation Night Vision System 6 (ANVIS-6) goggle to fly low and spot targets.

A 160th Forward Area Rearming and Refueling Point (FARRP) team parachuted into Río Hato with the 75th to be ready to refuel and rearm the helicopters supporting the assault. Pallets containing ammunition, JP-5 fuel, and refueling equipment were also parachuted in. A second 160th FARRP arrived later in 160th Black Hawks, and a MC-130 Combat Talon arrived to provide a wet-wing refueling point.

For three minutes, starting at 0100 on the 20th, the AC-130 gunships and the AH-6's launched a preparatory firing on selected targets in the Río Hato complex. Then, at H-hour plus 3 minutes, 0103 hours, the lead C-130 flew in from the sea, on a flight course from south to north, and began dropping its paratroopers into the tropical blackness in an area along the western edge of the Río Hato runway. The remainder of the fifteen-plane C-130 serial, with aircraft in trail, followed at close intervals. After the troops made their exits, two C-130's heavy-dropped four pallets onto which had been lashed four jeeps and four motorcycles. For reconnaissance, the 75th had replaced the horse with the motorcycle.[22]

The first jumpers were from 2/75 because their targets were the barracks complex to the south, near the shoreline. Colonel Kernan's headquarters were to assemble about midfield, so his command and control team—some twenty-one men, including his S-2, Major Inokuchi, his operations officer, Major Scroggins, and a small security force—followed 2/75. Because 3/75's targets were to the north and its drop zone was across the Pan-American Highway to the north, that battalion was the last to exit.

Night landings by parachute can be relatively easy if the trooper is relaxed and lands on a level piece of ground. On the other hand, the landing can be fraught with some difficulty because, even on a full-moonlit night, the ground rushes up unexpectedly and with unseen hazards, especially if the jump is from five hundred feet above ground level—as it was at Río Hato. Pfc. John Price, a member of 2/75, was killed when his parachute malfunctioned.

Colonel Kernan found himself in some difficulty after jumping out of Plane 4 over Río Hato. Instead of landing in a smooth, often practiced PLF (parachute landing fall), he found himself suspended some ten feet off the ground, entangled in the fence surrounding the "Bull Ring." In addition, however, he had fallen through the power lines that provided electricity to some of the Río Hato buildings. Above his head, his parachute was in flames. Unintentionally, he had knocked out the power to the surrounding buildings—an unexpected advantage, as it turned out. In some haste, Colonel Kernan unloosened his harness and lowered himself to the ground.[23]

The drop at Río Hato was not without other difficulties. The PDF 6th and 7th companies apparently had been alerted to the jump and were out of their barracks and deployed onto and around the airfield. The Rangers began receiving fire from two ZPU-4's (12.7mm) and small arms mostly from the area near the south end of the runway. One Ranger was wounded by rifle fire before he hit the ground. True to General Downing's fears, thirteen of the fifteen C-130's received .50-caliber fire from the ground, but the pilots held a steady course in spite of the tracers rising toward them. General Downing said after drop: "They hit the right DZ. The 317th from here at Pope dropped the Rangers on target. They nailed that drop zone. That was as fine a jump as I have seen. . . . I went out the next morning. The chutes were still laying where the men left them so you could see exactly where they landed. They [the 317th] did a great job."[24]

After a seven-hour flight from the States and finding the precise location of a small drop zone in the dark without the use of Pathfinders already on the ground is no small navigational task. The C-130 crews were flown by SOLL II- and AWADS-qualified aircrews. SOLL stands for special operations low level, and the II means that the crews are capable of making blacked-out landings; AWADS stands for all-weather air delivery system and gives a pilot the ability to drop totally by instrumentation. In earlier days, combat jump planes were guided into the drop zones by radio-equipped pathfinders who had either jumped in earlier or had infiltrated cross-country, under cover of night, to the drop zone.

A few of the Rangers had more than ordinary difficulties on landing. S. Sgt. Richard J. Hoerner jumped from the twelfth C-130 over Río Hato. His jump was fairly routine until shortly after he hit the ground. "Upon making contact with the ground," he wrote later, "my parachute was still fully inflated due to the winds and I was sitting in the middle of a road. I popped one of my cable loop assemblies in an attempt to deflate my chute. I noticed an enemy vehicle coming down the road at a high rate of speed and coming straight at me. I then attempted to get my weapon (M-16) out of my M-1950 so I could engage the enemy. I couldn't unzip the zipper so I detached my M-1950 from my D-ring on my harness. At the same time the enemy on the vehicle [pickup truck] opened up at me with *full automatic AK-47 fire.* I rolled out of the way of the truck and it drove through my parachute. My chute got attached to the vehicle during the driver's attempt to kill me. The vehicle was going so fast it slammed me to my back and started to drag me down the road, going north near the cadet barracks. I was dragged for about a hundred feet before I could get control of my other cable loop assembly and pop it so I could fall free from the enemy truck. During the drag, I dropped my weapon, lost my Kevlar helmet, and ripped my LCE (load-carrying equipment) in half. I got up, recovered all my gear, and drove on to my platoon assembly area down at Obj Silver."[25]

General Downing was proved correct also in his estimate that the PDF had and would use armed and armored vehicles against the Rangers both in the air and on the drop zone. Some fifteen CG-150's, armored vehicles, were estimated to be located in the vicinity of the airfield. One Ranger remembered that "while trying to get out of my equipment, there was a vehicle going up and down the runway with an M-60 machine gun blazing; luckily, he was not accurate. Bullets were everywhere. A short while later two M-72 LAW rockets were fired toward the enemy vehicle and didn't miss."

The airfield control tower at Río Hato was near the center of the airstrip where Specialist Kristops of B Company, 2/75, landed. During his short descent to the drop zone, he could see several vehicles on the runway and in a nearby wood line firing on the descending troopers. After he got out of his parachute and "before moving out to link up with my fellow Ranger comrades," he wrote, "I engaged a vehicle with my M249 SAW, which was firing on our descending troops. The vehicle was quickly taken out by one of our men with a LAW.

"I quickly got my equipment together and proceeded toward the control tower. When I rounded the back side of the tower, I came across a fellow Ranger, Specialist Benchwall, who was tangled in some concertina wire and was receiving fire from the top floor of the tower. I shot up the top floor and quickly got him out of the wire. We moved to the right side of the tower where we came across a lieutenant who was injured. Specialist Benchwall was on the casualty evac team and took care of him. I linked up with Sergeant Brackenbury and we cleared the tower."[26]

After landing on the runway just outside the 7th Company's compound, Staff Sergeant Brackenbury joined up with three other members of his squad: Sergeant Rice, Sergeant Hadfield, and Specialist 4 Houlihan. The quartet started to move off toward the assembly area of B Company, 2/75. When they passed the control tower, they realized it had not yet been cleared. "They made a quick search of the surrounding area," Staff Sergeant Brackenbury wrote. "They noticed that the main entrance to the tower was locked, so Sergeant Rice shot it off. The small team then entered the tower with their weapons at the ready. They found a large stairway leading to the top of the tower. At the top of the stairs, they found a suspected member of the PDF speaking to them in a mixture of Spanish and English. After a series of threats by the Ranger team, the man surrendered. . . . Staff Sergeant Brackenbury and Sergeant Hadfield proceeded up the stairs, clearing each level. No other personnel were found. Sergeant Brackenbury ripped the phones out of the main control board and smashed a large window. He then placed three chem lights in the shattered frame, signaling that the tower was all clear. The team then left the tower and moved on with their prisoner to the assembly area to face even a larger objective."[27]

Capt. Steven G. Fogarty, S-2 of 2/75, regrets a prescient thought he had prior to the jump. "Prior to rigging," he wrote, "I walked over to Sergeant Nieman, the B Company senior medic who had been in my jumpmaster class a month before, and wished him good luck. I jokingly told him that he was the last person I wanted to see on the ground. He replied that if anything went wrong, he was the person I would have to see first. After breaking both ankles in the jump, I started to low-crawl off the drop zone. After crawling for several hundred meters, the Rangers moving south noticed me crawling. They walked up and asked: 'What the fuck are you crawling for?' I replied that I had both ankles broken. One of the Rangers moved to examine me and I realized that it was Sergeant Nieman. He put me on his shoulder and carried me to the airfield tower before he moved to his assembly area."[28]

After the jump, the Rangers gathered on the move toward their assembly areas. The troopers formed into their attack configuration, checked weapons and personnel, and made ready to move out toward their assigned objectives. Getting to Río Hato had not been easy; nor would its takedown be.

16 | Río Hato Takedown

Although the 317th TAW (Tactical Air Wing) dropped the paratroopers at Río Hato accurately, once on the ground the Rangers found some difficulty in assembling in the dark and moving on to their objectives, principally the barracks areas of the 6th and 7th companies, the Military Institute, and the administrative buildings around the airfield. The mission was not made easier when the Rangers found the PDF deployed both on the ground around the airfield and barracks and racing around the area in armored cars and other vehicles, firing indiscriminately, filling the air with red tracers.

First Sergeant Mattison of A Company, 3/75, discovered a couple of the vehicles as soon as he landed. He remembered that "There was sporadic automatic weapons fire coming from the vehicle as well as occasional small-arms fire going toward the vehicle from the airfield area. . . . While still in my harness and laying over my reserve parachute, I obtained my LAW from my M1950. I immediately put it into operation. While doing this, the vehicle pulled up in front of me and stopped. I completed putting my LAW into operation and engaged the truck. I was only about twenty-five meters from the truck when I hit it. . . . Moments later a Staff Sergeant Gibbons or Gibson from 75th RIP (Ranger Indoctrination Program at Fort Benning) linked up with me. We identified ourselves and I asked him if he had a LAW. He said 'Yes' and I told him to get it ready.

"While he was placing it into operation, a second vehicle came up the road at a high rate of speed. This second vehicle smashed into the rear of the truck I had previously engaged. There was a momentary pause and then the second vehicle shoved the truck off to the side of the road. I engaged the second vehicle with my rifle, firing about half of a magazine at it. The staff sergeant who linked up with me began to sight in his LAW. He missed and the second vehicle continued toward objective Green, which was only about 100 to 150 meters farther north. . . . All of this occurred at night and within the first appx. twenty

148

minutes after TOT time. Later, after daylight, I went back to the truck and searched it.

"The entire side (right) and rear of the truck was badly damaged. The rear right side of the cab was badly damaged and some windows were blown or broken out. The cab of the truck had expended AK-47 brass in it. . . . The truck had an official vehicle tag on the rear and hung up on the rear of the truck and drive shaft was a parachute canopy." First Sergeant Mattison had knocked out the truck that had dragged Staff Sergeant Hoerner a hundred or so yards along a road just after the jump.[1]

Capt. Jonathan L. Beegle was the fire support officer (FSO) with C Company, 2/75. He found himself in hectic action shortly after he landed. "There I was on Río Hato, 20 December 1989," he recalled. "After maybe forty-five minutes of excitement—of jumping, getting out of the harness, linking up, moving to the assembly area—I was established at our company CP, wheeling and dealing on the radios, nonstop commo—with the gunship, the attack helicopters, the other FSO's, the FOs (forward observers)—it was hectic. And then to his everlasting credit, Lt. Jim Larsen, the executive officer, leaned over to me in the dark and waved a freshly opened can of Copenhagen underneath my nose. 'Wanna dip?', he asked. What a stud; instant gratification."[2]

The PDF vehicles that raced about the airfield and adjacent roads with machine guns blazing and with PDF soldiers in the back of pickup trucks firing at random through the blackness of the night caused the Rangers a great deal of concern, if not widespread injuries. One trooper reported that "While trying to get out of my equipment, there was a vehicle going up and down the runway with an M-60 machine gun blazing; luckily he was not accurate. Bullets were everywhere. A short while later, two M72 LAW rockets were fired toward the enemy vehicle; they didn't miss. Once up and out of the equipment, we collected up friendlies and gathered a fighting force, which finally moved to the assembly area. Once there we organized ourselves into our teams and moved to mission posture."

The 3d of the 75th had the mission of assaulting the camp headquarters, the communications center, NCO academy barracks, motor pool, and severing the Pan-American Highway. Capt. Raymond A. "Tony" Thomas, West Point '80, commanded Company A of 3/75. One of the objectives in the middle of his company sector was the main gate at Río Hato. He described the gate as "looking like a rook—a chess piece." On top of the gate was a .50-caliber-machine-gun position. Shortly after the drop, Thomas's executive officer, Lt. Loren Ramos; S. Sgt. Wayne Newberry, his fire support NCO; and Specialist Oler formed a three-man team to "take out" the gate. By firing and maneuvering, the team knocked out the gun and killed two of the defending PDF soldiers. In the process, an armored vehicle "came rolling through the gate and almost ran over Ramos as he went through the gate, the castle," Thomas remembered. "The wheeled vehicle, a B-150, ran out the gate and up toward Penonomé. We later found it abandoned."

In another part of his company sector, Captain Thomas found an "unidentified school building. It was not supposed to be occupied," he recalled later. "We had taken fire from this area when we first landed, so we proceeded against it with fairly good caution. The lead squad went in literally doing building clearing but turned it off on a moment's notice when they discovered unarmed noncombatants in there. The squad found 150 to 200 cadets all huddled in underneath their bunk beds. There were no KIAs as a result."[3]

B Company, 2/75, had the 2/75th's main effort: assaulting the military compound housing the 6th and 7th PDF companies. Capt. Joseph Anderson, B Company commander, assigned the mission to his 3d Platoon, with the specific instructions to "breach the east wall, assault the first building, establish a foothold, and continue to assault assigned buildings in sector," according to Capt. David B. Haight, the AS-4 of the 2/75. "They completed all assigned missions by 1700 hours on 20 December 1989 and then started the arduous task of clearing a housing area to the west that contained many PDF soldiers that had run from the compound. These soldiers were taken prisoner and sent to the rear."[4]

The assault on the building compound had been well rehearsed beforehand. The preparation paid off. "Once we assembled in the assembly area," one of the B Company, 2/75, Rangers wrote later, "weapons squad of 2d Platoon was designated support for the main assault on the objectives Cat and Lion (the barracks of the 6th and 7th companies) in Río Hato.

"We were to establish support position Banana not later than H+50 minutes. We were to have four M-60 MGs, one sniper, and a support team leader, assistant support team leader, for a total of fifteen pax [persons]. At H+30 we had everyone except for the support team leader. We started our movement to the objective. The jungle was incredible, thick, coupled with very heavy rucks made it a long two hundred or so meters. The terrain was up and down, very difficult, but we managed. During the initial movement we lost one MG crew. They went back to the assembly area and just after we reached the 9mm pistol range, just about the halfway point, we broke contact with guns two and three, which left me with one gun. I didn't find this out until we were occupying Banana. I looked at my watch and decided to go with what we had. The time was H+46 and I needed to be set up at H+50. There simply wasn't enough time to go back and find them so now my position consisted of one M-60 MG, one sniper, assistant support team leader: five out of fifteen. We had started to place sporadic fire on objective Cat. We received some enemy fire; however, we suppressed it with M-60 and sniper fire.

"It seemed like eternity but the assault force finally attacked and we went to a cyclic rate of fire with all weapons systems to cover their maneuver to the first building. Then we were ordered to shift our fires. Later we were told we had effective fires on the obj."[5]

The ability of the Rangers to proceed with their missions with only a portion of their assigned strength assembled is exemplified by the actions of some of the troopers as they attacked the barracks buildings and motor pool area of Río Hato. Sergeant Greene was in the 1st Platoon of A Company 3/75. After he landed, he stayed in "the prone position to avoid being hit in harness. . . . I got my weapon from the case (an M-16A2 rifle with Litton night sight attached)," he wrote later, "loaded a magazine into weapon. Looking through sight I observed a pickup truck west of my position with several personnel in the back firing on drop zone. I engaged them with my rifle fire to suppress or kill them. They were traveling south to north at a high rate of speed with headlights on. After I fired about thirty rounds at vehicle, it turned off its lights and continued to come to my position. I had to stop firing at it because of friendly personnel landing in between me and it. Shortly thereafter someone made a direct hit with a LAWs rocket—this stopping it. . . .

"I grabbed my ruck, as I was in front of Objective Green just east of it, and linking up with a Ranger from 2d Battalion began moving to my objective Silver [an area near the southern end of the runway], south about six hundred meters. We still had a lot of small-arms fire all around us but with no cover it was determined by myself to move out. Also, 2d Battalion had to assemble to Silver's south to stop mechanized threat of reinforcement onto drop zone.

"I made it to Objective Dog, where the enemy fire was so concentrated that I decided to ground my rucksack, after securing my second LAWs rocket, observed from the prone my objective still three hundred south. I found Sgt. D. Smith, 2d Platoon A Company 3/75 at his assembly chokepoint to the east of Dog [a barracks complex]. I could see no enemy through my scope on Silver so I took the 2d Battalion personnel and moved out skirting the runway to come into Silver from the northeast to southwest. However, as I was moving to my objective, I became engaged by a sniper on control tower before 2d Battalion cleared it. I did not engage due to the fact friendly Rangers were at the bottom of it. I crawled about twenty-five meters. When I was not taking fire, I moved on at a rush to the approx. vicinity of Silver's chokepoint assembly.

"I observed a Ranger coming south from north. I waited to challenge him. It was Sergeant Hine, 1st Platoon, A Company, 3/75. We made linkup and made a decision to locate the chokepoint at that time. I got a red chem. light bundle out and marked it with such.

"About four minutes after waiting for sufficient personnel to attempt to take objective I heard a vehicle coming at a high rate of speed from south to north. I threw up my Litton and observed a black BM-300 armored vehicle. I fired at it across Sergeant Hine's front. Told him to get down from the sitting position. I fired about ten more rounds at it. It stopped after about two hundred meters and began firing back onto objective drop zone, obviously assuming the fire was coming from drop zone. It fired about two hundred rounds, then left, still headed north. I later learned that Specter gunships blasted it with 40mm cannon fire.

"Having observed one armored vehicle go by Silver, Sergeant Hine and I decided to attempt to take objective (a fuel resupply-motor pool) with only the one 2d Battalion Ranger, Sergeant Hine, and myself. We moved by wedge to the fuel tank northeast of the motor pool. The reason we opted to attempt [takedown] of objective was due to the fact a secondary objective was to block any armor movement north from 6th and 7th company AO [area of operations] to reinforce drop zone or escape.

"We got into position to lob grenades onto row of parked vehicles then rush to clear. Then do the same to the long motor pool. However, by that time, the platoon leader with about five additional Rangers linked up with us. He took charge of assault and we moved across to take objective. Platoon leader opted not to frag vehicles or buildings due to possible secondary explosion, that is, fuel tanks. We cleared vehicles without incident. As I entered building on east end, I looked through my Litton and observed an enemy person attempting to stealthfully leave motor pool to the west. He was carrying what appeared to be an AK-47. He was wearing a white T-shirt. I centered the aim point of my scope and fired a single round into center mass of his back. He went down as my scope whited out. . . .

"By that time, all Rangers cleared to my position inside of building (west end). We observed a building, south (behind) main motor pool and a building across road to the west.

"Staff Sergeant Anta located himself to my right on a knee, where he fired a LAWs rocket into building west, then an M-203 HE round. Then he fired an M-203 HE round into building south. He took a fire team and cleared building south, a barracks-type building. He fragged into building using SOP [standard operating procedure] for clearing such. And he, along with Sergeant Griffin, captured a prisoner who escaped injury by cowering in concrete shower stall. Building was then secure.

"Sergeant Hine and myself were then instructed to go to building west and clear it. Bounding and running while platoon minus covered us from motor pool, we swung to right of it and came in from backside. I fragged an open bay-type room. No enemy presence. Sergeant Hine then went to front of building and fragged inside room through M-203 hole made in the wall by Staff Sergeant Anta earlier. Room was secure by lock on outside. We opted not to blow door because of no possible enemy personnel inside.

"We then went back to motor pool, where a defense vehicular ambush was established."[6]

A Company of 2/75 had the mission of clearing the barracks of the Military Institute. Spc. Michael M. Sonnenschein wrote about his part in the operation. "Alerted. Everything smooth. Don't really think president has the balls to go through with the mission. Nine-hour flight in the harness. Thirty minutes out jumpmaster from 2d Battalion recites Ranger creed. He's very nervous and bones it up. Bird is very crowded and it's hard to maintain good static line control. Two minutes out the word is passed. Bombs away! Loud and thunderous hoorahs!

"Jump out and immediately see tracers from enemy fire. Land on another inflated chute right in the middle of the airstrip. Weapon is put into action and fire on moving vehicles already drawing fire on the highway. Hear a fellow Ranger asking for a medic twenty-five meters away. Help him out and leave knife to cut any restricting material from his body. Later found out he had broken femur. B Company further assisted him when they cleared runway. Ran to the chokepoint hoping to make linkup with any fellow Rangers. Linkup with approximately five plus the lieutenant.

"We (Sergeants Smith, Hyde, Reynols) breach fence and head for first objective (Dog). Support is set in [McDougal] and just when we are ready to prep, a V-300 drives down the road behind us with the airstrip on the far side. It hits a vehicle already taken out with a LAW and slows down a bit. I get my LAW extended about five seconds too late as the V-300 continues toward objective Green. Later find out it was fired on by small-arms fire only, as it sped through Green and hung a left. The 60s prepped Dog and I moved a fire team-sized element (Smith, Hyde, Reynols, myself) up to a chain link fence to make a breach. The breach was successful and we moved up to commo building to clear barracks. Bars were on all the windows as we (myself, Smith, D.) moved around perimeter shooting out lights above that were illuminating us. Threw a grenade in one room causing power to cut off. The room was a dead end. Backup power source kicked in.

"Went back to support for demolitions that finally made it to Dog by someone in 2d Squad. Objective was obviously cold and the platoon leader was instructed not to blow door down and to move on the next objective (Steel). Supposed to be empty school buildings for future PDF officers. Moved over to objective Steel and stopped short to plan attack on buildings because we (Smith, C., Howle, Harrison, myself) approached from a different angle. Proceeded with one fire team (1st Squad) up to building and found three vehicles. Harrison cleared vehicles. I reported and [was] told to move on after check. Heard voices and what sounded like a weapon dropping on concrete. Enemy troops running through courtyard and going into doors. Smith, C., and Harrison fired two M-203 rounds through back wall. Call for a Spanish-speaking friendly back at the platoon hault. Enemy is warned to come out with hands up and no harm will come. Three times the warning was yelled. Smith, C., and I proceeded to clear the building 'hot.' Smith threw a frag in the first room, followed by Smith and Harrison spraying rounds to clear. The enemy was under the bunks and came flying up, yelling, with hands in the air. Eight enemy were injured. Quick thinking and reaction prevented students from getting killed. Holton and myself went into the room next to the first one. It was occupied, and students were hiding and yelling. We entered the room. One of the students spoke English and we used him to call out 159 others. We went from room to room escorting him and using him as lead man. All were put face down with hands on head in courtyard. Searched the entire building and [it] was cleared. One PDF instructor from the jungle surrendered to Staff Sergeant Friar and myself. He had dropped his weapon and was also detained in the courtyard. All prisoners taken in groups of twenty-five down to Silver. All injured patched up."[7]

Sgt. David R. Clifton, C Company, 2/75, was guilty of AWOL in reverse. On the drop at Río Hato, he injured his arm and was MEDEVACed to Howard Air Force Base. He saw two doctors, who informed him that "the nerve endings in his left arm were separated from the wrist down." The doctor gave him some medication and told him to wait.

About an hour later, he remembers, "a major and a captain came and got me. They started to escort me toward a C-5 that was being loaded with other wounded men. I turned and asked the captain where the plane was going; they told me it was headed for Texas and that I was going home. They then asked me for my weapon and gear. At this point I realized that I would be leaving my team and platoon for good; this definitely did not appeal to me. I started slowing down and hesitating about giving up my gear. The captain left me to talk to another officer near the plane, and the major was talking to some other NCO.

"At this point, I decided it was time to get out of there. The area around the plane was crowded and fairly confusing, and it was dark, so I had little problem departing undetected. I made my way over to the operations center and found a Ranger officer. I told him I needed to get to Río Hato, and he started to ask me questions about where I had come from. I was the only person in the hangar in full combat gear. He told me to sit down and that he would see what he could do. I waited for about thirty minutes when I saw the medical corps major come into the hangar. I figured if he saw me I would be in big trouble, so I left the hangar. As I walked outside I saw an MH-53 starting to crank up. I walked up to the ramp and asked the crew chief where he was going. He replied, 'Río Hato, buddy.' I said, 'Great, that's where I need to be.' Nobody on the helicopter ever asked me a question. They landed at Río Hato the morning of the twenty-first and I got off. After catching another ride in a truck, I finally linked back up with my platoon. There was no way that I was going home while they were still there."[8]

Because the Rangers dropped into Río Hato by parachute and had few heavy drop planes available (the regiment had heavy-dropped only four jeeps and four motorcycles), they were short of vehicles for use in resupply and general transportation between units. With some ingenuity, a few of the Rangers solved at least part of the problem.

Lt. Brian M. Drinkwine was the executive officer of A Company of 2/75. "As morning came on 20 December 1989," he wrote later, "and the heat tab in the sky rose along with the humidity, we were soon to find that all but a few canteens of water had already been used during the night and we were dangerously low and needed resupply quickly to maintain combat-readiness. Through the resourcefulness of my two young buck sergeants, we located a water spigot near a trailer to fill canteens and they presented me with a resupply vehicle. The vehicle . . . was a brand-new cream-colored Mazda RX-7 equipped with sunroof, AC, and all the options, the ultimate resupply vehicle. We set about resupplying the forward platoons by shuttling five-gallon cans back and forth to the front. I drove with Sergeant Ghormley standing between the seats through the sunroof, M-60 machine gun posed at the ready to defend us as Sergeant Thornhill held on desperately to the water cans.

"As I drove across Río Hato compound on that historic morn, I pondered for a moment of great moments in history—General Washington crossing the Delaware in a rowboat; Napoleon riding into battle on his trusty steed; Rommel bounding across Africa in his desert half-track; and me cruising around Río Hato in my brand-new RX-7. I couldn't help but think that I had to go as far as combat to finally drive a new car instead of the rusty old jeep that I normally drive on a daily basis."[9]

The 2d Battalion had acquired another local vehicle, a red station wagon, for use as transportation among battalion headquarters, the companies, and regimental headquarters. The automobile had been abandoned near the NCO academy. Because of damage to the vehicle, however, it would move only in reverse. Capt. Edward B. Daly was the battalion's S-5. Out of necessity, he decided to drive the car as it was. According to one observer, Captain Daly "opened up the back hatch for better observation, put an orange VS-17 panel on the hood to identify the vehicle as 'friendly,' and knocked the glass windows out. He, Capt. Robert Bell, the signal officer, 1st Lt. David Morrison, the battalion S-2, and S. Sgt. James W. Redmore, fire support NCO, were tasked to search the kunda grass near the Río Hato airfield to find and recover lost communications equipment. They loaded into the vehicle and, driving in reverse with Captain Daly at the wheel looking over his shoulder as he drove, they headed off—in reverse—to the airfield. They stopped and First Lieutenant Morrison remained with the vehicle parked on the taxiway while the others went into the kunda grass.

"First Lieutenant Morrison was watching a parachute recovery detail on the airfield when a 'boom' was heard in the distance. A few seconds later, an explosion erupted about a hundred meters away from the work detail. First Lieutenant Morrison thought that a soldier had tripped a booby trap. He saw the Ranger fall to the ground. Then there was another 'boom' in the distance followed by another explosion. It was indirect fire. First Lieutenant Morrison yelled for the party to return. Once back in the vehicle, Captain Daly tried frantically to drive it forward. It wouldn't go. He then put it in reverse and raced off the airfield. Captain Bell and First Lieutenant Morrison were sitting 'point' in the back of the station wagon as the vehicle proceeded around the taxiway in reverse. Once off the airfield, they proceeded to the Ranger regimental head-quarters near the Pan American Highway to report the incident. When they drove up to the headquarters, Colonel Kernan, the Ranger regimental com-mander, happed to be outside and was laughing as they backed down the taxiway toward him. 'What ya doing, Daly?' Colonel Kernan said, laughing. Captain Daly replied, 'Oh, nothing much, sir, just driving the 'back' roads."

A few days later, one of the Rangers at the 2d Battalion CP checked the car out. He "disconnected the car's parking brake, and, according to Capt. Mike Newcomb, the battalion adjutant, "once again the car could be driven for-ward."[10]

At 0240, Lt. Col. Joseph F. Hunt, commander of 3/75, notified Colonel Kernan that his battalion had secured Objectives Dog and Steel, the NCO academy, and the motor pool north of the 6th and 7th company barracks area. At 0430, Lt. Col. Alan H. Maestas, commander of 2/75, reported to Colonel Kernan that he had secured Objective Cat, the barracks nearest the end of the Río Hato runway; at 0628, he reported that he had secured Objective Lion, the barracks next door. These objectives, the garrison of the 6th and 7th Rifle companies, were the main efforts in Río Hato and, with their neutralization, resistance thereafter was "very light and sporadic."

Even though the fighting at Río Hato was over in a relatively short time, the Rangers did not escape unscathed. One man was killed when his parachute malfunctioned, and thirty-five other Rangers were injured on the jump. Spc. Philip Lear was killed during the attack on the PDF barracks south of the airfield. And S. Sgt. Larry Barnard and Pfc. Roy Brown were killed while they were assaulting a sniper position halfway down the west side of the runway.

Some twenty-seven other Rangers were wounded in their attacks on the various PDF installations around the airfield. The PDF suffered 34 soldiers killed in the action; 278 PDF soldiers were taken prisoner.

One hour, fifty-three minutes after the Rangers jumped on Río Hato, the first U.S. aircraft, carrying company support items and command and control vehicles, landed on the runway. Río Hato was secure.[11]

17 | The Airport

At precisely 0100 hours on 20 December, the silence of the morning was shattered by the staccato fire of an AC-130 gunship firing at three .50-caliber machine guns and a ZPU-4 antiaircraft position in the compound of the PDF 2d Infantry Company at the PDF Tocumen Airport. The early-morning blackness was sliced through by the flashes of tracers from AH-6 attack helicopters firing at Tocumen's guard shack.

The Tocumen PDF military airport is part of the Torrijos International Airport complex. The runways of Torrijos and Tocumen are parallel but in prolongation of one another. The southwestern tip of Tocumen's runways is roughly adjacent to the northeastern tip of Torrijos' and about a half mile apart. The international terminal lies in this area between the two airfields. Torrijos/Tocumen (T/T) is about ten miles northeast of Panama City and connected to it by Highway 1, the Carretera-Pan American Highway. From T/T, the highway then moves fifteen or so miles to the east and northeast to the Fort Cimarron area and then swings in an arc to the southeast along the center spine of Panama, terminating at Yaviza, about forty miles from the border of Colombia.

Lt. Col. Robert W. Wagner was the commander of the 1st Battalion of the 75th Rangers, normally based at Hunter Army Airfield, Georgia. For the Torrijos/Tocumen phase of the operation, Colonel Kernan had attached to the 1st Battalion Capt. Alfred E. Dochnal's C Company of 3/75 Rangers that, on the 18th, had moved from Fort Benning to Hunter; combat control teams; elements of the 4th Psychological Operations Group, including loudspeaker teams; and two civil affairs teams from the 96th Civil Affairs Battalion. In precise, militarese language, Wagner's mission was to "conduct an airborne assault D-day H+0003 (200103R December 1989) to seize Omar Torrijos/Tocumen Airport and eliminate PDF in sector; to clear Tocumen Airport for airland operations; to be prepared to conduct battle-turnover to JTFSOUTH (Joint Task Force South, General Stiner's command); to be prepared to conduct follow-on combat operations as directed; and, on order, to redeploy to CONUS." In short, knock out T/T, take on some other missions, and return safely home.

Ready to thwart Colonel Wagner's plans to accomplish those missions were 200 soldiers of the PDF's 2d Rifle Company, 150 men of the FAP (Fuerza Aérea Panamena—Panamanian Air Force), and some 30 security guards at the airport. In today's modern military parlance, Colonel Wagner had certain "critical nodes" to neutralize, in this order of priority: the 2d Rifle Company barracks, the FAP barracks, the Torrijos/Tocumen terminal, the Ceremi Recreation Center (which, in the early-morning hours of the twentieth, would prove to be a far more important but more frustrating target than anyone had at first suspected), the Torrijos International Airport terminal, and FAP aircraft. He was also cautioned that within a forty-five-minute reaction time were 200 soldiers of Noriega's favorite battalion, Battalion 2000, armed with, among other weapons, twelve mortars and nine V-300's (lightly armored cars).

In his CP at Hunter before the operation, Colonel Wagner and his staff studied the maps and photos of the area; read and reread the intelligence data; developed a plan of attack; "ran it" by Colonel Kernan and General Downing; briefed the company commanders, including Dochnal, and checked and rechecked item after item. The company commanders, in turn, briefed their platoons in painstaking detail, including troop-leading procedures.[1]

At H+55 minutes, five C-141's from Hunter Army Airfield heavy-dropped pallets loaded with twelve jeeps, twelve motorcycles, and two HMMWVs on the drop zone at Tocumen. Fifteen minutes later, Colonel Wagner and the 1st of the 75th jumped from seven C-141's on Tocumen Airport while Captain Dochnal led his C Company of 3/75 from four C-130's from Hunter onto the tarmac around Omar Torrijos International Airport. A total of 732 Rangers jumped onto the two-airfield complex. "The Air Force dropped the Rangers precisely on target," wrote one of the 75th Ranger staff officers. "Most Rangers landed within a few meters of where they had planned to land on imagery studied during the planning phases of the operation."[2]

On the ground, the troopers unbuckled their parachute and equipment harnesses, put on their rucksacks, readied their weapons, ran to their assembly areas, and prepared to accomplish their assigned missions. They knew that accomplishing their missions as rapidly as possible was important for two reasons: (1) They did not know the status of the motorized Battalion 2000, just fifteen miles away, and (2) a brigade from the 82d Airborne Division was due to parachute onto Tocumen forty-five minutes after their jump.

"Ranger fire control was remarkably disciplined," continued the Ranger staff officer, "as civilian (automobile) traffic continued well into the assault (one hour) with people using the perimeter road to escape the fighting. Ranger command and control elements were assembled in twenty to twenty-five minutes and operational in thirty to thirty-five minutes. In fact, an after-action comment made by many Rangers was that the assault went down by the numbers like the rehearsal they had conducted only one week earlier."[3]

The initial firing by the Specter gunship and the attack helicopters at H-hour on the twentieth was apparently Noriega's first indication that an attack on his country was under way. On the evening of the nineteenth, Noriega had left Colón, the port city on the Atlantic side of the canal, and had planned to spend the night with one of his female "companions" at Ceremi, a PDF military recreation center in the La Siesta Military Resort Hotel near the entrance to the Tocumen side of the airport complex.

"During this time (one to two hours before the drop) most PDF officers did not believe that the United States would actually initiate an invasion," a 75th Ranger after-action report concluded.

> though due to the killing of Marine lieutenant Paz on the sixteenth, the entire PDF was at a heightened state of alert. At 0100 an AC-130 gunship and two attack helicopters conducted preparatory fires on selected targets at the airfield. The PDF initially deployed two to four men in the ten known guard and machine-gun positions, a platoon-size element (approximately twenty-five militia men) of Dignity Battalion personnel (led by the 2d Rifle Company first sergeant) at Torrijos International Airport terminal and about thirty troops around the FAP area and military terminal. About thirty PDF and FAP soldiers tried to shoot down the two attack helicopters as they attacked the FAP communications and arms room buildings. The AC-130 fires destroyed the horseshoe-shaped 2d Rifle Company barracks. These prep fires had a significant effect on the PDF soldiers, causing the majority of the 2d Rifle Company and FAP defenders to run away. Three of the four machine-gun positions were suppressed by the attack helicopters.[4]

Noriega had received an earlier warning that U.S. aircraft were approaching, but, according to the after-action report,

> he did not regard the report as accurate. Once the planes roared overhead and the fighting started, he quickly fled his room (and concubine) and drove west toward the city on the road between Tocumen and Torrijos. Two PDF guards from the western gate of this road ran past him without their weapons. Approximately one kilometer to the west, the AC-130 destroyed a Dignity Battalion car at the entrance to Torrijos with a 105mm round. Noriega had his driver turn the lights off his car and escaped to the northeast into Tocumen. Noriega had come within three hundred meters of the advancing Rangers from C 3/75 and B 1/75.[5]

In his precipitate rush out of the rec center, Noriega left behind his briefcase, wallet, and uniform. No follow-up reports indicate with any certainty the disposition of his partner for the evening. Noriega's departure, although this time under pressure, was not unusual: For personal security reasons, he was in the habit of changing locales several times per night and had a number of luxuriously furnished and amply stocked beachhouses and mansions scattered around the isthmus for his exclusive and impulsive use. Other indications of his apparent paranoia were the facts that he had, in recent months, "taken to the bottle," occasionally drinking himself into a stupor, and that he refused to eat anything not prepared by the mother of his girlfriend Vicky Amado.

159

A number of PDF helicopter pilots were in a barracks near Tocumen at the time of the Rangers' jump. One of them, Raul Alberto Reyes, had heard the fires of the C-130 gunships. He looked out of the second-story window of one of Tocumen's BOQs into the darkness and saw, dimly, the Rangers parachuting quietly onto the tarmac. To no one in particular he said: "This does not look good." Goaded by that accurate summary of the situation, he and about forty of the pilots took off for the hills outside Tocumen. Five days later, on Christmas Day, the pilots came back into the airport complex and surrendered at Torrijos. While they were being interrogated, one of the American interpreters noted that Reyes spoke superb English. The interpreter asked him where he had acquired his unusual fluency. Reyes said, somewhat matter-of-factly, that he was a 1983 graduate of the U.S. Military Academy at West Point and that he had taken his flight training at Fort Rucker, Alabama.[6]

Captain Dochnal's mission was to isolate Objective Bear, the international airport terminal, eliminate enemy resistance, and prevent any interference with the follow-on operations. The troopers from Chalk numbers 13, 14, and 16, C-130's, landed on the runway of Torrijos International Airport while those from Chalk 15 landed in the kunda grass (elephant grass—ten feet high and razor-sharp) west of the runway, a minor deviation from the drop plan that slowed the company's assembly. Nonetheless, Dochnal regrouped his men and moved them quickly toward their assault objective.

Preliminary intelligence had estimated that there would be very few people in the terminal at 0100 hours. But, in fact, an international flight from Brazil had just landed. The passengers were in the process of off-loading and watched with some interest and trepidation as the parachuting men of C 3/75 landed all around their aircraft and the international terminal. The terminal shortly became fully operational, with almost four hundred civilians milling about the concourse. By this time the PDF and the airport security force were on general alert and patrolling in and around the area.

To "isolate" the international airport terminal, Dochnal had decided to move in on it from three sides: the 1st Platoon from the west, the 2d Platoon from the south, and the 3d Platoon from the north, with the weapons platoon setting up to support the three rifle platoons from a position on the infield a hundred meters east of the terminal. The plan was sound, but its execution was fraught with some difficulties—not totally unexpected.

About fifteen minutes after the jump, Lt. Mike Franck had assembled two squads from his 1st Platoon at a chokepoint south of the terminal. The 3d Squad joined up shortly thereafter. Franck's plan was to move to "battle position two," the entrance to Omar Torrijos International Airport. En route, the platoon moved to one of its preliminary objectives, a building used as a restaurant, south of the terminal. Franck assigned the 1st Squad the mission of clearing the building. The squad scaled a chain link fence surrounding the building and moved up next to one of the restaurant doors. The squad leader could see that there were only civilians inside. He called for one of his bilingual, Spanish-speaking men to tell the workers inside to open the doors and surrender and no one would be hurt. The workers followed the instructions. The squad members detained and "flexcuffed" eighteen civilian "detainees." (A "flexcuff" is a ⅜-inch plastic cord device about 24 inches long, one end of which passes through a metal device on the other end. When the knot is pulled tight around a person's wrists, it cannot be undone except by cutting. Flexcuffs are used instead of handcuffs when a number of people need to be temporarily incapacitated.) The squad then systematically cleared the building without fire or casualties.

Lieutenant Franck left his 3d Squad to secure the restaurant. He moved the 2d Squad, under Sergeant First Class Beam, toward the entrance to the international airport. To get there, the squad had to cut through two chain link fences. Once through, the squad found a guard shack, near the terminal entrance, with PDF soldiers' bodies strewn about. Fire from the Specter and the AH-60's had killed them. The 2d Squad cleared the guard shack and so marked it. Meanwhile, Lieutenant Franck and his 3d Squad moved to the west side of the main terminal and set up an observation post to "overwatch the terminal and its parking lot."

Captain Dochnal then ordered the 1st Platoon to enter the main terminal and establish an EPW (enemy prisoner of war) collection point on the second floor. The 1st Squad collected the original eighteen detainees plus thirty more from the Avis rental car facility and moved them to the civilian detainee point. The 2d and 3d squads also escorted another forty civilians to the EPW point. Lieutenant Franck's platoon controlled all of the civilians and EPWs found at the airport. Eventually the platoon gathered some 398 civilians and 21 EPWs.

Lt. J. Kashouty and his 2d Platoon had more than its share of difficulties— some unusual. One Ranger remembered that "On 20 December 89 at approximately 0200 hours, the 3d Squad proceeded to move across to the airport concourse. There was an Eastern airliner parked with the tailgate down that had had the lights on earlier. Sergeant Anderson, my squad leader, sent me, the Bravo Team leader, into the airliner to clear it. I took Private First Class Lopez with me and we went up the tailgate to clear the inside of the jet, which was pitch black inside. The front side door was closed and the airliner was empty. The 3d Squad then proceeded to go into the bottom floor of the concourse. We didn't find any personnel on the bottom floor so we proceeded to the main terminal."

The 2d Platoon entered the terminal from the south, with one squad going to each of the three floors. On the third floor, the 1st Squad came under fire. The squad chased the PDF soldiers into the airport security office, where they began to burn papers. The 3d Squad leader ordered the PDF soldiers to surrender. But the PDF were still belligerent. They responded to the order to surrender by firing at the 3d Squad Rangers. Then one of the Rangers from the 3d Squad threw in a grenade and waited for the PDF to acknowledge that they had had enough. That did not happen. When the office began to burn, the squad entered the room and tried to put out the fire. Fortunately, the sprinkler system came on and contained the fire. The squad then cleared the rest of the third floor.

On the first floor, after moving to the main terminal, Sergeant Anderson split his squad into two teams. The Bravo team leader recalled that "Sergeant Anderson took Alpha Team to the left and I took Bravo Team to the right. All the doors we checked were locked and we were told not to bust or blow them down. I moved down a hallway and found some steel double doors that were unlocked. I opened one of them and moved inside. It was dark but the PDF must have heard the door open because they started firing at me. My first reaction was to get low and return fire but some women started screaming in English not to shoot. I went back out the door and found Sergeant Anderson and told him of the situation. Sergeant Anderson sent the Psyop man to the hallway with me and then called the platoon leader to tell him of the situation. The Psyop man tried to talk them out but the PDF said they would kill the hostages if we came in. Sergeant Anderson left me and Private First Class Lopez and the Psyop man there while he took Alpha Team to clear the rest of the floor. Sergeant Anderson also was trying to find another entrance to the baggage claim area. I found out that there were at least two American female hostages and an infant baby among the hostages. The Psyop man told me that there were only one or two men holding the hostages. He asked me if I could go inside and take out the PDF guys and I told him that I probably could. I crept up on three of the PDF in the darkness but couldn't fire at them because I didn't see the hostages. . . ."

The electric power in the terminal had been cut off when Staff Sergeant Borja of the 3d Platoon had thrown a grenade into the power shack.

Once he became aware of the situation, Lieutenant Kashouty quickly had his squads isolate the area and sent for Captain Dochnal. When he arrived, Kashouty briefed him and told him that the airport security manager, a colonel in the security forces, anti-Noriega and very "pro-American," was willing to help to secure the release of the hostages. All Kashouty knew was that there were at least two American women detained by an unknown number of PDF in civilian clothes. One PDF soldier leaned out the door and fired in the direction of Sergeant Smith. He had gotten Sergeant Smith's attention. Smith jumped over the customs inspection counter and landed on top of one armed PDF soldier hiding behind the counter. Sergeant Smith quickly subdued that soldier without a fight.

To find out what was happening in the room, Sgt. Brad Beauchamp took off all of his equipment except his night vision goggles and, carrying a CAR-15, very quietly went into the blacked-out office. He could see the hostages and the PDF, but they could not see him. Beauchamp estimated that there were at least twelve PDF holding two American young ladies and one woman, apparently a Panamanian, with a baby. The American ladies were bilingual and kept screaming at the Rangers to leave the area so they would not be killed.

Beauchamp backed out of the room, and the security colonel tried to negotiate with the ringleaders of the PDF. Captain Dochnal used Specialist 4 Pagan, a Spanish-speaking Ranger, to ensure that there was no trickery in the shouted negotiations. After two hours of shouting back and forth, Dochnal lost his patience. He told the security officer to tell the PDF holding the hostages that if they didn't come out now, he would have them killed. That broke the ice, and the PDF put down their weapons and walked out. Dochnal's men discovered that the ringleader of the group was a Cuban, Bernardo Magesta, who had a diplomatic passport. The leader of the PDF was 1st Sgt. Luis A. Santos of the PDF 2d Rifle Company. In all, there were twelve PDF and

Magesta in the room with the hostages. The surrender of this group meant that the terminal was now completely cleared and secure.

Previously, on the north side of the airport, moving toward the terminal, the 3d Platoon, under Lt. Mark Gibbons, seized a fire station, where it captured about fifteen firemen. Then, as the platoon approached the terminal, two PDF soldiers in the terminal fired at the platoon through a glass window. The platoon rushed into the terminal and isolated the PDF in the latrine. What followed thereafter was, according to General Downing, who spoke later to one of the sergeants involved, "close quarters combat."[7]

Sergeant Reeves and Private First Class Farber followed the PDF into the men's room. One of the PDF in the first stall to the left of the door fired and hit Sergeant Reeves with three rounds. He fell to the floor, wounded. The PDF soldier stepped over Sergeant Reeves's body and started to "finish him off." Farber tried to fire, but his weapon malfunctioned. The two PDF soldiers moved to the far end of the latrine around the bank of washstands. Farber got out of the room and reported to Specialist Eubanks. Then Eubanks, Private First Class Kelley, and Sergeant Thorland went back into the latrine after throwing in two grenades that were ineffective because the blast went out the windows and destroyed only the porcelain sinks. Eubanks and Thorland pulled security while Kelley extracted Reeves. While Kelley was pulling Sergeant Reeves out of the door of the latrine, one of the PDF soldiers at the far end of the latrine shot Kelley three times in the back of the head with an FAL, a Belgian rifle similar to the M-16. But Kelley's Kevlar helmet saved him, and he was not injured. Outside the door, Reeves gave a "salute report" as Sergeant Thorland gave him first aid. Specialist Eubanks and Private First Class Kelley went back into the latrine and crouched down inside, Eubanks on the right and Kelley to the left front. Eubanks tried to fire his SAW, but the barrel dropped off because the locking lever was not fastened. He dropped his weapon and grabbed Sergeant Reeves's M-16 off the floor. One PDF soldier peeked out from behind the last stall at the far end of the latrine. That was all that Eubanks needed. With one accurately aimed round, Eubanks shot the man in the neck. Eubanks moved toward the wounded soldier to "secure" him. When he got near him, another PDF soldier leaped from a stall and wrestled Eubanks for his weapon. Eubanks backed him up against the wall.

According to General Downing, "They got into a fistfight. This private [Private First Class Kelley] who had been in the battalion nine months is trying to help his fire team leader. He backs up, leans over his shoulder, and shoots the PDF guy in the head at point-blank range. Simultaneously, another enemy soldier entered into the action. Private First Class Kelley kicked the PDF soldier through the window, and he lands right at the feet of another Ranger (Private First Class McKinney) lying out there in the prone position behind his M-16. He had no idea that the fight in the men's room had been going on." The PDF soldier who landed near McKinney attempted to draw a pistol; Private First Class McKinney killed him with the M-16.[8]

Two and a half hours after the jump at Torrijos/Tocumen, the terminal and the airports were neutralized. In the terminal, the Rangers separated the detainees and the prisoners and flexcuffed the EPWs. The Rangers guarded the

EPWs closely and simply had the detainees sit down in the terminal and "remain calm." After a few hours, some ten children, ages six months to ten years, became hungry. The Rangers arranged with the restaurant manager for food and paid for it with their own funds.

In the assault on the terminal, Captain Dochnal's company had killed five PDF soldiers and had collected 21 prisoners and 398 civilian detainees. No civilians had been killed or injured. With the surrender of the PDF holding the hostages, Captain Dochnal and his C Company of the 3d Battalion, 75th Rangers, had completed their mission—Objective Bear had been neutralized.

While Captain Dochnal and his company were clearing out the international airport terminal at Torrijos, Colonel Wagner and his 1/75 were operating along the flanks of the Tocumen runway. The PDF had fired very few shots at the jump planes or the Rangers in the air, but once on the ground and getting out of their harnesses, some ten or twelve PDF defending the old Tocumen military terminal "placed accurate fire onto the 1/75."

Colonel Wagner's main objectives at Tocumen were Tiger, the housing area of the FAP assigned to the airfield, and Pig, the old Tocumen multistoried military terminal and the H-shaped barracks of the 2d Rifle Company. Tiger and Pig were both at the northeastern end of the runway. The 75th's after-action report states,

> A small amount of rifle and light machine gun (squad size) came from objective Tiger (FAP area), the north end of military runway (northwest of Objective Tiger), numerous fleeing vehicles and Objective Pig. . . . Two PDF soldiers fired their rifles (AK-47's and M-16's) from the military fire house south of Objective Pig. Approximately ten to twelve PDF defended the . . . old Tocumen military terminal. . . . Neither runway was blocked. During the initial minutes of the assault, several cars and light trucks escaped to the northwest into the town of Tocumen (which bordered the west flank of the Tocumen runway). The PDF soldiers in the cars were firing pistols and rifles at the Rangers as they descended on the north end of the runway. One truck tried to escape to the south along the taxiway and ran into the bulk of C Company 1/75. During the ensuing firefight, Pfc. James Markwell, a medic, was killed in front of the military terminal, the only American fatality at TT2. Four PDF machine-gun positions (three MAG-58's and one .50-caliber) were found abandoned with their ammo belts fed into the machine guns.

At 0208, the first planes carrying the 82d Airborne Division troopers arrived over Torrijos/Tocumen and began dropping the paratroopers just to the east of the intended drop zones.

Just after 0245, Captain Allyn and his C Company of 1/75 had isolated Objective Pig. The PDF were not firing from it, but some remained in the building. Some 82d Airborne Division soldiers were, by this time, moving between buildings. At 0612 Captain Allyn reported that Pig was clear and that two PDF had been killed and ten captured.

At 0255 Captain Ritter and his A Company of 1/75 had isolated Objective Tiger against light resistance. In the firefight to take the area, two PDF were killed and twenty-four captured. At 0520 Colonel Wagner confirmed that the Tocumen runway was clear.

At 0300 the 75th made a radio linkup with the 82d on the 82d's command FM net.[9]

Captain Mathey and his B Company of 1/75 had had the mission of isolating Objective Hawk, a gasoline dump just to the east of the military terminal. At 0515 he reported that he had isolated the area against very light resistance—some sporadic rifle fire at his company while it was en route to the area. Mathey elected not to assault the objective because there were "numerous Panamanian civilians in the area and no PDF or resistance coming from it."

"At 0458," reported the 75th's journal, "the second 82d drop occurs. Air Force still dropped paratroopers too far east into the swamp."

At 0612 the regimental journal reported that all Torrijos/Tocumen objectives had been secured and all battle positions occupied with no further resistance. At 0650 Captain Dochnal reported that the hostage situation in the terminal had been resolved with the surrender of the last PDF defenders in the terminal.

Again from the journal, "0800—82d Abn third pass drops (Air Force places them on the runway this time.)" The journal continues:

- 0745—JSOTF CDR orders 1 Co of Rangers to be attached to TF Gator to clear La Comandancia. RCO radios DCO Frago (Fragmentary Order) for C Co 3/75 to conduct the mission.
- 0900—Ranger liaison officer to 82d Abn conducts linkup with Team Gold [75th's executive officer in command of forces at Torrijos/Tocumen] at Torrijos International Airport.
- 1000—82d Abn MPs and CA [civil affairs] elements take charge of POWs and civilian detainees.
- 1030—82d personnel begin to relieve C Co 3/75 from security positions on perimeter around Torrijos IAP.
- 1100—1/75 BPs around perimeter of Tocumen report Panamanian civilians beginning to come out of homes and talk to Rangers. Most seem friendly and anti-Noriega.
- 1115—82d elements in PZ posture for follow-on air assaults into Tinijitas and Cimarron.
- 1130—82d troops begin to expand perimeter around Torrijos IAP.
- 1200—C141's and C5A's begin to land at both TT2 airfields bringing in follow-on 82d Abn and 7th ID forces.
- 1330—C Co 3/75 is picked up by two CH-47's and one HH-53. They are lifted to Fort Amador for their mission to clear La Comandancia.[10]

In the operation at Torrijos/Tocumen, the 75th Rangers suffered 1 man killed in action and 5 wounded. Of the 750 Rangers who jumped on the international airport, 19 were injured in the jump. The PDF lost 13 men killed in action and 4 PDF officers, and 50 men were held as prisoners of war. Some 376 civilians were detained during the operation.

At Torrijos/Tocumen, the Rangers rounded up 384 rifles (mostly M-16's and

T-55's), 3 .50-caliber machine guns, 10 light machine guns, 5 75mm recoilless rifles, 110 pistols, 1 4.2″ mortar, 150 CS grenades, 1 million rounds of 7.62-caliber rounds, 12 Huey helicopters, and 13 fixed-wing aircraft.

With the collection of the weapons and ammunition, the Torrijos/Tocumen phase of Operation Just Cause was over. At 1000 on the twenty-first, A Company of 1/75 was airlifted by two CH-47's into Paitilla Airfield to relieve the SEALs who had seized it the night before. And on the afternoon of the twenty-first, to emphasize that Torrijos/Tocumen was in U.S. hands, several anti-Noriega Panamanians reported to the Rangers patrolling the area the location of weapons caches of the Dignity Battalions and PDF personnel.

18 | Task Force Pacific

On the afternoon and evening of Tuesday, 19 December, the weather at Fort Bragg and the adjacent Pope Air Force Base was North Carolina "winter miserable." The temperature was about thirty degrees, with the wind-chill factor much lower, the clouds hung low and dark, and a wind-blasted icy sleet storm covered the roads and land with a slick patina of ice. In the words of Col. G. A. Crocker, the 82d Airborne Division's chief of staff, "It was the worst North Carolina ice storm in fifty years." The aircraft parked at Green Ramp at Pope, ready to load the troopers of the 82d, were also being covered with a thickening layer of ice. And, unfortunately, Pope Air Force Base, in theoretically "mild" North Carolina, had few "deicers" available.[1]

By 2055 that evening, the ice problem was so bad that Gen. James Johnson, the 82d's commanding general, called General Stiner in Panama and requested that he delay H-hour by one hour so that the deicers could have more time to do their work. At 2208 word came back to Pope that General Johnson's request was denied—in effect, said General Stiner, do everything possible to take off as planned. The wing commander at Pope, Col. Daniel "Stump" Sawada, then recommended to General Johnson that the ten aircraft he thought he could deice on time depart on schedule and that the ten remaining depart as soon as they were deiced to catch up with the first aircraft en route to Panama.

Capt. Gary J. Ramsdell, twenty-eight, West Point '84, commanded C Company of the 2d of the 504th, part of Col. Jack Nix's (DRB) Division Ready Brigade on the eighteenth of December. The commander of the 2d of the 504th was Lt. Col. Harry Axson, a large "bear" of a man and, like so many large men, with a jovial sense of humor, an outgoing personality, and a self-confidence to match his physique. His figure was much like that of a four-star general who would win so much acclaim internationally in the United States' next war—Gen. "Stormin' Norman" Schwarzkopf. Admittedly, Axson was taller and less stocky than the commander of all the Allied forces in the Persian Gulf.

167

At 0915 on the eighteenth, Colonel Axson called his company commanders to his battalion headquarters and announced to them that N-hour was 0900. "Just another EDRE," thought Captain Ramsdell. EDREs (emergency deployment readiness exercises) were a way of life for the "always ready" 82d. In "normal" times, the division commander ordered a surprise EDRE for some unit in the division about every month. Thus Ramsdell and his company had taken part in one every six months or so as part of a one- or two-battalion jump into Fort Stewart, Georgia, for example, or Avon Park, Florida, Camp Mackall, North Carolina, or on one of the spacious drop zones at Fort Bragg itself. The EDRE tested a parachute unit's ability to deploy in eighteen hours from barracks to "wheels up" on the first aircraft taking off from Pope.[2]

"At 1100 hours, the N+2 brief was held at division headquarters for the division-ready brigade and other selected division elements," according to the division's historical summary.

Due to OPSEC (operational security) considerations, only brigade-level commanders were briefed that this no-notice EDRE was actually a cover for the execution of OPLAN 2-90.

At 1400 hours, the Division Assault CP (command post) occupied the PHA and continued planning and preparation for the EDRE. At approximately 1500 hours, the division assault CP was alerted to begin preparing for combat operations in Panama IAW 82d Div OPLAN 2-90. The DRB occupied the PHA and conducted rehearsals IAW the OPLAN. Rigging of HD (Heavy Drop) items continued throughout the day in order to prepare the 28 C-141 HD package for forward staging at Charleston AFB, SC.[3]

After the 0915 meeting with his battalion commander, Ramsdell went back to his company CP in the barracks area, alerted his men, went through a long checklist for an EDRE, and, by 1300, had moved his company in 2½-ton trucks from its barracks to the PHA. His men drew ammunition, extra water containers, mosquito repellent, sunscreen, and other necessities from the corps marshaling area, test-fired their weapons, and drew rations—MREs (meals ready to eat). (After months living on MREs in Saudi Arabia, some of these same 82d troopers, deployed there a few days after Saddam's rape of Kuwait, referred to MREs as "meals rejected by Ethiopians" or by even less flattering and more graphic terms.)

Ramsdell and the company spent the rest of the day reviewing troop leading procedures and rehearsing various phases of the operation. But even after he arrived at the PHA, he was still under the impression that this EDRE might just be another training exercise. "When we arrived at the PHA," he wrote later, "you could see mounds of live ammunition that were being prepared for issue. On a normal EDRE, we were issued blank ammunition only, so this was a positive indicator that it was a real operation. However, I do not think we truly believed it was the 'real thing' until an hour before drop time, when the message was passed from one end of the aircraft to the other that the Rangers had jumped and were encountering light resistance. Up until that time, I felt that the weather or diplomats would intervene and cancel the jump."[4]

By 1400 hours the entire 2d Battalion of the 504th Infantry was assembled in the PHA. At 1500 hours, Maj. Jon Chase, S-3 of the 2-504 PIR, assembled the battalion's "Orders Group A" and published the battalion warning order. At this time, everyone in the chain of command knew they were locked into the PHA and that this "EDRE" was the real thing. The warning order established the mission for the battalion: "TF 2-504 conducts airborne assault commencing 200145 to achieve PZ posture on Tocumen Airfield NLT 200245 DEC 89, conducts air assault to isolate, neutralize and, if necessary, destroy enemy forces vic OBJECTIVE AXE and HAMMER" (Panama Viejo)."

Major Chase also published the battalion's timetable for Phase I (alert, marshal, and deploy) of the operation:

TIME	CHRONOLOG ENTRY
2100	Brigade-level communications exercise
2230	CG backbrief
2400	Jumpmaster briefing
0100	Battalion operations order
0600	Air assault air mission commander's briefing
0800	Trial manifest/sustained airborne training
0900	ESIP (equipment and supply issue point) procedures
1330	Final manifest
1500	Move to Green Ramp
1600	Parachute issue (planeside)
1640	Rig/JMPI
1800	Load time
1845	Station time
1900	Takeoff
0145	Drop time[5]

On Monday night at 1900, Colonel Nix issued his brigade order in one of the Quonset tents at the PHA. Present for the briefing were about seventy-five officers and men, including the division commander, his principal staff officers, Nix's staff, his battalion commanders, and all the members of their staffs. Colonel Nix repeated in detail the brigade's plans, procedures, and sequence of operations to accomplish the brigade's missions: 2/504 to Panama Viejo; 1/504 to Tinajitas; 4/325 to Fort Cimarron. General Johnson was the last man to speak; he gave a "pep talk," outlining the importance of the mission, the U.S. president's concern about the operation, and the capability of the 82d Airborne Division. The entire briefing, including intelligence estimates and other details of the pending operation, took about 2½ hours.

At 2300 hours, Colonel Axson gave his battalion operations order backbrief to Brig. Gen. Richard Timmons, the assistant division commander for support. He was followed by Lt. Col. Richard Marable, commanding officer of the 1-504 PIR, and Lt. Col. John Vines, commanding officer of the 4-325 AIR.

At 0100 on Tuesday morning, in a continuing process of passing orders down the chain of command, Colonel Axson issued his order to his company

169

commanders and his staff in one of the PHA Quonsets. The other two battalion commanders did the same. Axson's discussion of his mission—the neutralization of the PDF at Panama Viejo—took about an hour. Axson detailed his plan of attack; after jumping into Torrijos and assembling, loading up in helicopters at Torrijos, flying to two LZs near their objective, the barracks at Panama Viejo, landing, and then isolating the barracks, with B and C 2-504 landing on the same LZ, BOBCAT, to the north and the rest of the battalion from the west ON LZ LION. B and C companies would have the mission of isolating to the north. Axson pointed out to his battalion officers that he wanted to accomplish the mission "through the measured application of overwhelming force and not the immediate application of full firepower indiscriminately." After cordoning off the area, Axson said that he would then give the PDF a chance to surrender through broadcasts in Spanish by the 6th Psyops Group's loudspeaker teams.[6]

Ramsdell got back to his company in the PHA at about 0330 and, at 0530, issued his company order to his platoon leaders. At 0630 the men of C 2-504 ate breakfast; at 0730, Ramsdell ran his company through a trial manifest. The 82d SOP required that companies avoid putting "all of their eggs in one basket." Thus Ramsdell's 120-man company was scattered among twenty "birds," six men to a "bird." This procedure prevented the loss of an entire unit if one of the "birds" were shot down, aborted in flight, or otherwise did not make it to the DZ. Each C-141 carried 120 jumpers. (By contrast, the C-47's of World War II fame carried only about 20 jumpers for parachute operations.)

Ramsdell's company worked on the manifests until about 1000. After that the company went to the ESIP (emergency supply issue point) and drew a basic load of ammunition. Soldiers who normally complained about the amount of ammunition issued for a "practice" EDRE could not get enough of it on this occasion. By making changes on the ESIP records, a practice discouraged by their NCOs and officers, soldiers could draw more than the basic load. Soldiers were also required to jump with an additional one hundred rounds of .50-caliber ammunition for D Company's gun-mounted HMMWVs.

From 1000 until 1300, the platoon leaders went through the plan at platoon and squad level, outlined the PZ (pickup zone) posture, and went through basic squad battle drills—drills they had practiced endlessly in the past so the men of the squads could perform their battle maneuvers in the dark or in any kind of inclement weather.

By 1400 the men of C Company were in final manifest formation in an area next to the PHA. They were more than delighted to be out of the PHA and ready to get on with their mission. The accommodations at the PHA were not exactly of Hilton or Marriott standard. Some of the heaters in the tents did not work, some of the latrines were stopped up, and the ammunition supply points did not have all of the types of ammunition for all of their weapons. To add to their misery, soldiers had to stand in long lines in the sleet to get their gamma globulin shots. Finally, due to the temperature in Panama, Colonel Axson issued the order to start taking off the cold-weather gear prior to chuting up and loading the aircraft. There would be no time to remove clothes once they hit the drop zone. The temperature in Panama was expected to be eighty-one degrees.

This was not the most popular order that the soldiers received, but the paratroopers did it quickly, quietly, and without complaining.[7]

They went through prejump training and thereafter ate a sack lunch. Jumpmasters, meanwhile, had gone to Green Ramp to inspect their aircraft. The sleet storm continued unabated until the very end of final manifest call, when it seemed to pause for just a moment. At that moment, Major Chase assembled the 2-504 troopers on his aircraft and had them look across the huge area being used for final manifest procedures. He told them to "take a close look at what it looks like to have twenty-two hundred paratroopers assembled and ready to jump into the history books. . . ." It was an awesome sight, Major Chase decided.

Colonel Axson decided to walk from the PHA to Green Ramp by chalk. Although the trip was only about a quarter mile, it turned into a journey. Laden with over a hundred pounds of equipment, the troopers proceeded quickly and quietly down the muddy road leading to Pope Air Force Base. At the gate was Lieutenant Colonel James Grazioplane, the commander of the 82d's armor battalion. With his battalion dropping only a company of tanks, he was not going to jump and take a parachute away from a "shooter." "Nonetheless, he was there to heighten the excitement and warm the soul," wrote one of Colonel Axson's staff officers.

Between 1730 and 1800, the men loaded the planes for an originally scheduled takeoff time of 1900 hours. They carried on board their rucksacks, each weighing eighty pounds or more and stuffed with an assortment of extra gear, claymore mines, special ammunition, and plenty of water. They stored the "rucks" under their pull-down canvas seats and "loose-rigged" their parachutes.[8]

Because of the storm and the requirement to deice, the takeoff was delayed 2½ hours. The troopers remained aboard. It was going to be a long delay followed by a very long flight. Many of the men dozed. They had had little sleep in the last thirty-six hours. "In the PHA (18 December 89)," Ramsdell remembered, "the leaders averaged about one hour of sleep and the soldiers averaged about three hours. On Tuesday night (19 December 89), very few soldiers got any rest. The first night we spent In Panama (20 December 89), we averaged about three hours of sleep, but this was accomplished by being up an hour and then sleeping an hour, and so on." Ramsdell's and Axson's actions in the time frame after the alert and prior to the jump were typical of those of the other company and battalion commanders in Jack Nix's brigade.

At 2130, after an all-out effort by the Air Force ground crews to deice the planes, the first C-141 rolled down the runway at Pope. General Johnson was aboard it; so was Captain Ramsdell. At 2230, General Johnson sent a report to General Stiner: "Eight (8) Pax a/c (passenger aircraft) are up (chalks 1-6, 9, 10); all heavy equipment a/c are up. All Bn and Bde Cdrs are airborne. The lift of eight will make the original TOT of 0145. The remaining 12 a/c will attempt to link-up en route to make the scheduled TOT; if no link-up occurs, they will drop on arrival."[9]

"At 2228, Chalks 7 and 8 departed Pope AFB. At 2327, direct communication was established between COMJTFSO (Stiner) and COMTF PACIFIC (Johnson)," reported the division's historical summary.

The C-141's carrying the heavy-drop loads that had staged through Charleston Air Force Base, South Carolina, had not been affected by the Pope–Fort Bragg ice storm. Consequently, twenty-eight C141's carrying heavy-drop equipment and three C-141's carrying CDS (containerized delivery system) bundles arrived over Torrijos International Airport at 0145, right on schedule, and dropped their loads. This drop of heavy equipment and bundles marked the commencement of the 82d Airborne Division's combat operations in Just Cause.

The heavy drop included seventy-two Hummvees (M998), eight Sheridan tanks (the M551), four M102 105mm howitzers, two M1038s, two supply platforms, and seventy-four CDS bundles. This equipment was for the three infantry battalions of the 1st Brigade plus A Company of the 3d of the 505th PIR, C Company of the 3d of the 73d Armor, C Battery of the 3d Battalion 319th Field Artillery, A Company 307th Engineer Battalion, and elements from the 3-4 ADA Battalion, 313th MI Battalion, 82d Signal Battalion, a Psyops team, and the 82d Military Police Company. The 3-504 PIR, a battalion of the 1st Brigade, was already in Panama at the Jungle Operations Training Center (JOTC). It was attached to a brigade in the 7th Infantry Division commanded by Col. Keith Kellog, a former commander of the 1-504 PIR, 1st Brigade, 82d Airborne Division.

Much of the heavy-drop equipment landed off the designated DZ. One M551 Sheridan tank was heavily damaged when its parachutes apparently failed to inflate properly. It landed in an almost inaccessible area, very difficult to reach with a recovery vehicle. General Johnson decided to blow it up so no part of it could be salvaged by the PDF. A second Sheridan was also damaged on landing, but a recovery vehicle carried it to Tocumen Airport, where the Sheridan mechanics cannibalized it for spare parts for other Sheridans, the HMMWV belonging to the S-3, 2-504 PIR (nicknamed "Gunther" by the battalion's assault command post) suffered a cracked frame during its heavy drop onto the airfield. "Ironically," said Colonel Axson, "it survived the entire operation and enjoyed the best communications ever off its vehicle-mounted radios."[10]

Captain Ramsdell said that the five-hour, forty-one-minute flight from Pope to Torrijos was "not rough." The planes' doors remained closed until three minutes out—effectively cutting out the thirty-degree weather from Pope at the start of the flight. Aloft, General Johnson had communication through a VHF Tactical Satellite with, among others, General Stiner at Fort Clayton, General Downing at Howard, an AWACS plane, and the Rangers at Tocumen. A follow-on report claimed that "En route communications were superb. The division commander was able to communicate with all aircraft en route to the objective."

The drop zone, Torrijos/Tocumen Airport, consisted of two colocated airfields, Tocumen, the civilian airfield, and Torrijos, the military airfield. The serial of C-141's carrying the first elements of the 82d flew over Panama, out into the Pacific, and then turned back and came over Torrijos Airport on a northeast heading from the Pacific side of the isthmus.

At about two hours before jump time, the jumpmasters alerted the jumpers, who put on their rucksacks and tightened their parachute harnesses. They had worn their reserves throughout the entire flight. At three minutes out, the air crews opened the jump doors, the 80-degree warmth of Panama blasted into the planes, and the jumpmasters began their prejump safety checks followed by the jump sequence: "Stand up and hook up, check equipment, and stand by."

On the first plane, General Johnson was the first man in the sixty-man stick, jumping out the right door; Captain Ramsdell was number eight, going out the left door. At 0211, and from an altitude of five hundred feet at a jump speed of 135 knots, the green light came on and General Johnson led his men into the warm, humid, clear night air of Panama. Behind him, paratroopers leapt out of both doors of the plane. The exits were fast—jumpers exited at double time, ignoring the 82d Airborne Division's SOP of one-second intervals between jumpers because the troopers had been briefed that it would be "one pass and one pass only." Second Lieutenant Helms, who jumpmastored one flight, said, "Jumpers were so close that the fronts of the jumpers' reserves were actually touching the pack tray of the paratrooper in front of him." The Air Force loadmaster on the aircraft with 2d Lt. Maurice Heisig, B/2-504, told the troops as they were getting ready to jump, "The Rangers have not secured the drop zone yet . . . the DZ is hot. . . . Good luck." Their target, the DZ along the eastern edge of the Torrijos runway, was approximately three miles long and "could be characterized as muddy and having high grass," said one of the jumpers later in what turned out to be an understated appraisal of the DZ terrain.

Once his chute opened, Captain Ramsdell had a brief look at tracers streaking through the black sky and saw firing on the ground about six hundred meters from where he was going to hit the ground. He and his stick of paratroopers landed about fifteen hundred meters to the right side of the Torrijos runway in kunna grass that was fifteen feet tall. The paratroopers, laden as they were with their parachute harnesses, rucksacks, and weapons containers—altogether weighing over 140 pounds—wrestled to untangle themselves from their chutes and other gear in the thick grass and then struggled to "load and lock" (put their weapons into operation) and then don their rucksacks before they were ready to move to their assembly areas. Captain Ramsdell said that because the kunna grass was so thick he felt that he was walking—or struggling to walk—two feet above the ground. It took him almost an hour and a half from the time he landed to move the five hundred or so meters to his battalion assembly area that was also the PZ (helicopter pickup zone) on the west side of the Torrijos runway. The assembly areas for the various units were marked by twenty-foot poles with four- by four-foot banners on top, color-coded for easy identification. These markers were referred to as "Stiner aids." The assembly areas were also marked with "chem lights," which, when bent and shaken, glowed like neon. The assembly area of 4/325 was at the northeast corner of the Torrijos main runway, the 1/504's was in the middle, and 2/504's was at the southwest end.[11]

One soldier, a radio operator, remembered most clearly the "elephant" or kunna grass that ran up to the edge of the runway. He said that he had jumped with the heaviest load he had ever carried—including two radios, his personal rucksack loaded with ammunition, extra clothes and food, a base station antenna, and his M-16 rifle. He landed about seventy-fve meters off the runway. "It was so bad that I could only take three steps and then fall down," he said after the jump. "And in the dark, I couldn't tell if the man only three feet away was a good guy or a bad guy, so I would lay very still until he went away."

"I was the number-one jumper on the sixth aircraft," wrote Capt. Steve Phelps later. "During the jump, I made my first tree landing about a half mile from the 2-504 assembly point. My PFL [parachute landing fall] was broken by another chute spread across the top of the tree. I slid off of that chute and became stuck in the tree. I jettisoned my equipment and later could not locate my rucksack due to the denseness of the underbrush. Later, Capt. Robert Krueger, the commander of Headquarters Company, 2-504, informed me that along with my rucksack a dead Ranger soldier was found in the same tree I landed in. When he told me that, I felt extremely lucky to have walked away from that landing."[12]

Relatively few men were injured on the jump, but typical of those who were was Sgt. Berry B. Kelly, a squad leader with B Company of the 1st Battalion of the 504th. He said that "his parachute collapsed when a fellow parachuter stole my air. [To steal air means a parachuter glided directly beneath another parachuter.] My chute collapsed about 150 feet off the ground and I kinda burned in." He tore some ligaments in his ankle when he landed on the concrete runway.

Behind General Johnson's plane were seven more C-141's in the first flight echeloned from side to side in their flight path rather than flying one directly behind the other. During the parachute drop, the PDF did not use any defensive antiaircraft weapons. The ZPU-4's reportedly at the airfield were never fired. However, the enemy did engage the C-141's with a considerable amount of small-arms fire. The C-141's received dozens of small-arms hits in the aircraft fuselage while flying over the airfield. "Enemy forces on the airfield consisted mainly of stragglers and security forces that had occupied the international terminal and taken civilians located there as hostages," reported the division historical summary.[13]

Several of the aircraft flew right (east) of the drop zone center line and put entire planeloads of paratroopers and equipment east of the DZ and into an adjacent swamp and sawgrass. A postoperation Joint "MAC/Army Hotwash," a review of the operation, stated,

> The crews were not briefed on the swamp. . . . DZs should be at least 800M wide for management/dispersion factors. . . . This DZ was 600M wide. . . ."Effective" DZ (right of active) was 400M wide × 500 long. . . . Crews were flying into a "black hole"; simply couldn't see features on the ground. . . . Featureless run-in after breaking land. . . . None of the crews have ever dropped at 500′ AGL and do not have a sense of timing/time warnings. . . . Bottom line: Crews not trained for this.[14]

However, Colonel Axson, in an after-action briefing to the division commander, said, "When twenty Air Force C-141 crews can fly five hours without communications, in total darkness and drop two thousand paratroopers in a soft swamp only eight hundred meters off the target, the airfield runway, who is going to complain? The crews did an outstanding job."[15]

The troopers who landed east of the runway, in the swamp, did not complain at all. Rather, as trained, they linked up into small groups, some as small as two or three. The 2-504 Battalion S-3, for example, linked up with an NCO from the 2-504 Scout Platoon, who jumped from another aircraft but landed in the swamp within two hundred meters of Major Chase. They made their way to the airfield using only a general compass heading, used their bayonets to cut a hole through the chain link fence surrounding the airfield, found a 2-504 50-caliber HMMWV from D Company, derigged it, and drove to the assembly area. "Actions like this were not uncommon as the troopers displayed great poise and discipline while moving over unfamiliar terrain, at night with an unconfirmed enemy situation," wrote one of Colonel Axson's staff officers later.

Second Lt. Paul Helms, platoon leader 3/B/2-504, and Sgt. Robert Chappuis, platoon sergeant 1/B/2-504, failed to make linkup at the battalion assembly area along with approximately five other B/2-504 soldiers due to an early green light. "The green light came on just as the C-141 cleared the ocean," wrote Captain Phelps. "Helms, who was the jumpmaster of the aircraft, tried to hold the jumpers up, having recognized that the green light was early. Nonetheless, due to the forward momentum caused by the paratroopers pushing forward toward the door once they saw the green light, Helms could not hold them up. As he tried, he was pulled out the door with them. Among these soldiers was a battalion commander who was the number-one jumper. Lieutenant Helms landed approximately two thousand meters short of the leading edge of the DZ and had to negotiate a thousand meters of coastal mangrove swamp, a creek twenty meters wide, and then a thousand meters of kunna grass to make the drop zone."[16]

Because of the abnormal, foul weather at Pope and the inadequate deicing equipment, the follow-on air package from Pope was forced to fly to Panama in five serials. The first eight arrived over the DZ at 0211, twenty-six minutes late; two more came over at 0350; three arrived at 0400; two more dropped at 0455; and the final five dropped their paratroopers at 0515. In all, 2,176 82d Airborne Division paratroopers made the jump; 30 men sustained jump injuries for a parachute jump injury rate of 1.38 percent—an excellent rate compared to an average 4 percent injury rate for similar peacetime parachute operations. During the heavy-equipment drop, one Sheridan drifted under another and "stole the air" of the higher tank, causing it to fall more rapidly than normal. But in spite of that problem, almost all of the airdropped equipment functioned normally once it had been recovered. And, according to Colonel Crocker, "All air crews performed with complete professionalism. Heavy-equipment drop is rated at 90 percent by the Military Airlift Command Scoring System." The total delay of 3½ hours from the scheduled H-hour to the time of the last drop naturally caused a delay in the ongoing combat operations of Task Force Pacific.[17]

On the ground, the paratroopers, faced with the sudden heat and humidity and the thick, entangling kunna grass, found the task of assembling quickly almost impossible. Captain Ramsdell's PZ time was 0300, but it was not until 0430 that he had assembled about 70 percent of his company; 90 percent of the 2/504 was assembled between 0530 and 0600. At 0615, the commander of the 1/504, Lt. Col. Renard Marable, reported to the Division Assault CP that his battalion was in PZ posture. As soon as he assembled enough of his company, Ramsdell organized his men into "chalks" for loading on the Black Hawk helicopters when they arrived. He set up security around his company area, checked out his men and their equipment, and waited for the helicopters.

At 0440, the division assault Cp, consisting of General Johnson and scaled-down G-2 and G-3 contingents, formed on the center west side of the Torrijos runway. Twenty minutes later, General Johnson reported to General Stiner, that he had made a linkup with the Rangers at 0500. (General Johnson assumed operational control of 1/75th Rangers at 0600.) He was now about ready to move out to attack his three assigned objectives.[18]

*   *   *

During these hours of darkness, the troopers of the 82d continued to ready their weapons, get out of their parachutes, don their gear, and struggle through the head-high, thick kunna grass toward their assembly areas.

By 0438, Colonel Nix decided that he was about ready to launch his three battalions in separate air assaults on Panama Viejo, Tinajitas, and Fort Cimarron. He requested the division assault CP to bring forward the command and control aircraft for the three air assaults.

By 0650, the runway at Torrijos had been cleared of men and equipment, and the lift and assault helicopters had arrived. The 2-504 PIR began to load immediately. Of the twenty Black Hawks that were planned to lift the 2-504 assault forces in one lift, one nine arrived initially, forming a first lift, with eight reported to be following in ten minutes. Although the troopers had rehearsed extensively in loading twenty to twenty-five troopers on each aircraft, the loss of these aircraft meant some sixty to a hundred fighters might not make it to the battle for Viejo. Major Chase decided to scrap the battalion's air assault "bump plan" SOP and packed the Black Hawks with as many troopers as possible. Several Black Hawks landed in Panama Viejo with as many as thirty combat loaded soldiers crammed aboard.

Colonel Axson's assault plan on the Panama Viejo barracks was to air-assault into two LZs—Bobcat, a "six-shipper" just to the north of the objective and covered with grass higher than the heads of the troopers, and Lion, a "four-shipper" on the south side along the shoreline. These forces would then seal off the Panama Viejo area with Capt. Paul Defleuri's A Company and Captain Ramsdell's C Company. Captain Phelps's B Company would be assigned as task force reserve, rear security for the assault forces as well as protection of the battalion's mortars and command post and finally linking up with D Company just to the north of the objective. Capt. Gregory Sawyer's D Company (−), which was traveling overland to Viejo, consisted of four, .50-caliber-mounted HMMWV's, two M551 Sheridan tanks, the remainder of the battalion's mortar platoon in one HMMWV, the battalion commander's HMMWV for command and control, and one cargo HMMWV carrying ammunition and medical resupply items. Intelligence did not report that

Bobcat was covered with ten-foot-high kunna grass nor that some of Lion was a muddy quagmire that could not support the weight of a Black Hawk.

Colonel Axson planned the use of a measured application of force to isolate, then neutralize, and, if necessary, destroy the forces at Panama Viejo. His rifle companies would isolate the enemy at Viejo while Colonel Axson issued his surrender ultimatum through task force interpreters and Psyops loudspeaker teams. Major Chase lettered each of the buildings in the Viejo complex and passed this sketch along with his operational graphics to the company commanders and through both the Army and Air Force fire support networks to facilitate fire support and command and control. The intent was to isolate the barracks complex and attempt to talk the PDF into surrendering while the D Company convoy and support element made their way to Viejo. If the PDF refused Colonel Axson's demands, he had the ability to continue tightening the screw until his demands were met. Colonel Axson expected to take Panama Viejo by noon on the twentieth of December.[19]

Panama Viejo, on the eastern side of Panama City, was a town established in the 1500s, was later burned by pirates, and then was rebuilt of stone in the 1600s. Now, many of the buildings had been reduced to piles of stone. The ruins stand on a scenic point of land looking out across the Bay of Panama. The ruins were the location of a PDF barracks and special operations (UESAT—Unidad Especial de Seguridad Antiterror) training center occupied normally by about 350 soldiers, 180 of whom were from the 1st Cavalry Squadron, a unit that provided guards for Noriega's residences and troops for ceremonies. In the compound, the squadron had a stable in which Captain Ramsdell counted 76 horses. Some of these horses were on the Panamanian Olympic Team. The remaining 170 soldiers were members of UESAT, Noriega's antiterrorist troops. UESAT, highly trained and dedicated soldiers, were originally stationed on Flamenco Island. During the October coup attempt, when Noriega realized that the troops at Flamenco were too remote to come to his aid rapidly, he moved them to Panama Viejo.

These forces were armed with a wide variety of weapons, including Uzi submachine guns with night sights, antitank missiles, sniper rifles, an automatic grenade launcher, and "state-of-the-art body armor." One room of the main barracks was stocked with explosives. On the roof of the barracks, a .50-caliber machine gun was mounted; on the shoreline sat a ZPU-4, an armored vehicle equipped with a four-barrel antiaircraft gun aimed over the water.[20]

After the Fort Amador operation, Lt. Lisa Kutschera and all eleven helicopters of A Company, 3/123d Aviation Regiment, had loggered in Empire Range north of Fort Kobbe to refuel and wait until the 82d troopers had landed, assembled, and were ready to move out to their first three objectives. It was a short wait until they got word to lift off for the pickup point at Tocumen.

"The sun was coming up over the horizon as we flew our approach to Tocumen Airport, the PZ," wrote Lieutenant Kutschera recently. "My aircraft was one of the last in the flight and I watched as some of the open parachutes scattered on the runway became airborne on the rotor wash of the first helicopters, creating a hazard for all the aircraft behind. Luckily, none of them got entangled in rotor blades or ingested by engines."

The first mission was an air assault by 2-504 into Panama Viejo. "The stiff resistance expected at Panama Viejo didn't materialize on the first lift," continued Lieutenant Kutschera. "Some of the crews heard small-arms fire and my door gunner said he heard some as we were departing the LZ, but no firers could be identified and none of the aircraft was hit. The second load of troops we picked up at the PZ wanted to go into Panama Viejo also, rather than to Tinajitas as per our mission brief. On the second trip in, we took more fire and two aircraft were disabled and had to shut down after returning to the PZ.

"One of these was flown by Pilot in Command (PIC) CW2 Debra Mann, who hadn't flown on the first assault into Amador and had linked up with us at the lagger site. Her aircraft had taken three hits, the most serious of which was in the tail rotor intermediate gearbox. The round went completely through the gearbox, leaving entry and exit 'wounds.' Most of the oil drained out of the gearbox, and if the gears had seized at the altitude we were flying at, they probably would have crashed because helicopters don't fly well at all without a tail rotor. Sikorsky helicopters must know what they're doing, because they made it all the way back to the PZ, where the oil spraying out of the gearbox caught the crew chief's attention and they shut down to check it out."[21]

The flight route, south from Torrijos, was out over the ocean and then back to the north from the southeast to the northwest and took about ten to fifteen minutes. Colonel Nix used one UH-60 for command and control. The flight route took the aircraft out of small-arms range but also carried the troopers along a route that was completely observable from the complex of buildings at Panama Viejo. At about 0645, the first lift of troopers from 2-504 touched down in LZ Lion, carrying men from A Company, the scout platoon of Lt. James J. Johnson (the division commander's son), the Psyops team, and Colonel Axson's assault command post. As part of the first lift, five Black Hawks continued on to LZ Bobcat, carrying troopers from the scout platoon, C Company, and a battalion command and control element led by the Battalion S-3, Major Chase.[22]

One of the Black Hawk pilots making his approach to LZ Lion spotted a fully operational 23mm antiaircraft gun on the road just off the beach. As the Black Hawk approached, the gunner dismounted and ran. "Fortunately for us," the pilot said later. "If he had stayed with the gun and engaged us, it could have been a nightmare."

Despite the fire covering the LZs and the air immediately above them, the two overwatching Cobras from the 7th Infantry Division (L) and an Apache from the 1st Battalion, 228th Aviation Regiment, held their fire unless they found a specific and clearly obvious enemy target.

Captain Ramsdell remembered that about five seconds from touchdown on LZ Bobcat, he heard rifle and automatic-weapons fire. Several of his soldiers said that an air defense artillery gun along the road north of the barracks had fired at least three shots and then apparently and fortunately jammed as the Black Hawks were landing. The proximity of the firing made him accelerate the unloading of his troops. The PDF covered LZ Bobcat with automatic fire from AK-47's, assault rifles, and pistols. In the tall grass, Ramsdell's troops had a hard time finding each other, let alone the enemy.[23]

Sgt. Michael Alexander of C Company was finally able to locate some of the PDF. He called for a grenade launcher and fired several rounds. The PDF were not silenced; they returned fire directly at him. In spite of the PDF rounds coming directly at him, Alexander directed the fire of a machine gun that shortly neutralized the PDF position and permitted C Company to move off Bobcat. Gen. Carl Vuono, the Army chief of staff at the time, later awarded Alexander a Bronze Star for valor for his actions at LZ Bobcat.[24]

LZ Lion would prove to be an even more difficult landing zone than Bobcat, but for a different reason. The helicopters that touched down near the beach were on solid ground. But the troops in the Black Hawks that landed farther out, toward the water, had great difficulty. The mud flats looked firm from the air, but as the men jumped out of the helicopters, some sank up to their armpits in what turned out to be soft, oozing muck. Seeing the problem, several Black Hawk pilots, in spite of the small-arms fire covering the LZ, hovered their ships just over the mud so that the troopers could grab the landing gear and be lifted free. Spc. Hector Martinez, B/2-504, who speaks Spanish, was a grenadier on the operation. He said that Panamanian civilians formed a human chain and used ropes to haul other men out of the mud.[25] He said that the civilians kept asking him why it had taken the Americans so long to arrive. "The first thing they told me was," he said, " 'We were waiting for you a year ago.' " Later Martinez said, because of his language ability, "We did a lot of going house to house, looking for tips. I got tired of speaking Spanish."

Within fifteen minutes, the second lift was on the ground. This time the remainder of A Company along with an element from the battalion's communications platoon led by Lt. Scott Geiger were set down in the mud just off LZ Lion. At the same time, the remainder of C Company, and troopers from the battalion mortar platoon led by Lt. Chris Miller, and part of B Company arrived at LZ Bobcat. During the first lift, Colonel Nix determined that the 2-504 would be completely lifted out of Torrijos before the 1-504 would board the aircraft for its flight to Tinajitas. This decision allowed the remainder of B Company to move into the objective area using four more Black Hawks on a third lift. Unfortunately, these aircraft landed the troopers from B Company on LZ Lion.

With the landings of the eighteen helicopters, Colonel Axson had on the ground about five hundred troopers from his battalion task force. Unfortunately, this distribution of troops between the two LZs was not exactly as planned. "The lift of the A/C which took soldiers of B/2-504 into LZ Lion should have gone into Bobcat," wrote Captain Phelps. "So as it turned out, I had my company split between the two LZs. I positioned my mortars and XO between the two LZs (S Sgt. John Negre—mortar section leader, and 1st Lt. Byron Echols—XO) in order to relay communications between Bobcat and Lion and to support with indirect fire if need be. Although the B/2-504 element left at Bobcat maneuvered on a sniper originally, the troops at Lion pushed out toward the bridge with the battalion scouts. There they took significant enemy fire." B Company was now split between the northern and western portions of the objective, and the B Company troopers who landed on LZ Lion were becoming intermixed with A Company.

179

As the skirmishing continued around Panama Viejo, Colonel Axson decided to leave the B Company platoon where it landed and place it under the control of Captain Defleuri until the platoon could link up with B Company. When Major Chase heard this decision over the battalion command radio, he told Captain Ramsdell to break contact and move east to seal off the northern portion of the objective. He then told Captain Phelps to move his troops to the east out of the kunna grass and toward the objective.

While these units were moving, the battalion scouts ran into a number of PDF and UESAT forces north and west of the objective, trying to disrupt the U.S. air assault. A Company on the west used the platoon from B Company to secure its western flank while it maneuvered toward the main barracks building at Panama Viejo. B Company linked up with the battalion mortar platoon and moved to the east until it crossed the road leading north out of Viejo.

After repeated attempts to call out any PDF still remaining in the headquarters building, Colonel Axson ordered Captain Defleuri to seize the building. While Colonel Axson directed A Company toward the main headquarters building, Major Chase sent B Company into a position behind C Company, where they could support C Company as well as fire on the main barracks building if necessary. Once A Company had achieved a foothold in the headquarters building, Major Chase linked up with the main portion of the assault CP. Still not hearing from D Company, Colonel Axson moved C Company into Panama Viejo and ordered them to commence clearing the remaining buildings.

Unknown to Axson and his men, at about 2300 on the night of the nineteenth, eighty of the PDF force that had been in the Panama Viejo barracks got out of their uniforms and into civilian clothes, took their weapons, and headed north out of the area to defend fixed sites nearby. At about 0600 on the morning of the twentieth, having gotten word of the parachute landings at Torrijos and Rio Hato, many of the rest of the Panama Viejo PDF garrison changed into civilian clothes and, with their weapons at hand, occupied more of the "civilian" buildings around the area. By the time 2-504 arrived, about eighteen soldiers of the PDF were still in the barracks and some twenty-five were dug in around the compound. It was this group and those in nearby buildings close to the compound who greeted the first 2-504 helicopters on both LZs with intense small-arms, mortar, and machine-gun fire.

The PDF had obviously vacated their barracks in some haste. When A Company went into the barracks to search it, they found a mess hall with half-eaten breakfasts on the tables and a gun room in shambles. On the second floor were the troops' living quarters. In each wall locker were personal weapons such as guns, knives, and steel knuckles.[26]

For the next forty-five minutes, the troops of the 2d of the 504th continued to receive a large amount of harassing fire from small arms and AK-47's from PDF on the dikes near the main barracks. An AH-64 Apache took the ZPU-4, on the road to the north of the barracks, under fire and knocked it out. Some civilians reported to Captain Ramsdell's men that a PDF tank was down the road to the north. When Ramsdell's men found it, one of his AT-4 missile gunners got into position and took aim at the V-300 armored vehicle, not a tank. As soon as the PDF crew saw the gunner take up firing position, they left running. The AT-4 round destroyed any utility the V-300 might have had.

While Ramsdell's company was landing on LZ Bobcat, they were fired on by PDF from the police station. Some of the helicopters took hits. Ramsdell sent a platoon to knock out the police station. The PDF in the police station, according to Ramsdell, "did engage in a small-arms firefight for several minutes before they fled."

By noon, most of the PDF had left the area. But in the afternoon, a number of PDF soldiers came down the main road to the barracks in civilian clothes in their automobiles—some BMWs and Mercedes—apparently reporting to work and seemingly unaware of the landing of 2/504. Some of the PDF carried Israeli Uzis, others AK-47's, some even LAWs. The carloads of PDF drove up to the fighting positions of the 2/504 blazing away with their assorted weapons. The battalion stopped or knocked out nine such impromptu fighting vehicles—hardly Bradleys, but perhaps "Noriegas." A 2/504 sniper stopped one car. In another encounter, Apaches from the 82d destroyed three V-300's. Intermittent sniper fire continued throughout the day, and three PDF mortar rounds landed harmlessly in the area occupied by the 2/504. By dusk, the battalion had established a perimeter around the area that was, by then, relatively quiet. But before that calm settled over the area, two men would be killed: Pfc. Martin D. Denson, twenty-one, of B Company, 1/504, and Spc. Alejandro I. Manriquelozano, thirty, of D Company, 2/504.

Throughout the day, a few diehard snipers had continued to take random "potshots" at the troopers in the area. One of them made his way to the top of a crane about three hundred meters from Ramsdell's position. One of Ramsdell's men took it under fire with an AT-4, wrecking the crane. Then some ten PDF snipers in "Ghille" suits, somewhat like strips of rags over their clothes and hats, fired sniper rounds from five hundred to eight hundred meters away. None found a mark. By late afternoon the main force of the PDF had melted into the civilian population. For a short time thereafter, they and the Digbats resorted to spasmodic and generally worthless hit-and-run guerrilla tactics on the various positions occupied by Ramsdell's men.[27]

Axson's troopers captured one fully loaded and operational ZPU-4 in the area near the barracks. They found some expended shell casings, but it was unclear whether this weapon was fired against the 2-504 in an antipersonnel or an antiair role. The PDF had hidden two V-200's and several 2½-ton trucks in a junkyard near the city. Apaches destroyed this miniature motor pool with 30mm AWS and Hellfire missiles.

At various times, Panamanian anti-Noriega civilians reported to Axson's men that Noriega was "here" or "there" in the city. One such report unearthed Colonel Mina, Noriega's secretary of economics. On 27 December, Axson's men picked up Mina, searched his house, and found there some $267,000 in U.S. currency.

At 0910 on D-day, a convoy of five vehicles and two M551 Sheridan tanks with some sixty troopers from Axson's D Company attempted to move out of the Torrijos Airport airhead area along Highway 1 to link up with the rest of the battalion near Panama Viejo. Forty PDF men armed with automatic weapons

181

and RPG-18's assaulted the convoy at a bridge over a small canal near the Torrijos international terminal. The bridge was blocked with two burned-out automobiles. The D Company commander dismounted his men and started an intense firefight with the Panamanians.

Sfc. Gene G. Wolf was the platoon sergeant of the 1st Platoon of D Company. The company commander assigned the 1st Platoon to clear the roadblock. After taking out the roadblock, the platoon came under heavy fire from automatic weapons in a two-story building two hundred meters west of the bridge. The platoon maneuvered around the building but was pinned down by the fire, and one trooper, Spc. Alejandro J. Mannique-Lozano, D/2-504, was killed. To eliminate the fire, the platoon leader, 1st Lt. Steve Hayden, had his men lay down a base of fire, and Sergeant Wolf moved close to the building. He fired a LAW into the machine gun position and wiped it out. Then Wolf and Lieutenant Hayden entered the building. The entire platoon followed and cleared it. Eleven PDF were killed in the building while fighting in close quarters room to room. Two PDF were killed by soldiers around the back of the building. "The actions of Lieutenant Hayden and Sfc. Wolf were heroic," wrote one of Colonel Axson's staff officers. "The two paratroopers were later awarded Bronze Stars for valor medals by General Johnson. Incidentally, Sergeant Wolf had been selected earlier in the year as the 82d Airborne Division NCO of the Year. He sure lived up to the honor."[28]

Fighting continued in the area of the roadblock. The company commander requested help from the battalion executive officer, Maj. Rick Ballard, who was still in the Torrijos airhead. He sent another M551 and twenty men to help D Company. With the added help, Capt. Greg L. Sawyer and his men repulsed the PDF, killing three more of them and wounding an unconfirmed number. Captain Sawyer remounted his men to continue his move to Panama Viejo. Colonel Nix, however, ordered Sawyer to return to Torrijos and link up with another convoy from the 1/504.

At 1155, Colonel Axson reported to Colonel Nix that he had secured his objective at Panama Viejo in spite of continuing harassment from random snipers and PDF who drove by shooting wildly from their civilian cars. The PDF also lobbed mortar rounds from a wood line near the barracks throughout the day. Axson directed Apache helicopters to the enemy mortar sites and eventually took the positions under fire and suppressed them.[29]

Panama Viejo was not out of the hands of the PDF. Axson's men consolidated on the objective and settled in to "stabilize" the area and its environs.

19 | The Marriott Incident

Freeing hostages held in a plush hotel in the middle of a large city was not exactly the type of mission for which the 82d Airborne Division had spent an inordinate amount of training time. But at 1807 on the evening of the twentieth, General Stiner's headquarters notified General Johnson that possibly the PDF had seized twenty-nine U.S. hostages at the Marriott Hotel in downtown Panama City and that he had the mission of securing the hotel and freeing the hostages. General Johnson knew his troopers were flexible and could handle this unexpected mission. He passed the task on to Colonel Nix, who, in turn, passed it to Colonel Axson and the 2-504.

Initially, at 1700 hours, Colonel Nix had told Colonel Axson to be prepared to conduct a company-size air assault on Paitilla Airport, where earlier four Navy SEALs had been killed. Axson's commanders were continuing to prepare positions in and around Panama Viejo as well as patrolling aggressively to set up a safe zone in the built-up areas surrounding the former PDF headquarters. Axson knew of the aborted attempt by D Company to reach Panama Viejo and that D Company would be linking up beginning at first light on the twenty-first. When Axson received a radio message that Colonel Nix was inbound with a change of plans, the 2-504 staff was making plans for the mission to Paitilla. At 2020 hours, Colonel Nix arrived with his assistant brigade S-3, Capt. Chuck Durr, and told Colonel Axson that his new mission was to rescue twenty-nine hostages from the Marriott Hotel by seizing the Marriott not later than midnight—tonight.

The origin of the mission to free the "hostages" in the Marriott is somewhat muddled. The fact is that an Eastern Airlines pilot, Capt. Jay Skinner, a guest at the Marriott, aware of the shooting and the miniwar zone around the hotel, called, via commercial phone, his corporate headquarters in Miami. The pilot summarized the situation at the time, stating that the PDF had taken hostages from the hotel at gunpoint to another location in town. The hostages were lectured and threatened, he said. Later the PDF soldiers seemed nervous when they brought the hostages back to the hotel. The PDF told the hostages to stay in the hotel. The PDF then "posted" the hotel grounds with soldiers. From Miami, an Eastern Airlines official called a staffer at the White House and passed the message about the deteriorating situation at the Marriott.

Mr. Skinner later said that because the PDF had not cut the phone service and could not watch all the phones at once, he was able to use a phone to relay facts to his corporate headquarters almost at will.

As the situation developed, the U.S. forces came up with the mission knowing that there was always the possibility that hostages were being held in other areas of the large hotel and that substantial problems could develop if the PDF decided to fight and hold the hostages at all costs.[1]

After Colonel Axson got the Marriott mission from Colonel Nix, Colonel Axson and his staff made a hasty mission analysis: How are we going to do this job? He postponed moving D Company until the next morning and decided to concentrate on getting the Marriott Hotel under control—and then plan for the evacuation of the hostages to Tocumen Airport. During this brief planning session, Axson peered at the map to locate the Marriott Hotel. Thinking out loud, he said to his Battalion S-2, Lt. Bob Cejka, "You're the intelligence officer. Where is the Marriott?"

"There it is, sir," responded Cejka, pointing across the bay to the well-illuminated marquis on top of the Marriott Hotel. Major Chase recommended to Colonel Axson that he send B Company on the mission along with a battalion command and control element. Then, when the battalion executive officer arrived at Viejo in the morning, arrangements could be made for the evacuation and processing of the hostages.

Axson's scheme called for a rifle company, with its engineer squad, to move by foot along the shortest and fastest route to the hotel. The force would leave its rucksacks at Viejo but carry its special-purpose equipment, such as night-vision goggles. B Company would also leave behind its 60mm mortar section, since it would slow the advance, and these small mortars would have minimal effect in such an operation. The battalion command post moving with B Company would include the commanding officer; the S-3; the S-2; the fire support officer, Capt. Glen Goldman; the Air Force tactical air controller, Capt. John Wittington; and the battalion's surgeon, Capt. John Marriott (no relation to the founder of the hotel chain). In support of this operation would be a commandeered white civilian van that would trail the walking formation to act as an ambulance.

At this point someone reminded Colonel Axson that Capt. Chuck Durr, who had come with Colonel Nix to Viejo, had left an assignment in Panama only six months earlier. Durr, when asked by Axson, said that he was still very familiar with the road network between Viejo and the Marriott. Intelligence reports indicated that there were several pockets of resistance and ambushes already set up by the PDF along the route to the Marriott. Colonel Axson realized that to maintain the speed of the attack and clear the hotel by midnight, he would have to avoid the enemy and perhaps change his route of approach. Colonel Axson immediately drafted Captain Durr and told him to guide the lead platoon of B

Company on the march. Captain Durr was as good as his word: Repeatedly on the march, he changed the route to avoid ambushes and traps.[2]

Major Chase assembled the company commanders at 2130 at Viejo and put out a brief but detailed oral operations order. He pointed out that the operation had to commence at 2215 to have sufficient time for B Company to move through the city and seize the hotel by midnight. He pointed out the route. He had already numbered the key buildings to provide a reference for the AC130 gunship that would overfly the operation. He gave copies of the reference map to Axson, the Air Force liaison officer, and Durr. Speed was of the essence, he pointed out more than once. Speed and the AC-130 overhead would provide the security for the mission. He also said that he would coordinate with the AC-130 by radio to conduct a reconnaissance of the route ahead of the advancing troops.

Back at his company area, because of the shortage of time before moving out, Captain Phelps had time to brief only the lead platoon on the route, tell the men what gear to carry, and set up the movement formation. Phelps selected the 1st Platoon to lead the way because its leader, 2d Lt. Kevin Stoddard, was "the most experienced platoon leader I had," said Phelps. Then it was time to move out. Any unexpected actions at the Marriott would have to be based on the soldiers' training and the response of the chain of command.

Axson left Ramsdell in charge of the perimeter at Panama Viejo and gave him the mission of linking up with D Company and the battalion executive officer, Major Ballard, the next morning. Axson told him to brief Major Ballard on the situation and to tell Ballard to prepare to receive the hostages and process them to Tocumen in accord with the battalion's noncombatant-processing SOPs. At 2215, B Company and the Battalion CP group left on the 2½-mile march (almost a run) to the Marriott.

Just as the column left the perimeter, it started marching past an auto repair shop on the right side of the street. The shop's lights lit up a large area about 150 meters from the battalion's perimeter at Viejo. Captain Durr, at the head of the column, decided on the spur of the moment to shoot out the lights. With his first shot, he sprung a PDF ambush that was waiting for U.S. vehicles to leave the Viejo compound. The result: a firefight. There was one PDF casualty, and the others fled into buildings along the route of march. Colonel Axson got the column moving forward again, "this time with a sense of urgency that only a shot of adrenaline can provide," wrote one of his staff officers.

Down the road another five hundred meters, the 1st Platoon of B Company heard what sounded like a large tractor trailer truck grinding through its gears. Although no one saw the vehicle, the noise made it clear that the truck was moving toward the column at high speed. Suddenly, from a side street, a truck the size of a UPS delivery truck roared into the column between the 1st and 2d platoons. The truck's aluminum sides had been cut open, and five Panamanians were in the rear firing at the advancing troopers with a variety of automatic weapons, some mounted on tripods bolted to the floor of the Tinkertoy APC. In the cab sat a driver and a passenger who, not to be outdone by the cowboys in the rear, was firing a pistol and throwing hand grenades wildly out the passenger side of the cab.

By this time, late on the evening of D-day, the battalion's troopers had been through a long preparation period at Bragg, a six-hour flight to Panama, a night parachute assault, and an opposed daylight helicopter landing; and on the ground, they had withstood snipers, drive-by shootings, mortar attacks, and sustained automatic-weapon firings. Now they were on their way, on foot, some thirty-six sleepless hours after their alert at Bragg, to rescue American hostages, and they were being heckled by this unexpected attack.

The B Company troops reacted swiftly with an "immediate action drill" and returned fire. The truck turned left and continued between the column of soldiers on either side of the road. Many of Phelps's men found themselves literally with their backs to the wall, a seawall next to the street. One trooper elected to jump over the dark wall for cover. Unfortunately, from the top of the wall to the mud flats below was a twenty-foot drop. The other troopers kept up a large volume of fire when the truck had turned so that they could see into the rear of the truck. The trooper who leapt over the wall was slightly injured and was missing for some time until he made his way back to the company—embarrassed and disheveled.

Spc. Walter Randall ("a super troop," according to Captain Phelps) was hit in the bicep as the truck passed the 1st Platoon. The truck roared on through the gauntlet of fire toward the company command element. As it passed by the 2d Platoon, Major Chase was hit in the face and his radio telephone operator was hit in the leg as they returned fire. A Spanish interpreter working with the battalion was blown over the seawall by a shotgun blast. The entire column, in turn, raked the truck with their weapons. "It was like a cone of fire," said Major Chase.[3]

Within the confusion of this mad, thirty-second engagement stood Specialist Harrod, an M-203 grenadier from the 3d Platoon. As the truck made its turn onto the main street, Harrod stepped into the middle of the street. With the truck headed directly toward him, he fired his rifle grenade at the cab of the truck. The round blew off the right arm of the cab's passenger, throwing it free of the truck and landing on the street below. The truck did not slow down but kept moving at a high rate of speed. With little emotion other than saying, "Shit, I'll get him with the next round," Harrod reloaded him M-203. Dropping to one knee, he took aim and fired again. This round hit the driver in the face. The truck veered off the street and crashed into a local café about twenty meters from where Colonel Axson had been watching the action.

The night air became still and quiet as the troopers hurriedly searched the truck's wreckage for survivors. There were none. Colonel Axson broke the silence when he said to Harrod, "Good shot, Harrod. You got huge steel balls, or what?"

The wounded were quickly brought to the vicinity of the battalion S-3, who handed Colonel Axson his map with the AC-130 checkpoints on it before he, too, was loaded, along with the other B Company wounded, into the makeshift ambulance. The rest of B Company—by now moving at the "airborne shuffle" pace—sped on toward the Marriott.

Throughout the remainder of the march, the AC-130 gunship cruised overhead, giving detailed intelligence to Axson, through his Air Force ground liaison officer, using the numbered building reference system that Chase had developed. Colonel Axson was well aware of the capability of the AC-130 with its advanced optics and weapons system. His extensive work with the aircraft in Grenada would prove invaluable to the success of the remainder of the mission.

Now, some fifteen minutes after the fight with the truck, the Air Force LNO received a message that the first bridge crossing was manned by eleven PDF soldiers. When Axson heard this, he told Durr to change the route and avoid the bridge. Durr turned north immediately and led the column quickly and quietly down another route. As they moved, Axson mentioned that he could still hear small-arms fire on the road to the rear. He said that he didn't know what was happening back there.[4]

The makeshift ambulance had been left behind with one of the company medics to evacuate the wounded. Sergeant Lucas, a member of the assault CP and a Vietnam veteran with thirty-six confirmed kills as a Marine sniper, volunteered to take command of the ambulance, get it back to Panama Viejo, and then return it to B Company before they got to the Marriott. On the way back to Viejo, Lucas and the ambulance met only sporadic fire from buildings along the way. The trip back was another story.

Spc. Richard Lucas, a small clerk-typist and RTO for the battalion S-3, was the driver of the ambulance. "Radar O'Reilly," one officer described him, but he did not hesitate to volunteer to drive the ambulance when the S-3 told him he was going to be left at Viejo to monitor the brigade radio net. His passenger and guide initially was a volunteer from the scout platoon, Specialist Juarez. He moved to the rear of the ambulance when Sergeant Lucas took charge. When Sergeant Lucas briefed Colonel Nix in Viejo that he intended to regain contact with Colonel Axson, he could see the Marriott Hotel sign across the bay and knew he had some catching up to do.[5]

Sergeant Lucas left the Viejo perimeter knowing the route he had to take. He told the ambulance driver (the other Lucas) to move out at breakneck speed—not only to catch the column but also to flash past any enemy ambushes before they could put effective fire on the ambulance. Unfortunately, he did not know that B Company had turned away from the possible ambush at the bridge and that it still might be manned.

When he hit the bridge, he sprung the ambush. The PDF fire blew out all the windows of the van. Both Sergeant Lucas and Specialist Juarez were able to return fire. As they left the ambush site, Juarez was wounded in the leg. In addition, Sergeant Lucas realized that they were being followed closely by another vehicle. It closed on the ambulance and started a running gun battle for several blocks. During the exchange of fire, Sergeant Lucas was firing across Juarez's front and into the Panamanian vehicle. Whenever the pursuing vehicle would slow enough for him to shoot, Juarez fired. This running street battle, Mafia movie style, continued until Specialist Lucas turned sharply to the left, down a side street.

Sergeant Lucas decided to return to Viejo to get Juarez attended to and to get himself a new set of glasses as well as a resupply of ammunition. During the gun battle, both lenses of Specialist Lucas's glasses were shattered, but the frames remained intact. Specialist Juarez wondered later why Lucas kept swerving off the road. Without his glasses, it turned out, Specialist Lucas was as good as blind.

Sergeant Lucas got the ambulance back to the Viejo perimeter and into the area of the headquarters building—now well set up as an aid station and resupply point. When he tried to leave again to rejoin the column, Colonel Nix stopped him and ordered him to stay at Viejo because Axson and B Company were about to enter the Marriott.

Ten minutes after Lucas and the ambulance activated the bridge ambush, the AC-130 reported to Colonel Axson that four snipers were on top of building seven. Axson asked the AC-130 to repeat the building number. Again the AF LNO confirmed it was building seven, which happened to be across the street from where Axson was standing. As the command group looked across the street, several rifle barrels disappeared from the top of the building. Axson decided that they were waiting for his small group to pass the building so they could take the rear of the formation under fire. At this point the first two platoons of B Company had already turned the corner, heading for the Marriott. Axson told the AC-130 to engage the snipers. The ALO asked Colonel Axson, "Say again?" Axson said, "Tell them to shoot 40mm and destroy the snipers on the roof." The AC-130 came back and said, "Roger, move over eight feet." B Company momentarily stopped their movement, and as soon as the troopers hit the sidewalk, the AC-130 sprayed the roof of building seven with 40mm fire—effectively putting an end to that threat.

The AC-130 continued to report enemy on rooftops with the next sighting on the roof of the Marriott. Axson told the AC-130 not to shoot the Marriott, that there were hostages somewhere in the building, and that he would take care of them in a few minutes. Ten minutes later, B Company unlocked the front door of the Marriott Hotel after shooting a hole in one of the large windows beside the door.

Captain Phelps remembers blasting open the door of the Marriott. "I laugh about it now and even found it humorous then," he remembers, "that the two front double doors were open the entire time. Yet we tried to shoot them down/open because we could not open them. We were pushing them toward the hotel and away from us. To open them, we merely needed to pull them toward us."

Once inside the hotel, Captain Phelps had one platoon secure the entrances. He ordered the remaining two platoons to clear the fifteen-floor building systematically—a standard building clearing drill. He assigned Lt. Maurice Heising and his platoon the specific task of moving to Room 1015, where the hostages were allegedly being held. Captain Durr went to the hotel switchboard and started calling each room. For everyone who answered the phone, the message was the same: "The Marriott Hotel is now under the control of U.S. Army paratroopers. We will be on your floor shortly. Unlock the door, prop it open with a pillow, and lay down on the floor face down. Do you have any questions?"

Every room was searched, and "hostages" were found everywhere. Twenty-eight hostages were found in one of the hotel elevators. Phelps's men moved any guests to a collection point in a windowless room behind the front desk. As the hostage count came to 80, Colonel Axson had the hotel disco opened by using two M-203 rounds. All the hostages were brought there for safekeeping. The final count was 106 people, who represented about every nation of the free world, as well as a group of hotel employees who feared for their lives if they would have been released.

While the building was being cleared, Lieutenant Cejka, the battalion intelligence officer, began interrogating the guests and dividing them into groups: confirmed U.S. citizens, people with valid passports and visas, and others. In the meantime, Capt. John Marriott, the battalion surgeon, tended to one soldier who was injured during the AC-130 mission on building seven, and another soldier who was injured during the initial assault on the hotel entrance. Later the surgeon treated one of the hostages who had gone into cardiac arrest.

Communications inside the building were less than ideal. Only radios on the fifteenth floor could contact the rest of the battalion. Axson set up the assault CP on that floor, while Phelps set up his CP in the offices in the lobby on the ground floor. When the building was cleared at 2330, Colonel Axson attempted unsuccessfully to contact his boss, Colonel Nix. He decided then to call the Fort Clayton EOC on a commercial phone. When he finally got through to the 82d Airborne Division CP, General "Smokin' Joe" Kinser, the assistant division commander, was on the line.

"Harry, where are you?"

"Sir, I'm in the lobby of the Marriott Hotel."

"Well, we thought that was a bridge too far. . . . What do you need?"

"Sir, we could use some claymores, LAWs, sniper match, and M-16 ammo. . . . We also need some medical supplies. I'll put my doc on the phone to give your folks the specifics. Also need transportation for about 106 hostages back to Tocumen."

"Okay, we'll get you the supplies . . . probably have to sling-load it to you, since the sniper fires have been pretty intense in your area . . . can't risk setting an aircraft down unless you have some critically wounded."

"No medical problems that won't keep until tomorrow. Sir, we'll take anything you can give us."

"What about chow, Harry?"

"Sir, don't need any chow. We're staying at the Marriott."

"Right, we'll get those hostages off your hands in the morning. Put the doc on and keep this line open."

"Wilco, sir. Here's the surgeon."[6]

Major Ballard flew in the supplies from Tocumen within a few hours. While the 2-504 was waiting for ground transportation to evacuate the civilians, numerous PDF "drive-bys" fired automatic weapons at the hotel. PDF or Digbats fired sporadically from nearby rooftops at the hotel windows and doors. At 1000 hours on 21 December, the evacuation force, led by Capt. Greg Sawyer and consisting of four .50-caliber mounted HMMWVs, one Sheridan tank, two cargo trucks from 1st Brigade, and two large civilian "Marriott" trucks from the airport, arrived on the scene. The force carried with its flak vests for all the hostages, and intelligence personnel with MPs to handle the hostages once they left the hotel. There was a short exchange of gunfire between Captain Sawyer's forces and lone gunmen on the rooftops both as the force approached the hotel and during the loading of the hostages into the transportation. Only one Panamanian civilian was hit during the exchanges. The gunfire actually sped up the loading process.

While Captain Sawyer was loading the hostages in the varied vehicles, he briefed Colonel Axson that Major Ballard was at Viejo and that the brigade CP was moving next to the battalion's main CP in the vicinity of the ruins at Viejo. By 1200 hours on 21 December, all the hostages were safely at Tocumen Airfield. Captain Phelps and his company stayed at the Marriott for the next few days to secure the hotel's valuables and maintain a military presence in the area. From this location, Colonel Axson could direct B Company's actions as the search for Noriega went on.

Captain Phelps and his company were still at the Marriott on Christmas Eve. "That evening," wrote Captain Phelps later, "three Panamanian special agents requested U.S. troops to help them capture Noriega. One of the men wore a hood. Another man said that this man was Noriega's personal bodyguard. He stated that the bodyguard had left Noriega just a few hours before and that he was at the home of a wealthy friend a mile or so away. He asked that U.S. soldiers isolate the objective (the house), and, if need be, use forced-entry techniques in gaining entry.

"I selected Lieutenant Helm and the third platoon for the mission. First, a select few soldiers did a recon in civilian clothing. (The clothing was taken from the luggage left by the hostages.) The B Company first sergeant called the battalion headquarters, explained the situation to Major Chase, and requested assistance. Twenty minutes later the battalion command group arrived at the Marriott.

"Major Chase immediately wrote up a plan, got it approved by Colonel Axson, and notified brigade headquarters.

"Before the actual movement of troops and in order to reduce the chance of fratricide, the Panamanians were put in military BDUs so they would not be mistaken. This was humorous, as the soldiers who turned over their clothing were left only in their underwear in the hotel lobby.

"Upon our arrival, a neighbor reported that a helicopter just departed, and we believe it was with Noriega. The homeowners denied everything. The ex-bodyguard took us to the guest room where he claims Noriega stayed.

"Later we identified the homeowner as a man wanted on an indictment by the United States. We apprehended him and turned him over to the military police.

"While at the home, we saw that one of the Panamanian men had a bandaged bullet wound. A car in the garage had bullet holes and was identified by Specialist Boaz, B/2-504, as a vehicle which participated in a drive-by shooting at the Marriott shortly after B Company secured it."[7]

Before that incident, the U.S. forces were, of course, still searching for Noriega. At 0500 on the twenty-first, Axson tasked Ramsdell with the mission of taking a platoon to search Noriega's golf house in the north-central part of the city. The golf house was one of Noriega's many residences in and out of the city. Ramsdell appropriated a couple of Panama civilian trucks, hot-wired them, and sent Lt. Louis Ortiz and his 3d Platoon to secure and guard the golf house.

The golf house was in an area of other large homes of well-to-do Panamanians who were in no way connected to any of Noriega's schemes. One of the owners told a U.S. officer, "We have felt like prisoners. You have released us from prison and we will always be grateful."[8]

The golf house was actually a compound of several houses. One, called the Delta, was apparently Noriega's personal residence, where his wife and daughters lived. It was about four thousand square feet in size and was surrounded by a concrete wall ten feet high. In it the platoon found three safes containing some $4 million to $5 million U.S. dollars and priceless works of art—but no drugs. Some Christmas presents were lying on the tables. In the rather extensive library, Ortiz and his men found one book of some interest: William Casey's *The American Revolution.* Inside the front cover of the book was a personal inscription that read: "To Manuel, Thanks for cleaning up a troubled region." Signed Bill Casey.

One room was a voodoo room; another resembled a Catholic chapel; still another was a weight and workout room. The compound also held three smaller houses for Noriega's guards. Ortiz's platoon moved into the main house and stayed there until time to return to Fort Bragg.

"Noriega is a junk collector," said Lieutenant Ortiz after spending four days in the house. "Using drug money, he collected a lot of expensive junk. And yet, at the same time, he has all these Christian icons and hides out with the Pope. As a general, I don't think he ever actually led his troops. He had, more or less, an army built up around protecting what he had. If you look around the house, at the way the house was built, you notice it wasn't built to be defended from attack. It was built to keep burglars out; that's about it."

Sgt. Gordon Pargellis was a weapons squad leader in the 2d Platoon. He remarked later that almost everything in the house was personalized by Noriega. His name was on every pen, knife, every plaque. "There's this desk plaque upstairs, engraved with a self-assessment of himself," Pargellis said later. "It says he's intelligent, not worried about himself. . . . I think he's really an insecure person who discovered he had a lot of charisma."

On a tip from one of the neighbors in the area, Ortiz's men found a large weapons cache not far from the golf house. Despite the fact that it was well stocked with assault rifles and mortars, there was no resistance to Ortiz's seizure of the cache and its contents.[9]

The Marriott and the golf house complex were now secure. But Noriega was still at large.

20 | Tinajitas

The Tinajitas Army Garrison was the home of the PDF 1st Infantry Company. Prior to the U.S. attack, the 1st Infantry Company was something of an enigma to the Southern Command because, during the 3 October coup attempt, it stayed in its barracks and did not rush to Noriega's rescue. The company may have been dormant during that brief interruption in Noriega's reign of power and terror, but when the helicopters carrying the 1st Battalion of the 504th descended on it, its reaction was far from passive.

The Tinajitas barracks, and the objective of 1-504, sits atop a five-hundred-meter hill whose approaches were limited by civilian buildings in close proximity. The barracks overlooked the slums of San Miguelito, an area about six kilometers to the northeast of the heart of Panama City and about nine kilometers due west of Torrijos Airport. Prior U.S. intelligence had determined that the 1st Infantry Company had 184 men armed with four 120mm mortars, six 81mm mortars, three 60mm mortars, and one ZPU-4 AAA weapon.

At 0800 on the morning of the twentieth, after it had assembled on PZ Center after parachuting onto Torrijos, the 1/504 took off in three helicopter lifts and landed on two LZs that were on a ridge line about seven hundred meters from the hilltop barracks. Before the arrival of the troop-carrying helicopters, two AH-64 Apaches and one OH-58C Kiowa had been overwatching the area. They approached San Miguelito from the northwest and overflew the objective. From that direction, they received no ground fire. But when they turned and headed back over the area from the southeast to support the air assault, all three aircraft took heavy and effective ground fire from a built-up area in the northern part of San Miguelito. To avoid collateral damage in the village, the team of attack helicopters did not return fire and flew to and made emergency landings at Howard Air Force Base.

Before they left the area, they gave a "target handoff to the next team which was simultaneously arriving on station," according to the division's after-action report. "The lead scout passed the enemy information to the air assault TF commander on the air assault FM net, who acknowledged while the flight was in the PZ at Tocumen." While the assault helicopters were bringing in the 1-504, one of the attack helicopters finally located, in a hilly area in northern San Miguelito, a PDF battle position of eleven soldiers armed with automatic weapons. CW-2 Flankey, flying the lead scout helicopter, an AH-64 Apache, requested and received permission to engage the target. He and his team made contact with the group with its laser range finder. They neutralized the enemy position with salvos from their 30mm cannons from a distance of some twenty-eight hundred meters. Subsequently, the 1/504 found ten PDF dead. A helicopter pilot saw one of the PDF running away.

At 0830, the first lift landed on LZ Leopard aboard five UH-60 Black Hawks and, at 0840, onto LZ Jaguar with one Black Hawk. The second and third lifts, each with six Black Hawks, landed on Leopard. The helicopter flight path had been from Torrijos to Panama City to a point near Panama Viejo and then north to San Miguelito. The 1-504 S-2 said later that the people in the city came out on rooftops to wave at them, but when they crossed over Highway 1 into the area of San Miguelito, people came out on the rooftops to shoot at them.

Once the first air assault helicopters had landed, it became obvious that the PDF 1st Infantry Company had had advance information of the U.S. attack. A stay-behind element of the PDF had surrounded LZ Leopard and engaged the helicopters and the emerging paratroopers with intense automatic-weapons fire and 81mm mortars. Even before the first lift touched down, the PDF took them under fire in the air from a number of positions in buildings to the west and southeast of the LZ, a definitely "hot" LZ. After they landed and were deploying into their attack formation, they came under heavy fire not only from the hilltop, which was covered with elephant grass, but also from the barrio around it.[1]

"The LZ at Tinajitas turned out to be the 'hottest' of all," Lieutenant Kutschera recalled. "Mr. Mann and I were made flight lead of a flight of three when we reorganized after losing the two damaged aircraft. As we flew over the start point of the route to the LZ, we could hear the radio traffic of the two flights preceding us, though they were too far ahead for us to see them. The first flight and then the second reported taking and returning fire from both sides as they approached the LZ.

"Suddenly the realization that we were in combat was brought home to everyone in A Company when CW-2 Vandenhueval, the PIC flying with Captain Muir, said on the radio that Captain Muir had been shot in the head and he was returning to Howard Air Force Base for medical aid. There was a moment of stunned silence on the radio as the message sunk in, then the necessity of completing the mission and getting out of the LZ reclaimed everyone's attention. About a minute later First Lieutenant Healy, one of my fellow platoon leaders and now acting company commander, reported as he took off from the LZ that his door gunner had been shot and he would return to the PZ as briefed to get medical aid from the medics there. We figured out later from the blood stains and holes in the floors of a couple of aircraft that some of the infantry had been wounded on the approach also, but they had either gotten or been taken off the aircraft at the LZ and stayed with their units.

"By this time I was within three kilometers of the LZ and not looking forward to what I was flying into. I found out later that as the second flight cleared the LZ, a Cobra fired on the area where most of the firing was coming from and the volume of fire decreased somewhat. Whatever the reason, only one of the aircraft in my flight was hit as we flew in low over the treetops and landed in the ten-foot-tall grass in the LZ, paused about ten seconds for the troops to get out, and took off on the steep climb over the two-hundred-foot high-tension wires on top of the hill on the departure end of the LZ. Whoever planned that LZ gave the PDF an easy shot at us as we departed the area. We couldn't go under the wires because of a shorter set running alongside the tall set.

"It was a subdued group of aviators who shut down back at the PZ to regroup and wait for the rest of the 82d to get into PZ posture. . . ."[2]

Spc. Andrew "Slats" Slatniske of B Company said later, "It was the longest seven hundred meters I ever did—up that hill in that elephant grass. It may have been seven hundred meters on the map, but it was about three thousand meters the way we had to go."

S Sgt. Joe Sedach, Slatniske's platoon sergeant, said, "The soldiers fought just the way they practiced back at Fort Bragg, but with a difference: Usually the 'live fires' we had at Fort Bragg are only one way." He added that if the PDF mortar crews had been better, "It could have been very bloody." He said that the paratroopers kept moving, so the PDF mortar crews kept having to adjust the fall of their shells.[3]

Lt. Col. Renard Marable was the commanding officer of 1-504. His plan of attack was to advance in three directions on the garrison—"One company advanced from the south of the garrison, one from the far east, and one from the far west," said the division's after-action report.

> The task force seized the hilltop next to the Tinajitas Garrison and attempted to gain line of sight with the enemy company. After two hours, two companies reached the top of the hill and they discovered that the 1st Infantry Company had abandoned the garrison. The battalion continued to receive sporadic sniper fire from all directions of the hilltop. This fire was from the slum areas that surrounded the area. The unit observed that the 1st Company abandoned Tinajitas in a very orderly manner and no evidence of a hurried withdrawal. 1-504 found three 120mm mortars set up in position in the garrison. Two of the tubes had hung rounds in them and were pointed toward Fort Clayton. The area was littered with mortar rounds that were apparently being prepared for firing.[4]

The 1-504 did not escape unscathed. Pfc. Jerry Scott Daves, twenty, was an infantryman assigned to B Company. He had been wounded from the PDF fire earlier, but he was killed by a mortar shell while a medic was working on his first wound. The medic was wounded. Pfc. Martin Denson, from B Company, was shot as he stepped off a helicopter and was later killed by mortar fire.

In spite of the superb physical condition of the paratroopers, a number of them fell victim to heat exhaustion during the attack up the hill, so steep that the paratroopers often fell to their hands and knees to climb through the thick and tall elephant grass. Heat, lack of water, and fatigue slowed the troops, yet the "Red Devils" of the 1/504 continued their advance. "The weather made a big difference," Sergeant Sedace said. "It was really hot compared to North Carolina," remembering the ice storm that had delayed the 82d's departure. Eventually their physical conditioning and aggressiveness pulled them through. They also knew that they had to keep moving to frustrate the PDF mortar gunners.[5]

"One of the interesting stories to come out of the assault on Tinajitas come not from the 82d, but from the UH-60 lift unit," reported a SOUTHCOM spokesman after the operation.

Whether or not female soldiers ever faced death in ground combat may be debated, but bullet holes in helicopters flown by female pilots cannot be denied. Both the #1 and #2 aircraft on the "hot" LZ at Tinajitas were piloted and commanded by female aviators. The debate concerning assignment policies for women is ongoing and will continue. However, the simple truth of the matter is that these women were assigned to units that had a mission to complete. The units completed their mission. No thought was given to precedent setting or the reality of women in combat. The men—and the women—of the units were too busy doing their jobs to concern themselves with either precedents or their impact on history.

In the aviation brigade of the 7th Infantry Division there were twenty females, of whom four were pilots, one was a crew chief, three were in aircraft maintenance, and one was the brigade communications officer.[6]

At 1433, Colonel Marable reported to the division CP that he had secured objective Tinajitas. Some additional firing went on during the afternoon, but by nightfall of the twentieth, the 1/504 had completed their physically demanding mission. The following morning, combat patrols eliminated remnants of the PDF still "sniping" at them from nearby buildings. Marable's battalion at Tinajitas was geographically isolated from the rest of the brigade and consequently found itself in an unexpected and unusual position. The civilians expected them to perform the government functions that were now in a state of chaos. The 1/504 reacted with style. The battalion's medics started health care programs while the rifle companies moved out to help workers restore the electrical power plant and distribute MREs to the needy.

The distribution of food to the poor from the slums of San Miguelito was a major undertaking for the battalion. More than ten thousand people were in line even before the trucks carrying the MREs for them arrived. When the flatbed trucks carrying more than fifteen thousand MREs did arrive in the area, they were greeted with loud cheers from the people. Marable's initial estimate was that he would be able to distribute two meals per day, per person, and in keeping with the gallantry of the American soldier, the "Red Devils" escorted pregnant women to the front of the lines and fed them first.

"It's amazing to see all these people," said Capt. Bart Physioc, the battalion chaplain. "Last week there was no one on the streets. They were hiding. Then we got here. We gave them liberty, then peace. Now, we're doing what we can to feed them. And they're so patient. They wait—and the line must be a mile or more long—then they come in and take what little we have to give them and leave with a smile. It just makes me feel good."

Second Lt. Eloy Mazo, an officer in the battalion's S-2 section, saw another side of the picture. "Being able to speak Spanish, you get an inside look into these people's lives," he reflected. "You get to know what's actually going on. These people are very, very poor and right now, very happy. They lead simple lives. If they have shelter and food, they're happy. Everyone who can walk in here is going to get an MRE."[7]

The actions of the battalion won the trust of the people, that, in turn, over the next few weeks, led directly to successful programs to recover weapons and persuade former PDF soldiers to turn themselves in.

21 | 7th Infantry Division (Light)

Because the units of the 7th Division did not parachute into Panama on D-day and because the only ground element of the 7th engaged in operations on D-day was on the Atlantic side of the canal, the division's major role in Operation Just Cause has been somewhat obscure and underreported. In reality, the 7th Infantry Division supplied more soldiers and equipment to the operation than any other comparable unit. By D+3, almost the entire division had deployed to Panama from Fort Ord, California.

Col. David Hale, commander of the 1st Brigade of the 7th, had deployed his brigade to Panama on 12 May 1989 as the Army element in Operation Nimrod Dancer. The brigade's headquarters, the 1st and 2d battalions of the 9th Infantry, the 2d Battalion of the 8th Field Artillery, and the forward area support team had moved into and occupied Fort Sherman near Colón on the Atlantic side of the canal. The brigade then began a series of "force projections" that permanently placed infantry forces in close proximity to the PDF's naval infantry at Coco Solo, the 8th Infantry Company at Fort Espinar, and the Colón Bottleneck. The brigade prepared and rehearsed detailed plans for its part in ensuring freedom of transit through the Panama Canal, the freedom to exercise treaty rights, and the possible overthrow of Noriega as part of Sand Flea exercises. On 16 October, the 3d Brigade relieved the 1st Brigade in place, and the 1st Brigade returned to Fort Ord.

The 7th's 2d Brigade, commanded by Col. Linwood Burney, was the 7th's ready brigade on 19 December. At 0749 on the nineteenth, Maj. General Carmen J. Cavezza, the 7th Division's commander, received the alert from the Joint Chiefs of Staffs' office to execute Blue Spoon and immediately triggered the notification system down his chain of command. He set "N-hour" for the 7th Infantry Division at 0900 on the nineteenth. Colonel Burney alerted his battalions in turn. At 1930 on the evening of the nineteenth, Lt. Col. Robert Cronin and his 5th of the 21st Infantry left Fort Ord for the trip to Travis Air

197

Force Base, 150 miles northeast of Fort Ord. The battalion's strength was 32 officers, one warrant officer, and 383 men. The first elements of the battalion arrived at Travis at 2158 hours.

At 0237 hours on the twentieth, the division's tactical CP—General Cavezza plus a scaled-down operational staff—left Travis, followed at 0310 hours by the 5th of the 21st, and at 0318 by the 2d Brigade's tactical CP. Lt. Col. Alan Rock's 2d Battalion of the 27th Infantry left Travis at 0615 hours. At 0123 hours on the twenty-first, another 2,104 troops, 95 vehicles, 16 trailers, and 56 supply pallets left Travis aboard 10 C-5's and 21 C-141's.

The 5/21st began arriving at Tocumen at 1515 hours on D-day and immediately assisted in securing the airfield. At about the same time, General Cavezza and his tactical CP arrived at Albrook Air Force Base and established a command post. Shortly thereafter, the 2/27th arrived at Tocumen. On arrival, the 2d Brigade came under the direct control of Task Force South, General Stiner's command.[1]

On the twenty-first, General Stiner assigned Colonel Burney an AO (area of operations) ranging west from the Panama Canal to the Costa Rican border. The primary objectives in the area included neutralizing the PDF in the area, securing key sites and facilities, protecting U.S. lives and property, restoring law and order, and demonstrating support for the emerging Panamanian government.

Colonel Burney began operations by directing Colonel Cronin and his 5th of the 21st Infantry to air-assault into the town of Coclecito on the 22d while the other two battalions of the 1st Brigade, 2/27th and 3/27th, relieved the 2/75th and 3/75th Rangers in Rio Hato. The 2d Brigade staged out of Rio Hato to continue a two-phased operation in the west. The first phase had B Company, 3/27th Infantry, air-assault into Las Tablas and secure the area. B Company captured two hundred prisoners. During the second phase, the 2d Brigade moved to the city of David in the western part of Panama to conduct stability operations until relieved by the 2d and 3d battalions, 7th Special Forces Group. On 8 January, after being relieved in the west, the 2d Brigade moved east to join the 1st Brigade in Panama City and relieve the 82d Airborne Division. On 13 January, the 2d Brigade assumed total responsibility for the city. During this phase, the 2d of the 27th Infantry returned to David by order of General Stiner to demonstrate the ability to reenter swiftly any area and show U.S. support for the new government.

The 2d Brigade expanded operations in the east toward the Colombian border from 24 January to 6 February. Primary objectives were to show a strong U.S. presence, support the new Endara government, and neutralize any remaining PDF elements.[2]

On 22 December, D+2, at 0900, Colonel Hale began deployment of his 1st Brigade from Fort Ord to Howard Air Force Base, Panama. On arrival, his brigade was attached to General Johnson's 82d Airborne Division, Task Force Pacific. General Johnson gave Colonel Hale the mission of clearing and securing a major portion of Panama City. By 24 December the brigade was establishing control of an area encompassing six-hundred-thousand residents. Over the next week, the brigade had some twenty-one separate engagements with elements of the PDF and Digbats while clearing and securing its AO. On 6 January the brigade relieved the 82d Airborne Division of security of the Papal Nunciatura. On 10 January the brigade reverted back to General Cavezza's control and expanded its AO in Panama City to control that area formerly held by the departing 82d Airborne Division. Subsequently the brigade transferred its AO to the 2d Brigade and combined U.S. MP/Fuerza Pública de Panama (FPP) control and deployed back to Fort Ord on 17 January.[3]

Lt. Col. William J. Leszczynski, Jr., thirty-nine, West Point Class of 1972, commanded the 3d Battalion of the 9th Infantry, part of the 1st Brigade. He had received his alert on the nineteenth. His first aircraft, a C-141B, was "wheels up" from Monterey Airport at 0130 on the twenty-third. The battalion used eight C-141's and landed at Howard at approximately 1200 hours the same day.

"We moved into an assembly area on the western side of the Panama Canal, a couple of miles from the Miraflores swing bridge," he wrote later. "At 232100 December, I linked up with Colonel Mike Snell, commander of the 193d Infantry Brigade, and he took me on a recon of the area so I could get the 'lay of the land' of the sector. (Note: Lesson 'Relearned': Nothing is better than a personal recon by commanders.) The next morning at 240700 December, the company commanders were taken on a recon of the sector's key sites. Later that day, we moved into the sector."

Less than twelve hours after his battalion touched down, Colonel Leszczynski had started to deploy his men in some sixty squad-size elements and individual snipers throughout his area of responsibility in Panama City and had moved part of his battalion to secure such key sites in the city as the Cuban, Nicaraguan, and Libyan embassies; TV Channel 4; and the Panamanian Ministries of Treasury, Health, and Foreign Affairs. The latter building was especially important because it was the temporary headquarters of the new Endara government. Lt. Col. Thomas Plant and his 1st of the 9th Infantry and Lt. Col. Charles Swannack and his 2d of the 9th Infantry had arrived at Howard within the same time frame on the twenty-third.[4]

On the sixteenth of October, when Col. Keith Kellogg's 3d Brigade of the 7th had assumed responsibility for all U.S. forces in the vicinity of Colón from the 1st Brigade, it also had become Task Force Atlantic. The task force spent the time in "hard training and planning, and in intense mission analysis, preparation, and rehearsals." Every three weeks, battalions rotated to the Jungle Operations Training Center and became familiar with Op Plan 90-2. Units conducted Sand Flea exercises primarily to exercise "U.S. freedom of movement rights" under the Panama Canal treaties and to rehearse contingency plans. The brigade conducted "freedom of movement" convoys twice weekly from Fort Sherman to Fort Clayton or from Howard Air Force Base and back to Colón.

By 0600 on D-day, Task Force Atlantic had cleared Coco Solo and Fort Espinar and had secured Madden Dam, neutralized the Cerro Tigre logistics site, cleared and defended the town of Gamboa, and seized Renacer Prison. The cadre of the Jungle Operations Training Center had secured the Gatun Locks and Fort Sherman.[5]

Colonel Leszczynski's experiences in Panama City were typical of those of the commanders whose units operated within the urban area. "Basically, when we went into Panama City," he wrote, "we conducted a linkup with elements of the 193d Infantry and relieved them. We were given a sector, and a number of key sites were located in the sector and needed to be secured/protected.

"We later took over the security of the American embassy and held this mission until we left for Howard Air Force Base for our redeployment to Fort Ord.

"Additionally we conducted active patrolling the entire time in Panama, with patrols going virtually twenty-four hours a day. We also ran checkpoints and roadblocks to capture any Panamanian Defense Force personnel, Dignity Battalion personnel, and personnel on the 'most wanted list.'

"Immediately after occupying our sector, we began to acquire intelligence and followed up on intel leads. We raided a local Communist Party headquarters and captured a number of documents, including the May election results. We also raided a DENI station and captured over fifty weapons (rifles, shotguns, handguns), assorted ammunition, small quantity of drugs, and three individuals. Additionally, the DENI station contained a roomful of records.

"There were a number of firefights. Most of them were small (squad/squad($-$)). Our biggest problem (and my biggest concern) was the sniper activity. The first week we were in our sector the streets came alive at night. The major road which runs by the American embassy, Balboa Avenue, was the boundary (eastern) of my sector and ran right by my initial CP. It was 'affectionately' knowns as 'sniper alley' and our vehicles were always being fired at from the vicinity of San Tomas Hospital, which we cleared/secured on 27 December.

"Probably the most significant firefight occurred on Christmas. A platoon ($-$) from C/3-9 was sent to reinforce a small element that was securing the DENI station, which had been raided earlier in the day. As the platoon ($-$) was crossing a street, it was engaged by two men firing automatic weapons from a nearby bank. The platoon ($-$) immediately hit the ground, found cover, and returned fire, killing one of the individuals and setting the bank on fire. The other individual escaped.

"I suspect the individuals we were up against were probably Dignity Battalion personnel still operating in the area. I think we killed five personnel total. They were not wearing uniforms.

"My soldiers did anything they were asked to do. For a number of my soldiers (new), the first time they *ever fired,* except for weapons qualification, was when they fired their weapons in Panama. They guarded embassies/secured key facilities twenty-four hours a day; *not very* exciting; pretty boring. They ran patrols twenty-four hours a day, seven days a week through some of the poorest and most crime-ridden areas of Panama City (Curundu). They never fired on a target unless the target was *positively* identified as being hostile. They always stayed in the proper uniform (which included flak jackets and Kevlar helmets) and camouflage. They cleared numerous buildings room by room. At the end of the mission (beginning 5 January) they helped train the new PPF (Panama Police Force), a mission which we continued until we left the sector and went to Howard Air Force Base.

200

"When we cleared San Tomás Hospital on 27 December, they searched operating rooms, maternity wards, the children's hospital, and *even* the caskets that were coming into and leaving the morgue with the dead bodies inside. This was not an easy task, but my soldiers did it without hesitation.

"When we cleared San Tomás Hospital on 27 December, the entire situation was very confusing. San Tomás is a large hospital complex with a large number of buildings. One of the buildings was the military hospital, which was known to contain over twenty patients, including some UESAT personnel. We had been receiving sniper fire from inside the hospital grounds and, needless to say, I was a little apprehensive and expected some fighting when we went inside.

"Our basic plan was to cordon off the buildings to prevent any PDF who may have still been inside from leaving and to use some loudspeaker teams to encourage any PDF to surrender.

"My plan was put together very quickly and I issued the plan to the B Company commander at 270700 December. When we went inside the hospital at approximately 1100 hours, we found a much different situation than we expected. The hospital was loaded with civilians (doctors, nurses, patients, workers, etc., etc.) and it was very confusing for the soldiers who had expected there would be some fighting, especially in the vicinity of the military hospital.

"The soldiers quickly changed focus and took charge, dealing with the civilian personnel firmly but professionally. There was not a single incident and we had soldiers in virtually every part of the hospital as we searched and cleared the complex. We even had soldiers clear the operating room. I can guarantee that there is nothing in any publication that tells a soldier how to clear a hospital.

"During building-clearing operations, a particular technique is always used to clear rooms. Demolitions are used (if necessary) to blow open the door. Once the door is opened, the first man enters the room and is immediately followed in by a second man—crisscrossing. We practiced this procedure a number of times during training and used the same technique for our room-clearing. Soldiers didn't even need to talk.

"At the American embassy (which we took over from the 3d Ranger Battalion) we were responsible for the 'outside' security. . . . The American embassy had been attacked by RPG-7's on D-day. Our mission at the other embassies was to prevent personnel on the most wanted list from entering or leaving. We stopped all personnel and vehicles entering or leaving. We searched the vehicles to ensure none of the most wanted people were inside. We were also looking for weapons and contraband."

"Our company helped secure the outside of the Cuban and Libyan embassies," said Cpl. William Stansberry, a team leader in A Company of the 3d Battalion, 9th Infantry. "Before General Noriega turned himself in to the papal nuncio, it had been rumored that he might seek asylum at the Cuban embassy, so we doubled our security there. On Christmas Day, a Panamanian vehicle tried to break through our barricades without any success. It was a scary moment, as we had received some sporadic sniper fire from the area."

"Our unit helped secure the Channel 4 TV station so that the Panamanian people could be informed on what was happening with the new government and the American forces," said S. Sgt. John Carter, a squad leader with B Company of the 3d of the 9th. "We set up barricades with the help of the Panamanian people."

"We were prepared for the search and patrol missions, but not the police role," said Command Sgt. Maj. Thurman Beaver of the 3d of the 9th. "Our soldiers were looking for aggressive action and didn't want to be policemen, but they accepted that role when it came. Our troops were very disciplined during their missions and didn't fire their weapons at animals, each other, or even at armed Panamanian shopkeepers, who were protecting their property from looters, especially during the first few days of Operation Just Cause. I'm proud of everybody in this battalion."[6]

Many newspapers reported and numerous TV shots depicted the widespread fires and destruction of neighborhoods in Panama City, especially in the Chorillo district, where Noriega's headquarters was located, and blamed the U.S. forces, either directly or by implication, for the devastation. Inevitably there were some fires started by U.S. gunships, artillery, and mortar fire. But the U.S. commanders insisted that their troops be careful with their fires and shoot only at known enemy targets to avoid unnecessary "collateral" damage. Roberto Eisenmann, the publisher and editor in chief of *La Prensa,* said in an interview in the April 1990 issue of *The American Legion,* "In Chorillo, where most of the damage occurred, there was extensive testimony from eyewitnesses indicating that most of the destruction was because of fires set by Noriega's troops. Many 'Dignity Battalion' members were seen throwing gasoline on buildings and then firing grenades into the area."

General Stiner insisted that all firing be held to the minimum essential and that a field-grade officer approve artillery targets and air strikes. The troops followed that guidance and sought to limit damage. In one instance, a young private first class from the 193d, a gunner on a Sheridan tank firing his tank gun at the corner of the Comandancia, moved his tank from one location to another. An officer asked him why he had moved. The young soldier said, "From here I have a better shot at the building, and I've got less chance of hitting those civilian buildings over there."[7]

*   *   *

On 18 December, two days before the beginning of hostilities, Col. Douglas Terrell deployed the tactical command post of his 7th Aviation Brigade from Fort Ord to Panama. Once there, the TAC assumed command and control over Task Force Hawk, a unit that had been organized to support Nimrod Dancer. He then formed Task Force Aviation, comprised of the 1st Battalion of the 228th Aviation, elements of the 82d's aviation brigade, and his own aviation brigade from the 7th. He then organized Task Force Aviation into four subordinate elements: Task Force Hawk, Task Force 1-228, Team Wolf, and later Team Candor.[8]

Combat operations began for Task Force Aviation with simultaneous battalion and company air assaults, flown by pilots with night-vision goggles (NVGs), in support of Task Force Bayonet to Fort Amador and Task Force Atlantic to Renacer Prison, Gamboa, and Cerro Tigre. Attack helicopters engaged targets at Rio Hato, La Comandancia, Fort Cimarron, Panama Viejo, and Torrijos

Airport. After daylight, Task Force Aviation flew air assaults into Panama Viejo, Tinajitas, and Ft. Cimarron in support of Task Force Pacific. Upon completion of these missions, Task Force South took over command of all aviation assets.

Task Force Aviation conducted resupply, command and control, reconnaissance missions, and support for the hostage rescue forces at the Marriott Hotel. On D+2 the AO expanded, with the air assault of the 5th Battalion, 21st Infantry into Coclecito in the west. Elements of Task Force Aviation also flew recce missions in Colón, on the Atlantic side.

On D+5, General Cavezza's TAC requested and was given air assets to support the 2d Brigade's operations in the west. TF Condor was formed and consisted of UH-60 Black Hawks, AH-1 Cobras, and OH-58 Kiowas. This support of the 2d Brigade in the west consisted mainly of air assaults and recce missions. As the 2d Brigade turned over the AO to Special Forces, Task Force Condor began a phased recovery from David through Rio Hato to Fort Kobbe. Task Force Aviation redeployed all augmentation forces and reduced Task Force Hawk to Team Hawk.

Lieutenant Kutschera summed up the operations of her 7th Division helicopter unit this way: "We continued to fly missions throughout Panama. . . . I spent Christmas Eve laggering at Rio Hato waiting to take troops to a new area just before dawn. On 27 December we deployed to David near the Costa Rican border to support operations throughout the mountains of western Panama. We returned to Fort Kobbe about 4 January and the next day we deployed to Fort Sherman on the Atlantic end of the canal with two other aircraft to support missions in that area for about a week. Captain Muir rejoined us on 15 January after convalescing in the States, and cheerfully accepted all the ribbing about being the hardest-headed commander in the Army. On 23 January I flew recon to La Palma on the eastern side of Panama not far from the Colombian border and in February we deployed the company to nearby Sante Fe for about a week to support 7th ID (Light) operations there. . . .

"B Company had returned to the States the first week in January . . . we finished our normal rotation. . . .

"Life at Fort Ord has gotten almost soft. We now get weekends off consistently and I even managed to get enough training time in to complete the Big Sur Marathon. I've also taken up sky diving and in the past year have managed to make 150 freefall jumps."[9]

Lieutenant Kutschera seems to suggest that some women, at least, are ready for combat.

III | FINISHING THE JOB

22 | Follow-on Operations

Prior to the operation, the SOUTHCOM intelligence picture depicted Fort Cimarron, the home of the elite Battalion 2000, the outfit that had come rapidly to the aid of Noriega during the 3 October coup, as one of the most difficult objectives that the 82d Airborne Division would have to neutralize. According to best estimates, Battalion 2000 had three companies at Fort Cimarron along with eight V-300 armored cars, fourteen mortars of assorted calibers, four 107mm rocket launchers, and perhaps three large 120mm mortars. It could be a formidable force if it were dug in a strong defensive position. But fortunately that was not to be the case.

At 1205 on the twentieth, Lt. Col. John R. Vines led his 4/325 on an air assault into the Fort Cimarron area from its PZ at the northern end of Torrijos. The first lift of eleven Black Hawks, escorted by two Cobras, landed part of A Company on LZ Cougar and part of B Company on LZ Tiger. The second lift repeated the first.

Once on the ground, B Company conducted an aggressive patrol south and west of the area to determine enemy positions. The company found scattered PDF soldiers at Paso Blanco and Naranjal. The battalion's scout platoon screened to Paso Blanco and found some additional enemy troops in civilian clothes. The result of the encounter was a firefight in which five enemy were killed. The firefight went on into the evening.

A Company went to the west of the Fort Cimarron airfield into an overwatch position. They were not unobserved. Some enemy troops in the Battalion 2000 barracks fired on them. A Company reacted according to a very positive plan. The company commander first directed his Psyops team to warn the troops in the barracks that if they did not "lay down their arms" he would call in an air strike. The warning went unheeded, so the commander did as promised: He called in an AC-130 to suppress the fire from the barracks. The AC-130 stayed on station from 2100 to 0100 the next morning, firing almost continuously at the area. The barracks was "neutralized."

At 0730 the next morning, Colonel Vines reported to the division tactical CP that he had secured Fort Cimarron. Vines moved a task force into the garrison area and found the barracks deserted. Throughout the twenty-first, the battalion searched the area and set up a perimeter for an expected counterattack that night. During the evening, Battalion 2000 troops did attempt to probe the position to the south near Naranjal, but they were repulsed by the paratroopers. During the twenty-first, the 4/325 cleared the area and found an arms room in each of the company areas. But the small PDF probes were the extent of the enemy action at Fort Cimarron.

This was a surprise to the 4/325. Subsequent to the operation, Battalion S-2 learned that, starting in early December, Battalion 2000 troops had routinely displaced from their barracks area during the night to a position about three kilometers north of the barracks. But they did not make any attempt to counterattack the 4/325 with any large force from the remote position.

After the battle with the remnants of the Battalion 2000, patrols from the 4/325 found that thirteen PDF had been killed, ten vehicles destroyed, and three 120mm mortars were unharmed. A and B companies consolidated their positions and awaited the linkup with the remainder of the battalion.

On the twenty-second, at about 1750, the 4/325 less B Company, which remained at Fort Cimarron, but with A Company of 3/505, which had been in reserve at Torrijos, air-assaulted into Punta Paitilla Airfield in Panama City "to secure that area for future extraction operations." Colonel Nix also gave the battalion the responsibility for the security of the district containing the Papal Nunciatura.[1]

The first night the battalion was in Paitilla, Pvt. James Allen Tabor, eighteen, a .50-caliber machine gunner assigned to Headquarters Company, was shot and killed when his patrol moved toward the main part of Panama City. Spc. Glenn Lame of A Company said, "The first night, we started out the gate (of Paitilla) on patrol and started taking sniper fire immediately. Lame also had some kind remarks for the ability of the Hummvee to run on flat tires. "They really run on flat tires, just like they are advertised. We had one come in running on the rim, not the rubber. It just came right in."

Pvt. Tony Moore, a member of a forward observer party from C Battery, 3d Battalion, 319th Field Artillery, who was with A Company 4/325, said his worst moment came when his sergeant and lieutenant adjusted artillery fire by sound. "That was a bit hairy," he claimed. "Other than that, it has been pretty quiet around here."[2]

Another episode that received some press coverage was the "Smithsonian rescue." The Smithsonians were a group of five Americans, four Panamanians, one Venezuelan, and one Pole. The Americans included Dr. Nancy Knowlton and her four-year-old daughter, Rebecca; Preston Hardison, graduate student at the University of Washington; Steve Travers, a research assistant to Eric Fischer, deputy director of the Smithsonian Tropical Research Institute; and Greg Summers, a research assistant and student at the University of Washington.

The group had been conducting research on "Smithsonian Tupu" Island in

208

the San Blas group on the Atlantic side of the canal. The PDF "captured" them by dispatching a twenty-foot patrol boat and crew to the island, forcibly loading them up, and transporting them as far as Carti Airstrip on the mainland. Two Smithsonian Boston whalers followed the PDF boat. From Carti Airstrip, the PDF marched the Smithsonians overland some twenty-one kilometers to the Cuna Indian Research Station at Nasugrande. Apparently during the land march, the PDF lost interest in the whole project and faded away. For two days the group stayed in a remote schoolhouse between the towns of Carti and Llana. "Rescue" came when the party was able to contact U.S. forces and arrange to be picked up by helicopter on 22 December.[3]

As December faded into New Year's Day, the U.S. forces spread out around the countryside, intent on returning the country to its legally elected administration and assuring the Panamanians that Noriega and his thugs were no longer in power. General Thurman still had one more objective to achieve: finding and arresting Noriega.

The D-day operations were a success from a number of standpoints. At a breakfast-hour briefing on the morning of D-day, Gen. Colin Powell said that Noriega was "not running anything, because we own all of the bases he owned eight hours ago." At the end of the operation, Lt. Gen. Tom Kelly, General Powell's director of operations, said, "It is among the most professionally executed operations that I have seen in thirty-three years of military status. . . . It looks like the organized resistance is a thing of the past. . . . We have a concern that they have gone off into the jungle. There is every chance that we will go after them." And "go after them" they did.

On D-day, thousands of American troops from the United States and Panama had converged from widely scattered bases in the United States and Panama to defeat a spread-out, in-place force with "rapid and overwhelming combat power." By the end of D+2, over twenty-seven thousand U.S. troops were in Panama, under the operational control of one headquarters and had accomplished over twenty-seven separate missions in various spread-out locations. Two hundred forty-five U.S. Air Force airframes supported the U.S. forces on D-day as transports for paratroopers and heavy equipment, as transports for air-landed troops primarily from the 7th Infantry Division, as gunships, as airborne command and control ships, or as air warning platforms. It had been a massive, rapidly executed undertaking both in the planning phase and in the operation itself.

With the end of D-day and the defeat of the majority of the PDF units, there remained a less spectacular but perhaps far more important phase yet to be executed: the stabilization of the Panamanian people and their institutions, the "going after" and capturing of former PDF and Digbat leaders (including El Jefe himself—Noriega); the provision of humanitarian relief and assistance; the restoration of basic services to include, most especially, law and order; and the insuring of the security of U.S. citizens and key facilities.

By the end of D-day, no major PDF unit had mounted a counterattack. But Panama "remained a very lethal environment for U.S. forces," according to a Southern Command spokesman. "Sunset found every objective secured. . . . The Blue Spoon operations order had been executed nearly flawlessly."[4] Now it was time for follow-on operations. As General Johnson, commander of the 82d Airborne Division, reviewed the situation, members of his Task Force Pacific occupied key locations at the eastern end of Panama City.

On D+1, the twenty-first of December, sniping and drive-by attacks, similar to what the 2d of the 504th had endured, persisted throughout the city. By that morning, B Company of the 2-504th had rescued twenty-nine civilians who had been trapped in the Marriott Hotel and feared of being taken hostage. Additionally, eleven employees and family members of the Smithsonian Institution were rescued from near the continental divide east of Panama City. Other elements began moving into the city to assert a U.S. presence. As PDF members, or more commonly, Dignity Battalion members were encountered, they were captured and moved to detention centers. On D+2, the highly publicized "attack on Quarry Heights" occurred. Although the media indicated the attack was aimed at the Southern Command's home base, the attack actually disrupted activation activities of the new Public Forces at the bottom of Ancon Hill.

During the first couple of days after the operation began, anarchists had reigned in the streets of Panama City. Vandals set a supermarket warehouse on fire. Thugs stole cars and then abandoned them after turning them upside down. Digbats roamed the streets, rattling off bursts of automatic-weapons fire at random. "You could see the fires and the Molotov cocktails," reported Sgt. Jeffrey Newport of Springfield, Massachusetts. "You could hear the screams. It was amazing what they were doing to themselves."

The president of the Panamanian Chamber of Commerce, Alfredo Maduro, put losses by looting at $50 million to $1 billion.

Melquiades Dominguez was a security guard at an American-owned electronics warehouse in Panama City. For five days he was a one-man police force, using a 12-gauge shotgun to try to drive off a mob of thieves and hoodlums who ransacked his warehouse and terrorized the civilians in the area. One night he stood atop his warehouse and watched thieves across the street loot the Superior Products warehouse and litter the area with crates from stolen refrigerators, TV sets, and shoes. Felix Larringa was an insurance salesman. He watched helplessly from his apartment balcony as marauding bands on the street below him ripped off all the cars from a Hertz parking lot and blasted the door of a jewelry store.

"Small bands of armed thugs wandered through the barrio," wrote one reporter, "raping, stealing, and murdering at will . . . a man got out of his car, walked to another parked beside it, drew a gun, and killed the driver."

"Have you ever seen a BMW going down the street on a forklift?" asked Lt. Col. Johnny Brooks, whose men tried to stop the theft.

A number of concerned citizens tried to generate some order out of the chaos created in the policeless city swarming with violent, unruly, armed mobs. Some residents dragged abandoned cars, stones, poles, and old refrigerators into their areas to block the roaming looters. The residents developed shifts "to man the barricades." Mr. Larringa said, "We had no choice. We were our own security."[5]

In early January, Gen. Ed Scholes, the chief of staff of XVIII Airborne Corps, took Gen. Carl Vuono, the Army's chief of staff, on a tour of some areas in

Panama City. In one section, where some wealthy Panamanian civilians—doctors, business owners, other professionals—lived, they were greeted warmly. One of the homeowners in the area said, "We feel as if we have been released from prison. In our own country, we feel like prisoners." The people in the area had showered the American soldiers with soft drinks and food.[6]

After a couple of days, the situation in Panama City gradually returned to some sort of normalcy as U.S. soldiers spread out through the city and patrolled the streets, generated a sense of calm and order, and filled in the wide gap in the police ranks left by the surrender and desertion of the PDF who had formerly doubled as the civilian police force.

"We're trying to establish a police force as opposed to a paramilitary organization like the old PDF," said Col. Larry Brede, the commanding officer of Fort Bragg's 16th Military Police Brigade. Colonel Brede had command and control of some eleven hundred MPs who came to Panama at various times during the crisis from posts across the United States. In an effort to change the way the Panamanian people think of their police forces, the Southern Command has brought into Panama eleven thousand sets of green, Vietnam-style jungle fatigues from Fort Bragg for the reconstituted police force. Colonel Brede said that this change in uniform was an attempt "to remove the taint" of the PDF's old blue uniform. He added, "I don't want this new organization to be the old PDF in new uniforms."

When his MPs checked some of the PDF's old police stations in and around Panama City, they found cattle prods and rubber hoses among other devices used to coerce and control the populace. The devices were mute testimony as to why the people feared the Noriega regime.

The MPs from the various units under Colonel Brede's command performed many more duties than just trying to control traffic and prevent looting. They enforced basic laws and operated "detainee" camps for looters, former prisoners, and PDF members. They are "detainees" rather than POWs because, while Noriega declared war on the United States, the United States did not declare war on Noriega. "We're transitioning from pure combat to nation-building," Colonel Brede explained. "We will stay here longer than everyone else."

In the days following the operation, the MPs had processed over 4,000 Panamanian prisoners at a converted rifle range north of Panama City on the Panama Canal. They used 105 tents and 780 rolls of concertina wire to transform the range into a semblance of a detention camp. By the middle of January 1990, less than 1,000 "detainees" remained in the camp. Capt. Kerry Skelton, commander of the 65th MP Company from Fort Bragg, said, "For a couple of days, this place was wall-to-wall people coming through as fast as they could. . . . Some of them were people who performed patrols with my MPs four months ago. We had MPs that worked with PDF members they recognized. They very well may work together again in the future."

"We've got them under control," said Sgt. Michael Hare, a member of Skelton's company. "We take them for chow and showers."

In the operation of the camp, the 65th MP Company was augmented by fifty-six MPs from Fort Lee, Virginia, thirty from the Missouri National Guard, and the 519th Military Intelligence Battalion.

211

Some of the Fort Bragg MPs have spent so much time away from their home base, in places such as St. Croix and Panama, that they consider a return to Bragg "R&R." "The demand for bilingual soldiers is tremendous," said Colonel Brede. He added that he has an Hispanic mechanic whose Spanish is more valuable than his MOS.[7]

SOUTHCOM's goal was to reconstitute the Panamanian police force. The MPs, of course, work along U.S. lines in their methods to reestablish law and order. "We're trying to show that if people are arrested and taken to the police station, they're not going to get beaten with a hose," Colonel Brede explained. "When we are down there alone, people cheer and clap and want autographs and to take pictures. When we're with Panamanians, people tend to get sullen and see our association with the old regime. We're trying to diffuse that."

But in spite of the whooping and hollering, the celebrations and the pot-banging on the street corners, there was still chaos and anarchy in many parts of the nation, especially in Panama City itself. Because many foreign countries wanted to evacuate their citizens, the United States had to open an airport to receive relief supplies and to permit the resumption of some sort of routine air travel. Commercial flights out of Tocumen were resumed on 30 December.

The needs of the Panamanians in Chorillo were most urgent. Their homes and businesses had been burned, in most cases by the looting and ravaging Digbats, but in some cases by battle. The people of the district fled into Balboa. In the Balboa High School athletic stadium they found a refuge where Maj. Michael Lewis and his D Company of the 96th Civil Affairs Battalion had established a "displaced persons" camp. After it had been in operation a few days, the makeshift camp received high marks from Panama's surgeon general and the International Red Cross. The Chorillo mayor acted as camp mayor, and the camp residents had set up their own administrative systems. At the camp, Major Lewis and his men processed and screened almost eleven thousand Panamanians; his camp had an average population of thirty-five hundred at any one time.

"It's a daily battle to control sanitation and health," Major Lewis said, "but we're winning the battle. They have no discipline problems or control problems. They're poor people and probably didn't have much before the fire. A lot of people may be living better now than they were before."[8]

When the humanitarian assistance program was under way about three days after the operation began, there were thirteen military distribution sites (they were closed out on 3 January), at which the U.S. forces in each of the task force areas distributed, to long lines of Panamanians, 75,000 cases of MREs and 1,120,000 pounds of bulk food, including baby food, liquid and dry milk, and dried beans.

In the field of medical assistance, during and just after the operation, the U.S. forces found a paucity of medical supplies in the Panamanian hospitals. As a consequence, the U.S. forces shipped in some 615,920 pounds of medical supplies and treated over 15,000 civilian sick and wounded at fixed and improvised hospitals and aid stations. But the tragedy of the situation was that, during the operation, the U.S. forces found a large PDF warehouse in the

212

Balboa engineering complex where the PDF warehouseman had hoarded over 150,000 pounds of medical supplies. He had been in the habit of demanding bribes before he would distribute any of his wares to legitimate customers. Such was the legacy of Noriega.

Besides the effects on the nation of the political instability caused by Noriega's harsh regime, the prewar U.S. economic sanctions, and the battles of Just Cause, the Panamanian economy had been battered by a deepening recession. A depositor run on the banks prior to the operation had caused bank deposits to drop from $40 billion to $15 billion.

"To keep from having to do this again in five to ten years, it's important to create a strong infrastructure and conclude this conflict on favorable terms to our national interest—a stable, democratic government in Panama," said Lt. Col. Dwayne Aaron, civil-military operations officer for the joint task force and assistant chief of staff for civil-military operations of XVIII Airborne Corps.

"The way this place was organized before, Noriega ran it all and the PDF was in charge," said Lt. Col. Michael P. Peters, 96th Civil Affairs Battalion commander. "You had civilians in nominal charge, but the military was the real authority in the country. They worked independently from the civilian government. The military was so in charge the civilian sector had atrophied. You didn't have a loyal opposition to take its place."

Capt. Ken Carter is the principal adviser to the government of Colón Province, on the Caribbean coast. "He's helping them do everything from collect the garbage to setting up the police force," said Colonel Peters. He added that Capt. Dave Heckert is working with officials in the town of David, on the western coast. These two captains are examples of the civil-affairs world that grew throughout Panama in the days after the demise of the PDF.

The 96th Civil Affairs Battalion is part of the 1st Special Operations Command at Fort Bragg and is the Army's only active-duty civil-affairs unit. About 97 percent of the Army's civil-affairs personnel are in the reserves. Colonel Peters said that it is the reservists, with their in-depth expertise—from air traffic control to banking to police administration to law to medical support—who will provide the long-term care and monitor the various programs set up by the active-duty combat forces and civil-affairs teams. For the first time in its history, the 96th Civil Affairs Battalion deployed in its entirety. In the first stage of the operation, civil-affairs officers and men parachuted into Rio Hato with the Rangers to assist in dealing with civilians from the beginning of the operation. "Commanders here have been made believers in how valuable civil affairs can be," Colonel Aaron said. "Battlefields are not clean. The real world is full of civilians and they're always in the wrong place at the wrong time."

"The challenge is to build a security force that is competent and yet has credibility with the people and understands its role in society and is responsible to the civilian leadership," said Colonel Peters. "If we get the military too efficient too fast and the civilian structure doesn't mature, you'll be in the same situation you were in before."[9]

During the operation and immediately thereafter, the U.S. forces collected over 52,000 weapons from the Noriega regime. They also picked up 28 armored vehicles, 7 ships, almost $8 million, 600 tons of ammunition, almost 14,000 canisters of chemicals (type CS/CN), and 417 kilograms of drugs valued at about $6.8 million.

But by the morning of Christmas Day, Noriega was still at large. The thinking in the Pentagon and in SOUTHCOM prior to the operation had been that Noriega would "take to the woods" with any of his PDF forces who could escape the U.S. forces and fight a guerrilla war à la Robin Hood.

In his office on the twenty-third, General Powell had said, "We will destroy his Robin Hood image."

23 | Winning the West and Noriega's Surrender

But now it was the time to "win the West."[1]

Lt. Col. Luís A. Del Cid was a close Noriega associate who, like Noriega, was wanted by the United States on drug charges. Del Cid was the Noriega-appointed "boss" of the PDF military operations in Panama's western frontier who ran the operation from his headquarters in David, the capital of Chiriquí Province, the area that was the Panamanian version of the "Wild West." The D-day attacks triggered Del Cid's long-standing, Noriega-approved plans to fade into the jungle with a ragtag band of PDF regulars and criminals he had released from jails and continue armed resistance against the Americans.

Maj. Gilberto Pérez was the Spanish-speaking commander of A Company, 1st Battalion, 7th Special Forces Group. His Special Forces unit was "oriented" toward Latin America, and he was well steeped in the history of Panama, its institutions, its military forces, and its culture. On the twenty-second of December he received a warning order through his chain of command to "pacify the districts of Herrera, Coclé, Los Santos, and Veraguas," all provinces to the west of Panama City. His mission was to operate with the 75th Rangers and elements of Colonel Burney's 2d Brigade of the 7th Infantry Division (Light) to cause the commanders of scattered PDF *cuartels* throughout western Panama to surrender their arms and men with as few casualties as possible on both sides. As soon as he received the mission, Major Pérez contacted Colonel Burney at Albrook Air Force Base, sketched the outline of a plan, and then flew his Special Forces company to Río Hato to begin the detailed planning.

From his knowledge of the terrain and military forces of Panama, Pérez was aware that a *cuartel* was the generic term used throughout Latin America for a military base of any kind. Frequently a *cuartel* is an area the size of some four to six city blocks surrounded by a solid wall of varying height and thickness. Perez also knew that the *cuartels* were manned by PDF forces whose size and dedication to El Jefe were not constants.

215

To accomplish his mission over the wide area he had been assigned, Pérez developed a two-phased concept, later referred to as the "Ma Bell approach."[2] In phase one, he planned to insert Special Forces teams into the towns of Santiago, Chitré, and Las Tablas. He selected the airfield in each town as the initial landing zone for his men. An AC-130 Specter gunship would be available in the air to provide close air support. He had arranged with Colonel Kernan and Colonel Burney to have one of their infantry or Ranger battalions standing by with helicopter lift as a quick reaction force should he encounter any resistance his small forces of Green Berets could not handle.

Once he and his team were in place at the town's airfield, Pérez planned to telephone the commander of the local *cuartel* and ask him to meet him at the airfield. When he appeared, Pérez would then tell him that he had an infantry or Ranger battalion standing by and that he wanted the commander to surrender his *cuartel*. There were three terms to the surrender, Pérez would tell the local commander: One, the surrender would be unconditional; two, all weapons would be placed in the *cuartel*'s guard room; and three, all of the PDF in the *cuartel* would assemble on the *cuartel*'s parade ground. Then Major Pérez would "invite" the commander to fly with him over the parade ground to ensure that all of the terms of the surrender had been met. If Pérez detected any hesitancy or reluctance by the commander to comply, Pérez would have the AC-130 fire a few inhibiting 105mm rounds into an unoccupied open part of the *cuartel*. Pérez felt that it was essential to use all available means to gain a peaceful surrender with minimum casualties on either side. That was phase one of the "Ma Bell approach."

In phase two, Pérez and some of his Special Forces would move into the *cuartel* to search the area and to process the PDF soldiers. At the same time, a backup 7th Infantry Division or Ranger company would move into the town to establish law and order. The company's mission would be to prevent looting and reprisals that the citizens might be inclined to take against the surrendering PDF, whose past transgressions of varying degrees against the civilian population might have warranted considerable revenge and retribution.

At 1400 hours on the twenty-third, Pérez launched his first mission. He and his Special Forces flew into the town of Santiago in the province of Veraguas in helicopters from Task Force Hawk of the 7th ID and 617th Aviation Company. As soon as his helicopter set down, Pérez and his team captured three PDF who were at the field. Then Pérez tried to contact the local *cuartel* commander but could not find him. Pérez then decided to fly to the *cuartel* with five of his men. When he got there, he found that the PDF were prepared to surrender and were already assembling on the parade field. One dissatisfied PDF took a shot at the helicopter as it was landing but did no damage. Pérez's men quickly took the misguided youth under control. Pérez then called forward the rest of his SF Company and searched and cleared the *cuartel*. He also brought in Captain Stone and his 7th ID Company and gave him command of the *cuartel*. Pérez left behind with Stone a small Spanish-speaking SF detachment to assist Stone in his work with the local community. Pérez gave Stone four missions: One, gather intelligence on the weapons caches of the PDF and the Digbats who had not yet surrendered; two, assist the local civilian community leaders in gaining control of the town; three, assess the condition of the local infrastructure—hospital, public utilities, law and order, and establish priorities for follow-on civil-military operations; and four, conduct joint Panamanian-U.S. patrols throughout Santiago. For the next few days, Stone and his company followed the instructions carefully, with the resultant restoration of order in Santiago.

At 0630 on the twenty-fourth, Pérez launched his second mission, this one into the town of Chitré, in the province of Herrera. At the airport, he and his men captured one PDF soldier. Pérez then phased into his plan and telephoned the *cuartel* commander, who surrendered his force without any resistance. Colonel Burney's troops followed and accomplished, without serious incidents, the same missions that Stone had accomplished in Santiago.

At 0900 on Christmas Day, Pérez and his team flew into Las Tablas, the capital of Los Santos Province, on a Panamanian peninsula that juts into the Pacific Ocean about due south of the Pacific end of the canal. He landed in an open field and immediately went to a nearby house and telephoned the local commander, who surrendered with no difficulty. Pérez and his small team entered the *cuartel.* When they had finished checking and securing the area, Pérez noticed that a large number of civilians had gathered outside the wall. Pérez made a quick decision. He ordered the PDF to assemble on the parade ground with his own troops lined up beside them. Then Pérez called the combined force to attention, ordered "present arms," and had the Panamanian flag raised on the *cuartel's* flagpole. With this small but symbolic ceremony, Pérez demonstrated that the United States was not a conqueror but a liberator. His impromptu ritual gained the support of the civilians for the follow-on U.S. efforts in the area. An ancillary result was a steady flow of valuable intelligence from the civilian populace.

Meanwhile, at 1000 on Christmas Day, Lt. Col. Joseph Hunt and his 3d Battalion of the 75th Rangers had air-assaulted into Malek Airfield in the town of David, the capital of Chiriquí Province, which abuts the eastern boundary of Costa Rica. David is about fifty miles from the border. Hunt's mission was to seize the airfield for use by follow-on forces, to accept the surrender of PDF forces in the area, and to locate and secure cache sites. By 1100, Hunt's men had secured the airfield. Five hours later, Hunt moved one company into the city of David and began searching for and securing suspected cache sites.

Lt. Col. Robert Cronin and his 5th of the 21st Infantry from the 7th ID arrived at Río Hato on 21 December and relieved the 3d Battalion of the 75th Rangers. In the early morning hours of the twenty-third, the 5th of the 21st took over control of the 6th Zone Police headquarters in Penonomé, about 62 miles southwest of Panama City, from the 3d of the 75th. Capt. John Fieder commanded B Company of the 5th of the 21st Infantry. He said that his mission at Penonomé was multipurpose: to relieve the Rangers, to secure the PDF who were surrendering themselves, and to gather and secure arms and equipment from the PDF and the Digbats.

Inside the prison at Penonomé, Fieder's men found a small cache of weapons, including the ubiquitous and rugged AK-47, some ammunition, and some

Molotov cocktails. The 5th of the 21st debriefed the detainees, fed them, and separated them into three groups according to rank. Civilians gave the gate guards leads on the location of other PDF members and arms caches.

On the night of the twenty-sixth, the 5th of the 21st flew out of Río Hato aboard C-130s and arrived at Malek Airfield in David early the following morning. Within an hour of landing, the battalion was in the process of relieving the Rangers in David. One platoon finished securing the airfield, while another platoon moved to a nearby rock quarry to confiscate a reported weapons cache. A third platoon helicoptered to an area in David secured by the Rangers. When the platoon landed in the helicopters, it was surrounded by about a hundred Panamanians trying to "get a good look at the machine and the passengers. As the crowd formed around the aircraft, the Light fighters slipped into the city streets on the way to relieve the Rangers." The citizens were definitely friendly and welcoming.

Colonel Cronin became the commander of the district. Major Pérez served as his adviser and interpreter. During the next few days, Cronin and his men visited all the *cuartels* and towns in the region. They established liaison with the newly appointed Panamanian commanders of the *cuartels* and the governors and mayors throughout the district. Colonel Burney and the entire 2d Brigade operated throughout the central and western portions of Panama and provided support to the governments in Río Hato, Santiago, and David. Their efforts paid off in a number of ways. One was very important: Major Pérez and his team accepted the surrender of Del Cid.

The surrender of Del Cid was accomplished more easily than Pérez and his men had at first thought possible. On Thursday, the twenty-first, Del Cid had had second thoughts about fighting from the jungle with his motley crew of renegades. He contacted some Catholic priests in his area and through them arranged to talk to Gen. Marc Cisneros, the Spanish-speaking commander of the Army's forces in Southern Command, who was acting as General Stiner's deputy. They agreed on the phone to the unconditional terms of the surrender and, by Friday, a white flag flew over Del Cid's camouflaged jungle headquarters. This somewhat unexpected action negated the need for an American foray into the jungle and saved the lives of many men on both sides of the battle.

Another payoff: Lieutenant Colonel Cronin and Major Pérez convinced the governors in the area to permit the new Panamanian security forces to carry weapons and thus begin to take over the role of maintaining law and order. They also established a program to train the security forces to deal with the population as a "protecting police force and not a dominating military force."

Major Pérez was still not satisfied with the pace of the pacification and felt that there were not enough U.S. forces present to bring peace to the region. From one of the outlying areas, he flew to David and convinced Colonel Burney to redeploy a battalion to Río Hato to conduct "reconnaissance in force operations" throughout the region. These incursions into the areas outside the towns resulted in the capture of several weapons caches and a number of former PDF soldiers and Dignity Battalion troops. Major Pérez continued to conduct strike operations in the same successful way that he had in Santiago, Chitré, and

218

Las Tablas. In one location, his Special Forces team captured 180 members of the Macho de Monte.

He also used his Psyops men and their equipment and techniques to great advantage. One communiqué, read over the local radio, urged Digbat members in Chiriquí to turn in their weapons. Within an hour, a large number of them were lined up ready to surrender their weapons in exchange for a bounty of $150 promised by the United States.

In addition to Del Cid, four other regional commanders formerly intensely loyal to Noriega and beholden to him for their positions, pledged loyalty to the new president, Endara, by the end of the week and were allowed by the U.S. commanders in the area to retain their posts—at least temporarily.

On Saturday, the twenty-third, the reign of looters and thieves in La Chorrera, about twenty miles west of the canal, came to an abrupt halt. A unit from the 7th ID moved into the empty PDF headquarters and quickly restored order to the area. The PDF headquarters had sustained surprisingly little damage during the earlier fighting. By dawn on Saturday, groups of Panamanian civilians were forming outside the headquarters, and by midmorning the crowd had swelled to thousands, ready to thank the United States for the intervention of its armed forces. People hollered, flashed peace signs, and waved at the soldiers. Women and young girls hugged and kissed the grinning and embarrassed soldiers.

Noriega's grip was loosened. But he was still "AWOL" as far as the U.S. troops were concerned.

*   *   *

Max Thurman had had four objectives to achieve during Just Cause: Protect American lives, safeguard the integrity of the Panama Canal, restore democracy in Panama, and capture Noriega. On Christmas morning he had accomplished only three quarters of his missions; Noriega was still loose.

In the early developmental stages of Blue Spoon, the planners at the Pentagon and in SOUTHCOM had allocated Special Forces teams to trail Noriega, totally surreptitiously, and to capture him when the National Command Authority made that decision. The tracking began weeks ahead of the actual D-day for Just Cause. General Thurman said later that the teams knew of Noriega's whereabouts 80 percent of the time.

One spokesman for the U.S. Special Operations Command, Gen. Jim Lindsay's outfit, said in a wrap-up of the operation:

> An additional force that can only be mentioned in passing is Task Force Blue and Task Force Green. These forces, supported by quick-reaction helicopters and AC-130 gunships, had the difficult task of capturing the elusive Noriega. Our intelligence efforts greatly narrowed the possibilities for his location and allowed this force to apply pressure to him commencing at H-hour. This pressure never let up, with our force systematically pursuing each substantive lead. This effectively denied Noriega a place to hide and prevented his escape from Panama.[3]

Noriega had a series of plush apartments, condos, and beach houses scattered throughout Panama. One of them, the Farallon beach house, was on the shore of the Gulf of Panama near Río Hato. At H + 2 hours, Buck Kernan dispatched a team from his 2d Battalion, which had jumped onto Río Hato, to investigate the beach house. The team found a palatial, beautifully furnished house—without Noriega.

Noriega's other homes and offices were equally luxurious. One office, at Fort Amador, was windowless and drab on the outside but well appointed on the inside. "Noriega was a conditioned drinker," according to a SOUTHCOM speaker,

> and well-stocked bars were centerpieces of each of his various residences. The beach house at Río Hato reportedly had a bar in every major room. As the fine furnishings attest, Noriega liked the good life. His corruption and drug money allowed him to indulge in expensive furniture and pieces of artwork. He enjoyed all this while his country's economy went to ruin.
>
> True to his image of machismo, Noriega was also a womanizer. Despite the jealousy of his wife, Felicidad, Noriega kept several women. His favorite apparently was Vicky Amado—the person he called first in this office during the October coup attempt. Another mistress was identified in Santiago and, of course, he had planned to spend the night with a temporary liaison the night of the invasion.
>
> Despite Noriega's devotion to his daughters and his propensity for high living, dark hints of depravity are evident. TVs and VCRs with pornographic tapes still seated, were found in several of his homes. Rumors had circulated of Brazilian witches. A set of quarters on the causeway at Fort Amador yielded proof of the rumors.[4]

From H-hour on, General Thurman had kept General Powell informed of the details of the search for Noriega. Just before midnight on the nineteenth, General Powell went to the Crisis Situation Room in the Pentagon's National Military Command Center (NMCC). There he had direct communications with General Thurman in Panama. Throughout the early-morning hours he kept track of what was happening, especially of Noriega's whereabouts and the rescue of Kurt Muse. The news from Thurman was good and bad: Good—the drops at Torrijos and Río Hato were going well; the initial assaults by the in-country forces were proceeding generally as planned; the Comandancia was in flames; the PDF were surrendering in droves; bad: three SEALs had been killed at Paitilla Airport; the Muse helicopter had crashed; Noriega was still at large.

General Thurman told General Powell that the Rangers who jumped on Tocumen had almost captured Noriega in the Officers' Club at Tocumen. But when Noriega heard the aircraft and saw the parachutes, he jumped into his clothes and ran to his ever-present getaway car. He roared away from Tocumen and headed for Panama City where, for the next few days, he moved from one hideout to another, collecting IOUs from his various cronies.[5]

In its frustration, the U.S. administration put a $1 million bounty on Noriega's head, hoping to encourage a PDF trooper or some member of the opposition to put the finger on the dictator. General Powell, by now referring to Noriega as "a dope-sniffing, voodoo-loving thug," was becoming increasingly vexed that, with the success of the military operation in Panama, neither the troops spreading throughout the countryside nor the Special Forces who had been targeted on Noriega had been able to find him.

But the relentless tracking had an effect. At about 1530 on Christmas Eve, a car drove up to the residence of the Vatican's representative in Panama, the papal nuncio, Monsignor Sebastian Laboa. Out of the car emerged General Noriega, wearing a T-shirt and shouldering two AK-47's. Noriega went inside the nunciatore and requested political asylum.

Prior to Noriega's arrival at the nunciatore, the U.S. forces had been overwatching other embassies in the hopes that Noriega might seek asylum in one of them, particularly the Cuban embassy. His selection of the papal nuncio's quarters had a double deterrent: It was both an embassy and church property.

But both Max Thurman and Carl Stiner reviewed the methods by which they might get Noriega out of the nunciatore. Monsignor Laboa met with Max Thurman and Stiner and told them that if shooting started in the nunciatore, they were authorized to make an assault to rescue as many people as possible. Stiner got on the hot line to Kelly in the Pentagon and asked for new rules of engagement that would comply with Monsignor Laboa's statement. Kelly went to Powell and Cheney and got the rules changed. Throughout the time that Noriega was holed up in the nunciatore, Thurman was frequently on the hot line to the Pentagon discussing the "what ifs." What if a hostage is taken? What if there was shooting in the nunciatore? By this time, over a hundred U.S. soldiers surrounded the nunciatore.

On 27 December, Max Thurman ordered loudspeakers placed in a parking lot next to the nunciatore and blasted the building with rock music. The noise was not specifically intended to force Noriega out of the building, as some Panamanians reasoned; rather, it was to prevent eavesdropping on SOUTHCOM's negotiations with the papal nuncio. Some of the rock numbers included "I Fought the Law," "Voodoo Child," and "You're No Good." Reporters could hear the music from the twelfth floor of a nearby hotel, and people walking the streets could hear the music for blocks.[6]

By the twenty-seventh, the Panama Canal was returning to normal operations, and officials said that they hoped to go into a twenty-four-hour-a-day operation to clear up a backlog of some 125 ships.

In Rome, Vatican spokesman Joaquín Navarro said that there was no legal way for the Holy See to turn Noriega over to the United States because the Vatican and the United States had no extradition treaty. He added that the Vatican was studying the case in its "judicial, diplomatic, and humanitarian, and therefore ethical considerations." At one point General Thurman tried curbside diplomacy, talking to Monsignor Laboa outside the embassy. General Thurman did not neglect the military side: He had the embassy tightly surrounded with troops and ordered helicopters and AC-130's to patrol the sky overhead constantly. U.S. troops shot out the street lights with pellet guns

(M-16's would have endangered nearby Panamanian civilians), erected concertina wire around the area, blocked the streets in the area with APCs, and mowed the grass outside the embassy compound to improve the view. Noriega appeared not to notice.[7]

During the ten days Noriega stayed in the nunciatore, the U.S. administration became more and more concerned and even felt that the standoff might continue indefinitely. President Bush said that if the Vatican refused to turn over Noriega, "that complicates things." To preclude other countries from granting Noriega asylum, the U.S. Justice Department filed papers in four countries to freeze bank accounts in which Noriega was thought to have stashed more than $10 million in "illegal drug money." Cuba and the Dominican Republic, where one of Noriega's daughters lives, had been mentioned as possible havens. But the Dominican foreign minister, Joaquín Ricardo, said that his country had an extradition treaty with the United States and that Noriega could be extradited if he went there.

During Noriega's incarceration, President Bush seemed to have left open the possibility that Noriega could be tried in Panama. He mentioned that Noriega might regain power if left in Panama "unless he were in total custody and sentenced to the prison sentence he deserves."

In a little-noticed footnote to the events of the twenty-seventh was the item that Vicky Amado, Noriega's longtime mistress, had been arrested along with hundreds of PDF soldiers. And Benjamin Colomarco, the head of Noriega's Dignity Battalions, surrendered on 11 January 1990 and was in U.S. custody.

Life inside the Vatican embassy had not been pleasant for the deposed dictator. Monsignor José Sebastian Laboa, the papal nuncio, who had once served in the Vatican as the "devil's advocate," taking the negative side when the Vatican examined the veracity of miracles, tried various means of pressure to force Noriega to surrender to the U.S. authorities. In the white stucco embassy, Laboa assigned Noriega a white room decorated only with a broken TV set and a crucifix. The one window was opaque. Initially Laboa shut down the air conditioning, resulting in an almost unbearably hot and humid room. He allowed Noriega only one alcoholic drink—a beer—during his entire ten-day stay.

Among other means of pressuring Noriega, Laboa arranged for two diplomats to hold a stage-whispered conversation outside Noriega's door, during which the diplomats discussed the fate of deposed Nicaraguan dictator Somoza, who died in exile in an ambush in Paraguay. The monsignor told Noriega that he had authorized the U.S. Army to "storm the embassy if a hostage situation arose." The priests in the embassy reminded him that he was an unwelcome guest and provided only minimal hospitality. He was given nothing special, said embassy spokesman José Cubillas. "He was a vegetarian but did not get vegetarian meals." He also mentioned that for most of the time Noriega had carried on very few conversations.[8]

Monsignor Laboa kept up the psychological pressure. He told Noriega, "You could be lynched like Mussolini and exposed in a plaza as the laughingstock of the people. That would be less than a dignified end for you." He also told him that the Panamanian bishops had written to Pope John Paul II and that the pope had agreed with the bishops that Noriega was a common criminal and ineligible for political asylum.

But then Monsignor Laboa became more conciliatory. He turned on the air conditioning in Noriega's room and invited him to eat the New Year's Eve dinner with embassy personnel and some Noriega cronies who had also sought sanctuary. At the dinner, Noriega and embassy personnel sat at a large table and ate pasta. Monsignor Laboa said that the conversation was strained because no one wanted to discuss the circumstances of Noriega's presence. After dinner, they all attended Mass in the embassy's chapel, with Noriega sitting in the last pew by himself.

During the four days that the U.S. Psyops team pummeled the nunciatore with loud rock music, Noriega, an opera lover, could hear the blasting music that pounded his ears. And he also heard news over the loudspeakers—that his top aides were surrendering to the U.S. forces and that his millions of dollars in foreign banks were being frozen. For a time he had access to a phone, but it was pulled to prevent his manipulation of his fortune. The last day of his stay in the nunciatore was perhaps his worst: Twenty thousand people filled the streets shouting "Assassin!," "No More!," and "Out of the nunciatore!" Panamanians hung him in effigy. The figure was in full military uniform, and the face was a pineapple—reminiscent of Noriega's pockmarked face. Often during his ten-day stay, to show their contempt and hatred for the man, Panamanians smashed pineapples to pulp in the streets. In a poll taken during the first week of January 1990 by CBS News and a Washington research firm, 92 percent of Panamanians interviewed approved of the "invasion."

One of Noriega's last conversations before his surrender was with Vicky Amado. General Thurman's office had tried to get her to convince Noriega to come out. But she didn't. During that ten-minute conversation, she told him, in effect, "The decision is in your hands."

Monsignor Laboa's last words to Noriega were, "You have to decide." Noriega, increasingly withdrawn and silent, finally said, "That solution of yours is best."

Before Noriega walked out of the nunciatore, he had made three requests of the United States: that he be allowed to make a few phone calls, that his decision to leave be kept secret until the actual time of his arrest, and that he be permitted to wear his uniform. The administration had earlier given assurances to Noriega that he would receive a fair trial and that he would not be tried on a federal drug kingpin statute that carries the death penalty. Because the administration did not deal directly with Noriega, all communications were through the Vatican nuncio. Because Noriega did not have a uniform with him, General Thurman's headquarters delivered one to the embassy.

At 2044 on the evening of 3 January 1990, General Noriega, accompanied by Father Villanueva, walked the twenty yards from the Vatican embassy front door to Avenida Balboa and surrendered to Delta Force troops outside the embassy gate. He was escorted across the street to the elementary school that the U.S. Special Operations troopers used as a headquarters. Noriega carried a Bible and a toothbrush. One senior U.S. official on hand said that Noriega "really looked like a whipped and beaten little man." Noriega was immediately handcuffed. "I will pray for you every day," said Father Villanueva, the parish priest who had been helpful in getting Noriega to give himself up. *"Gracias,"* said a visibly shaken, fully uniformed Noriega.

General Thurman said later that U.S. officials had only a few minutes' warning that Noriega would leave the embassy. He said that Gen. Henry Cisneros received a telephone call at his CP across the street asking him to "report to the gate." No Panamanian officials were present, but the Endara government was aware of what was going on.[9]

Noriega was escorted to a UH-60 Black Hawk helicopter waiting on the soccer field behind the school building and flown to Howard Air Force Base, where the helicopter landed on the tarmac in front of the small field medical hospital set up there. Noriega was escorted from the helicopter to a waiting MC-130 Talon aircraft, engines running, and was turned over to the DEA agents and U.S. marshals waiting aboard. It was 2131, just forty-one minutes from the time he had left the nunciatore. He was on his way to the U.S. District Court in Miami on federal drug trafficking charges.

Once inside the plane, the agent in chief told him to undress completely. At the time, he was wearing a dress uniform without hat. Underneath, he wore a white T-shirt and two pairs of underwear—one set of white boxer shorts over a set of bright red Jockey undershorts. Two Special Operations physicians then gave him a complete physical examination, asked him for pertinent medical history, and found that he had no physical complaints besides being tired and thirsty.

After the physical, the agents gave him brown Army boxer shorts, a brown T-shirt, a green Army aviator coverall-type flight suit, Army green socks, and hospital patient slippers. After he dressed in that outfit, he was handcuffed and manacled by U.S. marshals, and seated and strapped into the nylon jump seats set up in the forward part of the aircraft just behind the radio and navigational consoles. DEA agents photographed him and asked him a number of questions after formally placing him under arrest and reading him his Miranda rights—in Spanish. One special operations physician stayed aboard for the 5½-hour flight to Florida.

During the flight, Noriega appeared anxious and very tired; the only time he smiled was when a DEA agent told him that the physician stayed aboard to take care of him on the flight. He slept for nearly four hours sitting upright after agents gave him more water and told him what to expect on landing in Florida.

An hour before touchdown, Noriega asked permission to get dressed again in his military uniform. The U.S. marshals found the uniform in the luggage but discovered that they did not have a key to open the handcuffs. They finally broke the chain connecting the two cuffs. Noriega dressed in his uniform. The marshals again manacled him and put him into another set of handcuffs (with the separated cuffs from the first set still on his wrists). Once again he sat down, and the marshals strapped him to the seat. After the plane landed at Homestead Air Force Base in southern Florida, DEA and other U.S. officials interviewed him in the back of the plane. Then he was led to one of a caravan of black limousines that took him to a nearby taxiway, where a small government Learjet was waiting to fly him to Miami International Airport. From there he was transported to the jail in downtown Miami.[10]

As word of Noriega's departure from the nunciatore and his surrender to the U.S. officials spread across Panama City, horns honked; fireworks shot into the black sky; and people laughed, yelled, and raced up and down the streets, waving U.S. and Panamanian flags. Hundreds of cars jammed Fiftieth Street, near the center of what had been a thriving international financial center.

Max Thurman had accomplished the last of his missions.

24 | The New Military

The post-Vietnam doldrums were over. The military forces of the United States—all volunteers—had proved, in combat, that they were highly trained, superbly equipped with the latest and best arms and equipment available to any nation's military, that they were disciplined and dedicated professionals who knew their business—the business of war.

Gen. Edward Meyer, Army Chief of Staff from 1979 to 1983, said that Operation Just Cause "was probably the best-conceived military operation since World War II." A senior Pentagon officer said that "the Panama invasion was a test of manhood."

Dan Rather, in a CBS Radio news analysis and commentary on 28 December 1989, said,

> The men and women of the United States armed forces have done a superb job. They have performed efficiently and professionally. . . . The men and women of the armed forces of the United States were given a mission by their commander in chief. They had their orders. They were given a job to do, and they did it well. In the words of Tennyson's poetry, "Theirs was not to reason why, theirs was but to do or die." They did and some of them died.
>
> It is easy to blow bugles, have the band play marches and wave flags. It is hard to storm the beaches, hit the silk, and blow the barracks. Very hard and very dangerous.
>
> Before the smoke clears in Panama, before the politicians and the propagandists complete weaving their self-serving spells, it would be well for the rest of us to note and ponder the brave, efficient, professional service our citizen-warriors have given our country in the streets and jungles of Panama.[1]

Will and Ariel Durant have written that "War is a constant of history. In the last 3,451 years of recorded history, only 268 years have seen no war." In the

215 years of its history, the United States has been involved in 11 major wars and over 171 battles. The U.S. armed forces have lost over 650,000 men and women in battle and have had nearly 2½ million wounded. Since World War II, worldwide, there have been almost 400 revolts, coups, and small wars, and 69 major wars, including Afghanistan, Iran-Iraq, the Falklands, the Yom Kippur War, and the Vietnamese invasion of Kampuchea.

Since World War II, the United States has been involved in six major engagements, including Korea, Vietnam, Panama, and the Gulf War, and has resorted to the use of or the threat of the use of force for political effect some 219 times. These include the air attack on Libya, the stationing of forces in the Sinai, the *Mayaguez* affair, and the dispatch of Marines to Lebanon.

The road back from the victories of World War II has been long, difficult, and circuitous. The Korean War started with a weak, undisciplined Army used to the easy life of occupation duty. By the end of the Korean stalemate, the Army had regained some stamina, discipline, and esprit. But the politically designed end of the war—an armistice—left the Army with a feeling of frustration and skeptical of the worth of its sacrifices and losses.

Vietnam started out with a will and a determination—"Ask not what the country can do for you" enthusiasm. It ended with another political solution and a military establishment shot through with defeatism, marginal discipline, an "anything goes" philosophy, and barely functioning as a fighting machine.

On 20 November 1970, a group of Green Berets led by the stalwart and battle-experienced Col. "Bull" Simons raided the Son Tay Vietnamese camp allegedly holding American prisoners of war. The raid was carried out with surprise, skill, and courage by a singularly well-trained, disciplined, well-led group of volunteers. Unfortunately, the North Vietnamese had moved the U.S. POWs, and the raiders found the Son Tay camp empty.[2]

In April 1980, the United States launched an airborne raid to rescue the U.S. embassy personnel held hostage by Iran. On the night of 24 April, the plan began to disintegrate in Desert One—a blinding dust storm made helicopter navigation difficult, the Marine helicopters arrived late, a fiery accident in the desert cost eight American lives, and eventually there were not enough helicopters to complete the mission successfully. Col. Charlie Beckwith decided then and there to abandon the rescue attempt.

In 1983, commanders in Lebanon failed to build a barricade that could have prevented just one explosive-laden truck from crashing into a Marine barracks and snuffing out the lives of 241 Marines. As a result, the United States was forced to pull out.

In 1983, the United States invaded Grenada, an ultimately successful operation against a motley crew of 680 Cuban construction workers, of whom only 50 or so were soldiers. But the operation was fraught with difficulties—19 Americans died and 152 were wounded, communications between services did not work, and the command structure was multiheaded and ill-defined. In addition, the tactical plan was fraught with difficulties—no surprise, piecemeal commitment of forces, little maneuverability, no unity of command.

The Grenada strike was thrown together rapidly just a couple of days before the assault. Vice Adm. (Ret.) Joseph Metcalf III, who commanded the Grenada task force, said: "In Panama they had a lot of time to prepare, and they did a hell of a job; they were able to tailor things a lot better."[3]

Operation Just Cause in Panama was different. The work, the training, the revitalization of the U.S. armed forces during the eighties was evident. TV shots of the troops in action in Panama showed soldiers properly clad in their uniforms, wearing helmets, and handling their weapons expertly. But that was only part of the metamorphosis of the post-Vietnamese U.S. military establishment. The men and women who fought in Panama were all volunteers. Almost all of them had at least a high school education. Recruiters could be "choosy" about whom they would select for enlistment. The military's leaders had reinstated discipline in the ranks. NCOs and officers were well trained in their specialties. Training was not a hit-or-miss proposition. The National Training Centers at Fort Irwin, California, and Fort Chaffee, Arkansas, forged men into units who knew how to fight the AirLand battle specified in *FM 25-100*.

Just Cause was one of the largest and most sophisticated joint airborne and ground contingency operations in modern history. (The 1982 British invasion of the Falklands is by far the longest. It was, for the most part, a British Navy, Marines, and Army operation.) Just Cause represented integrated planning and execution among joint forces—Army, Navy, Marines, Air Force. It demonstrated that the mixing of special forces and conventional forces was not only possible but also enhanced the success of the operation. It showed the practicability of the use of joint communications-electronics operating instructions. It validated the necessity for small-unit drills and training in urban terrain. It proved that troops fight to the standards to which they are trained. It showed that night operations have a great advantage, and that night-vision devices are essential for night air assaults. It proved that live fire exercises are imperative for soldier confidence, fire control, and fire distribution. It certified the worth of the AH-64 Apache on night operations and the Hellfire missile as a "surgical weapon." It proved the value of using Psyops and electronic warfare and the necessity of training Psyops troopers with conventional forces. And it proved that U.S. military planners could tailor and package a force of paratroopers, special forces, light infantry, mechanized infantry, marines, sailors, airmen, psyops units, military police, and civil affairs units to the task immediately at hand. It proved that obedience to the oft-repeated but oft-ignored principles of war—surprise, mass, objective, unity of command, maneuver, offensive, and economy of force—paves the way for success in battle.

The commander in chief of the U.S. armed forces, the president of the United States, gave his military forces a job to do and then let them do it without second-guessing or "tying one hand behind their backs." President Bush did not pore over maps and select targets for air strikes the way President Johnson did during the Vietnam War. President Bush was not in direct communication with the commander in the field to give suggestions or orders, as President Carter allegedly was. And the Pentagon let the field commanders fight the battles. General Powell was upset, for example, that the forces in the field could not find Noriega immediately after H-hour. But he let the plan unfold and permitted Max Thurman to "run the show." General Stiner had full command in the field. Every "trooper who carried a gun" was under his command. He was the sole commander, even though the commanding general of Fleet Marine Forces, Atlantic, did want General Stiner to use more Marines and to set up a separate Marine headquarters for the operation.

A spokesman for SOUTHCOM said,

> Operation Just Cause was the largest use of strategic air assets to introduce tactical forces directly into combat in the history of the U.S. military. In the initial operations, it delivered the equivalent of a division minus onto tactical drop zones and had delivered an entire division within the first thirty-six hours. Strength figures peaked out at just over twenty-seven thousand soldiers, sailors, airmen, and marines. Enemy personnel losses are difficult to categorize due to the use of the paramilitary Dignity Battalions and the proclivity of many of the uniformed PDF to become nonuniformed as soon as possible after hostilities initiated.[4]

The operation was not without its costs. Twenty-three U.S. servicemen were killed and 324 wounded. The reported enemy losses were 314 killed in action and 124 wounded. The estimated civilian casualties were 202 killed and 1,508 wounded. The exact figures will never be known.[5]

General Thurman went to extraordinary measures to determine the number and type of civilian casualties. For a month after the surrender of Noriega, General Thurman's teams of experts went to morgues, hospitals, churches, schools, and even cemeteries to try to track accurately the civilian casualties. His teams worked closely with the Panamanian Red Cross. The Panamanians also did substantial research on casualties and actually came up with figures less than Thurman's teams. General Thurman assigned his civil affairs/military government units to assist the government of Panama "in any way possible."[6]

There were, of course, difficulties. General Stiner alleged at a Washington meeting with defense writers on 26 February 1990 that, while he had "no direct knowledge" but "had heard" of them, he cited three "possibilities" that the operation had been compromised. One was that "A call went from someone in the State Department to a friend of his who was a member of the Panama Canal Commission that said, 'Tonight is the night. One o'clock in the morning is the time.' This individual (in Panama) began to call around to his buddies . . . and word spread.

"The second thing that I heard, and this is being looked at at the National Security Agency level, was that there was a burst broadcast [a message sent out in less than a second and decoded at the other end] that went out of Cuba to the south toward Nicaragua and Panama. I don't know what that said, and I don't know if anybody knows what that said, but I heard it.

"There was speculation (about the U.S. military action) on the evening news at 2200 that night (19 December) . . . that the 82d Airborne had left Fort Bragg and it is expected that they headed to Panama."

A few days later, chief Pentagon spokesman Pete Williams released a statement saying General Stiner was wrong in just about everything he said to reporters about how leaks had "compromised" the operation.

The Army's commanders in the field also recognized some faults. They saw the need for better equipment to prevent fratricide—"antifratricide equipment," they call it. At Río Hato, for example, during the hours of darkness, a "Little Bird," a Hughes 500 helicopter, fired on a squad of men moving forward along the ground in the same area where it was strafing. Two men were killed. In another case, the Specter firing near the Comandancia on D-day wounded a number of men assaulting the building.

There were some difficulties on the ground in Panama during the operation. For example, a number of paratroopers and some of the 82d's heavy-drop equipment missed their designated DZs. And, of course, the miserable weather at Pope Air Force Base postponed the arrival of the 82d's paratroopers at the scheduled time, causing a delay in the start of their ongoing missions.

Civilians were killed and civilian areas damaged. But the media seem to have exaggerated the extent of the deaths and the damage. CBS's *60 Minutes* in the summer of 1990 quoted sources that as many as four thousand civilians may have been killed. Sgt. Lewis A. Matson, who was present in the area after the cessation of hostilities and who took many photos for the Department of the Army, wrote that CBS's claim "is ridiculous. American soldiers would have been involved in the burial of these bodies or the elimination of these bodies. American soldiers have been unable to hide such facts."

Sergeant Matson also wrote, "As the fight for the Comandancia began, PDF soldiers took refuge in El Chorillo, the dense neighborhood of makeshift housing, cardboard boxes, all around several high-rise buildings adjacent to the Comandancia. Vulnerable from all sides, American soldiers fired back when fired upon, and while capturing the Comandancia, the neighborhood was set on fire. By whom? There's no saying. It could have been the PDF themselves. So the fight to take the Comandancia resulted in the destruction of one neighborhood, and at that the high-rises are still standing. . . . But that's it—no other large-scale destruction took place in Panama during the invasion. . . . Any destruction downtown was brought on by the Panamanians themselves. Americans didn't loot Panama City—the Panamanians did."

I. Roberto Eisenmann, Jr., is the crusading publisher of *La Prensa,* a Panamanian newspaper that in February 1988 was forced to shut down when some of Noriega's "thugs" wrecked its offices. He is now back on the job running the paper. In an interview published in the April 1990 issue of *American Legion Magazine,* he was asked about the charge that U.S. troops caused extensive damage and destroyed entire civilian neighborhoods, especially in the Chorillo district of Panama City.

"In Chorillo," he said, "where most of the damage occurred, there was extensive testimony from eyewitnesses indicating that most of the destruction was because of fires set by Noriega troops. Many 'Dignity Battalion' members were seen throwing gasoline on buildings and then firing grenades in the area."

To underscore the fact that the Panamanians did in fact do some destruction themselves, no one less than President Endara himself took a sledgehammer to the wall of the Comandancia on Thursday, 11 January 1990. The Panamanians who were watching President Endara grit his teeth and swing the sledgehammer shouted "Harder! Harder!" Vice President Ricardo Arias Calderon, who accompanied Endara to the symbolic destruction of Noriega's old headquarters, said, "The demolition indicates in concrete terms to our people that Noriega's regime is over." Endara said, "For us, it is the end of an era of militarism."

The Comandancia, a bullet-scarred, four-story building, was razed and replaced by housing for families who were left homeless by Just Cause, government officials said.

"The invasion forces targeted with unprecedented accuracy the PDF and their locations," continued Sergeant Matson. "On the night of 19 December, the DNI . . . located in a heavily populated residential area of Balboa about a mile north of the Comandancia was targeted by Air Force gunships. The internal walls of the DNI were completely destroyed; however, the external walls were left standing as were the palm trees on the front lawn. Across the street from the DNI is a three-story 'Young Men's Christian Association' building. The YMCA received not a single piece of shrapnel."[7]

Some armchair tacticians, with twenty-twenty hindsight and little knowledge of military tactics or capabilities, questioned the advisability of dropping, instead of airlanding, the 82d's paratroopers on airfields that the Rangers had already secured. But to the commander of the 82d, Maj. Gen. James Johnson, there was no question about his method for introducing the 82d into Panama. "Given the choice, I can tell you on my watch we will always airdrop," he said when questioned about the drop versus airland issue. As far as he knew when he left Fort Bragg, the airfield was probably "hot," and it was not until about 0530 on 20 December that the Rangers told him the field was secure. And, he added, "It's usually faster and safer—given the possibility that the enemy can launch a surprise attack on taxiing planes—to parachute."[8]

As the division chief of staff, Col. G. A. Crocker, said after the operation, "The 82d Airborne Division combat parachute assault into Torrijos was a large success. The assault rapidly introduced a fully capable combined arms brigade task force into a combat environment with accuracy and minimum injuries. The operation validated joint Army/Air Force doctrine and training."

By and large it was a winner, an operation executed as planned with vigor, daring, and success. The Vietnam doldrums were over. The president of the United States could order his military forces into combat and within fifty-three hours the lead elements of the attacking force would be in action. Execution of contingency plans was not only a possibility but also, proven in Panama, a certainty. The next display of U.S. armed might, about a year later, would be a roaring, TV-centered, hero-worshiping, chest-thumping, flag-waving, parade-making, military success. Desert camouflage fatigues became a fashion.

The Gulf War was yet to come, however, when 1,924 XVIII Airborne Corps and 82d Airborne Division paratroopers, led by General Stiner and General Johnson, parachuted back onto Sicily DZ at Fort Bragg at 0800 on 12 January 1990 on their return from Panama. They dropped from eight hundred feet from twenty C-141 Starlifters. Gen. Carl E. Vuono, the Army chief of staff and a former member of the 82d himself, was on the DZ to greet the troopers, who formed into five columns and marched toward the stands where over five thousand families, soldiers, and friends awaited them. The jump was symbolic and represented the other men and women who had made the Panama operation such a success. General Vuono congratulated the soldiers on their "unqualified success." For the 82d soldiers, the battle was over. But for many of the troops still in Panama, there was the problem of nation-building still to be done. As General Stiner told the troops in formation on Sicily Drop Zone just after the drop, "The mission in Panama was a difficult one. We were literally to decapitate a government and then shake hands with the same people who we fought the night before and say, 'We want to help you now.'"

General Stiner had full praise for his troops. "You would have been very proud of your soldiers," he told the assembled crowd on the edge of the DZ. "They're dedicated and motivated by all the things the American flag stands for, the very flags you were waving. Everyone knew there would be danger, but not a single one hesitated to go or enter battle time and time again. They were well trained for the mission, and they fought the way they trained."[9]

The Panama operation proved that the military forces of the United States had turned a corner. The military technology developments and the buildup of the volunteer forces in the eighties, the dedication of the leaders from corporal to chairman of the Joint Chiefs of Staff, and the resurgence of the U.S. military were now realities. Resort to war is a difficult decision for a president to make. And as any combat-tested soldier knows and believes, the resort to war should be the last and only solution to the salvation or the protection of the nation's interests. "War is still hell," and no one knows that better than a soldier who has fought in one.

One can debate the wisdom of Just Cause as a solution to the problems of the United States with Noriega. One cannot debate that when the military forces of the United States were given a mission, they accomplished it with new fervor, dedication, self-confidence, and professionalism. Today's U.S. military forces are without doubt the best the country has ever built.

The U.S. military was now a force capable of carrying out the will of the commander in chief. Just Cause proved it; Desert Shield and Desert Storm would further validate it.

Notes

1. Noriega's Rise to Power

1. John Dinges, *Our Man in Panama* (New York: Random House, 1990), p. 31. Dinges's book covers the career of Noriega in detail.
2. *Current Biography Yearbook 1988,* pp. 428–31, contains a concise biographical sketch of Noriega, including his relationship with Torrijos.
3. Frederick Kempe, *Divorcing the Dictator* (New York: G. P. Putnam's Sons, 1990). Extracts of this book appeared in "The Noriega Files," *Newsweek* (15 January 1990). The book covers minor parts of Noriega's career in enough detail to paint an accurate portrait of Noriega and his "peculiar" personality.
4. *Current Biography Yearbook 1988,* pp. 428–31.
5. *Facts On File* contains a number of references to Noriega's drug deals.
6. *Current Biography Yearbook 1988,* pp. 428–31.
7. Ibid.
8. Sally Quinn, interview of Noriega published in *Washington Post* (8 March 1978).
9. Kempe, *Divorcing the Dictator.*
10. Dinges, *Our Man in Panama,* p. 118.
11. Oliver L. North, *Under Fire: An American Story* (New York: HarperCollins 1991), p. 226.
12. Kempe, *Divorcing the Dictator.* As quoted in *Newsweek,* "The Noriega Files," Jan. 15, 1990, pp. 23–24.
13. *New York Times* (12 June 1986).
14. Spadafora's career and assassination are covered in some detail in Dinges's *Our Man in Panama.* They are also covered in Georges Fauriol, *Security in the Americas,* pp. 223–24.
15. *Current Biography Yearbook 1988,* p. 430.
16. *New York Times* interview with José I. Blandon (26 November 1988).
17. *Insight* (8 January 1990), p. 27.
18. U.S. Southern Command briefing.

2. 1989: The Climactic Year

1. *Facts On File* (12 May 1989) covers the 7 May elections and the irregularities and fraud underscored by President Bush, who called on Noriega to resign. Former President Carter later told reporters that he did not advise any hasty moves by the United States such as abrogating the Panama Canal treaties, or taking military action.

233

2. *Insight* (8 January 1990), photo on p. 27.
3. *Facts On File* (12 May 1989).
4. *Insight,* p. 28.
5. U.S. Southern Command briefing.
6. Lt. Col. Dave Huntoon reviewed and amended this paragraph.
7. U.S. Southern Command briefing.
8. *Facts On File* (12 May 1989).
9. Col. C. E. Richardson, the commander of the Marines in Panama at the time of Just Cause, sent me six letters covering the part played by the Marines before and during the operation.
10. *Facts On File* (8 September 1989), pp. 650–51.
11. *Time* (27 February 1989), p. 45.

3. A Tightening Noose

1. *Army Times* (6 August 1990) ran a cover story by Margaret Roth and an editorial on General Maxwell Thurman. Both pieces summed up the career of a dedicated, unusually hardworking, self-disciplined Army officer and his modus operandi. I know both Generals Thurman and can vouch, in general, for the authenticity of the cover story. Newsweek (16 July 1990) also ran a piece on the career and personality of Gen. Maxwell Thurman. Bob Woodward also discusses General Thurman in *The Commanders* (New York: Simon & Schuster, 1991).
2. Personal knowledge.
3. *Army Times* (6 August 1990).
4. *Register of Graduates,* USMA, 1991, p. 479. The *Register* contains biographical data on all West Point graduates.
5. *Facts On File* (6 October 1989), p. 734.
6. USSOCOM briefing. Dinges also covers the coup in *Our Man in Panama,* pp. 304–5.
7. *Facts On File* (6 October 1989) covers the failed coup in some detail.
8. Woodward explains Thurman's reaction to the Giroldi coup attempt.
9. Woodward, *The Commanders,* pp. 121–22.
10. *U.S. News & World Report* (30 July 1990).
11. *Facts On File* (6 October 1989), p. 734.
12. USSOCOM briefing.

4. The Planning Phase

1. Interviews with Maj. Gen. (then Brig. Gen.) Ed Scholes, XVIII Airborne Corps chief of staff on Operation Just Cause.
2. Interview with Brig. Gen. (then Col.) Thomas Needham, XVIII Airborne Corps G-3 on Operation Just Cause.
3. Interview with Lt. Col. (then Maj.) Dave Huntoon.
4. USSOCOM briefing.
5. Personal knowledge and General Stiner's biographical sketch.
6. Oliver L. North, *Under Fire: An American Story* (New York: HarperCollins 1991), p. 211.
7. JTF SOUTH command briefing.
8. Discussions with Col. (then Lt. Col.) Dan K. McNeill, then the G-3 of the 82d Airborne Division.
9. When Lt. Col. Dave Huntoon reviewed this section, he included this paragraph.
10. Report of General Stiner's preparations and movements have been verified by XVIII Airborne Corps staff officers.
11. *Facts On File* (22 December 1989), p. 941.
12. Woodward, *The Commanders,* pp. 158–59.
13. *Facts On File* (22 December 1989), p. 942.
14. Frederick Kempe, "The Noriega Files," *Newsweek* (15 January 1990).
15. Joint Chiefs of Staff briefing following Just Cause.

16. Joint Chiefs of Staff briefing notes.
17. USSOCOM briefing.
18. Kempe, "The Noriega Files."
19. Douglas Waller, writing in *Newsweek* (17 June 1989).
20. Lt. Col. Huntoon reviewed this entire section and added a number of comments.
21. XVIII Airborne Corps briefing notes.
22. USSOCOM briefing.
23. Lt. Col. Huntoon reviewed this entire section and added a number of comments.

5. The Decision

1. Bob Woodward, *The Commanders* (New York: Simon & Schuster, 1991), p. 85.
2. USSOCOM briefing.
3. Lt. Gen. Tom Kelly, Joint Chiefs of Staff chief of operations, furnished the chronology to the author.
4. This meeting is covered in some detail by Woodward in *The Commanders,* pp. 162–67.
5. Woodward relates in *The Commanders,* p. 173, that "Blue Spoon" became "Just Cause" during a telephone conversation between General Lindsay, the cigar-chomping, marathon-running, down-to-earth commander in chief of Special Operations Command, and General Kelly. After Jim Lindsay knew that "Blue Spoon" had been approved for implementation, he called Kelly on Sunday afternoon and said that "Blue Spoon" was a terrible name for the operation they were about to launch. "Do you want your grandchildren to say you were in some war called 'Blue Spoon'? he asked the ex-tanker Tom Kelly. Apparently not, because Kelly took immediate steps to change the name. He asked his deputy for current operations, Joe Lopez, "How about calling it 'Just Action'?" Lopez said, "How about 'Just Cause'?" Kelly thought that was a much better idea and then took whatever steps were necessary to get the name changed.
6. Lt. Gen. Tom Kelly and one of his officers, Maj. Raymond Melnyk, reviewed and amended this entire chapter and made necessary corrections.

6. Alerts

1. Lt. Gen. (then Maj. Gen.) Wayne Downing reviewed this entire section and made a number of comments and additions.
2. Letter from Lieutenant Colonel Maestas, undated.
3. Letter from Sergeant Spano, undated.
4. Letter from Private First Class Bunch, undated.
5. Discussions with Major General Scholes at Fort Bragg.
6. Lt. Col. Dave Huntoon and other members of the XVIII Airborne Corps staff have reviewed and commented on this section.
7. Discussions with 82d Airborne Division staff officers at Fort Bragg.
8. Lt. Col. Gerald L. (Jay) Behnke escorted the author through the PHA and explained the functions of the various buildings and elements of the PHA.
9. 82d Airborne Division briefing notes.
10. Letter from Maj. Steven Hill, chief of public affairs, 7th Infantry Division (Light) (6 September 1990).
11. *Salinas Californian* (20 December 1989).
12. *San Francisco Examiner* (21 December 1989).
13. Discussions with Maj. Gen. Ed Scholes at Fort Bragg.

7. Initial Deployments

1. U.S. Southern Command briefing.
2. Interview with General Downing; he also reviewed this section of the book and made some changes and additions.
3. Letter and comments from Colonel Snell detailing the part played by Task Force Bayonet.

4. Letter from Colonel Richardson.
5. Article in *Marine Corps Gazette* (September 1990) by Capt. Stephen J. Linder.
6. Article in *Marine Corps Gazette* (September 1990) by Capt. G. H. Gaskins and 1st Lt. Brian C. Colebaugh.
7. Article in *Marine Corps Gazette* (September 1990) by Lt. Kenneth M. DeTreux.
8. Letter from Colonel Richardson including his Just Cause narrative.
9. General Downing reviewed and commented on this section dealing with the initial deployments.

8. The Attacks Begin

1. Letter from Maj. Kevin M. Higgins. He reviewed the Pacora River Bridge section of the book and inserted some eighteen comments, corrections, and explanations.
2. Interview with Capt. Stuart Bradin in Beaufort, South Carolina. He provided most of the details of the operation later verified by Major Higgins.
3. U.S. Special Operations Command briefing.
4. Ibid.

9. Task Force White

1. Joint Special Operations Command briefing
2. *The Warriors: Operation Just Cause,* published by U.S. Southern Command, a series of articles about various elements of the forces engaged in Just Cause. One article, "TV Whiskey, Balboa Harbor PDF Patrol Boat Operation," covers this section of the book.
3. *Time* (1 January 1990).

10. The Rescue of Kurt Muse

1. XVIII Airborne Corps staff officers have reviewed this section and made some changes and additions. I also had some knowledge of the Son Tay raid because the men on that operation were all selected by Colonel Simon from my command—the Special Warfare Center at Fort Bragg.
2. Bob Woodward, *The Commanders* (New York: Simon & Schuster, 1991), p. 183.
3. The rescue of Kurt Muse, as described in this book, is based, with permission, in large part on a magazine article, "Danger in the Air," by Neil C. Livingstone and published in the *Washingtonian* issue of June 1990. The quotations are from that article, which is copyrighted by the *Washingtonian*. The entire section on the rescue of Kurt Muse was reviewed by officers in the Special Operations Command at Fort Bragg.

11. The Comandancia

1. Colonel Snell's summary of Operation Just Cause.
2. Letter dated 12 February 1991 and summary of Operation Just Cause from Lt. Col. James W. Reed Commanding Officer of the 4th Battalion (Mechanized), 6th Infantry, 5th Infantry Division, Fort Polk, La.
3. *The Guardian,* Fort Polk, La. (5 January 1990), p. 2.
4. Colonel Reed's letter of 12 February 1991 gives a complete description of his battalion's operations.
5. David Harris, Reuters Information Services.
6. Recommendation for posthumous award of Silver Star for E-4 Ivan D. Perez from his commander, Colonel Reed, 4th Battalion, 6th Infantry, dated 20 January 1990; also letter from Colonel Reed dated 12 February 1991.
7. *The Guardian,* Fort Polk, La. (5 January 1990), p. 10.
8. Recommendation for award of the Silver Star from Colonel Reed, Commanding Officer, 4th Battalion, 6th Infantry, and his 12 February 1991 letter.
9. "A Night at the Comandancia," pp. 18–19 of DA pamphlet, Command Information publication, *Soldiers in Panama.*

10. Colonel Reed's letter of 12 February 1991 and summary.
11. Interview with General Downing.
12. Colonel Reed's letter of 12 February 1991 and summary.
13. Letter and comments on the Comandancia final "takedown" from Maj. (then Capt.) Albert E. Dochnal.

12. Fort Amador and Balboa

1. Personal knowledge gained after almost thirty-six years of continuous active duty.
2. An article in DA pamphlet *Soldiers in Panama* titled "The Fight for Fort Amador," pp. 12–13.
3. Letter from Colonel Snell.
4. Article in *The Warriors,* USSOUTHCOM publication, "Reduction of PDF 5th Rifle Company."
5. Tab P of note 7 following.
6. Memo from Lt. Col. Bob Fitzgerald to Lt. Col. Dave Huntoon commenting on this chapter of the book and adding and correcting details.
7. Lt. Col. Bob Fitzgerald's after-action report is very detailed. Each of his company commander's reports is included. At Tabs A through S are missions, commander's intent, concept of the operation, chronologies, maps, organization charts, company rosters, and other reports. It is the most complete battalion after-action report on Just Cause that I have seen.
8. Letter from Lt. (now Capt.) Lisa M. Kutschera (23 May 1991).
9. U.S. Southern Command briefing.
10. *Soldiers* (the official U.S. Army magazine) (February 1990), pp. 38–39; "Operation Just Cause" by Donna Miles.
11. After-action reports by company commanders in the 5th Battalion, 87th Infantry.

13. Task Force Atlantic

1. U.S. Southern Command briefing.
2. Just Cause command briefing and after-action report and journals from the 82d Airborne Division and 7th Infantry Division (L) cover the general outline of this chapter.
3. Article in *Fort Ord Panorama: Operation Just Cause Perspective,* "4/17 Completes Five-Part Mission," by Bob Britton.
4. Article in DA pamphlet *Soldiers in Panama,* "Conquest at Coco Solo," pp. 25–27.
5. "4/17 Completes Five-Part Mission."

14. Madden Dam, Cerro Tigre, and Renacer Prison

1. Article in DA pamphlet *Soldiers in Panama,* "Raid at Renacer Prison."
2. *Fayetteville Observer* (3 January 1990), p. 44; article by Rich Browne.
3. *The Warriors,* "The Action at Renacer Prison," Tab A.

15. The Jump on Río Hato

1. Letter from Colonel Kernan (23 August 1990).
2. Letter from Lieutenant McCown (11 January 1990).
3. Memo from Pfc. Richard Fox (undated).
4. Memo from Spc. Steve Stadelman (undated).
5. 75th Ranger SOP.
6. Letter from Colonel Kernan (31 October 1990).
7. Letter from unidentified 75th Ranger.
8. 75th Ranger briefing notes.
9. Letter from Lt. Tim Nye (undated).
10. Letter from Pfc. Leon Erickson (undated).
11. Letter from Capt. John A. Davis (undated).

12. Letter from Lieutenant Dichairo (undated).
13. Letter from Maj. Clyde M. Newman (undated).
14. Letter from Lt. Jeffrey A. Bouais (undated).
15. Letter from Capt. William A. Doukas (undated).
16. U.S. Southern Command, briefing.
17. 75th Ranger command briefing.
18. Interview with General Downing at Fort Bragg.
19. Letter from Twenty-first Air Force historian, Clayton H. Snedeker (5 July 1990).
20. *Aviation Week & Space Technology* (1 January 1990); article by John D. Morrocco.
21. Letter from Capt. Philip D. Colahan (undated).
22. 75th Ranger command briefing.
23. Discussion with Colonel Kernan.
24. Interview with General Downing.
25. Letter from S. Sgt. Richard J. Hoerner (undated).
26. Letter from Specialist Kristops (undated).
27. Letter from Staff Sergeant Brackenbury (undated).
28. Letter from Capt. Steven G. Fogarty (undated).

16. Río Hato Takedown

1. Letter from 1st Sgt. Joseph L. Mattison (undated).
2. Letter from Capt. Jonathan L. Beegle (undated).
3. Interview with Capt. Raymond A. Thomas at Fort Bragg. At that time he was the aide de camp to General Downing.
4. Letter from Capt. David B. Haight (undated).
5. Letter from an unidentified soldier in the 75th Rangers.
6. Letter from Sgt. Greene (undated).
7. Letter from Spc. Michael A. Sonnenschein (undated).
8. Letter from Sgt. David R. Clifton (undated).
9. Letter from Lt. Brian M. Drinkwine (undated).
10. Letter from Capt. Mike Newcomb (undated).
11. 75th Ranger staff memo, "Summary of Ground Action at Río Hato—20–24 December 1990."

17. The Airport

1. 75th Ranger command briefing notes.
2. 75th Ranger memo, "Summary of Ground Action at Torrijos-Tucumen."
3. Ibid.
4. Ibid.
5. Ibid.
6. Interview with Col. Dan K. McNeill, 82d Airborne Division G-3, on Just Cause.
7. Capt. (now Maj.) Albert E. Dochnal reviewed this entire chapter and added his comments and corrections.
8. Interview with General Downing.
9. 75th Ranger after-action report.
10. 75th Ranger journal.

18. Task Force Pacific

1. Memo from chief of staff, 82d Airborne Division, to chief of staff, XVIII Airborne Corps.
2. Interview with Capt. Gary J. Ramsdell.
3. 82d Airborne Division historical summary.
4. Interview with and letter from Captain Ramsdell.
5. Chronology from the S-3 of the 2d Battalion, 504th Infantry.
6. Lt. Col. Harry Axson and his staff reviewed this entire chapter and added parts in which he

was personally involved. On 7 February 1992 he wrote, "This is the rewritten copy. My S-3 (Maj. Jon Chase) and I were able to reconstruct some more facts and details."

7. Interview with Captain Ramsdell.
8. Colonel Axson et al. review and additions.
9. Interview with Captain Ramsdell.
10. 82d Airborne Division historical summary.
11. Interview with Captain Ramsdell.
12. Letter from Capt. Steve Phelps.
13. 82d Airborne Division historical summary.
14. Joint "MAC/Army Hotwash," review of Operation Just Cause.
15. Colonel Axson et al. review and additions.
16. Letter from Captain Phelps.
17. Memo from chief of staff, 82d Airborne Division, to chief of staff, XVIII Airborne Corps.
18. 82d Airborne Division after-action summary.
19. Input from Colonel Axson and his staff, who reviewed and commented on this entire chapter.
20. *The Warriors,* "Days of Stars—Bronze, That Is."
21. Letter from Capt. (then 1st Lt.) Lisa M. Kutschera (23 May 1991).
22. Input from Colonel Axson et al.
23. Interview with Captain Ramsdell.
24. "Days of Stars."
25. Ibid.
26. Ibid.
27. Interview with Captain Ramsdell.
28. Input from Colonel Axson et al.
29. Ibid.

19. The Marriott Incident

1. Lieutenant Colonel Axson and his staff also reviewed this chapter and rewrote many portions of it. The comments about Mr. Skinner are Colonel Axson's input.
2. Ibid.
3. *The Warriors,* "Days of Stars—Bronze, That Is."
4. Colonel Axson et al. review and rewriting.
5. "Days of Stars."
6. Colonel Axson et al. review and rewriting.
7. Letter from Capt. Steven Phelps.
8. Interview with Maj. Gen. Ed Scholes.
9. Article in *Fort Bragg Paraglide* (28 December 1989), p. 2A.

20. Tinajitas

1. 82 Airborne Division after-action report.
2. Letter from Capt. Lisa M. Kutschera (23 May 1991).
3. *Fayetteville Observer* (11 January 1990), p. 1D. The *Observer* of 28 December 1989 also carried a description of the action at Tinajitas, on p. 3D.
4. 82d Airborne Division after-action report.
5. *Fayetteville Observer* (11 January 1990 and 28 December 1989).
6. U.S. Southern Command briefing.
7. 82d Airborne Division summary of Operation Just Cause, and 82d Airborne Division *Notebook.*

21. 7th Infantry Division (Light)

1. 7th Infantry Division (Light) chronology of events for Operation Just Cause.
2. Operation Just Cause retrospective (16 February 1990), p. 7.

3. 82d Airborne Division historical report.
4. Letter from Lt. Col. William Leszczynski (10 March 1990).
5. Operation Just Cause retrospective, p. 10.
6. Letter from Colonel Leszczynski.
7. Conversation with Colonel McNeill after the operation.
8. 7th Infantry Division (Light) chronology.
9. Letter from Capt. Lisa M. Kutschera (23 May 1991).

22. Follow-on Operations

1. 82d Airborne Division after-action report.
2. *Fayetteville Observer* (11 January 1990), p. 1D, "Panama Notebook" by Rich Browne.
3. Letter from Dr. Robert K. Wright, Jr., XVIII Airborne Corps historian (24 May 1991).
4. U.S. Southern Command, briefing.
5. *Fayetteville Observer* (28 December 1989), p. 3D; article by Douglas Jehland and Bob Secter.
6. Conversation with Maj. Gen. Ed Scholes.
7. *Fayetteville Observer* (10 January 1990), pp. 1–4A.
8. *Fayetteville Observer* (11 January 1990), p. 4A; article by Harry Cunningham.
9. *Fayetteville Observer* (10 January 1990), pp. 1–4A—a long article covering the part played by civil affairs units in the postfighting period in Panama.

23. Winning the West and Noriega's Surrender

1. DA pamphlet *Soldiers in Panama* covers this chapter in an article, "Winning the West." The same general subject is covered in more detail in *The Warriors*—also called "Winning the West."
2. I first heard about the "Ma Bell approach" during my interview with General Downing.
3. Special Operations Command briefing.
4. U.S. Southern Command briefing.
5. Bob Woodward, *The Commanders* (New York: Simon & Schuster, 1991), p. 186.
6. *Fayetteville Times* (28 December 1989), p. 1A.
7. Ibid.
8. *Fayetteville Times* (5 January 1990), pp. 1–4A.
9. *Fayetteville Times* (4 January 1990), p. 1A.
10. Memo from Maj. Gen. Ed Scholes (undated).

24. The New Military

1. Dan Rather, CBS Radio News analysis and commentary (28 December 1989).
2. Personal knowledge. The Special Forces soldiers selected by Col. Bull Simon for the Son Tay raid came from the Special Warfare Center of which I was the commander at the time.
3. *Time* (8 January 1990), p. 43.
4. U.S. Southern Command briefing.
5. Telephone call from Lt. Gen. Tom Kelly, Joint Chiefs of Staff operations chief.
6. Conversation with Maj. Gen. Ed Scholes.
7. Letter from Sgt. Lewis A. Matson (3 January 1992).
8. John Monk, "Did the 82d Look Before It Leaped?" *Savannah News Press* (4 February 1990).
9. *Fayetteville Observer* (12 January 1990), p. 2A.

Sources

Interviews

A number of officers who participated in Just Cause were generous with their time and granted me interviews in person or on the telephone. Among them were Lt. Col. Gerald L. Behnke (who also escorted me around the 82d's marshaling area); Capt. Stuart W. Bradin; Maj. Donald K. Bridges; Lt. Gen. Wayne A. Downing; Lt. Col. Michael Franks, USMC; Lt. Col. David Huntoon; Lt. Gen. Thomas W. Kelly; Brig. Gen. William F. (Buck) Kernan; Col. Dan K. McNeill; Brig. Gen. Thomas H. Needham; Cmdr. David Porter, USN (Ret.); Capt. Gary J. Ramsdell; Maj. Gen. Edison E. Scholes; Capt. Raymond A. Thomas; and Dr. Robert K. Wright.

Private Papers, Letters, and Personal Communications

A number of officers and soldiers, and others wrote about their personal and unit experiences on Just Cause. Among them were Maj. Dorian T. Anderson; Pfc. R. T. Anderson; Staff Sergeant Arta; Maj. Charles W. Barker; Maj. Craig D. Barta; Capt. Jonathan L. Beegle; S. Sgt. Kurt Boehm; 1st Lt. Jeffrey A. Bouais; Staff Sergeant Brackenbury; Maj. Donald K. Bridges; Lt. Col. Robert V. Bryant; Private First Class Bunch (a letter nineteen handwritten pages long); Spc. Steven L. Clark; Maj. Stan Clemons; Sgt. David R. Clifton; Capt. Philip D. Colchar; Ms. Mary Ellen Condon-Rall; Capt. George R. Copeland; Capt. Edward B. Daly; Capt. John A. Davis; Sgt. Steven L. Denelsbeck; First Lieutenant Dichairo; Capt. (Dr.) William C. Doukas; 1st Lt. Brian Drinkwine; Pfc. Leon Erickson; Capt. Stephen G. Fogarty; Pfc. Richard Fox; Capt. (Chaplain) Peter J. Frederick; Lt. Col. Robert L. Granville; Lt. Col. James J.

Grazioplene; Sergeant Greene; Mr. George B. Grimes, PAO office, USSOCOM; S. Sgt. Frank A. Grippe; Capt. David B. Haight; Col. John W. Handy; Capt. Louis E. Herrera; Maj. Kevin M. Higgins; Maj. Steven R. Hill; S. Sgt. Richard J. Hoerner; Capt. Samuel H. Johnson; 1st Lt. Paul Kelly; Brig. Gen. William F. (Buck) Kernan; First Lieutenant King; Private First Class Kovac; Specialist Kristops; Capt. Lisa M. Kutschera; Lt. Col. William J. Leszczynski, Jr.; Gen. James J. Lindsay; Lt. Gen. Gary E. Luck; Lt. Col. Alan H. Maestas; Spc. Richard Malvarose; Col. Donald P. Maple; Spc. Paul Margeaf; Sgt. Lewis A. Matson; 1st Sgt. Joseph L. Mattison; 1st Lt. Kerry D. McCown; Specialist McKinnon; Brig. Gen. Charles W. McLain; Maj. Raymond Melnyk; Capt. John W. Metz; 1st Lt. Joseph A. Mullally; Capt. Mike Newcomb; Maj. Clyde M. Newman; 1st Lt. Tim Nye; Specialist Oler; Capt. Steven Phelps; Capt. Gary J. Ramsdell; Lt. Col. James W. Reed; Col. C. E. Richardson, USMC; Col. Peter J. Schoonmaker; Pfc. Paul Signonetti; Mr. Clayton H. Snedeker, Twenty-first Air Force historian; Col. Michael G. Snell; Specialist Sonnenschien; Col. Daniel E. Sowada; Sgt. Andrew A. Spano; Spc. Steve Stadelman; Pfc. William Stasburg; Maj. L. D. Walker; and Sergeant White.

Military Documents and Publications That Provided Many Facts and Background

After-action report, Southern Command Network
Capt. Donald K. Bridges, 75th Ranger Regiment summary of operations
Bulletin No. 90–9 (October 1990), *Operation Just Cause Lessons Learned*
Volumes I, II, and III, U.S. Army Combined Arms Command, Fort Leavenworth, Kansas
Maj. Gen. Carmen J. Cavezza's biographical sketch
Chronology of events for Just Cause, 7th Infantry Division (Light)
Capt. Mark Conley, B Company, 5/87th Jungle Cats after-action report
Capt. Don Currie, C Company, 5/87th Panthers after-action report
DA *Field Manual 100-5* (September 1954)
Maj. J. M. Donivan, 4–6th Infantry, Citation for Army Commendation Medal
XVIII Airborne Corps Briefing Charts for JTF South
82d Airborne Division: Operation Just Cause briefing charts and notes; SOP for airborne operations; operational summary (23 December 1989–5 January 1990); memo, chief of staff
82d Airborne Division to chief of staff XVIII Airborne Corps (undated); historical summary (17 December 1989–12 January 1990)
Lt. Col. B. R. Fitzgerald, 1/508 unit history, Operation Just Cause
Capt. Bill Flynt, A Company, 5/87 Jaguars after-action report
Lt. Col. James J. Grazioplene, history of 3/73d armor and briefing charts. Also "Armor Support to Infantry in Contingency Operations"
Lt. Col. William H. Huff III, 5/87th Infantry after-action report
Joint Chiefs of Staff chronology entry log (16 December–20 December 1989)
Joint Special Operations Task Force (JSOTF) briefing charts

Just Cause briefing notes and charts; chronology of Panamanian crisis (February 1988–January 1990)
Just Cause "Hotwash Agenda" with comments
Brig. Gen. William F. Kernan, 75th Ranger Regiment, briefing charts and notes; biographical sketch; 75th Rangers SOP
Col. Dan K. McNeill, 82d Airborne Division G-3, on Just Cause: personal diary and notes
Maj. Raymond Melnyk, office of Joint Chiefs of Staff, information paper
"Panama—Just Cause," JTFSOUTH (20 December 1989–13 January 1990)
Operation Just Cause, DA PIO releases, Section B
Operation Just Cause retrospective, *Fort Ord Panorama* (16 February 1990)
E-4 Ivan D. Pérez, 4/6th Infantry Battalion, citation for Silver Star
E-4 Roderick B. Ringstaff, 4/6th Infantry Battalion, citation for Silver Star
7th Infantry Division (Light), chronology log (12 December 1989–10 February 1990)
Soldiers (February 1990)
Col. Michael G. Snell, after-action report, 193d Brigade
Soldiers in Panama, chief, Public Affairs Command Information Division, U.S. Army
General Carl W. Stiner, career résumé
Task Force Bayonet overview of Operation Just Cause
U.S. Special Operations Command, briefing and charts for Just Cause
U.S. Southern Command, briefing and charts

Magazines That Have Been Quoted from or That Proved Useful for Background

American Legion Magazine (April and August 1990)
ARMY (February 1990)
ARMY TIMES (ten issues between 2 February 1990 and 29 October 1990)
AVIATION WEEK & SPACE TECHNOLOGY (1 January 1990)
Current Biography Yearbook 1988
Current History ("World Affairs Journal," December 1988)
Facts On File, Vol. 49, No. 2529, May 12, 1989; Vol. 49, No. 2550, Oct. 6, 1989; Vol. 49, No. 2561, Dec. 22, 1989.
Fort Ord Panorama (Operation Just Cause retrospective, 16 February 1990)
INSIGHT (29 January 1990)
Marine Corps Gazette (February 1990, September 1990)
Marine Magazine (January 1990)
Military Life Style (July–August 1990)
Newsweek (1 January 1990, 15 January 1990, 25 June 1990, 16 July 1990)
TIME (1 January 1990), 8 January 1990, 16 October 1990, 23 October 1990)
U.S. NEWS & WORLD REPORT (30 July 1990)

SOURCES

Published Sources from Which Facts or Quotations Have Been Taken

Dinges, John, *Our Man in Panama*. New York: Random House, 1990.
Donnelly, Thomas, Margaret Roth, and Caleb Baker. *Operation Just Cause*. Lexington Books, 1991.
Kempe, Frederick, *Divorcing the Dictator*. New York: G. P. Putnam's Sons, 1990.
North, Oliver L. *Under Fire: An American Story*. New York: Harper Collins, 1991.
Woodward, Bob. *The Commanders*. New York: Simon & Schuster, 1991.

Articles That Have Been Quoted from or That Proved Useful

Akers, Col. Frank, "The Warriors," a DA summary of Just Cause operations
"Did 82d Look Before It Leaped?," *Savannah News Press* (4 February 1990).
Fauriol, Georges, "Security in the Americas," National Defense University Press, Washington, D.C., 1989.
"Focus on Panama," a section of Marine Corps Gazetteer (September 1990) featuring articles by Marine officers who served in Panama during Just Cause. Included were Col. Robert P. Mauskapf, Maj. Earl W. Powers, Capt. Stephen J. Linder, Capt. John S. Dunn, Capt. Gerald H. Gaskins, 1st Lt. Brian C. Colebaugh, Capt. Richard R. Huizenga, and 1st Lt. Kenneth M. DeTreux.
Hammond, Capt. Kevin J., and Capt. Frank Sherman, "Sheridans in Panama," *Armor* (May/April 1990).
Livingstone, Neil C. "Danger in the Air," *The Washingtonian* (June 1990).
"Misuse of SEALs in Panama," Chicago *Tribune* (9 February 1990).
Quinn, Sally, "Interview with Noriega," *Washington Post* (8 March 1978).

Reviews and Comments

A number of officers reviewed pertinent portions of the text and made comments and corrections. Among them were: Lt. Col. Harry Axson; Capt. Stuart W. Bradin; Maj. Albert E. Dochnal; Lt. Gen. Wayne A. Downing; 1st Lt. Byron K. Echols; Maj. Kevin M. Higgins; Lt. Col. David Huntoon; Maj. Raymond Melnyk; Brig. Gen. Thomas Needham; Capt. Gary J. Ramsdell; and Maj. Gen. Edison E. Scholes.

Index

About the Author

Lt. Gen. Edward M. Flanagan, Jr., U.S. Army (Ret.), was born in Saugerties, New York, and graduated from West Point with the World War II class of January 1943. In World War II he served with the 11th Airborne Division in combat as a battery commander and division staff officer in the Philippines and later with the occupation forces in Hokkaido, Japan. During the Korean War he commanded the parachute artillery battalion of the 187th Airborne Regimental Combat Team. In Vietnam, he served in Chu Chi as assistant division commander of the 25th Infantry Division, in Saigon with the staff of MACV, and at Da Nang as the operations officer of the 3d Marine Amphibious Force. He commanded the 3d Armored Division Artillery in Germany, the JFK Center for Special Forces at Fort Bragg, the 1st Infantry Division at Fort Riley, Kansas, and the Sixth Army at the Presidio in San Francisco. He was the deputy commander of the Eighth Army in Korea. He served two tours in the Pentagon, first as a lieutenant colonel in the Army's Secretary of the General Staff and later as a lieutenant general as the Army comptroller. He is a master parachutist with one combat jump and an Army aviator. His military decorations include two Distinguished Service Medals, two Legions of Merit, a Bronze Star, two Air Medals, and nine battle stars. He has had published five books on military history and writes a monthly column and other articles for *Army* magazine. He and his wife, Peggie, have five children.